INVESTMENT & SAVINGS HANDBOOK

1999/2000

General Editor:

Paul Wright

Investment Marketing Manager

Allied Dunbar Assurance plc

PEARSON EDUCATION LIMITED

London Office:
128 Long Acre, London WC2E 9AN
Tel: +44 (0) 171 447 2000
Fax: +44 (0) 171 240 5771
Website: www.pearsoned-ema.com

First published in Great Britain in 1999

© Allied Dunbar Assurance plc 1999

The right of Paul Wright to be identified as author of
this work has been asserted by him in accordance with the
Copyright, Designs and Patents Act 1988.

ISBN 0 273 64175 1

British Library Cataloguing in Publication Data
A CIP catalogue record for this book can be obtained
from the British Library

All rights reserved; no part of this publication may be reproduced,
stored in a retrieval system, or transmitted in any form or by any means,
electronic, mechanical, photocopying, recording, or otherwise without either
the prior written permission of the Publishers or a licence permitting restricted
copying in the United Kingdom issued by the Copyright Licensing Agency Ltd,
90 Tottenham Court Road, London W1P 0LP. This book may not be lent,
resold, hired out or otherwise disposed of by way of trade in any form
of binding or cover other than that in which it is published,
without the prior consent of the Publishers.

Typeset by M Rules
Printed and bound in Great Britain by Biddles Ltd, Guildford and King's Lynn

*The Publishers' policy is to use paper manufactured
from sustainable forests.*

No responsibility for loss occasioned to any person acting or refraining
from action as a result of the material in this publication can be
accepted by Allied Dunbar, the author or publishers.

The views and opinions of Allied Dunbar may not necessarily coincide
with some of the views and opinions expressed in this book which
are solely those of the author and no endorsement of them by
Allied Dunbar should be inferred.

CONTENTS

Preface ix

Some favourite investment maxims x

Contributors xii

1 AN OVERVIEW 1

  1.1   Introduction 1

  1.2   The investment adviser 2

  1.3   Types of investor 2

  1.4   Ways of arranging and holding investments 3

  1.5   The nature of an investment 3

  1.6   Investment policy — general principles and special factors 5

  1.7   Trustees 8

  1.8   Overseas investors 10

  1.9   Conclusion 12

  1.10 Income tax rates, allowances, and National Insurance rates from 6 April 1999 12

  1.11 Capital gains tax 13

2 UNLISTED INVESTMENTS 15

  2.1   Types of unlisted security 15

  2.2   Review of 1998–99 15

  2.3   Types of unlisted investment 16

  2.4   Comparing different types of security 31

  2.5   Preview of 1999–2000 33

3 LISTED INVESTMENTS 34

  3.1   Introduction 34

  3.2   Review of 1998–99 35

  3.3   Comparing different types of security 38

  3.4   The Stock Exchange 42

  3.5   Listed public sector securities 53

  3.6   Listed company fixed interest securities 60

  3.7   Ordinary shares 63

3.8   Preview of 1999–2000   76
3.9   Conclusion   77
       Useful addresses   78

4 MAJOR OVERSEAS MARKETS   80

4.1   Introduction   80
4.2   Opportunities overseas   80
4.3   Choosing a market   89
4.4   The mechanics of investing overseas   91
4.5   Conclusion   94

5 EMERGING MARKETS   95

5.1   Introduction   95
5.2   What are emerging markets?   95
5.3   World of change   96
5.4   Performance   100
5.5   Individual markets   102
5.6   Constant change   103
5.7   Factors to consider   105
5.8   Country versus geographically diversified funds   109
5.9   Choosing a fund manager   109
5.10   Timing   110
5.11   Conclusion   111

6 DERIVATIVES DE-MYSTIFIED   112

6.1   Introduction   112
6.2   'Surely derivatives are very risky?'   112
6.3   What is a futures contract, and how does it work?   113
6.4   Dealing in futures and stocks compared   115
6.5   Pricing futures contracts   115
6.6   What is an option?   116
6.7   Pricing options contracts   117
6.8   Over-the-counter options   118
6.9   What is a swap, and how is it priced?   119
6.10   Conclusion   120
       Sources of further information   120

7 INVESTMENT TRUSTS 121

7.1 Introduction 121
7.2 Historical background 121
7.3 Recent developments 122
7.4 Legal nature 124
7.5 Conditions for purchase 128
7.6 Characteristics 128
7.7 Taxation 134
7.8 Unapproved investment companies 136
7.9 Suitability 137
7.10 Mechanics 137
7.11 Maintenance 138
7.12 Preview of the year ahead and conclusion 139
Useful addresses 139

8 OEICS, UNIT TRUSTS AND OFFSHORE FUNDS 140

8.1 Introduction 140
8.2 Historical background 141
8.3 Authorisation 141
8.4 Highlights of the previous year 142
8.5 Pricing of units 143
8.6 Legal nature 144
8.7 Conditions for purchase 146
8.8 Characteristics 146
8.9 Taxation 150
8.10 Suitability 152
8.11 Mechanics and maintenance 152
8.12 Open-ended investment companies 154
8.13 Unauthorised unit trusts 155
8.14 Exempt unit trusts 155
8.15 Preview of the year ahead 155
8.16 Conclusion 156
Sources of further information 156

9 REAL PROPERTY 158

9.1 Introduction to real property 158
9.2 Legal, taxation and cost factors of real property 160
9.3 Property valuation 162
9.4 Role of advisers 163

10 RESIDENTIAL PROPERTY   164

10.1   Highlights of the past few years   164
10.2   The alternatives   164
10.3   Preview of the year ahead   168

11 AGRICULTURAL LAND, WOODLANDS AND MISCELLANEOUS   169

11.1   Introduction   169
11.2   Agricultural land   170
11.3   Woodlands   179
11.4   Miscellaneous land uses   181
     Useful addresses   189

12 COMMERCIAL PROPERTY   191

12.1   Introduction   191
12.2   Types of commercial property   194
12.3   Shops   200
12.4   Offices   201
12.5   Industrial   203
12.6   Hi-tech   204
12.7   Agriculture   204
12.8   Leisure   205

13 BUSINESS VENTURES (WITHOUT PARTICIPATION IN MANAGEMENT)   206

13.1   Introduction   206
13.2   The current business climate   207
13.3   Minority holdings in private companies   208
13.4   Private investment companies   218
13.5   Enterprise Investment Scheme   219
13.6   Dormant partnerships   228
13.7   Membership of Lloyd's   231
13.8   Investment in another's expertise   235
13.9   Racehorses   237
13.10   Backing plays   239
13.11   Options on books   240
13.12   Preview of the year ahead   240
     Useful addresses   241

14 LIFE ASSURANCE   242

14.1   Introduction   242
14.2   Highlights of the previous year   242

14.3   Life assurance policies   243
14.4   Purchased life annuities   258
14.5   Preview of the year ahead   261
14.6   Conclusion   262
       Useful addresses   262

15 PENSION CONTRACTS   264

15.1   Introduction   264
15.2   Highlights of the previous year   264
15.3   The State pension scheme   267
15.4   Contracting-in and contracting-out   268
15.5   Types of pension contracts   269
15.6   Characteristics of pension contracts   270
15.7   Eligibility, taxation, contribution limits and benefits   271
15.8   Wefare reform   280
15.9   Suitability   281
15.10 Preview of the year ahead   281
15.11 Conclusion   283
       Useful addresses   283

16 COMMODITIES   284

16.1   Introduction to commodities: what they are   284
16.2   Types of commodities   285
16.3   Characteristics of commodities   287
16.4   Methods of participation in the commodity markets   288
16.5   Review and outlook for commodities in 1999–2000   293

17 GOLD AND OTHER VALUABLES   302

17.1   Introduction   302
17.2   Highlights of the previous year   316
17.3   Counterfeits and frauds   321
17.4   Opportunities and costs   323
17.5   Taxation   325
17.6   Preview of the year ahead   326
17.7   Conclusion   330
17.8   Other valuables   331

18 ART AND ANTIQUES   337

18.1   Introduction   337
18.2   Prevailing trends   339
18.3   National Heritage issues   347
18.4   Highlights of the previous year   358

18.5   Purchasing art and antiques   360
18.6   Characteristics   368
18.7   Taxation   373
18.8   Mechanics   380
18.9   Maintenance   386
18.10   Preview of the year ahead   388

19 COLLECTABLES   391

19.1   Introduction   391
19.2   Developments in collectables' markets   396
19.3   Future developments   415
19.4   Purchasing collectables   418
19.5   Taxation   420
19.6   Suitability and mechanics   422
19.7   Conclusion   425
        Sources of further information (Chapters 17–19)   426

20 TAX BENEFICIAL INVESTMENTS AND SAVINGS   430

20.1   Introduction   430
20.2   Tax privileged investments   431
20.3   Conclusion   440

21 INVESTOR PROTECTION   441

21.1   Introduction   441
21.2   Highlights of the previous year   442
21.3   Basic framework   444
21.4   Rules and regulations   447
21.5   Complaints and remedies   450
21.6   Overseas aspects   451
21.7   Preview of the year ahead   452
21.8   Conclusion and future developments   452
        Useful addresses   454

INDEX   457

PREFACE

Welcome to the last *Allied Dunbar Investment & Savings Handbook* of this Millennium. I hope this latest edition – the 20th – exceeds your expectations. Although I've yet to be swept up by the fervour and tumult that awaits the up-coming celebrations, I do foresee a myriad of exciting opportunities for savers and investors as we approach and enter the 21st century.

All the chapters in this year's edition have undergone an update. Once again, the respective authors have worked hard to ensure relevance and accuracy. Whatever your savings and investment objectives, whether it is a leisurely stroll through fixed-interest securities or a rollercoaster ride through the derivatives market, you should find what you're looking for within these pages.

Ultimately, the silver thread which holds this tome together is risk and your atti-tude towards it. Your definition of a 'risky' investment could be very different from the next reader. Take, for instance, bank and building society accounts. One view is that they are as 'safe as it gets'. However, it's incorrect to say there are risks in leaving significant sums on deposit for the long term – for example, the impact of inflation on the purchasing power of capital. Let the debate begin!

Over the last few months, the big investment news has been the launch of Individual Savings Accounts (ISAs). Though masses of column inches have been dedicated to championing, explaining and recommending them, current public perception suggests they are viewed as a complex animal – rather ironic given the fact the Government hailed them as the new and simpler way to save and invest. However, it's still early days. I believe ISAs will, in the next few years, have a significant impact.

As we approach 2000 and beyond, consumers have access to an ever wider band of information. The rise of e-commerce generally, and the Internet in particular, are inevitable and welcome phenomena. Consequently, there is more choice and, equally, there is now a greater chance of making the wrong decision. Hence, my recommendation, whatever your savings and investment aims, is to seek out professional advice.

Another point to bear in mind: although Scottish law varies from English law on many subjects, in most aspects of tax, trusts and domicile the two systems coincide.

Finally, I would like to say a big thank you to all of this year's contributors, not only for their hard work, but also for their punctuality.

Enjoy the read.

Paul Wright
July 1999

Some favourite investment maxims from our authors

'Buy low, sell high.' (Anon)

'If it's obvious, it's obviously wrong.' (Joe Granville)

'Market dogmatists frequently bark up the wrong trees.' (David Fuller)

'Beware of company chairmen who either:
    a) wear more gold than is in the balance sheet
    b) have an all-year-round sun tan.' (David Ballance)

'A fool and his money are soon parted. What I want to know is how they got together in the first place.' (Cyril Fletcher)

'There was a time when a fool and his money were soon parted, but now it happens to everybody.' (Adlai Stevenson)

'Money is better than poverty, if only for financial reasons.' (Anon)

'Endeavour to chain-link decisions. Before dealing in a stock look back at what has happened (if anything) since your previous transaction in that stock, and relate this to the change in the share price.' (idem)

'It should take only one fund manager to change a lightbulb – assuming they still have the receipt.' (Paul Wright)

'All markets are cyclical and short-term performance is more about timing of investment and sale decisions than anything else.' (Geoff Abbott)

'When all advisers and commentators are in agreement be warned – the market is approaching the top or the bottom of its current cycle.' (idem)

'When property value falls below the cost of the bricks and mortar on site – start buying.' (idem)

'In depressed markets lenders will always try to support you through into the recovery phase – so as to be sure of getting all their money back.' (idem)

'When you observe a strong consensus, take the opposite view.' (David Fuller)

'Trust in a sufficiency of wealth as the by-product of a good life.' (John Train)

'Soar not too high to fall; but stoop to rise.' (Philip Massinger 1583–1640, from *The Duke of Milan*)

'When choosing an investment for tax reasons follow the "Yellow Box Principle". Do not enter the box unless your exit is clear.' (Stuart Reynolds)

'Learning from your own mistakes is all very well, but learning from the mistakes of others is cheaper.' (Oscar Wilde)

'Experience is the name everyone gives to his mistakes.' (idem)

'An economist is an expert who will know tomorrow why the things he predicted yesterday didn't happen today.' (Prof L J Peter)

'The riskiest place to leave your long-term investments is in a deposit account.' (D W Adams)

'The best time to invest is when you have the cash.' (Sir John Templeton)

'The closest you can come to safety in investing is to buy shares in many countries and many industries.' (Sir John Templeton)

CONTRIBUTORS

Geoffrey Abbott, Dip FBA (Lon) FRICS, is Agricultural Investment Consultant and Head of Purchases & Sales Department in Smiths Gore (Chartered Surveyors) based in their London Office. He was assisted by a number of the partners in their sixteen offices throughout England & Scotland.

Douglas W Adams, MA, MBA, is Business Planning Director at Templeton Investment Management Ltd, the UK subsidiary of the world-wide Franklin Templeton Group. Templeton manage over £6bn in emerging markets portfolios. Mr Adams is an economist by profession.

Martin Squires is Head of Research at Rudolf Wolff & Co Ltd; the company was one of the founding members of the London Metal Exchange in 1876.

David Ballance, MA (Oxon), is Head of the European Investment Department at Threadneedle Investment Managers Ltd, and also has previous experience in UK equities.

William Bourne, MA (Oxon), MSc (Finance) London Business School, was formerly a Director of Threadneedle Investment Managers Ltd with responsibility for Strategic Research. He now works in Tokyo for Scudder Kemper Investments.

Andrew Bull, ARICS, is a Partner at Jones Lang LaSalle, the world's largest independent property consultants with specific responsibilities for the investment strategy and implementation of two UK pension funds.

Peter Grimmett is the Marketing Compliance Manager for Threadneedle Investment Managers Ltd and is responsible for the approval and monitoring of advertisements and marketing material issued by Threadneedle. He has spent a number of years in the industry, initially in marketing and latterly, in regulation, within the Collective Investment Schemes Department of the Financial Services Authority.

Peter Howe, LLB, Barrister, is Company Secretary and an Executive Director in the legal department of Allied Dunbar Assurance plc. The legal department provides a complete legal and technical service to companies in the Allied Dunbar Group. Financial Services legislation is his principal area of specialisation.

Vince Jerrard, LLB, ACII, Solicitor, is the Legal Director of Allied Dunbar Assurance plc. Mr Jerrard has contributed chapters to other Allied Dunbar publications, including the *Tax Handbook*, *Capital Taxes Guide* and the *Business Tax and Law Handbook*.

Malcolm Kemp is the Director in charge of derivatives and quantitative research at Threadneedle Investment Managers Ltd. He gained a first class Honours Degree from Cambridge University in 1981, qualified as an Actuary in 1987 and was a partner in the investment consulting practice of Bacon & Woodrow, Consulting Actuaries, before joining Threadneedle in early 1996.

John Myers and Helen Baird are from Solon Consultants, a specialised research firm that focuses on property and alternative investments. John Myers is also a visiting professor at Sheffield University and has been a contributor to the *Allied Dunbar Investment and Savings Handbook* since it was first published in 1980.

Stuart Reynolds, LLB, is a Director in the Legal Department of Allied Dunbar Assurance plc where his primary responsibility is in relation to the development of new life assurance and pension products for the Company.

John Smithard, LLB, formerly a Member of The Stock Exchange and now a Member of the Securities Institute, is with stockbrokers James Capel Investment Management, a division of HSBC Investment Bank.

Mike Wilkes is a Senior Tax Manager with Pannell Kerr Forster, an international firm of chartered accountants. He specialises in the taxation of Lloyd's underwriters and foreign domiciled individuals, but also deals with the general taxation affairs of a number of other personal clients.

Paul Wright, BSc (Hons), MBA is Investment Marketing Manager for Allied Dunbar Assurance plc with particular responsibilities for communication and product development.

Other titles in the Allied Dunbar Handbook series

TAX HANDBOOK 1999–2000

Whether you are a financial adviser, accountant, solicitor, company secretary, finance director or private individual who wants to find out about your own tax situation, this thorough guide has to be your first choice for shrewd advice and tax saving hints. Fully revised and updated, this edition incorporates all the latest changes following the Finance Act 1999. It offers sound advice on how to cope with self assessment, as well as offering detailed information on the complete range of taxes including CGT, VAT, stamp duty, inheritance tax, life assurance and national insurance.

ESTATE PLANNING & TAXATION OF CAPITAL HANDBOOK

The 1998 budget introduced sweeping changes, specifically in the areas of capital gains tax and inheritance tax. The *Allied Dunbar Estate Planning & Taxation of Capital Handbook* is an accessible guide to estate planning, which you can use to understand the legal obligations and minimise the tax strain.

BUSINESS TAX & LAW HANDBOOK

With detailed information and astute advice, the *Allied Dunbar Business Tax & Law Handbook* makes business planning easier. It details the important taxation and legal considerations that affect a business; and considers both the legal environment in which businesses operate and the taxation obligations which must be met.

--- AVAILABLE SOON ---

RETIREMENT PLANNING HANDBOOK (7th edition)

The *Allied Dunbar Retirement Planning Handbook* is an essential addition to your bookshelf. It ensures that you are fully aware of long and short term investment opportunities and examines the options available for improving retirement prospects.

EXPATRIATES TAX & INVESTMENT HANDBOOK (7th edition)
'Expat's bible' – *What Investment*

Written by experts, the *Allied Dunbar Expatriate Tax & Investment Handbook* gives you comprehensive coverage of every aspect of expatriate tax and investment from the effect of the single currency to advice on working abroad. It is the essential guide for expatriates wishing to manage their financial affairs to their greatest possible advantage.

PENSIONS HANDBOOK (7th edition)

This is the complete guide for business owners, company directors, the self employed and professional pension planners. It gives you a detailed investigation of all the choices available for successful pension planning.

**For further information contact your local bookseller
or telephone Pearson Education Ltd on 01704 50 80 80.**

AN OVERVIEW

PAUL WRIGHT

Allied Dunbar Assurance plc

The *Allied Dunbar Investment & Savings Handbook* was first published in 1980 and is aimed primarily at the investment adviser. It is designed to give an annual update on the various types of investment. Most chapters include a section designed to cover highlights of the previous year, a preview of the coming year and a view on the next year or two based on current thinking.

This chapter covers the following topics:

- the investment adviser
- types of investor
- ways of arranging and holding investments
- the nature of an investment
- investment policy
- trustees, and
- overseas investors.

1.1 INTRODUCTION

The basic principles of investment do not change. It is only the influences on investment policy that are likely to alter over the years. These influences are primarily of a political and economic nature, that is to say, the world economic climate and, for the UK investor, the economic and taxation policies of the government of the day.

The investment adviser's task is always to ensure the client's asset portfolio is well balanced and robust in the face of changing investment conditions. When interest rates are exceptionally high, as they have been from time to time over the last two decades, the appeal of short-term deposits can be hard to resist. However, as we have seen more recently, interest rates can fall sharply, leaving clients with the twin problems of declining real value and declining income. Advisers must always be prepared, if necessary, to lean against the winds of investment fashion to ensure that clients achieve the right balance of risk and reward to suit their personal circumstances.

1.2 THE INVESTMENT ADVISER

Today's investment adviser has the unenviable burden of coping with more and more information about an increasing array of investments. Nowadays, more investment products exist than ever before, described in an ever growing mass of literature, commented on by experts of varying experience and qualifications in an environment of proliferating legislation.

Against that background, the investment adviser – solicitor, accountant, stockbroker, insurance broker, bank manager or anyone else – has five main responsibilities:

(1) To know which investment products are available and to establish which are suitable for individual clients (particularly so following the passing of the Financial Services Act 1986).
(2) To know which questions to ask about investment options and where to find the answers.
(3) To be able to support the investment decision and, if necessary, show that the advice is not influenced by the method of remuneration.
(4) To be able to make arrangements for a particular investment (or disinvestment) to be made on behalf of clients.
(5) To keep up to date on a fast-changing regulatory framework which applies to all those in the business of providing investment advice.

Most importantly, advisers have to recognise their own limitations and to look for advice themselves. That, in the main, is the purpose of this book. It identifies the main investment media, identifies the investor for whom they are suitable or unsuitable (posing the main questions which should be asked about each medium) and provides signposts to the specialist consultants or dealers and to the legal, fiscal and other technicalities.

1.3 TYPES OF INVESTOR

This book helps people advising individual investors (including trustees and family investment companies). It is essential that advisers identify the particular category of investor to which their client belongs. It would be impossible to devise a precise categorisation which is exhaustive and so it follows that advisers must take into account a number of personal factors in appraising both investors and also the investment and disinvestment situations with which they are concerned. These factors will include the investor's age and health, his or her intention with regard to place of

residence and/or domicile, willingness to accept risk, willingness to participate in the choice of investments and capacity to delegate.

1.4 WAYS OF ARRANGING AND HOLDING INVESTMENTS

All the foregoing assumes considerable sophistication on the part of
investment advisers and also a willingness to give their time, for which
they will obviously expect to be remunerated. The fact that investors of
moderate means are usually unwilling to pay for this level of individual
attention has meant that collective investment media have developed
hand-in-hand with the relative decline of individually tailored investment
portfolios. A corollary of this development is that an ever-growing body
of legislation and regulation (see Chapter 21) has had to be developed to
protect the small saver against fraud.

For many of the specific investments, comment is made on methods of
arranging and holding those investments, although a number of such
methods are common to many investment media. It is beyond the scope
of this book to give detailed explanations or advice on either the mechanics of establishing and conducting the particular 'vehicle' or its tax
implications. The investment adviser will be aware that the principal
ways in which investments can be arranged and held are:

(1) by personal direct investment by the individual;
(2) through a trust or settlement (including a will trust);
(3) in partnership with others;
(4) through a family investment company.

1.5 THE NATURE OF AN INVESTMENT

1.5.1 Capital and income

The two basic elements of investment are capital and income. At one end
of the scale, the capital remains constant while the income produced
may vary (eg bank and building society deposits); at the other end, there
are non-income-producing assets (such as commodities and works of
art) where no income is produced but the capital value fluctuates.

Between the two extremes are many variations. Gilt-edged securities
can produce a constant level of income and a known repayment value at
maturity. Short dated securities will have more certainty over the rise (or
fall) in capital values to maturity whereas values of long-dated gilts will
vary considerably as interest rates rise and fall. Investments in property

or equities will produce variations in both capital value and income. Life assurances, such as single-premium bonds, in theory produce no income while they are held as an investment, but in practice this disadvantage can be overcome by the various withdrawal plans which are available (see Chapter 14).

1.5.2 Inflation

An essential third element in evaluating investments is inflation. For most of the past ten years, inflation has been viewed by many governments as public enemy number one. Although currently under control, high inflation harms investment, damages prosperity and can destroy jobs.

The need for a hedge against inflation has had a strong influence on investment policy since the 1960s. As inflation rates fluctuate, opinions will vary widely on what represents an effective hedge; inflation has different consequences for different people. Commodities, works of art or tangible assets may turn out to be a good hedge against inflation, but the same hope of finding a good hedge often underlies investment in land, buildings and shares in companies, both domestic and overseas. The list is endless; and investors must take their pick, according to their own philosophy or judgement.

This is an area where fashion can play a part. The current view is that inflation provides only a modest threat to markets (indeed, some would argue that deflation currently poses a greater risk). The fact that inflation has been below 4 per cent for the past few years does not mean it will not return. People with not particularly long memories will recall inflation at four times that level and the impact this had both on individual savings and the economy.

1.5.3 Time

A fourth investment dimension is the time factor. In most, if not all, of the following chapters, references are made to fluctuations, trends and fashions affecting the various markets. Within a long-term trend, there are likely to be many short-term fluctuations, caused by a myriad of factors. When to buy and when to sell are therefore difficult decisions for the investor. Investors can be guided by professional advisers who have knowledge of the technical factors affecting a particular market, but who can only express an opinion on political factors and the general state of the economy, and who can therefore make only intelligent general forecasts not amounting to precise predictions. For those who invest overseas, fluctuations in exchange rates form a further element in the evaluation of investments.

1.6 INVESTMENT POLICY – GENERAL PRINCIPLES AND SPECIAL FACTORS

1.6.1 Diversification

The first maxim for practically every investor should be diversification (indeed, for trustees the Trustee Investments Act 1961 prescribes diversification, although its provisions can be excluded when a trust is created). You achieve diversification by investing in varying kinds of investments and also within a particular class of investment.

There will always, of course, be investors who have to commit, or to leave committed, a substantial part of their capital in one particular way (eg the man who has built up a substantial business). It might also be thought that the small investor with little money to invest would have little scope for diversification, but unit trusts (see Chapter 8) or bonds (see Chapter 3) indirectly provide significant diversification.

1.6.2 Balance

Investors should, as far as possible, have a balanced portfolio. A part of their capital should be earmarked for security and invested in, for example, building society or bank deposits. However, all investors should also look for a measure of capital appreciation as a hedge against inflation, so a part of their capital should be invested in equity-type investments. The precise balance will depend on the individual circumstances and inclinations of the particular investor.

1.6.3 Advice of specialists

The investor should be guided by the advice of the various specialists in the markets discussed in this book. They all provide a service which, if well performed, is a valuable one, for which they quite properly charge fees. However, they all wish to sell their wares and another reason for diversification is to avoid total dependence on the judgement and integrity of any one particular specialist.

Any investor investing overseas should pay particularly close regard to the advice of specialists familiar with the markets in the countries concerned. The additional advice required will cover such things as marketability, banking arrangements and (particularly in the case of purchase of property) legal advice to ensure that the investor obtains a good title.

1.6.4 Taxation

The general rule is that, while full account should be taken of likely tax implications, investment policy should not be dictated by tax. For example, it is often the case that decisions tend to be unduly influenced by capital gains tax considerations. The investor has to balance the right time to sell an investment which is showing a profit against a loss of use of the money required to pay the tax. In general terms, investors should not be deterred from realising investments simply by capital gains tax considerations alone.

Investments with favourable tax treatment include national savings certificates (see Chapter 2) and life assurances (see Chapter 14) which continue to have capital gains tax benefits and, in the case of certain trust policies, inheritance tax benefits as well. Another tax-efficient investment worthy of consideration is the new Individual Savings Account (see Chapter 20).

These tax benefits are a good reason for investing in this way. However, there is no guarantee that, over a given period, they will necessarily produce a better return than investments which have no tax benefits at all. Not only may these other investments have compensating benefits (eg better capital appreciation), future tax legislation could alter or even nullify tax benefits that are now available – yet another reason for a policy of diversification.

1.6.5 Commission and expenses of buying and selling

At one end of the scale, there is no explicit cost at all in investing money in a building society or bank deposit. Commission on the purchase of gilt-edged securities is small, while for equities it is reasonable, although stamp duty on purchases will also be payable (see Chapter 3). Commissions on equities vary from broker to broker following the abolition of fixed commissions in 1986.

At the top end of the scale comes the art market where the total commission can be as high as 20 per cent + VAT (see Chapter 18). The investor hoping to make an eventual gain must realise that, immediately after purchase, the item may be worth only around 80 per cent of the amount paid (or even less, where VAT is taken into account).

1.6.6 Buying and selling prices

On The Stock Exchange, separate buying and selling prices are quoted, the difference between these prices being the market-maker's turn or potential profit. The same principle can apply to other markets and, with certain assets (eg jewellery), the fact that the asset has only second-hand value the moment it has been purchased must be taken into account.

1.6.7 Other benefits

Investments should not be considered only by reference to pure investment criteria. Property may be purchased as a home or, if it is a farm, to provide a livelihood. Life assurance brings with it the element of family protection. Works of art (unless stored away in a safe deposit) bring pleasure to the owner and collector.

1.6.8 Methods of investment

The normal method of investment is for investors, either personally or through an agent, to buy and sell individual investments (and they could give their agent discretionary power to buy and sell on their behalf). Investors can either buy the investment outright or acquire options to buy at some time in the future. Alternatively, they may be able to buy a 'future', which effectively gives full exposure to fluctuations in the value of the underlying asset, but at a much lower cost.

The same type of investment can sometimes be acquired through different means. For example, investment in property can be by direct purchase of property (see Chapters 9–12), shares in a property company (see Chapter 3) or property bonds (see Chapter 3). Overseas investment can be through investment trusts, unit trusts or open-ended investment companies (either based in the UK or offshore) holding overseas investments, or in UK companies with substantial overseas activities.

1.6.9 Gearing

For the smaller investor, borrowing can only be a sensible strategy if tax relief is available on the loan interest. Under the present law, tax relief for loan interest is available for loans for the purchase of a house as a principal residence (the ceiling being £30,000) but this relief has fallen in value as the rate of tax relief was reduced to 20 per cent in the 1994–95 tax year, 15 per cent for the 1995–96 tax year and 10 per cent for the 1998–99 tax year. The relief will be withdrawn from April 2000.

Borrowing, however, will only appeal to investors with free assets who think they can invest these assets so as to produce greater capital appreciation. It would be pointless, for example, for the cautious investor to borrow from a building society and then reinvest the amount borrowed in a building society (or other equally safe investment) because the interest paid would exceed the interest received and the only beneficiary would be the building society itself.

For the wealthy investor, borrowing has often been less a question of tax relief than of altering the shape of the asset portfolio. For example, consider an investor with £250,000 who buys a house for £150,000. If Mr Smith buys the property without a mortgage, he will have a £150,000 stake in the property market and £100,000 invested elsewhere. If he takes a £100,000 mortgage, he will have an unchanged stake in the property market but £200,000 invested elsewhere.

1.7 TRUSTEES

Trustees are usually appointed by a settlement or a will. They can, however, be bare trustees, nominees or attorneys for others (under a power of attorney) who might well be infants or persons under some disability. They also include anyone who owes a fiduciary duty of care to others.

For investment purposes their 'bible' is the Trustee Investments Act 1961, although its provisions are often expressly varied by the trust instrument itself. The principles that the Act lays down are discussed below.

1.7.1 Suitability of investments for the trust

Normally the question of what investments are suitable for a particular trust involves considering the interests of the beneficiaries under that trust. If there is a life tenant and 'remaindermen', then the trustees must ensure that the income produced for the life tenant is reasonable, but at the same time they must consider security of capital and possible capital appreciation for the remaindermen. Where there are infant beneficiaries, a special duty of care is required.

1.7.2 Diversification

In a normal trust, the trustees could be in breach of trust if they do not diversify the trust investments. In a small trust, diversification can be achieved through the medium of, for example, unit trusts or investment trusts. However, diversification can be a problem in the fairly common case where a settlor has built up a business through a company and settled shares in that company upon trust for his or her children. In this case the trust instrument should include the appropriate authority for the trustees to continue to hold that investment even though that approach does not lead to diversification.

1.7.3 Expert advice

Trustees must obtain and consider proper advice from a specialist in the relevant field of investment. This principle is seldom expressly excluded. Unless there is a specific provision in the trust instrument to the contrary, trustees must make investment decisions personally (and cannot delegate this to the expert adviser).

1.7.4 Authorised investments

The Act specifies the kinds of investment in which trustees are authorised to invest and states that at least half the trust fund should be invested in the 'narrower range' and that the balance can be invested in the 'wider range'. Investments in the 'narrower range' include deposits with approved banks and building societies, gilt-edged securities, mortgages on property and debentures of companies that, first, have an issued and paid-up share capital of at least £1m and, secondly, have paid dividends (however small) on the whole of their ordinary share capital in each of the previous five years. The 'wider range' includes unit trusts and ordinary shares in companies satisfying the conditions stated above for debentures in the narrower range.

Nowadays it is general practice for trust instruments to confer express powers of investment, overriding the provisions of the Trustee Investments Act 1961 in this respect, and it is quite usual for the trustees to be given very wide powers in the interests of flexibility. The investment clause will always require close examination because, either by design or as a consequence of bad drafting, the powers actually given may not be so wide as appears at first sight. An investment in its narrow legal sense is an income-producing instrument. Consequently, if trustees are to be given powers to buy houses as residences for beneficiaries or to use capital for improving or repairing them, specific powers must be included. Again, if trustees are to be permitted to invest in assets such as capital shares with no participation in the profits of the company or chattels or commodities or currency, specific powers must be given. Specific powers must also be given for insurances and assurances.

1.7.5 Caution

In their own interests, trustees should tend to be cautious and adopt a conservative policy. They must act within the principles laid down in the trust or settlement deed and the 1961 Act. Their first duty is to familiarise themselves with the powers of investment that they have been given – specifically, whether these investment powers are restricted as specified in the Act or whether, as is often the case, they are given the powers of an absolute owner. Even then they must ensure that they are given *all* the powers of an absolute owner.

If a known liability arises (and this commonly occurs on the death of a testator, where a liability to inheritance tax may arise), the trustees or the personal representatives should set about covering that liability. If necessary they should realise investments and place the money on deposit with a bank or with building societies or even invest in short-dated gilts. A prudent trustee who does this cannot be criticised if the market in those realised investments then goes up, but, conversely, a trustee who does not do this is open to criticism if the market goes down.

1.8 OVERSEAS INVESTORS

1.8.1 Exchange control

UK investors can invest in any country in the world without restriction, although they will be subject to whatever restrictions the country in which they plan to invest may impose. Conversely, overseas investors can freely invest in the UK. However, they may be subject to exchange control provisions imposed by their country of residence.

1.8.2 Taxation

Detailed advice on taxation is outside the scope of this book and so the comments made below are necessarily only in very general terms. Overseas investors (and also immigrants and emigrants) have to be particularly aware of taxation considerations, which for them depend on domicile and residence.

For tax purposes, a person is regarded as resident in the UK if he or she is physically present there for 183 days or more in any tax year, or, if over a period of four such years, present there for an average of three months or more in each tax year.

Individuals will be regarded as 'ordinarily resident' if they are habitually resident in the UK year after year and will continue to be regarded as ordinarily resident if they usually live there but are in fact physically absent (eg on a long holiday) for even the whole of any tax year.

Inheritance tax

Liability to UK inheritance tax depends basically on domicile. Investors domiciled in the UK will be subject to inheritance tax on their worldwide assets, whereas investors not domiciled in the UK will be subject to inheritance tax on UK property or investments only.

Domicile is a concept of general law and is determined by a range of factors. Broadly speaking, domicile is where individuals have their permanent home. It is distinct from nationality or residence and an individual can have only one domicile at a time.

Individuals would normally acquire a domicile of origin from their father when they were born, though this may change if the person on whom the individual was dependent at the time changed his domicile before the individual was aged 16.

Married women who married before 1974 automatically acquired their husband's domicile, though they may now change it to a domicile of their choice.

Anyone over the age of 16 has the legal power to apply for a new domicile of choice. However, it is not that easy to do and will usually require proof that the individual has severed all connections with his or her existing country and intends to settle permanently in a new country.

Capital gains tax

Liability to capital gains tax depends on UK residence or 'ordinary residence' for tax purposes. The general rule is that the investor ordinarily resident in the UK is subject to capital gains tax and the investor not ordinarily resident in the UK is exempt from it. Investors immigrating to or emigrating from the UK should take advice on the timing of the sale of assets so as to avoid any liability to capital gains tax.

Income tax

Liability to income tax depends on residence, but there are certain concessions for people not domiciled in the UK. Many factors, including the provisions of double taxation agreements, are relevant and the investor must take professional advice.

1.8.3 Other restrictions

Normally, an overseas investor can invest in any form of UK investment without problems. However, difficulties might arise where the investor ultimately wanted to export the investment (particularly where it is a work of art) or where the investment involves a liability in the UK (which could arise with, say, an investment in leasehold property as the landlord might require a UK-resident guarantor).

1.9 CONCLUSION

When it comes to investment, nothing is constant. Continual review and permanent vigilance are essential. The investment strategies appropriate to one investor may not be right for another and those suitable for one particular generation of investor may be wholly inappropriate for the next generation, when the investment climate and the law may have changed. Even a strategy appropriate now may be inappropriate in the future by which time the investor will have aged and his or her needs and family circumstances will have changed considerably.

1.10 INCOME TAX RATES, ALLOWANCES, AND NATIONAL INSURANCE RATES FROM 6 APRIL 1999

Table 1.1 Income tax rates 1999–2000

Bands of taxable income £	Rate %	Tax on band £
0–1,500	10	150
1,501–28,000	23	6,245
Over 28,000	40	–

Table 1.2 Personal allowances

(1) Personal and married couple's allowances
   The rates which will apply for 1999–2000 (equivalent figures for 1998/99 in italics) are:

Age	Personal allowance £		Married couple's allowance £	
Under 65	4,335	*4,195*	1,970	*1,900*
65 to 74	5,720	*5,410*	5,125	*3,305*
75 and over	5,980	*5,600*	5,195	*3,345*

Note: The income limit for persons aged 65 and over is £16,800. Where the taxpayer's total income exceeds this limit, the age-related allowances are reduced by £1 for every £2 of income over the limit. The allowances are not reduced below the level of the basic personal or married couple's allowances.

(2) Additional allowance and widow's bereavement allowance – £1,970.

(3) Blind person's allowance – £1,380.

National Insurance contributions 1999–2000

Table 1.3 Contracted-in

Employer contributions		Employee contributions	
Earnings £pw	% of all earnings	Earnings £pw	% of all earnings
0–83	0	0–66	0
83.01–500	12.2	66.01–500	10
over 500	12.2	over 500	No further NI payable

Table 1.4 Contracted-out

Employer contributions			Employee contributions	
Earnings £pw	(a)%	(b)%	Earnings £pw	%
0–66	0	0	0–66	0
66.01–500	9.2	11.6	66.01–500	8.4
over 500	12.2	12.2	over 500	No further NI payable

Self-employed contributions

Class 2 Contributions: where profits are over £3,770, flat weekly rate increased from £6.35 per week to £6.55 per week.

Class 4 Contributions: 6 per cent on profits between £7,530 and £26,000 per annum.

These rates take effect from 6 April 1999.

1.11 CAPITAL GAINS TAX

Capital gains tax is charged on real capital gains. A person who makes a gain is allowed to deduct not only his actual acquisition value (in addition to the costs of acquisition and disposal) but also a proportion of the acquisition value which represents the increase in the RPI between the month of acquisition and the month of disposal.

Up until the November 1993 Budget, it was permissible to use indexation relief to create or increase a capital loss. From 30 November 1993, indexation relief may only be used in this way for transactions prior to 30 November 1993.

The intention of the new rules was that, in all future transactions, indexation relief should only be used to reduce or extinguish a gain, not create or increase a loss. The rule was relaxed as the Finance Bill made its way through the committee stages; indexation may continue to be used in this way but only for the 1993–94 and 1994–95 tax years and only up to an overall limit of £10,000.

The capital gains tax rates, taper relief, exemptions and retirement relief are as follows:

Individuals taxed:

Where gains plus total income are below basic rate limit	20%
Where gains plus total income exceed basic rate limit	40%
Trustees and personal representatives	34%

Tapering scale:

Complete years asset held after 5 April 1998 — *Percentage of chargeable gain*

	Business assets	Non-business
0	100.0	100
1	92.5	100
2	85.0	100
3	77.5	95
4	70.0	90
5	62.5	85
6	55.0	80
7	47.5	75
8	40.0	70
9	32.5	65
10	25.0	60

Annual exemptions:

Individuals	£7,100
Trusts, in general	£3,500

Retirement relief:

Exempt gain	£200,000
50% exempt on next	£600,000

2

UNLISTED INVESTMENTS

JOHN SMITHARD

James Capel Investment Management

2.1 TYPES OF UNLISTED SECURITY

This chapter deals with the most commonly available forms of investment which do not have an official quotation or market price. It includes investments issued by the government through National Savings, by local authorities, by building societies and by other financial institutions wishing to raise money, and in general can only be redeemed by the borrower.

With some exceptions, these securities provide investors with interest until they mature, whereupon they receive the return of their original capital. Although the rates of return on some of these investments might not always compare favourably with returns on other forms of investment, some have taxation advantages up to a specific amount, particularly for the higher rate taxpayer. Other investments covered in this chapter may produce no income in the course of their lives, but give a guaranteed improvement in capital value on maturity. Premium bonds give no guarantee of income or capital appreciation but offer the holder a chance in draws for tax-free prizes. A comparison of rates of return, the limitations on amounts invested, and conditions of withdrawal are set out in Table 2.1 on pp 18 and 19.

2.2 REVIEW OF 1998–99

In another year in which the overall public borrowing requirement fell, National Savings raised a net total of just over £360m on total sales of over £12bn. The figures were sharply down from just three years ago when in 1996–97 the total net cash raised after redemptions had been nearly £4.8bn on sales of just over £15.8bn. Increasing competition, withdrawals to fund PEPs and TESSAs, and the Treasury's sharply reduced need for new money were the main causes of the downturn, with interest rates being set at uncompetitive levels especially compared with new entrants to the cash savings market such as Prudential's Egg. Indeed, in the early part of 1999 there was a net outflow of funds from National Savings from its peak in January as almost £440m moved towards the successful launch of Egg, to PEPs and to TESSAs.

The year to 5 April 1999 was the last occasion for subscribing to a TESSA, and while those in place at that date remain so until they mature, new money now has to be directed towards an ISA, for which most of the old tax benefits remain.

Despite the overall decline in interest rates throughout the year, a number of entrants brought new products to the cash savings market. Standard Life, Virgin and Prudential's Egg all had successful launches by keeping their rates temporarily high while they were generally declining elsewhere.

After a splendid year for demutualisations in 1997, last year was very downbeat and carpetbaggers certainly had a disappointing time. The vote at the Nationwide went against floating the building society on the Stock Market. There was very little activity on the take-over front, the most noticeable exception being the acquisition by Halifax of the Birmingham Midshires, managing to beat off the offer by Royal Bank of Scotland.

2.3 TYPES OF UNLISTED INVESTMENT

2.3.1 National Savings Bank accounts

The National Savings Bank is guaranteed by the government and is operated by the Post Office as agent. Two types of account – ordinary accounts and investment accounts – are available.

Anyone aged seven years or over can open an account in his or her own name, and an account can be opened on behalf of a younger child by a parent or legal guardian although withdrawals and encashments are not allowed by the child until the child is seven. Friendly societies and other classes of investor can also open accounts.

Interest on both types of account is credited annually on 31 December. In the case of ordinary accounts, this is for each complete calendar month. For investment accounts, interest is calculated from the day funds are deposited until the day prior to withdrawal. There is a maximum amount which can be withdrawn daily from an ordinary account, and all withdrawals from an investment account require one month's notice, although withdrawal can be made without notice subject to 30 days' loss of interest.

Interest is paid gross (ie without deduction of tax at source). In the case of ordinary accounts an individual is given exemption from basic and higher rate income tax for the first £70 interest. If a husband and wife each have an account, they can each claim exemption up to this level, although if they hold a joint account the exemption is £140. However, there is no such exemption for the higher gross interest earned on investment accounts.

Although the limit on income tax exemption for ordinary accounts is relatively low, a holding up to this level may be attractive for higher rate taxpayers.

Accounts can be opened by completing a simple form available from almost any branch of the Post Office. The account holder receives a pass book in which all deposits and withdrawals are entered. The minimum for each deposit is £10 (ordinary account) and £20 (investment account) and the maximum holding is £10,000 (ordinary account) and £100,000 (investment account).

The pass book no longer needs to be sent in once a year for the adding of interest, as this will be done on the next occasion that it is received by the National Savings Bank.

2.3.2 National Savings certificates

National Savings certificates are guaranteed by the government. They cannot be sold to third parties. A number of different issues of certificates have been made over the years.

A maximum individual holding is specified for each issue of national savings certificates. Trustees and registered friendly societies and charities approved by the director of savings can also buy certificates.

No interest is paid, but after a stated period of time the certificates can be redeemed at a higher value than the original purchase price. The total rate at which the value appreciates during this period is indicated on the certificate and in the prospectus. However, the value builds up by the addition of increments at the end of the first year and each subsequent period of three months. The full table, showing how the value rises more steeply towards the end of the period and levels off after the end of the period, is available from the details issued by the Department of National Savings. Certificates from the seventh issue earn interest at the general extension rate after maturity. The general extension rate is a variable rate of interest for matured certificates when they have completed their fixed period terms and is currently only 2.49 per cent gross.

Table 2.1 Current rates of return and conditions (August 1999)

Investment	Return (% pa)		Amount invested		Withdrawal notice (days)	Notes
	Gross*	Net*	Min	Max		
1 National Savings Bank:						
Ordinary accounts	1.0–1.1	0.8–0.9	£10	£10,000	£100 on demand	Depending on balance, first £70 free of tax
Investment accounts	3.3–4.6	2.6–3.7	£20	£100,000	30	
2 National savings certificates (52nd issue)	3.85[1] (tax free)		£100	£10,000	8	[1]Equivalent to 6.4% to basic-rate taxpayers:
3 National savings index-linked certificates (13th issue)	Increase in RPI[2] (tax free)		£100	£10,000	8	[2]Paid on withdrawal if after one year, with tax-free interest.
4 National savings children's bonus bonds	4.85 (tax free)		£25	£1,000	8	If held for 5 years
5 National savings income bonds	4.6–4.8	2.8–2.9	£2,000	£250,000	3 months	
6 National savings capital bonds	5.15	3.1	£100	£250,000	8	
7 National savings FIRST option bonds	4.65–4.9	2.8–2.9	£1,000	£250,000	8	
8 National savings pensioner's guaranteed income bonds	5.0–5.15	3.0–3.1	£500	£50,000	2 months	

Table 2.1 cont

	Chance of prize (tax free)					
9 Premium savings bond	5.8	3.5	£100	£20,000	8	Monthly prize fund; one month's interest at 5.0% on each bond eligible for draw
10 Local authority mortgage bonds: 1 year						Other terms available
11 Commercial banks: Deposit accounts (7 day)	0–1.0	0.0–0.8	25p	None	7[3]	[3]But may be withdrawn on demand demand subject to deduction of 7 days' interest from balance
High Interest cheque	3.5–6.0	2.1–3.6	£1,000	None	None	
Certificates of deposit	5.1[4]	3.1	£50,000	None	Marketable security	[4]3-month term and 6-month term
12 Building societies: Share accounts	5.3–5.8	3.2–3.5	£1		On demand[5]	[5]Up to £300 in cash or £5,000 by cheque; above £5,000 branch refers to head office
Premium accounts	5.3–6.3[6]	3.2–3.8[6]	£500	None	0–12 months	[6]Rates vary according to size
13 Certificates of tax deposit	2.0–4.0[7] 2.0	1.6–2.4[7] 1.6[8]	£2,000	None	0–12 months	[7]If withdrawn for payment of tax [8]If withdrawn in cash
14 Treasury bills	4.8	2.9	£5,000	None	Marketable security	

*Based on tax at the basic rate of 23%

The capital appreciation is free from both income tax and capital gains tax. The minimum holding is £100 and the maximum £10,000 in the current issue, but holders may have a further unlimited amount of certificates if these arise from reinvestment of holdings of earlier issues.

The certificates can be a suitable form of savings for children, although parents and children should also consider capital bonds or children's bonus bonds (see **2.3.7**). For the pure investor they are not suitable for non-taxpayers or for short-term savings; but for the investor paying tax at the higher rate, the certificates may be attractive. Application forms are available from most post offices.

Holdings should be reviewed from time to time, particularly since new issues may carry more attractive rates of capital appreciation than those already held. A review of holdings should certainly be made at the end of the specified period as the general extension rate is usually unattractive.

Any number of certificates can be cashed at one time, on at least eight working days' notice, and repayment forms are available at most post offices and banks. No interest is paid if the certificates are redeemed within one year of purchase.

2.3.3 National Savings index-linked certificates

As with National Savings certificates, these certificates are guaranteed by the government. They cannot be sold to third parties.

There is no lower age limit for holding these certificates, although encashment is not allowed until a child reaches the age of seven, except in special circumstances. No more than 400 certificates of £25, ie £10,000 at initial purchase price can be held in the current issue unless they came from a reinvestment of mature certificates in which case there is no limit. The minimum holding is four certificates, costing £100.

If a certificate is encashed within the first year, the purchase price only is repaid, unless it is a reinvestment certificate. If the certificates are held for more than a year, the redemption value is equal to the original purchase price, increased in proportion to the rise in the RPI between the month of purchase and the month of redemption. In the event of a fall in the RPI, the certificates can be encashed for the original purchase price in the first year, and not less than their value at the previous anniversary otherwise. After the death of a holder, indexation can continue for a maximum of 12 months. Certificates can be inherited.

The latest issue guarantees a return above the rate of inflation for a five-year term by offering extra tax-free interest as well as indexation.

After the fifth anniversary, certificates continue to earn interest and index-linking, but on such terms as the Treasury may decide. As with national savings certificates, capital appreciation is exempt from income tax and capital gains tax.

Certificates are suitable for individuals who do not need immediate income but are seeking protection in real terms for the amount invested. Higher rate taxpayers in this category will find the certificates particularly attractive. Application forms are obtainable from most post offices.

2.3.4 National Savings income bonds

As with National Savings certificates, these bonds are guaranteed by the government. Anyone aged seven years or over can buy income bonds and they may be bought for children under seven, but there are two special conditions:

(1) interest is normally credited to a national savings bank account in the child's name;
(2) the bond is not normally repayable until the child reaches seven.

Friendly societies and other classes of investor can also buy these bonds.

Gross interest is paid on a monthly basis but the interest is subject to tax. Investors may cash in part of their holding in multiples of £1,000, but they must keep a minimum balance of £2,000.

Three months' notice of repayment is required. The maximum holding is £250,000. If the investor dies, the money can be withdrawn without any formal period of notice and with interest paid in full up to the date of repayment.

A slightly higher interest rate is given for amounts exceeding £25,000. Rates of interest are variable.

The bonds are particularly suitable for investors who require high regular income, who can afford to tie up at least £2,000 and are not subject to tax. Income is paid monthly, on the fifth of each month. The first payment is made on the next interest date after the bonds have been held for six weeks. Application forms are obtainable from post offices. Investors aged 60 or over should also compare the rates with those available on pensioner's guaranteed income bonds.

2.3.5 National Savings capital bonds

The bonds are guaranteed by the government. They may be held by individuals, by children and by trustees of a sole individual.

Bonds are bought with a £100 minimum and a £250,000 maximum and give a rate of return fixed at the date of purchase. Although called capital bonds, they accrue interest which is capitalised on each anniversary of the purchase date, and this accrued interest must be notified to the Inland Revenue on the individual's tax return (and income tax paid, if necessary, before actual receipt of the capitalised interest at the date of maturity). An annual statement of value, showing the capitalised interest, is sent to the bondholder shortly after the end of each tax year.

The capitalised interest accrues at an increasing rate during the bond's life and the full advertised compound rate is received only if held to maturity. This occurs on the fifth anniversary of the purchase date, before which the bondholder will have been reminded by the bond office of the imminence of maturity.

Repayment can be requested at any time for a minimum amount of £100, provided this leaves at least the minimum holding. No capitalised interest accrues before the first anniversary.

Depending on the level of interest rates available elsewhere, capital bonds may prove an excellent investment for an individual who pays little or no income tax and who can tie up funds for five years, assuming that interest rates will move downwards in the intervening period.

2.3.6 FIRST option bonds

FIRST option bonds are a means of lump sum saving in a government security, the returns on which are guaranteed for one year at a time. The interest rate for the first year is set at the time of purchase and the interest, net of basic rate tax, is capitalised within the bond on the first anniversary. At the same time, holders are notified of the next year's interest rate and this accrues, again net of basic rate income tax, on the value of the bond, being added to the capital at subsequent anniversaries.

The amount held in the FIRST option bond must not be reduced by subsequent withdrawals to below the minimum holding of £1,000, but up to £250,000 may be held in total in one or any number of bonds.

FIRST is an acronym for Fixed Interest Rate Savings, Tax-paid. Interest accrues daily but is added only on the anniversary; an improved rate is given on a bond exceeding £20,000, although an amalgamation of a number of bonds to make £20,000 or over would not qualify. Bonds may be purchased and held by anyone aged 16 or over, and by trustees.

Withdrawals should be made only on anniversary dates for, if not, only half the stated interest rate accrues since the last anniversary on the capitalised interest at that date. No interest is given on a withdrawal in the first year.

FIRST option bonds have been designed for basic rate taxpayers looking for a competitive return who can make lump sum payments which they intend to hold for at least one year. Non-taxpayers, who would need to reclaim tax deducted at source, might find other national savings instruments paying gross interest more convenient. Higher rate taxpayers, who will need to find a further tax payment, might consider tax-free investments.

Applications for bonds are made to National Savings on prospectus forms available from post offices.

2.3.7 Children's bonus bonds

These bonds are guaranteed by the government and are designed to encourage children to save. They can be bought to a maximum of £1,000 by or for children under 16, although they can be held to the age of 21. The minimum holding is £25 and the bonds are available in multiples of £25. After five years, holders receive a bonus payment and the bonds then attract interest at extension terms yet to be announced.

All interest, and the bonus, is exempt from income tax and need not be declared to the Inland Revenue. The proposed return should be in excess of that available on normal five-year fixed rate certificates. Repayment is normally made to a parent or guardian only if the holder is then still below the age of 16.

They may prove attractive to parents wishing to give capital to children, for there is no liability to income tax on the interest which in most other circumstances is deemed still to belong to the parent if it exceeds a token level of £100.

2.3.8 Pensioners bonds

This National Savings product has been designed to produce a competitive income return for older investors who wish to fix a monthly return for a period of five years despite any change in the level of interest rates during that period.

Interest is paid without deduction of income tax, although it is subject to income tax. This will be of certain benefit to non-taxpayers, who need not make a reclaim of tax already deducted at source. Interest is paid monthly on the 19th of each month, but only to a bank or building society account.

The bonds can only be bought by individuals of 60 years of age or older, or held in trust for a beneficiary who has reached that age. The minimum limit for each purchase is £500, but any amount above this level can be bought, up to a maximum of £50,000 for each individual for each series of bond. Up to £100,000 bonds can be held jointly. Application forms are available at post offices, with applications being made to National Savings.

Interest is earned on each day that the bonds are held. Repayment is subject to 60 days' notice, although no interest is paid for the notice period. However, there is no loss of interest on the repayment of the bonds on their fifth anniversary, or on a holder's death. The amount of each repayment must be at least £500, and there must be at least a £500 minimum holding retained after any withdrawal. Applications for repayment are also made direct to National Savings.

At the time of the bond's fifth anniversary a holder should receive a reminder notifying him of the rate of interest for the next five-year period. The holder then needs to make a decision whether to leave the bonds in place or to have them redeemed and reinvest in an alternative investment. This depends on the bondholder's needs at that time and the prevailing level of interest rates, although it is the intention to offer pensioners a competitive return for their savings.

2.3.9 Premium bonds

Premium bonds are guaranteed by the government. They cannot be sold to third parties.

Any person aged 16 or over can buy the bonds, and a parent, grandparent or legal guardian may buy bonds on behalf of a child under 16. A bond cannot be held in the name of more than one person or of a corporate body, society, club or other association of persons. Prizes won by bonds registered in the name of a child under the age of 16 are paid on behalf of the child to the parent or legal guardian.

Bonds are sold in units of £1 and purchases must then be in multiples of £10 subject to a minimum purchase at any time of £100 up to a maximum of £20,000 per person.

No interest is paid, but a bond which has been held for one full calendar month is eligible for inclusion in the regular draw for prizes of various amounts. The size of the monthly prize fund is determined by applying one month's interest at a predetermined rate to the total value of the eligible bonds at that time. This rate is reviewed from time to time. Bonds can be encashed at any time. All prizes are free of income tax and capital gains tax. Every month over 500,000 prizes are paid, ranging from £50 to £1m.

Premium bonds are suitable for higher rate taxpayers who do not wish to receive income and can set aside some savings with no guaranteed return but with the chance of receiving a tax-free prize. They are also a 'fun' investment for those investors who wish to take the chance of a prize, knowing they can always have the return of their cash investment, and so can be favourably compared to the National Lottery. The odds against winning any prize are currently 24,000 to 1 for each unit.

Application forms are available at post offices and on the Internet. Winning bondholders are notified in writing at their last recorded address and lists of winning numbers are advertised in newspapers. Repayment forms are also available at post offices.

2.3.10 Government stock

Gilts, gilt-edged or government stock represent a loan to the Bank of England, repayable on a fixed future date and, with the exception of index-linked gilts, on which a fixed rate of annual interest is payable to the holder. By far the largest active market for gilts is through The Stock Exchange, but they can also be bought and sold across post office counters. There are certain benefits to individuals in doing so, although transactions take slightly longer to process.

The full range of gilt-edged stock is now available to individual applicants. Potential investors must decide whether to buy stock which has a high income return with perhaps restricted capital growth prospects, or even a guaranteed fall in value if held to redemption; a low income return and a guaranteed rise in value until maturity; or a balance between the two. In the majority of cases, investment in index-linked stock will protect the capital against inflation until redemption, while providing a low, but inflation-proofed, income.

Gilts can also be bought when offered by the Bank of England through application forms published in the national newspapers.

Interest on gilts is paid without deduction of income tax and so gilts can certainly be considered by non-taxpayers and, depending on their return, by others who normally pay tax. Basic rate and higher rate taxpayers must account for the tax due on the interest at their marginal rate. There is no liability to capital gains tax on profits made on the redemption or sale of gilts.

The main characteristics of gilts are described in **3.5.1**.

Application forms are available from post offices. Investors can buy either a fixed nominal amount of stock, or they can invest a certain amount of cash. The maximum that can be invested on any one day is £25,000, but there is no maximum holding in one or any stock. When buying or selling, the delay between sending the application and the purchase or sale of the stock means that no guarantee can be given to the price paid or received as the market value of gilts fluctuates throughout the day. Sales are made by sending in the appropriate completed application form and the stock certificate. Commission charges are often considerably lower than those charged by stockbrokers.

Since July 1998, in an effort to save administration costs, the Bank of England has become responsible for the functions formerly exercised by National Savings.

Since July 1998, in an effort to save administration costs, the Bank of England has become responsible for the functions formerly exercised by National Savings.

2.3.11 Local authority mortgage bonds

These borrowings are secured on the revenues of local authorities, which have the power to levy the council tax. It is generally assumed that the government would stand behind such borrowings, although it has no legal commitment to do so.

A minimum investment is usually specified: this varies between authorities but is smaller than for local authority negotiable bonds (ie less than £1,000).

Local authority mortgage bonds are issued for a fixed term, usually between two and seven years. Unlike local authority negotiable bonds, in which there is a market on The Stock Exchange, they cannot normally be sold to third parties.

Interest is subject to income tax and is paid after deduction of basic rate tax. Non-taxpayers therefore have to claim a rebate of tax, while higher rate taxpayers are assessed for the balance of tax due.

Deposits are suitable for investors seeking a competitive rate of interest and prepared to tie up capital for a fixed term. Investors who may require to realise their investment more quickly should explore the possibility of negotiable bonds.

Authorities seeking deposits advertise in the national press, stating the period, rate of interest paid and details of where applications should be made. Deposits are acknowledged by the issue to the holder of mortgage bonds.

2.3.12 Commercial banks – current, deposit and savings accounts and certificates of deposit

Deposits with banks carry no government guarantee and their security therefore lies in the reputation and viability of the bank concerned. Certificates of deposit (CDs) are bearer documents and can be sold to third parties, whereas deposit and savings accounts represent a non-assignable debt from the bank to the holder.

There are normally no pre-conditions to opening a deposit or savings account with a commercial bank. However, the minimum sum for an investment in CDs is usually fairly high.

Interest, which is paid at regular intervals on accounts, can be varied by the bank as the general level of interest rates and the bank's own base rate change. Generally, seven days' notice of withdrawal is required for deposit accounts. The interest on CDs is fixed for the duration of the certificates – normally between three months and five years.

Interest on deposit and savings accounts is paid net of basic rate tax which may be reclaimed if tax deducted at source exceeds the total tax due. Higher rate taxpayers are given credit for the tax at basic rate.

Deposit and savings accounts are useful means of investing funds which may be needed at short notice. CDs are suitable for large deposits and consequently earn a higher return than deposit or savings accounts. Since 1 January 1991, banks have been able to offer tax exempt special savings accounts (TESSAs) – see **2.3.14** and Chapter 20.

Deposit and savings accounts may be opened, and CDs purchased, by instruction and transfer of cash to the bank concerned. Bank account statements should be kept for reference. Since CDs are bearer documents, they should be held in safe custody.

2.3.13 Building society accounts

Building societies offer share accounts, various higher interest accounts, term bonds and save-as-you-earn (SAYE) contracts. None of these investments can be sold to third parties. Security lies in the reputation and viability of the building society concerned. Since 1 January 1991 building societies have been able to offer tax exempt special savings accounts (TESSAs) – see **2.3.14** and Chapter 20.

The minimum age for entering into an SAYE contract is 16, but any of the other forms of savings may be undertaken by children aged seven or over. For younger children an account may be opened in the name of trustees (normally the child's parents). SAYE contracts are open only to individuals and cannot be undertaken on joint accounts.

Building societies compete for deposits not only with banks but also with each other (their offices are often open to the public for longer hours than the banks during the week and are also open on Saturday mornings). On lump sum investments, interest is usually paid every six months, although in some cases monthly. On SAYE contracts the bonus is fixed at the outset and paid at the end of the fifth and the seventh years, but other savings plans bear interest rates which, although specified at the time of investment, vary from time to time with the general level of interest rates. A period of notice is specified for withdrawals from share accounts but is in practice seldom required except for large sums. There may be penalties for early withdrawal from term bonds.

Since April 1991 basic rate tax is deducted from gross interest, but this can be reclaimed if tax deducted at source exceeds the total tax due. Higher rate taxpayers are liable for the balance of tax at those rates on the gross amount.

Since February 1989 building societies have been able to pay interest gross to depositors in certain instances.

The simplicity of building society deposit and share accounts and the ease with which small withdrawals can be made on demand, coupled with the sound record of building societies, make them attractive for basic or higher rate taxpayers. Application forms are available from local branches of the building societies. Passbooks are issued for most types of investment, although certificates are issued in some cases for fixed term contracts.

2.3.14 Tax exempt special savings accounts (TESSAs)

No applications for new TESSAs can be made following the introduction of ISAs on 6 April 1999. However, TESSAs in place at that date can continue to run their five-year life.

TESSAs were introduced on 1 January 1991. They provide a means of longer-term saving, tax free, and are operated on a commercial basis by banks and building societies. A total of £9,000 could be placed in a TESSA, either by monthly deposits of £150, or by lump sum payments of up to £3,000 at the start of the first year, followed by annual payments of up to £1,800 in the three succeeding years and up to £600 in the final year.

On the maturity of a TESSA on its fifth anniversary the full capital amount – a maximum of £9,000 – could be transferred into a new TESSA. This is no longer the case following the introduction of ISAs. The accrued interest cannot be reinvested if it brings the total above the £9,000 limit.

Interest accrues during the five-year period and is credited net of basic rate tax. At the end of the five years a bonus of the basic rate tax is credited to the account so that in effect the deposit interest is tax free. During the life of the TESSA up to the full amount of the net income can be withdrawn but any repayment of capital will bring the account to an end, without the bonus. Interest on a TESSA does not need to be declared on tax returns.

Although there is a five-year life to the TESSA account, an investor can withdraw capital and net accrued income at any time (but losing the right to the tax bonus), so the position is not dissimilar to an ordinary deposit account. However, except in cases where the accrued income has been continually withdrawn, an investor thinking of closing an account early should give consideration to the fact that all accrued income will be deemed to have been paid at the time of closure and may increase that year's income tax liability (see **20.2.1**).

2.3.15 Individual savings accounts (ISAs)

Following the success of PEPs and TESSAs, the government introduced ISAs from 6 April 1999. They supersede both, although holders of PEPs and TESSAs will be able to continue to hold their investments in a tax-free manner. The ISA is guaranteed to run for ten years and provides investors with a simple and flexible way of investing in a tax-free manner.

ISAs have three component parts. A saver is allowed to subscribe a maximum of £5,000 in any one tax year, of which up to £1,000 can go into a cash account, and up to £1,000 into life assurance policies. The balance goes into a share account. In effect, there are three 'mini' ISAs. A 'maxi' ISA can be made up entirely of stocks and shares, similar to a PEP. Investment in a mini ISA precludes investing in a maxi ISA. However, for the first year of ISAs, a total of £7,000 can be subscribed, with a maximum of £3,000 into the cash element. There is no official minimum limit but individual ISA managers may well introduce these to bring down costs.

The tax benefits are broadly similar to those for PEPs in that there is no liability to income tax or to capital gains tax while the investment is within the fund. For the first five years of ISAs, a 10 per cent tax credit will also be paid to the fund on the UK dividend stream. Withdrawals from the ISA can be made without giving rise to a tax penalty, but once the full £5,000 has been subscribed in any one year, no further topping up can be made in that tax year to make up for any withdrawal.

Investors can choose one manager to cover each of the three components, or individual managers for each part.

2.3.16 Certificates of tax deposit

Certificates of tax deposit are not strictly speaking a form of investment but a scheme operated by the Inland Revenue whereby future tax liabilities can be provided for in advance. The deposits are therefore guaranteed by the government.

Certificates are available to any taxpayer – individual, trustee or corporate – and can be surrendered to meet tax liabilities of any kind, except PAYE income tax or income tax deducted from payments to subcontractors. Different rates apply to deposits below £100,000; there is no maximum deposit.

Interest is paid for a fixed maximum period at a rate specified by HM Treasury when purchased, but the rate varies in line with money market rates. If the deposit is not used to meet tax liabilities but is instead withdrawn for cash, interest is paid at a much lower rate. Interest is paid gross and is subject to income tax.

These certificates are suitable only for taxpayers facing known future tax liabilities, although such taxpayers should consider whether a better return could be obtained by investing elsewhere until such time as the liability has to be met.

Deposits are made by applying to any Collector of Taxes, who issues a certificate specifying the date of receipt and the amount of the deposit. Any request for a deposit to be withdrawn for cash should be made to the Collector, accompanied by the relevant certificates.

2.3.17 Treasury bills

Treasury bills are bearer documents issued by the Bank of England and guaranteed by the government. There is a £5,000 minimum holding.

A Treasury bill is initially a 91-day loan to the Bank of England. No interest is paid but bills are issued at a discount. The difference between the discounted price and £100, the redemption price, is the capital gain accruing to the investor, and the annual rate of discount which it represents is called the Treasury bill rate. Although the holder may not encash the bills at the Bank of England before the due date, they can be sold through the discount market at any time at the prevailing market price.

The difference between the discounted price and the price at which the bills are redeemed at the Bank of England or sold in the market is subject to tax. In the unlikely event of a private investor holding a Treasury bill, the gain would be liable to income tax. Treasury bills are suitable for companies rather than individuals and confer total security on short-term deposits.

Tenders for Treasury bills must be made on printed forms (available from the Chief Cashier's Office, Bank of England) and must be submitted through a London clearing bank, discount house or stockbroker. The value of bills tendered for and the price at which the investor is prepared to buy them must be specified. On the day tenders are received the Bank notifies persons whose tenders have been accepted in whole or in part. Since Treasury bills are bearer documents, they should be held in safe custody.

2.4 COMPARING DIFFERENT TYPES OF SECURITY

The investor, in making a choice between different types of security, should take into account not only the relative importance of income and of capital gain but also:

(1) the degree of security against default;
(2) the expected rate of return;
(3) the tax advantages or disadvantages attaching to the security (see also Chapter 20);
(4) the convenience and cost of dealing in the particular security;
(5) the ability to realise the investment; and
(6) the prevailing rate of inflation.

2.4.1 Security against default

The British government has the power to levy taxes and to print money and it is in the highest degree unlikely that it would ever default on any of its borrowings, which include National Savings certificates, National Savings Bank deposits, premium bonds and government guaranteed fixed interest stocks. It is generally assumed that the government would stand behind borrowings of local authorities, which in any event have the power to levy local charges. All these securities, therefore, have an intrinsic safety which the private sector cannot emulate.

2.4.2 Rate of return

The rate of return on securities may be specified and fixed, as it is for conventional National Savings certificates, local authority deposits, Treasury bills and fixed interest stocks issued by public and private sector organisations. In most other cases the rate of return is specified initially but may be subject to variation to reflect the general movement of interest rates. Returns on some investments may be linked to the prevailing rate of inflation.

2.4.3 Tax advantages

Certain securities carry tax advantages, which may be of particular benefit to higher rate taxpayers. Examples are National Savings Bank ordinary accounts (up to a specified limit), national savings certificates, index-linked national savings certificates and prizes on premium bonds. British government guaranteed stocks are free of capital gains tax (see also Chapter 20).

2.4.4 Convenience and cost of dealing

The securities described in this chapter can (with the exception of certificates of tax deposit and Treasury bills) be negotiated conveniently through high street outlets such as post offices, banks, building societies and the Internet. In many cases no commission or other dealing costs are incurred.

2.4.5 Ability to realise the investment

With the exception of Treasury bills and certificates of deposit, the securities covered in this chapter cannot be sold to third parties. Thus the investment can be realised only by withdrawing the money from the borrowing organisation. This can be done on demand or at fairly short notice in the case of National Savings Bank accounts and certificates, national savings index-linked certificates (after one year if indexation is required), premium bonds, government stock, and bank and building society accounts. In other cases the capital initially invested is tied up for a particular period: this applies to local authority deposits and building society term investments as well as national savings income bonds. If certificates of tax deposit are encashed instead of being used to meet tax liabilities, a lower rate of interest is paid. Early withdrawal in these cases will either be impossible or entail a financial penalty. This disadvantage also applies to commitments to save regular amounts through yearly plan schemes.

2.4.6 Maintenance

The investor should retain safely all documents (particularly bearer documents) relating to the investments covered in this chapter. If the investor changes address he or she should notify the appropriate body.

2.5 PREVIEW OF 1999–2000

The Chancellor's forecasts for public finances, announced in the Spring 1999 Budget, seem to combine caution for the present with growing optimism for the future. However, his view that public finances will remain broadly in balance over the medium term rests heavily on an optimistic outlook for the economy. The 10p starting rate on income tax, and the prospects of basic rate tax falling to 22 per cent in the 2000–01 tax year, should keep consumer spending reasonably buoyant, but there are still some doubts on the level of future economic growth and it may be that further interest rate reductions are needed to keep sterling from strengthening against the euro, to help British industry and to nudge the consumer if spending slackens off.

The forecasts seem to suggest that the 1998–99 year – during which the budget surplus was £4bn – was the high point as far as the fiscal position was concerned, with all measures of borrowing needing to rise from now on, although only modestly. Public debt was repaid to the tune of £1bn last year. For each of 1999–2000 and the following year, borrowing of £3bn will be needed based on Treasury figures at the time of the Spring 1999 Budget. National Savings will tend to feature in this. The launch of its Individual Savings Account, a mini ISA initially paying out 5.75 per cent per annum tax free with a guarantee at least to match base rates until 5 April 2000, is bound to take in new cash and see some switching from other products. Most other deposit-taking institutions, building societies and banks will also be issuing their own cash mini ISAs, so as always it will pay to compare rates and withdrawal penalties along the high street.

National Savings is also launching a new shorter term two-year fixed rate Pensioners Guaranteed Income Bond paying a fixed monthly income for those aged 60 or over, running alongside the five-year Pensioners Bond.

Some useful addresses can be found at the end of Chapter 3.

3

LISTED INVESTMENTS

JOHN SMITHARD
James Capel Investment Management

3.1 INTRODUCTION

This chapter is concerned with securities created when bodies such as the government and individual companies wish to raise money. These securities can be traded on The Stock Exchange, where they are listed. However, this chapter does not deal with shares in private companies. Unlisted securities are covered in Chapter 2.

This chapter contains an introduction to The Stock Exchange and also deals with the distinction between market-makers and agency dealers, the mechanics of dealing in listed UK and overseas securities, as well as those traded on the Alternative Investment Market, and sources of information.

Sections **3.5** and **3.6** cover fixed interest borrowings ('stocks'); **3.5** deals with those issued by the public sector and which are traded on The Stock Exchange, and **3.6** with analogous private sector stocks. Purchasers of either kind of stock know precisely what interest payments they will receive during the life of the stock, since, with very few exceptions, these are fixed. They also know what they will receive if they retain the stock until redemption, and since this amount is normally more than the purchase price, they will realise a known capital gain. Investors also have the option of selling in the market before redemption, although the price obtainable in the market fluctuates from day to day.

Section **3.7** covers companies' ordinary shares traded on The Stock Exchange. Shareholders normally receive dividends the total of which may vary from year to year, reflecting the company's changing profitability. In addition, the market price of shares may also fluctuate from day to day. There is thus no certainty of the level either of income return or of capital gain, although the hope is that over a period of years the general level of share prices will rise to reflect inflation and growth in the economy.

3.2 REVIEW OF 1998–99

The investor in equities suffered a nervous year in 1998, experiencing the usual spring rise, a dull summer as the market tracked sideways, a scary autumn as markets around the world plummeted in unison, and a strong recovery into the winter and the New Year, as markets pulled themselves back up to record levels. Again, it was the US that gave the lead to UK equities. By the end of the year, however, the All Share Index had still managed a significant overall rise of nearly 11 per cent against its starting level. Gilts also showed an excellent return, with the All Stocks Index almost matching the All Share Index, while hiding a significantly higher overall return due to its income yield premium.

With the US economy entering its seventh successive year of growth, unencumbered by inflation and with short-term interest rates at low levels, the US market could continue its long-term climb and by April had passed the 9000 mark for the first time. Predictions for 10000 by the year 2000 looked ever more likely to be met. The UK market was brought along in its wake, passing through 6000 on the FTSE for the first time in March. Against a background of a thriving bond market, as much a result of low levels of issuance of new and replacement gilts as a reflection of muted inflation, equities were bound to rise as bond yields fell. The FTSE rose to a then record of 6179 on 20 July. Unfortunately, lethargy started to creep in during the summer months, not helped by the continuing poor economic performance of the Far Eastern economies and the June quarter point rise in base rates to 7.5 per cent.

It then all turned rather nasty, and not just in the UK. Comments that the Russian rouble was overvalued caused a sharp plunge in the currency and in its stock market. A decision not to repay capital, let alone interest, on government debt had ramifications around the world and especially to US and European banks, large lenders to the fledgling Russian economy. The yen was also starting to trend down against the dollar, forcing China and smaller Asian nations to consider devaluing their currencies in order to keep their competitive status against Japan. Latin America was thought to be the next problem area. A hedged fund, Long Term Capital Management, which was on the verge of collapse and which would have been a forced seller in a falling market, was bailed out by a group of major banks after some persuasion from the US financial authorities. The chairman of the US Federal Reserve was making cautious noises on the excessive level of world equity markets. The US President was about to be impeached. Talk was of a world recession. But nerves held, and the world's major markets put in a strong recovery from the low point reached in early October, helped by world-wide cuts in interest rates and a Japanese rescue package for its troubled banking sector. The FTSE had slumped to 4648 by then, a fall of 1530 points, or just under 25 per cent from its July high.

35

Because of the worries that this wealth-reducing fall would rein back consumer expenditure at a time when the industrial economy was feeling the double effect of a high sterling rate and a sharp decline in many of its export markets, the UK's Monetary Policy Committee put into train a series of short-term interest rate cuts, bringing base rates down from 7.5 to 6.25 per cent by the year end, with more cuts to follow in early 1999. Shares responded immediately, rising to close the year again close to the 6000 level.

On a PE ratio of 23 times earnings, UK equities were looking expensive by the year end, certainly in a historical context. That said, with little new equity being launched onto the market either through flotations or corporate capital raising exercises, and Government finances being such that new borrowing through the gilt-edged market was unnecessary – indeed, redemptions of gilts were tending not to be re-borrowed, leaving institutional holders with the problem of an ever-increasing pot of investment money chasing an ever-reducing amount of stock – share prices (and gilts, for that matter) could only rise, if only on basic theories of supply and demand. With the problems of money pouring into institutional investors' hands through pension contributions and final-year PEP contributions on the one hand, and by cash take-overs and share buybacks on the other, any short-term setback in the market had to be seen as a good buying opportunity to be grabbed before it disappeared.

Unfortunately it continued to be a two-tiered market, although the second-liners did have something of a recovery at the start of 1999. The 10.9 per cent rise in the All Share Index through 1998 somewhat camouflaged a further polarising of the market between the large caps and the smaller. While the FTSE 250 index was only up by 1.4 per cent in the year and the FTSE SmallCap fell by 10.5 per cent, the FTSE 100 rose by 14.5 per cent. Even that was under-performance against the world, with the FT/S&P world index in sterling terms improving by 17.7 per cent. The most representative US index, the S&P Composite, improved 26 per cent, Germany rose by nearly 18 per cent, France by over 31 per cent, and Italy by almost 41 per cent. Against this, Japan was down over 9 per cent and Hong Kong down by 6 per cent.

In terms of sector and company performances, it tended once again to be the telecoms and pharmaceutical stocks which made much of the running. Indeed, of the seven best performing stocks in the FTSE index by the year end – including stocks which moved into the FTSE during the year – six were telecom stocks, if one also includes Securicor with its 40 per cent ownership of Cellnet. Colt Telecom easily outshone its rivals, rising by over 480 per cent. Others in the top ten performance table included the contract caterer Compass, building materials concern Hanson, corporate outsourcing company Rentokil Initial, and Imperial Tobacco. On the other side of the coin, industrial stocks tended to be the weakest performers reflecting their difficult times, with ICI down 45 per cent and BTR (soon to merge with Siebe, also in the list of FTSE 100 worst performers) down 35 per cent, but also including Marks & Spencer, suffering from a slump in high street sales and with its shares off 31 per cent on the year.

There were a number of bids and deals during 1998. Admittedly, the most significant came in the US market with the Citicorp and Travelers merger producing a banking organisation with assets of $700bn and a market capitalisation of $133bn, dwarfing the $75bn oil merger at the end of 1998 of Exxon and Mobil. This in turn led to the merger of British Petroleum and Amoco of the US as we turned into 1999. This corporate activity in the oil sector coincided with a slump in the crude oil price to a level not seen since 1986, and perhaps can be seen in hindsight as one of the catalysts for the oil price recovery. In this sector, as in most others where bids were taking place, cost-cutting was the main aim. Daimler-Benz bought Chrysler for $38bn, while later in the year Volkswagen bought Rolls-Royce Motor Cars for a much cheaper £480m. The UK's largest potential merger, Glaxo Wellcome and SmithKline Beecham, was abandoned in the spring amid rumours of personality clashes at the highest levels, although potential Monopolies Commission difficulties of merging the two companies could well have been much more instrumental. Following the merger in spring 1999 of Astra of Sweden and the UK's third largest pharmaceutical company Zeneca, thought of a link between the two largest companies within the sector is never far from fund managers' thoughts. The costs savings would be immense.

Mergers which did come off included the formation of the £14bn CGU from the two insurance companies Commercial Union and General Accident. Scottish Hydro-Electric and Southern Electricity came together to form Scottish & Southern, at £4.8bn the largest company left in the UK electricity sector. In the same sector earlier in the year, Texas Utilities took over The Energy Group (which had initially been floated off as Eastern Electricity before being acquired by Hanson) for £4.5bn, and PowerGen acquired East Midlands Electricity for £1.9bn in July. Great Universal Stores bought Argos for just under £2bn in April, while there was a good deal of activity within the chemicals sector with Ciba buying Allied Colloids for £1.4bn and Akzo Nobel taking over Courtaulds for £1.8bn.

In the background, the London and Frankfurt stock exchanges agreed to form a strategic alliance to lay the foundations of a pan-European stock market, committing themselves to harmonise the two markets and deliver a low-cost, efficient and accessible infrastructure, while welcoming the participation of other major European exchanges. In time there will be a true pan-European market for the 300 leading shares. Following some criticisms of the electronic SETS order-matching trading system, especially of the problems of poor liquidity and unrepresentative prices at the start and close of the dealing day, the Stock Exchange decided to delay the opening of the dealing day to 9 am and to harmonise its close with that of the derivatives markets. However, one area still to be addressed is that of having to match the opening of the London market with the 7.30 am of Germany. SETS still has its problems, the greatest of which is the unwillingness of the major market participants to use it, preferring the lack of visibility associated with dealing off-screen. However, resistance is gradually being eroded.

The graphs on pages 39–41 illustrate:

(1) the performance of ordinary shares measured by the FTSE 100 Share Index;
(2) the performance of government securities (gilt-edged stocks), measured by the FT Actuaries All Stocks Index;
(3) the movement in UK interest rates and the inflation rate;
(4) the movement of sterling on a trade-weighted basis;
(5) the sterling-adjusted performance of New York, Tokyo and continental European equities.

3.3 COMPARING DIFFERENT TYPES OF SECURITY

The investor, in making a choice between different types of security, should take into account not only the relative importance of income and of capital gain but also:

(1) the degree of security against default;
(2) the expected rate of return;
(3) the tax advantages or disadvantages attaching to the security;
(4) the convenience and cost of dealing in the particular security; and
(5) the ability to realise the investment.

3.3.1 Security against default

The British government has the power to levy taxes and to print money and it is in the highest degree unlikely that it would ever default on its borrowings whether as National Savings (see Chapter 2), gilt-edged securities or Treasury bonds. It is generally assumed that the government would stand behind borrowings of local authorities, which in any event have the power to levy rates and the council tax. All these securities, therefore, have an intrinsic safety which the private sector cannot emulate. The safety of private sector borrowing lies in the reputation, integrity, viability and good management of the body concerned.

Figure 3.1   FTSE 100 index

FTSE 100 – PRICE INDEX
HIGH 6105.5 10/4/98, LOW 2765.1 15/1/93, LAST 5929.7 10/7/98

Source: *Datastream*

Figure 3.2   London FTA Government all stocks index

FTA GOVERNMENT ALL STOCKS – PRICE INDEX
HIGH 158.37 31/12/93, LOW 134.26 16/9/94, LAST 155.18 10/7/98

Source: *Datastream*

39

Figure 3.3   London clearing banks base rate and UK inflation rate

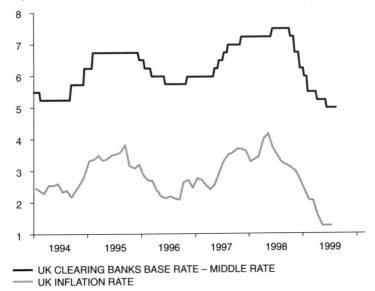

——— UK CLEARING BANKS BASE RATE – MIDDLE RATE
∙∙∙∙∙∙ UK INFLATION RATE

Source: *Datastream*

Figure 3.4   Bank of England trade weighted sterling index

——— UK £ INDEX 1990=100 (BOE) – TRADE WEIGHTED
HIGH 108.30 27/3/98, LOW 82.30 17/11/95, LAST 105.50 10/7/98

Source: *Datastream*

Figure 3.5   New York, Tokyo and Continental indices in sterling (rebased to 100)

■■■ DOW JONES INDUSTRIALS – PRICE INDEX (~£)
▓▓▓ NIKKEI 225 STOCK AVERAGE – PRICE INDEX (~£)
░░░ FT/S&P WORLD EUROPE EX-UK – PRICE INDEX

Source: *Datastream*

3.3.2 Rate of return

The rate of return on securities may be specified and fixed, as it is for fixed interest stocks issued by the government and by public and private sector bodies. In many other cases the return is specified initially but may be subject to variation to reflect the general movement of interest rates. Returns on some investments may be linked to the prevailing rate of inflation. Finally, the return may be dependent, as in the case of ordinary shares, on confidence in and the performance of the company. The more uncertain the return, the more attractive it has to be to compensate for the risk of underperformance. On the other hand, the investor should beware of overvaluing the certainty of return in money terms, since the real value of such returns can be eroded by inflation.

3.3.3 Tax advantages

Basic rate income tax payers are likely to find little tax advantage in individual forms of listed security and must choose whether the emphasis in their portfolio is to be on high income, the prospect of capital gain, or a balance between the two. Naturally, both among fixed interest stocks and ordinary shares, the investor will find a range of income yield from which to choose, and a stock which offers a good net return to a basic rate investor may not appeal so much to an investor who pays the higher rate. In terms of capital gains tax, British government stocks are exempt, no matter how long they have been held, and individuals will find that they have an exemption also for the first £7,100 of capital gains on disposals in the 1999–2000 tax year, after the indexation of book cost up to April 1998. Now that separate taxation of married couples has been introduced, each spouse has his or her individual capital gains tax allowance. Most trusts have an exemption of the first £3,550 of indexed capital gains on disposals in this tax year. An individual can also take advantage of an Individual Savings Account, in which dividend income is free of all income tax and capital gains are exempt from capital gains tax, by investing up to £5,000 a year in stocks and shares in a maxi ISA (£7,000 in 1999–2000), including unit and investment trusts, and some qualifying corporate bonds.

3.3.4 Convenience and cost of dealing

In general, investments listed on The Stock Exchange are liquid within reason and no investor should feel tied into any holding unless it is of unmarketable size. Dealing on The Stock Exchange, whether direct through a stockbroker, or indirect through an agent, will generally involve the payment of commission and other expenses (see pp 45 and 48).

3.4 THE STOCK EXCHANGE

3.4.1 Constitution and regulatory role

Historically, the burden of supervision of the securities industry has lain with The Stock Exchange. However, under the Financial Services Act 1986, Stock Exchange member firms must now be monitored by a self-regulatory organisation (SRO) which, in turn, is approved by the Financial Services Authority (FSA). In the FSA's hands rests the responsibility, delegated by the Department of Trade and Industry, for the entire securities industry – this includes Stock Exchange business, life assurance, unit trusts and commodities – both to regulate and to defend standards. Rules of any SRO must be equivalent in effect to those of the FSA and the remainder of the industry.

From its earliest origins in the coffee houses, through the establishment of an elected membership at the beginning of the nineteenth century, practice and regulation have developed together. The rules had evolved to meet changing circumstances and to deal with abuses. Under the Financial Services Act 1986, the position has now changed in that the Securities and Futures Authority (as SRO) has taken over a number of the regulatory roles, such as the authorisation of members, their conduct of business with clients and compliance matters. The Stock Exchange (as the Recognised Investment Exchange) remains responsible for the dealing rules, the listing of new securities and the provision of market related information services amongst many other matters. There is a close working relationship between the two bodies.

3.4.2 The primary and secondary markets

The Stock Exchange provides the main securities market in the UK, representing both a new issue and a trading market. The new issue, or primary, market provides the mechanism for the raising of capital by means of the issue of securities. Users of capital, be they government, local authorities or public companies, all seek funds of a long-term nature, and a large part of these funds is obtained by the issue of securities through the primary market.

Suppliers of capital, whether they are institutional or individual savers, need to invest their money in such a way that it is readily realisable – hence the existence of the secondary, or trading, market in which it is possible to deal in several thousand securities listed on The Stock Exchange. It is also possible to deal in traded options (see **3.7.2**).

3.4.3 Alternative Investment Market

The Alternative Investment Market (AIM) was launched in February 1995 as a means by which small unlisted companies could raise capital in a relatively inexpensive manner and investors become involved in expansion-minded and growth-orientated companies in their infancy. Regulation is much lighter in this market with much of the work falling on the shoulders of the sponsoring intermediary, and with costs much lower than for a full London listing, many companies on the former Unlisted Securities Market have moved to AIM, with some smaller companies even moving down from full listing. There has also been a progression of companies whose shares were formerly traded on rule 4.2. With reporting levels less onerous, and with companies on the market often much younger – not even requiring a trading record on entry – potential investors must not lose sight of the risks of the market, but its arrival has certainly been welcomed.

3.4.4 Overseas securities

This chapter is primarily concerned with UK securities, but British investors should remember that they can also deal in foreign securities, not only those listed on The Stock Exchange in London, but also those listed on foreign exchanges (see Chapters 4 and 5).

Residents of the UK are no longer required to deposit all foreign currency securities with an authorised bank or other authorised depositary in the UK, although on grounds of security and to protect the investor's interests on dividends and stock issues, it is still advisable for some foreign stocks, in particular those which are in bearer form, to be held by a bank or agent, either in the UK or overseas. Neither should investors overlook the withholding tax of the country in which they invest, since this is not always allowable against UK tax. Should bearer bonds be lost, the expenses incurred and work involved in obtaining duplicates can be considerable.

3.4.5 Dealing on The Stock Exchange

Following Big Bang in October 1986, the distinction between firms acting as stockbrokers and stockjobbers became blurred. Formerly, a member firm of The Stock Exchange would deal only as one or the other: as a broker it would advise and transact business for its clients, either individuals (private clients) or institutional, with a jobbing firm whose role was to buy and to sell securities owned by it for its own profit. Investors could not deal direct with a jobber, but were obliged to deal through a stockbroker who would charge a commission for this (the amount being laid down by The Stock Exchange). This commission also covered ancillary services such as advice, valuations and tax calculations.

The current position is that broking and jobbing (now called market-making) subsidiaries can belong to the same parent. Institutional investors can now deal direct with market-makers. However, many institutions, and all private clients, continue to use the broking arm of a firm exercising both roles, or a firm which concentrates solely on broking. Broking continues in the same manner as before: advice, recommendations, dealing at best price, settlement and protection of benefits accruing to the investment until registration.

The minimum rates of commission (formerly set by The Stock Exchange) have been abandoned and firms have been left to charge their own rates. For the private client, it may be that the commission charge has changed very little, and firms are now moving towards charging for ancillary services to keep dealing commissions competitive.

Figure 3.6 Dealing on The Stock Exchange

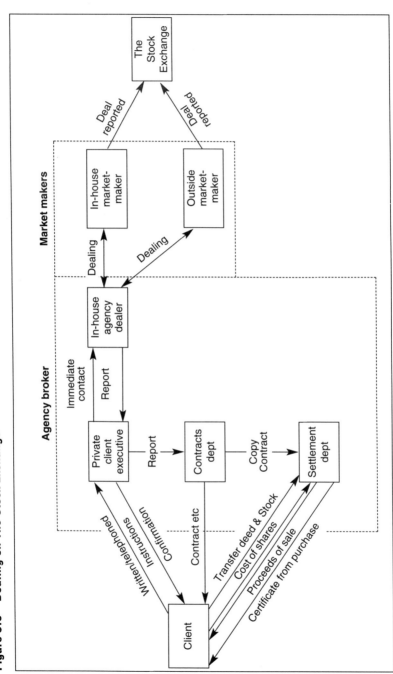

Generally, the method of dealing in stocks and shares is as shown in Figure 3.6, on p 45. The client will speak or write to the stockbroker looking after his or her affairs and is likely to discuss what the client wishes to do. The initial contact might alternatively have been made by the stockbroker. At this stage, if a sale is intended, it may be necessary for the broker to estimate potential tax liabilities as this may have some bearing on the discussions – many brokers will keep a running record of earlier transactions for the client to help them. By referring to sources of information to hand, primarily the screen-based price service, the broker will be able to give some indication of the current trading price. If an order is given by the client, it will be attempted immediately unless an unobtainable price limit has been set.

The broker then contacts the dealing staff whose function is to deal with the market-maker in that share who is offering or bidding the best price in the size (number of shares) required by the client. The change from face-to-face encounters on The Stock Exchange floor to a screen-based system means that agency dealers need only to look at their monitors to find the best price available in the most frequently traded stocks where market-makers' two-way quotes are firm; but those shown for the smaller-capitalised stocks are often indicative only and are not necessarily true dealing prices. The dealer will complete the order, occasionally with reference to the private client executive if there is some difficulty in dealing, with one or more market-makers including, in many cases, the in-house market-making side. The dealer should always try to improve on the prices quoted by the market.

The Stock Exchange electronic trading service (SETS) was introduced in 1997 with the aim of replacing the Stock Exchange automated quote (SEAQ) system with an automated order book through which buyers and sellers of more actively traded shares could be matched by computer. At present SETS accounts for a large proportion of trading in the FTSE 100 stocks but in due course its net may be widened to include more of the active FTSE 250 constituents.

For private investors there will seem little difference in practice, but they should see the benefits of SETS in keener spreads between selling and buying prices. This stems from the fact that the middleman – formerly the jobber, now the market-maker – is excluded from the system and in effect the investor now sets the price at which he wishes to deal. Of course, the investor's order may not always be satisfied on the SETS system but, if it is, he or she may be content in the knowledge that, for the moment at least, the deal has been struck at the level where buyers and sellers match and so has received 'the market price'.

Investors still place their orders through a broking firm, which still charges a commission for transacting the business, either on SETS or 'away from the order book'. As SETS is limited at present to the shares of the major companies and to dealing for standard five-working-day settlement periods, private investors may well find their business being transacted under the old method through a market-maker or a retail service provider (RSP). RSPs guarantee to give the same price as could have been attained if the order had been dealt on SETS.

An order remains on the order book until it is completed or withdrawn. Brokers must be instructed to deal either 'at best', in which case they enter the order immediately and complete at the best price currently available on the order book, or at a price limit. Unfortunately, dealing at best can have its hazards, especially at times when the market is opening or closing or when a full order book is otherwise unavailable; then, orders can often be matched against very uncompetitive business. It is sensible to check the current market price to ensure the dealing spread between the best bid and best offer is small enough at the time to make it worth dealing on SETS. Otherwise a limit order should be given to the broker, who will immediately enter it onto SETS. If it can be matched straight away, the transaction takes place if the order on the other side is for at least the number of shares requested; if not, it is part matched and remains on the order book until it is fully satisfied, or withdrawn. The risk is in a rapidly moving market where one can be chasing the price upwards (buying) or downwards (selling) and finding that other buyers or sellers are leap-frogging with ever more competitive orders entered onto the system. An order can be withdrawn at any time and resubmitted at a different price.

Investors should also be wary of leaving business on the order book at a limit price at a time when the entire market moves sharply. The order is transacted automatically if matched, without referring back to the investor, who might not have wanted to buy the stock too early in a sharply falling market, or vice versa.

With investor protection being of paramount importance, any deal for a client transacted through the in-house market-maker has to be done at the best price available in the market at that time, whether made by the in-house team or others. It will often be the case that the in-house team will match the best available price elsewhere, when they are not making it themselves, as the private client order is on average relatively small set against the size of institutional orders.

The dealer, having completed the bargain, will report to the private client broker who in turn, if requested, will contact the client with oral confirmation. The time of dealing will appear on the contract note so that no confusion will arise as to price, especially important in shares whose prices are volatile. The contract note, which will indicate whether the bargain has been made with a connected party, will then be produced

Figure 3.7 Contract note

Name and address
of stockbrokers

Bargain ref:

Bargain date:
Time of deal:

As agents we have bought for Mr J Smith

20,000 United Sprockets ord 25p at 56p   £11,200.00

Commission at 1.5%	£168.00
Stamp duty	56.00
PTM levy	0.25
	224.25
	£11,424.25

Bargain effected with connected company

Settlement date:

Subject to the rules, customs, usages and
interpretations of The Stock Exchange

(Signature of stockbrokers)
Members of The Stock Exchange

together with any other documentation required to cover a sale. An example of a bought contract note appears opposite (Figure 3.7) – a sold contract note would not include stamp duty, and the costs would be deducted from the sale consideration, rather than being added.

The settlement date appears on the contract note. Generally, settlement for a gilt is made on the next working day if stock is held in a broker's nominee name within the Central Gilts Office system; otherwise it is on a five-working-day basis, although delayed settlement can be agreed in advance.

Rolling settlement for equities, the greatest change in Stock Exchange settlement practice in 200 years, was introduced in 1994. The settlement date was then set for a ten working-day basis (T+10). Since 1995, the settlement period has been shortened further to five days (T+5). The cost of purchases, and the proceeds from sales, should then be available on this fixed date after dealing (sales, of course, only if the paperwork has been returned to the broker or stock is in the broker's nominee name).

Special provisions will be available for settlement for any date between T+2 and T+30 to tie in with clients' requirements, although the dealing price may reflect this change to the normal pattern. This will help investors wishing to close a position already opened just a few days earlier.

When selling, a client can expect to receive immediately in the post the contract note, which should be kept for tax purposes, and a transfer form if the stock is not held in the broker's nominee company. The transfer must be signed by the registered holder of the investment and returned to the brokers (together with the certificate representing the holding). Sales of unit trusts are covered by a standard transfer form, or through endorsing the reverse of the certificate. However, most unit trust groups are now moving to a form of uncertificated holding.

Transfer of bearer shares – mostly overseas companies – passes on good delivery. North American shares are in bearer form once the registered holder has signed the pre-printed form on the reverse of the certificate.

The buying client will not see a transfer form but will immediately receive a contract note. This should be kept for taxation purposes. If so arranged, investors may also be sent a dividend mandate form, to be signed and passed to their bank, which will authorise the company (or the Bank of England for a gilt) to pay all dividends direct to their bank account instead of their registered address. There is little more for them to do, except to arrange payment to their broker on settlement day. Depending on the speed of registration (usually out of the broker's hands) they would expect to see a certificate for their new holding within eight weeks of purchase. The company's registrars must be informed of any change of an investor's address.

CREST

Following the abandonment of TAURUS owing to its cost over-runs and huge delays in its implementation timetable, market participants and the Bank of England still felt it necessary to produce a system of settlement of Stock Exchange trades which reduced the risk of the financial failure of one of the parties to the transaction. CREST provides a highly secure system for the simultaneous exchange of securities and irrevocable payment obligations: it will provide delivery of stock against payment (DVP), with registration and full legal title being provided within two hours of settlement. This does away with much of the counterparty risk in settlement, and revolutionises the entire market process by removing paper from settlement and improving its efficiency and cost.

The efficiency of holding certificates in a private individual client's own name is gradually being whittled away. There is undoubtedly a move towards the use of brokers' nominees – most brokers will be direct or sponsored members of the CREST operation – so as to eradicate what is perceived as the weakest link in the system, the delivery of share certificates and signed transfers by the client, or the provision of funds for value on the correct date to cover purchases. A two-tier system has been developed to allow clients to retain certificates in their own names if they wish, although the cost of transacting business through their brokers may reflect the extra work involved in settling paper-based transactions.

Dividends

When a company intends paying a dividend, it must temporarily halt the registration of new shareholders in order to produce dividend warrants and tax vouchers in time for the dividend date. The registration process for that dividend stops on the 'record' or 'books-closing' date. Dealings in cum-dividend form include the right to the forthcoming dividend; dealings in ex-dividend form do not include the right to the dividend and it belongs, when paid, to the seller. Even under the CREST system, shares bought cum-dividend are occasionally not able to be re-registered in time for the record date and the company is obliged to pay the seller, as his or her name still appears on its books. It is then for the seller's broker to claim the dividend from the client and for the buyer's broker to pay the dividend to their client. The dividend will be passed from selling broker to buying broker.

Capitalisation and rights issues

If a company makes a capitalisation issue (often called a scrip, bonus or free issue) or a rights issue, a record date is used once again, although

The Stock Exchange will not usually mark the shares ex-entitlement until the working day immediately after new certificates or documents of title are posted. It is the buying broker's duty to claim from the selling broker any entitlement received by the seller which belongs to the buying broker's client. Where a seller is unable to produce documents of title for a rights issue by the time that new shares have to be accepted, then the broker must protect the buyer's entitlement so that those new shares do not lapse.

Stamp duty

Stamp duty is payable on purchases of shares, warrants and convertible loan stocks: it is collected by the buying broker and accounted for on the bought contract note. With CREST settlement, the rate is 0.5 per cent of the consideration. There is no stamp duty payable on purchases of gilts or corporate loan stocks. For unit trust purchases, the stamp duty is covered by the initial charge. Stamp duty at differing rates may be charged on purchases of overseas shares. In certain transactions, eg purchase and sale by an investor of the same shares for the same settlement date or purchase of renounceable letters of acceptance or allotment, stamp duty reserve tax is payable at the rate of 0.5 per cent on the amount or value of the consideration.

Commission

The scale of minimum commissions set by The Stock Exchange has been abolished and brokers are able to charge competitive rates. New clients should ensure that they know what rate of commission will be charged on their dealings; firms have started to charge non-advisory clients, requiring only a dealing service, different rates from those charged to clients needing advice and periodic valuations.

PTM levy

Deals showing consideration of £10,000 or more also attract a flat 25p levy to help fund the costs of the Panel on Take-overs and Mergers. This is only charged on dealings in UK equities and UK registered convertibles.

3.4.6 Stockbroker services

Stockbrokers, market-makers, licensed dealers in securities and all others in the industry are subject to regulation by self-regulatory organisations, answerable to the Financial Services Authority with wide-ranging powers.

Stockbrokers provide a variety of services in addition to buying and selling on behalf of clients. Brokers act on the specific instructions of their clients and give advice when called on to do so. They can also provide valuations of a portfolio at regular intervals and make recommendations. Alternatively clients may choose to give their broker discretion to manage investments on their behalf, buying and selling when the broker considers it to be advantageous and reporting their actions to their client. Charges, if any, for these services (over and above the commission that they charge for dealing) vary from firm to firm.

Stockbrokers, with access to economic and analytical material, often produced by their own firm's research department, are able to advise on investment policy and help in the choice of securities which best match their clients' objectives. Investors can approach a firm of stockbrokers direct, or can instruct their bank, accountant, solicitor or other financial adviser to approach a stockbroker on their behalf.

3.4.7 Sources of information

Every weekday the previous day's dealing prices and closing quotations of listed securities are published in The Stock Exchange Daily Official List. The last recorded marks are also shown for securities traded on AIM. The *Financial Times* and other newspapers also give a list of closing prices – generally the middle market price of each (ie the average of the buying and selling prices).

A number of indices are published, of which the FTSE 100 Share Index is the best known: it is widely quoted in the press and used as a barometer of price movement of shares. More sophisticated indices are published for government securities, fixed interest and gold mining shares. The FTSE 100 Share Index is an arithmetically weighted index of 100 leading UK shares, revalued each minute, giving an immediate picture of market movements. The companies appearing in the index are, in general, the largest in market capitalisation terms and account for almost 70 per cent of the total capitalisation of the UK equity market.

The most representative indices for ordinary shares are the FTSE Actuaries Share Indices, covering at present around 800 shares and 39 different sections of the market. These are compiled daily. To give a broader picture of equity price movements the *Financial Times* and the Institute of Actuaries also produce daily indices for the next 250 highest capitalised companies after the components of the 100 Share Index, an index for the top 350 companies, a Small Cap index and a Fledgling Index.

Daily indices of government securities, corporate fixed interest securities and gold mining shares are published in the financial press, together with indices of overseas markets.

Apart from primary sources of information such as political and economic news and statements, and annual accounts and other reports and circulars issued by companies, a wide range of information and comment is available from financial columns in newspapers, financial journals and newsletters. In addition, the results of stockbrokers' research covering both individual companies (most of which have been visited by the stockbroker) and sectors of the market are published together with economic forecasts, and various publicly available statistical services provide immediate access to relevant information. All this information provides the raw material for what is termed 'fundamental analysis'.

Technical analysis – the use of charts – provides data expressed in three forms: line, bar and point-and-figure charts. It is not the purpose of this chapter to explain these three forms of chart in detail, still less to comment on methods of interpreting them. However, charts are often a useful source of further information: for instance, apart from displaying the levels of the main markets, they can also be used to show a price level of a particular share or stock in relation to an appropriate index and how the performance of the particular investment has changed over a period of time in relation to the market generally.

Information issued by The Stock Exchange, such as the total number of daily bargains and the volume of equity turnover, has for some time been used as a measure of the current level of activity in the market. Other more sophisticated charts, such as confidence and over-bought/over-sold indicators, are now increasingly used and from these and many others the technical analyst tries to assess what is likely to happen in the future. In essence, chartists use technical analysis as a tool for demonstrating the existence of complex interrelationships between events and expectations, with a view to determining from established trends and patterns the direction in which the market generally, or a particular share, will move.

3.5 LISTED PUBLIC SECTOR SECURITIES

3.5.1 British government stocks

Legal nature

British government stocks (also called 'British funds' or 'gilt-edged securities' or simply 'gilts') represent borrowings by the British government or borrowings of certain nationalised industries which are guaranteed by the government. The investor can be entirely confident that interest will be paid and the principal repaid in accordance with the terms of the loan. A number of names are used for specific stocks – Treasury, Exchequer, etc – but these have no practical significance for the investor.

Pre-conditions

Gilt-edged securities listed on The Stock Exchange may be held by all categories of UK investor – governmental, personal, corporate or trustee. However, friendly societies or trustees acting without specific investment powers in their trust deeds must observe the Trustee Investments Act 1961.

Characteristics

British government stocks, with certain limited exceptions, carry a fixed rate of interest (the 'coupon') which is expressed as an annual rate on £100 nominal of the stock. Thus the holder of £100 nominal of Treasury 8½ per cent 2007 will receive £8.50 per year until that date (subject to deduction of income tax at the basic rate where requested by the holder, paid gross otherwise), irrespective of the price which may have been paid or of the market price from time to time. In March 1981 the first issue of an index-linked gilt-edged stock was launched on which both capital and interest were linked to the RPI and currently stocks are available with redemption dates ranging to 2030. With the exception of Consols 2½ per cent, on which interest is paid quarterly, interest on all British government stocks is paid at six-monthly intervals.

In addition to paying interest during the lifetime of the stock, the government has an obligation to redeem its stock, ie to repay each loan at the nominal, or par, value of £100. The precise nature of this obligation is different for different stocks: it may be to redeem either:

(1) on a fixed date (eg Treasury 7½ per cent 2006 must be redeemed on 7 December 2006); or
(2) within a specified range of dates (eg Treasury 8 per cent stock 2002/06 must be redeemed at some time between 5 October 2002 and 5 October 2006); or
(3) on a small number of low coupon stocks (eg Consols 2½ per cent, Treasury 3 per cent and War Loan 3½ per cent) at any time chosen by the government.

The government is unlikely ever to redeem the stocks in the last category unless the general level of interest rates falls below the coupon. They are purchased mainly for the interest payments, which give a high level of fixed income; but capital growth on them depends on interest rates falling rather than on the passage of time to a certain redemption date. The government is also unlikely to redeem a stock in category (2) above before the last date for redemption if the general level of interest rates remains higher than the coupon.

The period still unexpired before redemption is used to classify government stocks, as follows:

(1) Short-dated stocks ('shorts') are defined as stocks with less than five years until redemption.
(2) Medium-dated stocks ('mediums') are stocks with between five and 15 years still to run to redemption.
(3) Long-dated stocks ('longs') are stocks with over 15 years until redemption.
(4) Undated or irredeemable stocks are those with no final date specified for redemption.

Although all the irredeemable stocks have low coupons, there is a wide choice of different coupons in the other categories, ranging from $3\frac{1}{2}$ per cent to 13 per cent. Investors should therefore be able to find a stock which combines the redemption date which they are seeking with their preferred rate of coupon.

The two benefits of buying gilt-edged stocks are (1) the interest received and (2) the capital profit which can be made when a stock bought below par is repaid at par or when a stock is sold through The Stock Exchange at more than the purchase price. Two kinds of yield can be calculated to help in assessing the benefits: running yield and redemption yield.

The running, flat, or interest yield ignores the possibility of capital profit and takes into account only the interest. It is calculated by dividing the coupon by the price paid by the investor, ignoring any accrued interest, and multiplying by 100 to produce a percentage.

The redemption yield takes account of both the interest and the capital gain (or, in most cases, loss) which would occur if the stock was held until redemption. The most common form of redemption yield is the gross redemption yield, which ignores the effect of income tax. Redemption yields cannot of course be calculated for undated stocks, since there is no realistic prospect of redemption.

The price of gilts is determined by such factors as the amount of new stock which the government might have to issue to fund its borrowing requirement, the amount of new money flowing into the institutional investors (such as pension funds), and the attractiveness of gilts compared with other investment opportunities. Thus, if the general interest rates and yields on other investments rise, the yields on gilts will also rise, ie the price of gilts will fall. With the probable exception of index-linked stocks, gilt prices will also fall if inflationary expectations rise.

Any kind of political, economic, financial or industrial news may affect gilt prices, in so far as it affects the market's expectations about inflation, interest rates or the government borrowing requirement.

Although gilt prices do not tend to fluctuate as much as those of ordinary shares, the timing of both purchases and sales still requires careful consideration.

Accrued interest

Following the introduction of new rules in February 1985 designed to prevent 'bond-washing' or the substitution by investors of tax-free capital gain for taxable income, the market price of all gilts excludes the interest which has accrued since the last interest date and a separate payment is made in respect of this. In a 'cum-dividend' transaction (one where the purchaser will receive the next dividend payment) the purchaser pays to the seller the amount of interest which has accrued to the date of sale since the last interest payment, as the purchaser will later be receiving interest for the full six-month period. In an 'ex-dividend' transaction (where the seller will receive the next dividend payment) the seller pays to the purchaser the amount of interest which will accrue between the date of sale and the next interest date.

Index-linked gilts

In March 1981, the government made its first issue of an index-linked gilt, whose redemption value and annual income return were linked to the change in the RPI in order to compensate the holder to maturity for the effects of inflation. Since this date, and with inflation at lower levels, these stocks have been a cheaper method of finance for the government than conventional higher-coupon fixed interest gilts and a number of further issues have been made.

Income from index-linked stocks is relatively low as the main advantage to a holder is through the inflation proofing afforded to the invested capital. The income payments increase every six months to reflect changes in the RPI.

The timing of market purchases and sales requires consideration since dealing prices do not necessarily reflect the underlying value of the stock. A comparison might here be made with index-linked national savings certificates which increase in value each month in line with the change in the RPI (see **2.3.3**).

As with conventional gilt-edged stocks, the market price of index-linked stocks will not include interest which has accrued since the last payment date.

Taxation

New rules on the payment of interest have come into effect since April 1998. Before then, interest was paid by the Bank of England after deduction of income tax at the basic rate; now, interest is paid without deduction of tax on all new purchases of gilts, unless the Bank is specifically requested to do otherwise. For those who hold stock which was acquired before April 1998, the holder can ask the Bank to pay it without deduction of tax, but the Bank will otherwise continue to pay interest as before, with income tax deducted at source.

Interest received by individuals is treated as investment income and if received without deduction of tax may be liable to basic and higher rate tax. If received after deduction of tax at source, interest may still be liable to higher rate tax in the hands of the individual.

With some exceptions, overseas holders of gilts who are both resident and ordinarily resident outside the UK are exempt from all UK taxes on a large number of British government securities.

For transfers of certain interest-bearing securities made on or after 28 February 1986, the provisions of the accrued income scheme, introduced by the Finance Act 1985, apply. The securities affected include any loan stock or similar security (but not shares in a company) whether of the UK government, any other government, any public or local authority in the UK or elsewhere, or of any company.

Where such securities are transferred, the scheme provides for apportionment of interest on a daily basis with the result that, for tax purposes, the seller is treated as having received interest accruing up to and including the settlement day and the purchaser is treated as having received the interest accruing thereafter. Interest is therefore deemed to have been received by the seller on a sale 'cum div' and by the purchaser on a sale 'ex div' and, in each case, there is a corresponding rebate for the other party to the transaction. The charge to tax is calculated by reference to interest periods which usually end on each normal interest payment date. If deemed interest exceeds rebates for a given interest period, the difference is chargeable to income tax under Schedule D Case VI (or, where the securities are non-UK securities, Schedule D Case V).

No charge arises if the taxpayer concerned is an individual and at no time in the year of assessment in which an interest period ends, or the previous year of assessment, does the nominal value of securities held by him exceed £5,000. Husband and wife are treated separately for this purpose.

Stamp duty is not payable on purchases of British government stock.

Suitability

Investment in British government stocks is a convenient way of providing for future commitments, the timing and size in money terms of which are known or can be confidently predicted. On the other hand, if the size of the commitment is uncertain because of the impact of inflation in the intervening period, the investor should consider a portfolio comprising both fixed interest stocks, index-linked stocks and ordinary shares.

Because default is virtually inconceivable and interest and redemption value are both fixed, with the exception of the irredeemable issues and the index-linked stocks, gilts are also ideal for the investor for whom security is paramount. Most investors through The Stock Exchange will place some value on security and are therefore well advised to include a proportion of such stocks in their portfolios. Trustees, if they have not been given express powers by their particular trust deed, are obliged by the Trustee Investments Act 1961 to invest a proportion of the trust funds either in this sector of the market or in other fixed interest stocks carrying 'trustee' status.

Further, the advantages of ready marketability and reasonably high yields should not be overlooked.

Mechanics

There are four ways of dealing in gilt-edged stocks:

(1) by a direct approach to a stockbroker;
(2) by an indirect approach to a stockbroker;
(3) through the Post Office; or
(4) by application for newly issued stock direct to the Bank of England.

Direct approach to a stockbroker

An investor may place his order to buy or sell with a stockbroker who will execute the transaction on The Stock Exchange for a commission. For information on dealing see **3.4.6**.

Indirect approach to a stockbroker

Investors can instruct their solicitor, accountant, bank or other financial adviser to place the order to buy or sell on their behalf with a stockbroker. The stockbroker may share the commission earned from an agent's client with that agent.

Dealing through the Post Office

Members of the public can buy all stocks through branches of the Post

Office, from which application forms can be obtained, or by direct application to the National Savings Stocks and Bonds Office in Blackpool. Interest on stocks purchased in this way is paid gross. The maximum amount that may be invested in any one stock on any one day is £25,000, but there is no limit to the total amount of stock which may be held. Execution of orders takes longer than if they are placed direct with the stockbroker, leaving the price paid or received more open to chance. Moreover, the Post Office, unlike stockbrokers, will accept orders to buy or sell only at the best price obtainable, and it cannot give advice, manage portfolios or take orders to buy and sell when prices reach particular levels. On the other hand, fees charged by the Post Office on both purchases and sales may be considerably lower than Stock Exchange commissions. See also **2.3.10**.

Purchase of newly issued stocks

The above methods of dealing in stocks concern those already issued and trading on The Stock Exchange. When a new stock is first issued by the Bank of England, application forms (obtainable from the Bank of England, banks or stockbrokers or cut out from newspaper advertisements) must be sent to the New Issue Department of the Bank of England.

The names of holders are registered with the Bank of England, and holders receive certificates which are evidence of registration.

The direct cost of dealing is limited to the commission charged by the stockbroker, the Post Office or other agents. For dealing on The Stock Exchange see **3.4.6**.

Safe custody

The contract note, which constitutes evidence of a sale or purchase, is relevant, *inter alia*, for taxation purposes and should be kept in a safe place. For stocks where a register is maintained, certificates are evidence of title and should also be kept in a safe place. If certificates are lost, duplicates can be obtained only against an appropriate form of indemnity.

3.5.2 Other public sector stocks

Certain public boards are entitled by Act of Parliament to borrow on the security of their revenues without government guarantees, stated or implied. Examples are the Agricultural Mortgage Corporation, the Metropolitan Water Authority and the Port of London Authority.

Commonwealth stocks carry no British government guarantee and are the obligation of the issuing authority.

Commission on both public board stocks and Commonwealth and overseas government stocks is likely to be charged by the stockbroker. In most respects they are similar to debenture stocks (see **3.6.1**). For dealing on The Stock Exchange see **3.4.6**.

3.6 LISTED COMPANY FIXED INTEREST SECURITIES

3.6.1 Legal nature

Fixed interest stocks issued by companies are a form of borrowing. There are three basic types of security:

(1) debenture stocks;
(2) loan stocks; and
(3) preference shares (which are not borrowings).

Debenture stocks

These are either mortgage debentures, secured by a fixed charge on the company's properties, or debentures secured by a floating charge on some or all of the company's assets.

For all debenture stocks (and, nowadays also, all listed unsecured loan stocks), a trustee is appointed to supervise the performance of the company's obligations and to act for the holders in the event of default. The trust deed sets out the rights of the lenders, including limitations on the company's freedom to act in ways which might undermine their security (eg borrowing limits are imposed and changes in the nature of the business and substantial disposals of assets are restricted).

Loan stocks

Loan stocks are unsecured obligations. If the borrowing company fails to meet its obligations, loan stockholders are in the same position as other unsecured creditors: they can sue for their money, but if the company's assets remaining after creditors ranking ahead of the unsecured creditors have been paid off are insufficient to meet the claims of all unsecured creditors, stockholders receive only that proportion of the remaining assets which the outstanding principal amount of the loan stock bears to the company's total unsecured debts.

An important variant is convertible loan stock, which carries the right of conversion into the company's ordinary shares (see further **3.6.3**).

Preference shares

Preference shares are not debts but are part of the share capital of the company, issued on terms which are usually set out in the company's articles of association. Before any dividend is paid to ordinary shareholders, preference shareholders are normally entitled to receive a fixed dividend, provided that sufficient profits are available to cover it. If the company is wound up, preference shareholders rank ahead of ordinary shareholders up to the nominal value of their capital, but have no further rights unless expressly provided for in the articles.

An important variant is convertible preference shares, which carry the right of conversion into the company's ordinary shares (see **3.6.3**).

3.6.2 Pre-conditions

Fixed interest stocks listed on The Stock Exchange may be held by most categories of UK investor, although friendly societies and trustees acting without specific investment powers in their trust deeds must observe the Trustee Investments Act 1961.

3.6.3 Characteristics

Like dated government stocks, dated debentures, dated loan stocks and redeemable preference shares carry a fixed rate of interest for a specified number of years, at the end of which the principal amount becomes due for repayment. However, unlike the government, the company may have the right to repay before the stated redemption date and may do so if general interest rates fall substantially below the coupon. Thus the actual life of the investment may prove to be shorter than the originally stated term.

Private sector securities are less easily marketable than gilt-edged stocks and, with the exception of most convertible stocks, can normally be purchased on higher yields than government securities paying the same rate of interest over the same number of years. This yield differential also reflects the value given by the market to the weaker level of security offered by the loan stock.

Convertible stocks

Convertible stocks, sometimes referred to as 'deferred equities', have certain additional characteristics. Essentially they are securities issued with a fixed interest payment and fixed redemption date, but conferring the right to convert on a certain date or dates into a stated number of ordinary shares of the company.

Convertible stock usually provides a much higher running yield than the ordinary shares of the company concerned, in addition to being slightly more secure, although an investor who exercises his conversion right will not share in any capital gain achieved up to that point by an investor who had originally invested in the ordinary shares. Until the first conversion date, the market price of convertible stock tends to maintain a fairly steady relationship to the market price of a corresponding block of ordinary shares. However, the price of the convertible stock will not fluctuate to the same extent as the share price, since it will also be influenced by the general level of yields on non-convertible fixed interest securities.

Holders of convertible stocks will receive notification of the conversion option and advice should be sought at that time. It is most important to take action by the final conversion date, either exercising the conversion option or selling the convertible stock. Once the right to convert is lost, the stock will then be valued as a straightforward fixed interest security, which often results in a sharp drop in value.

The decision to exercise the right to convert on one of the conversion dates will largely depend on whether the income on the stock is likely to be less than the prospective return, in the form of dividends, on the holding of ordinary shares into which the stock can be converted.

The majority of the convertible securities in issue are convertible loan stocks, but some convertible debenture stocks and some convertible preference shares exist (see **3.6.1**).

3.6.4 Taxation

Stamp duty is not payable on transfer of debentures and non-convertible debenture or loan stocks, but it is payable (by the purchaser) on transfer of convertible stocks and on preference shares, whether convertible or not.

Fixed interest non-convertible stocks bought after 13 March 1984 and fulfilling the requirements for 'qualifying corporate bonds' in s 64 of the Finance Act 1984 are treated in a similar way to government securities (see **3.5.1**) and disposal or redemption gains are exempt from capital gains tax. Losses are not offsettable.

Gains on disposals of convertible stocks and on disposals of shares received following conversion of convertible stocks are subject to capital gains tax.

Interest on loan stocks is paid after deducting income tax at the basic rate. Holders not liable to tax may reclaim it, while those liable at the higher rate will be assessed on the gross amount of the interest, credit being given for the tax already deducted at source. The provisions of the accrued income scheme described in **3.5.1** may apply to the transfer of loan stocks.

In the case of preference shares, the 'imputation system' results in a slightly different treatment. The dividend paid is not subject to deduction of tax; instead it carries a 'tax credit'. The recipient's tax liability is calculated on the total of the dividend and the tax credit, with the result that for a basic rate taxpayer there will be no further liability to tax after allowing for the credit. Higher rate taxpayers will be liable to tax on the total of the dividend and the tax credit, the credit satisfying the basic rate part of their liability. The tax credit is being progressively abolished, falling initially from 20 per cent to 10 per cent. The 10 per cent tax credit will be deemed to satisfy the tax liability on the grossed-up dividend for basic and lower rate taxpayers, while higher rate tax on dividend income is reduced to 32.5 per cent.

3.6.5 Suitability

Fixed interest stocks are suitable for investors who have known future commitments to meet or who want to maximise the return on their invested capital through a mixed portfolio of stocks and ordinary shares. Private sector debentures or loan stocks may represent a cheaper route to these goals than gilts if the investor is prepared to forgo the additional security offered by gilts.

Convertible stocks are a means of keeping the investor's options open as between investing in ordinary shares or in fixed interest stocks.

3.6.6 Mechanics

The method of dealing is shown at **3.4.6**.

3.6.7 Safe custody

The contract note, which constitutes evidence of the sale or purchase, is relevant, *inter alia*, for taxation purposes and should be kept in a safe place. Certificates are evidence of title and should also be kept in a safe place, although if certificates are lost, duplicates can usually be obtained against an appropriate form of indemnity.

3.7 ORDINARY SHARES

3.7.1 General

Legal nature

A company is a legal person, capable of perpetual succession and distinct from its proprietors, namely the persons who contributed the original capital, or their successors. Ownership of a company takes the form of 'shares' in the capital of the company. All companies listed on The Stock Exchange, or the subject of trading on AIM, are limited liability companies, and the shareholders usually have no liability to creditors if the company defaults on its obligations.

Shareholders are the proprietors (or members) of the company. Subject to a company's memorandum and articles of association, and to whatever dividends the company in fact pays, ordinary shareholders have the right to all profits after payment of prior charges on the company's revenue, such as interest, wages, other running expenses, taxes and dividends on preference shares. In the same way, if the company is wound up they are entitled to all assets remaining when prior claims have been met. Thus they own the residual assets or 'equity' of the company – hence the term 'equities' to describe ordinary shares.

Ownership of most shares listed on The Stock Exchange is established by registration; the owner's name is entered on a share register by the company's registrars (sometimes an agent office of the company and sometimes a bank or other specialist organisation), which then issue share certificates.

Extensive and up-to-date information is required from companies when they seek an initial listing on The Stock Exchange, issue new shares or other securities for cash, make a take-over offer, or seek to effect a merger or reconstruction. Such information requirements may be prescribed by legislation, by The Stock Exchange or by the Panel on Take-overs and Mergers.

Pre-conditions

Shares listed on The Stock Exchange can be held by most categories of UK investor, although friendly societies and trustees acting without specific investment powers in their trust deeds must observe the Trustee Investments Act 1961.

Characteristics

Ordinary shares are a company's risk capital; the investor expects a reasonable and rising level of dividend income and a rise in the share price, but there can be no certainty about this. If investors' expectations are fulfilled or exceeded, they are rewarded for taking the risks that dividends might have been low or non-existent and that the share price might have fallen.

Dividends are paid out of profits, normally following the recommendation of the directors.

The market price of a company's shares will fluctuate from day to day and will in part reflect objective data such as its past records on profits and dividends and its assets; but prices will also be affected by subjective judgements about the company's probable future performance. News about the company (including its regular profit announcements) will influence the price, but so too will news concerning the sector or sectors in which the company operates and, indeed, news affecting the political situation and/or economy as a whole. Prices are also influenced by the amount of new money which the institutional investors, in particular, have to invest, some of which is likely to find its way into company shares, the proportion depending on how attractive shares are considered by comparison with other investments.

Scrip dividends

In order to conserve cash flow and to give shareholders a method of accumulating more shares, many companies now allow their shareholders to elect to take dividends in the form of shares in lieu of cash. This is commonly known as a scrip dividend. As the company is issuing new capital direct to its shareholders there are no brokers' costs nor stamp duty, but there are no tax savings for the recipient. Although the individual is treated as having received gross dividend income of an amount which, when reduced by basic rate income tax, is equivalent to the 'cash equivalent', this latter figure (the net dividend on his holding) only is used to acquire new shares at a pre-ordained pricing formula. The tax credit on the dividend cannot be reclaimed. Higher rate taxpayers must also eventually find the difference between the tax credit deemed to be theirs and the tax liability on the dividend's gross equivalent out of cash from other sources as they will have received no cash from the company, save perhaps for a small balancing item. The active share investor ought also to bear in mind before accepting scrip dividends that records will need to be kept completely up to date for the purposes of capital gains tax as each new allotment of shares requires an updated book cost.

Some companies now offer enhanced scrip dividends, to a value greater than the underlying cash dividend, and may offer a cheap broker option for selling the dividend shares at a premium value to the underlying cash dividend.

Dividend reinvestment plans (DRIPs)

When authorised by their shareholders, many companies buy back their own shares in order to improve earnings per share on the remainder of the equity. In these circumstances, further issues of scrip dividend shares would not seem to make sense. As an alternative, many companies have introduced DRIPs through which shareholders can use their net dividends to buy further shares. These are not issued by the company, but bought from the stock of already issued shares trading in the market. Stamp duty and small brokers' commission is generally charged. In contrast to scrip dividends, the price of the shares is unknown until bought.

B shares

Many companies wish to return excess and unrequired capital to their shareholders, but the efficiency of a large special dividend in the hands of a tax-free institutional investor was ended by the July 1997 budget. Many companies now return cash to shareholders through the issue of an additional form of share capital, normally known as B shares, which are then bought back by the company for cancellation. The sale of the B shares back to the company is deemed to be a capital, rather than an income, event and is tax-efficient for investors who are either not liable to capital gains tax, or whose gain on the sale is within the annual CGT exemption.

Taxation of income and capital gains

Ordinary shareholders in receipt of dividends also receive a tax credit. The liability of basic rate taxpayers is satisfied by the credit. For those liable to tax at the higher rate, tax is calculated on the total of the dividend and the tax credit, and the tax payable is reduced by the amount of the credit. The tax credit is being progressively abolished, falling initially from 20 per cent to 10 per cent. The 10 per cent tax credit will be deemed to satisfy the tax liability on the grossed-up dividend for basic and lower rate taxpayers, while higher rate tax on dividend income is reduced to 32.5 per cent.

Capital gains realised from the sale of shares may be liable to capital gains tax, and capital losses can be used to offset other gains. As a general rule capital losses can only be carried forward, but they may be used to offset earlier capital gains where they all occur in the same fiscal year.

Capital gains tax considerations are important and investors should try to make full use of the annual exemption for capital gains tax available in each tax year to individuals. This implies that an investor should endeavour either to switch from investments where the income or growth potential has run its course to others where the return is likely to be greater. The 1998 budget has effectively put an end to bed and breakfasting. Investors were able to use up their CGT exemption, or bring down their net gains for the tax year to a figure within the annual exemption, by selling an investment one night and buying the investment again the following morning. The identification rules now match a purchase of stock, within 30 days of a sale, with the sold stock. In effect, the investor is deemed to be selling the stock which he later buys, and so is not taking the gain (or crystallising a loss) on a holding which had been acquired some time before. Investors now wishing to buy back sold stock must wait for the 30 days to pass. Market movements can sometimes make this worthwhile, but investors now should consider reinvesting in an alternative investment, perhaps within the same sector, or where the growth prospects are better.

The Finance Act 1982 provided for indexation relief on capital gains from the 'appointed date'. The 'appointed date' is 6 April 1982 in all cases with the exception of companies, for which it is 1 April 1982. Indexation relief runs to the month of disposal, or to April 1998, whichever is the earlier. The calculation of the indexation relief, where there has been a single purchase of shares, is straightforward. For shares bought after March 1982, their historic cost is increased by a factor equal to the change in the RPI from the month of acquisition to the month of disposal or to April 1998, if earlier. For those bought before April 1982, the Finance Act 1988 brings forward the deemed acquisition date to 31 March 1982 and the deemed book value of the holding to the value on that date, as adjusted by capital issues made by the company in the intervening period, provided an election to do this has been made to the Inland Revenue. Some sales will produce indexed gains under the new system where these would have been losses under the old, and *vice versa*, and these will be treated as 'no gain, no loss' situations. Indexation relief can only be used to reduce a gain, and cannot increase a loss nor turn a gain into a loss.

Where a shareholding has been built up in a company over a period, the calculation of the capital gains tax position on disposal including any indexation relief can be extremely complicated, and accurate records of dates of purchase should be kept by all investors. This is especially the case where scrip dividends have been taken in lieu of cash.

Suitability

Ordinary shares are suitable for investors who are able to accept an element of risk and are looking for rising income and a hedge against inflation, particularly if they follow attentively the fortunes of companies in which they invest.

For investors who need to estimate with a degree of confidence the timing and size in money terms of their future commitments, shares are not as suitable as fixed interest stocks.

Unlike some of the fixed term savings schemes described in **2.3**, most ordinary shares in public listed companies are readily marketable at a moment's notice. However, since share prices are subject to a considerable degree of fluctuation (greater than that in fixed interest stocks), an investor who is likely to be faced suddenly with unexpected commitments should endeavour not to rely on ordinary shares to meet such commitments.

Mechanics

For the mechanics of dealing see **3.4.5**.

Safe custody and maintenance

The contract note, which constitutes evidence of the sale or purchase, is relevant, inter alia, for capital gains tax purposes and should be kept in a safe place. Share certificates are evidence of title and should also be kept in a safe place, although if certificates are lost, duplicates can usually be obtained against an appropriate indemnity. Company registrars are likely to make a small administration charge in replacing lost certificates and a bank or insurance company will also charge a fee for 'joining in' the indemnity.

In the case of bearer shares no register is maintained and possession is evidence of title. Bearer shares should therefore be held in safe custody.

The investor is well advised to keep his or her portfolio under review, either continuously or periodically. Some stockbrokers and other agents automatically review and revalue the portfolios of their private clients at regular intervals and are prepared to offer advice. Between these reviews they may also contact their clients to make recommendations affecting individual holdings or the balance of the portfolio between the main investment areas.

In addition to regular reviews, which are essential, investors who follow the economic, industrial and financial news and who are prepared to buy when a good investment opportunity arises at a reasonable price or to sell a share when its prospects have dimmed or its price is high, will do better than more passive investors, provided of course that their judgement and the advice that they receive are good.

All registered shareholders will receive the annual report and accounts of the company in which they hold shares. Companies listed on The Stock Exchange or the subject of trading on AIM also have to make an interim report, normally containing profit figures for the first six months of the company's financial year and reporting any interim dividends declared. The interim dividend, which is paid at the board's discretion, and the final dividend which is recommended by the directors at the company's year end (subject to the approval of its shareholders at the annual general meeting), normally make up the total dividend for the year. Some major international companies issue interim statements every quarter.

Although annual and interim reports provide natural occasions on which to consider increasing or reducing shareholdings, such action should not necessarily be taken straight away, since the impact of the report will immediately be reflected in the share price. Few tactics can be worse than trying to sell when others are selling and the price is low, or trying to buy when the price is high. Having formed a judgement on whether to buy, sell or merely retain an existing holding, the prudent investor will await a suitable opportunity before acting.

Nominees

Most stockbroking firms offer the use of a nominee facility to their clients. When bought, shares and other Stock Exchange investments (as well as unit trusts) are registered into the name of a nominee company instead of the client's own name. This makes for administrative ease both on the part of the stockbroking firm – which does not then have to chase clients for paperwork following a sale of investments, merely producing a contract note as proof of the transaction – but, more importantly, for the client. Using a firm's nominee company does not mean giving the firm discretion over one's investments; a client will often retain an advisory relationship, although in most cases firms will require the use of their nominee services if handling clients' investments on a discretionary basis.

The benefits to the client are numerous. No longer responsible for the safe-keeping of certificates, nor expected to pay the bank for holding them, the investor also does not need to sign transfer forms when completing sales. This becomes very important under rolling settlement, especially with the settlement period now at five working days and likely to move in due course to a shorter period still. It becomes the broker's responsibility to advise on rights issues and other corporate actions relating to the client's holdings, for which the documentation is handled by the nominee company. Dividend income can be mandated direct to the investor's bank, either straight from the investment company if 'designated' nominees are used or, at intervals, from the stockbroking firm when investments are held in 'undesignated' nominees. Brokers can produce a composite tax voucher, acceptable to the Inland Revenue, at the end of each tax year, listing all dividends received by the nominee company on behalf of the investor during that year, and can provide capital gains tax calculations.

It is important, however, to ensure that the security of the nominee company is of the highest order and, especially, that the company has adequate backing over and above any investors' protection schemes in case of fraud within the nominee company.

Personal equity plans (PEPs)

PEPs were introduced in the 1986 Budget, but the ability to subscribe to new PEPs ended on 5 April 1999, to be superseded by ISAs. However, PEPs open at 5 April 1999 can remain so for the foreseeable future.

Investment changes within the plan are allowed. The tax advantages continue until the investor ends the plan.

UK registered shares listed on The Stock Exchange may be included in the plan as direct equity holdings, but the full £6,000 of a general PEP may be invested in investment trusts or authorised unit trusts which themselves are at least 50 per cent invested in UK and EU equities. To reflect the advent of the single European market, the PEP rules have been changed to allow direct investment of up to £6,000 in equities of EU companies. Certain preference shares and convertible preference shares are included as acceptable investments, allowing an element of fixed 'interest' into PEPs. Cash may be held in a PEP and interest is credited net of basic rate tax, which is reclaimable by the PEP manager to produce a gross figure, provided the cash is eventually invested in qualifying shares or unit trusts.

Between January 1992 and 5 April 1999, individuals were also able to invest £3,000 in a single company PEP issued either by a listed UK company (in which case only shares in that company are acceptable) or by a recognised Plan Manager (allowing switches from time to time between shares of differing companies).

There is no liability to income tax at basic rate or higher rate on dividends on shares held in the PEP, nor is there any liability to capital gains tax on any disposal in the duration, or at the end of the plan. However, with the changes in the rules on tax credits from 6 April 1999, the full amount is no longer reclaimable, and only a 10 per cent credit can be returned to the plan. PEPs are therefore an advantageous method of saving through risk investment for all equity investors, but especially so for those on the higher rate of income tax or who generally have an annual capital gains tax liability. The advantages to basic rate or non-tax-payers who do not pay capital gains tax were not so obvious, especially if management charges are high.

PEPs can be held by anyone aged 18 or over who is resident and ordinarily resident in the UK or, though non-resident, is a Crown employee serving overseas.

Each plan must be managed by an investment adviser, authorised under the Financial Services Act 1986, and registered with the Inland Revenue. The manager may arrange for investors to receive annual reports of each investment, although often charging a fee for this service, and ensure that all rights of that shareholder are made available to him. All records, dealing and other paperwork would be the responsibility of the manager, who should liaise on the investor's behalf with the tax authorities (see also Chapter 20).

Individual savings accounts (ISAs)

These were introduced from 6 April 1999 and supersede PEPs and TESSAs. For a full discussion, see **2.3.15** above.

3.7.2 Warrants and options

Legal nature

An alternative to buying a security outright is to purchase the right to buy a security (see also Chapter 6). There are three ways of doing this:

(1) Warrants give holders the right to buy a particular company's ordinary shares at a fixed price. The right can normally only be exercised between two specific dates in the future.
(2) Conventional options confer the right to deal in a specified number of company's shares at a fixed price (the 'striking price') at any time during the option period (normally three months). To obtain an option the investor pays a price ('option money' or 'premium'), often expressed in pence per share. A 'call' option confers the right to buy at the striking price. A 'put' option confers the right to sell at the striking price. A 'double' option entitles the investor either to buy or to sell at the striking price.
(3) Traded options – 'calls' or 'puts' – are available in a limited but increasing number of leading companies, the FTSE Index and the Euro-FTSE Index, and, in the case of company shares, take a standardised form, each unit normally representing 1,000 shares in the underlying equity. At any time before the expiry date (either three, six or nine months after the commencement of the option), the holder can exercise the option. Alternatively, the option can be sold on The Stock Exchange, where another investor can buy it.

Pre-conditions

Before dealing in traded options it is essential for the investor to have read the brochures prepared by The Stock Exchange which cover in detail this specialist area of the market. Investors will also need expressly to authorise the stockbroking firm in writing before it can transact traded options business on their behalf. There are no other special pre-conditions to investment in warrants or conventional options over and above those applying to ordinary shares. However, such investment would not ordinarily qualify under the Trustee Investments Act 1961.

Characteristics

There are clearly two sides to any option transaction. On the one hand, the purchaser of the option is paying a premium in the hope that the underlying share price will rise or fall depending on the type of option. Since the premium will be low relative to the share price, the investor is able to obtain gearing (buy the option to acquire or sell more shares than if he dealt in the underlying shares). At the same time, should the share price decline substantially, the investor's risk is limited to the option money (which can be lost entirely).

On the other hand, there must be a writer of such an option, who will take the option money and any dividends on the underlying shares (if a covered writer and already holds the stock) in exchange for an agreement to supply to, or take up, the shares from the option buyer if the price rises or falls sufficiently. This role will appeal to the shareholder who wishes to hedge.

Taxation

The short-term nature of transactions in traded options may involve their being treated for taxation purposes as trading rather than capital transactions or even possibly as transactions falling within Schedule D Case VI. The full cost of acquisition is taken into account in the capital gains tax computation. The abandonment of a traded option is treated as a disposal.

Suitability

Options are suited to active investors, prepared to risk a small premium on his judgement about likely movements in share prices over the short-term. If they have little capital to invest, they might well consider traded options. The longer-term investor wishing to back a judgement that a particular company's shares will improve might consider purchasing warrants, although the number of companies with warrants is limited.

Mechanics

The mechanics of investing in options are similar to those applicable to private sector stocks (see **3.4.6**), except that for traded options the London Clearing House supervises the registration and settlement of transactions.

Safe custody

Warrant or option contract notes should be kept for tax purposes and certificates for warrants should be kept in a safe place.

3.7.3 Offers from companies

Whereas earlier sections were concerned with dealings by an investor in the market on his own initiative, this section is for the most part concerned with opportunities which may arise suddenly and may require an investor to respond rapidly to them. However, an application for shares under an offer for sale has often, though not always, to be actively sought out by an investor, and a take-over offer comes not from the company in which the investor has invested but from some other company.

It is a common feature of all the transactions referred to below that strict time limits are laid down for the taking of decisions by the investor, who should therefore allow adequate time for taking advice.

Offers for sale

Although there are several ways in which a company may obtain an initial listing of its shares, only one of them, the 'offer for sale', normally involves the private investor, although very occasionally the private investor is given an opportunity to participate in a private placing of shares on an initial listing or on entry to the AIM.

In the most normal type of offer for sale, an unlisted company seeks an initial listing (or permission for trading to take place on the AIM) for all its shares and makes a substantial proportion of its issued share capital (normally not less than 25 per cent) available to the general public. The shares may be made available either by means of a sale by existing shareholders of part of their holding or by the offer of subscription for new shares, the subscription moneys being paid into the company. Sometimes an offer for sale combines a sale and a subscription.

The offer is made by means of a prospectus, usually prepared by the company in conjunction with an issuing house or a firm of stockbrokers and with the help of professional advisers. The prospectus and accompanying application form are available from the issuing house, the stockbrokers acting for the company and selected branches of banks, and are also advertised in newspapers. If members of the public wish to participate in the offer, they must take steps to obtain a copy of the prospectus and complete and lodge the application form, with the application monies, within the (very short) period prescribed by the prospectus.

Occasionally investors receive an opportunity to participate in an offer for sale by reason of a holding of shares in another company which is 'floating off' a subsidiary.

Rights issues

A company wishing, subsequent to obtaining its initial listing or permission to enter the AIM, to raise capital by the issue of new shares or of securities convertible into shares will normally have to do so by means of an issue by way of rights to its existing shareholders. If it wishes to issue shares to third parties for subscription in cash, it will normally, in accordance with the requirements of The Stock Exchange, have to seek the prior approval of shareholders.

An issue by way of rights will almost invariably be made on terms considered to be favourable to the shareholders, with a view to persuading them to take up the offer. Generally, a shareholder who does not wish to take up the whole of the offer (whether because he does not have available funds or for some other reason) may sell, prior to the payment of subscription monies (ie nil paid), the rights subscribed, either through the market or privately, or simply fail to accept the offer, leaving it to the company to sell the rights on the shareholder's behalf and account for any premium. Shareholders may, if they wish, accept the offer in part.

However, there has been a discernible move towards a form of disguised rights issue, known as a placing with clawback, where a company making an acquisition will raise sufficient funds, subject to agreement by its shareholders in general meeting, by placing new shares with institutions while allowing current shareholders to apply for these shares in proportion to their present holdings. Entitlements not taken up by shareholders may be transferred but cannot be sold through the stock market in nil paid form. The higher the level of acceptance shown by shareholders, the greater the clawback from the institutional placees.

A rights issue is made by means of a prospectus, which typically consists of a provisional allotment letter and an accompanying, or earlier, circular. The provisional allotment letter is a temporary bearer document of title, which is negotiable for the period during which the offer is open for acceptance (a minimum of three weeks) and for a further period of weeks when the shares are dealt in on these documents. Thereafter, the shares become registered.

Capitalisation issues

From time to time companies also make capitalisation issues – from the company's viewpoint, merely a book-keeping exercise, reflecting the incidence of accumulated and undistributed profits and/or the effects of inflation. Although shareholders receive 'free' shares, which can be dealt in on a temporary bearer document of title (either a fully paid renounce-able allotment letter or a renounceable certificate) for a period of weeks, the issue of these shares represents no more than a rearrangement of existing shareholdings and any disposal of the new shares may give rise to a liability to capital gains tax. Special rules apply for arriving at the acquisition cost for capital gains tax purposes, depending on whether all or part of the underlying holding was acquired before 5 April 1982.

Demergers

The growth of companies through acquisition is occasionally reversed by demerger, allowing a subsidiary to be managed more effectively without centralised control. In terms of shareholder value, it is probable that the sum of the demerged parts initially will be more than the consolidated holding prior to the demerger. The separated companies will sub-sequently pay to their shareholders (who immediately on demerger will be the same) dividends recommended by their own boards. Dealings on The Stock Exchange in the demerged companies will commence, with the share price of the parent company adjusted downwards to take into account the distribution of assets. The book cost of the original holding is apportioned between that holding and the demerged company in accor-dance with their first day values so that the book cost of the demerged company is equivalent to the reduction in cost in the original holding. It is deemed to have been acquired at the same date or dates as the original holding for capital gains tax indexation purposes.

Take-over offers

From time to time shareholders in a particular company may receive offers from another company wishing to acquire their shares in exchange for cash and/or shares and/or other securities of the other company. Most take-over bids are conditional upon a reference not being made to the Competition Commission. Under the Fair Trading Act 1973 and the Competition Act 1998, the Director General of Fair Trading has the power to recommend to the Secretary of State for Trade and Industry that a proposed merger be referred to the Competition Commission if he believes the matter referred was against the public interest. If the merger involves parties with a combined turnover of approximately £4bn, it can be subject to the control of the European Commission provided the EC turnover exceeds approximately £200m. Whether the take-over proposal has or has not been agreed with the directors of the target company, the directors of that company will have to give to shareholders a recommendation as to whether to accept the offer. Shareholders can expect to receive not only that recommendation, but also offer documents and (particularly in the case of a contested take-over offer) a flood of circulars. The prudent course for the shareholder is to take careful note of the timetable for accepting the offer prescribed in the offer document and to delay taking any decision or action until a day or two before the closing date under the offer, in the hope that a higher offer may be forthcoming either from the original offeror or from a counter-bidder. If a higher offer is made by the original offeror, an earlier acceptance of the offer at the lower level will not preclude the shareholder from accepting the higher offer, and if a competing offer is made by a third party, an earlier acceptance of an offer can be withdrawn in certain circumstances.

Maintenance

The investor should retain safely all documents (particularly bearer documents) relating to the investments covered in this chapter. On each change of address the investor should notify the appropriate body.

3.8 PREVIEW OF 1999-2000

The UK equity market is likely to continue to track the US and its health will depend a good deal on the course of interest rates there. Indications on rates are that the next move is likely to be up, but the US economy continues to grow at a reasonable pace, and inflation does not seem to be much of a problem, so the US equity market is likely to remain much in demand. With worries of a UK recession falling into the background and the economy ever-more likely to experience a soft landing instead, UK equities continue to offer reasonably good value against the usual alternatives of cash or fixed interest stocks, even though they are highly priced in an historical context. With a distinct lack of supply of new equity coming to the market, and many companies seeking opportunities to pay back unneeded cash to their shareholders through share buybacks, rising long-term institutional cash to liquidity needs to find a home and, for the moment at least, equities retain their growth potential and attractions. As we move away from thoughts of recession, companies will be able to push their dividend payments at a faster rate again, helping to boost the market level.

Sector rotation seems to have been a feature of the first part of 1999, with some of the high return areas of the previous year losing out to industrial stocks and other cyclical sectors which had suffered from under-performance over the previous 12 months. This may continue to be a feature of 1999. Who knows, it might even be the first year for many that small cap stocks have out-performed the FTSE, although there still tends to be an underlying polarisation towards large caps as the UK market becomes pan-European through its link this year with the German, and perhaps the French, bourses.

Mergers and take-overs are likely to continue as a major feature of the market, with consolidation and cost-cutting given as the overriding reason. Sectors such as banks, insurance, investment management, telecoms and pharmaceuticals are all likely to see this, but there may also be selective corporate activity in the engineering sector if companies continue to go through a quiet period before their markets pick up and while sterling remains strong against the euro.

At the time of writing, it seems that the take up of ISAs has been a little disappointing, mainly because of complications of the product compared to PEPs, but perhaps also a need for potential investors temporarily to build up their cash reserves before committing more to the market, especially when it is standing so close to record levels. No doubt sales will pick up during the year to 5 April 2000.

Preparations will continue to be made for the Millennium. All stock exchange participants will have checked their computer records, dealing and settlement systems well in time for the end of the year. It would be too embarrassing to have a systems failure in what is one of the world's most important financial markets. As to the effect on individual listed companies, investors can only hope that enough of their funds have been set aside in writing replacement software and checking the hardware. Worried investors should take up the matter direct with their companies and, if their concerns persist, sell their holdings in those companies who cannot put up a convincing argument that they will be unaffected.

The amount of information readily available to investors through increased coverage of the market in newspapers and the Internet is bound to alter the way that investors manage their financial affairs. The days of reliance on stockbrokers for company information and market views are gone. With time on one's hands, the knowledge of where to find the sources of information and a cheap execution-only dealing service, an investor can now easily fend for him- or herself, leaving old-style stockbrokers perhaps to become investment managers to those who still lack the time or confidence, or who are willing to pay a reasonable rate to delegate the responsibility.

3.9 CONCLUSION

Historically, listed investments have presented a good means of saving with the flexibility of choice between income or growth, or a balance of the two. However, potential investors must give full regard to the detrimental effect that inflation can have on the return on fixed interest securities, and the damage to capital values that a decline in the general level of a stock market can create even to a quality list of blue chip equities. Most investment is on a long-term basis, regard being given to the real economic growth potential of the chosen investment area, and provided that the individual can accept the risks involved in this form of investment, balanced against the twin benefits of the potential for reward and the ease of encashment, if necessary, listed investments would seem an excellent place for savings over and above more immediate cash requirements. The spate of privatisations during the 1980s has done a lot to draw back the veil of mystery over equities in particular; they can now be accepted as part of the savings of all individuals as, especially in the case of PEPs and ISAs, the level of entry is now within the reach of so many more people. No longer can equity investment be thought to be limited to the very rich.

USEFUL ADDRESSES

The Public Relations Department
The Stock Exchange
Old Broad Street
London
EC2N 1HP

Tel: (020) 7797 1372
www.londonstockex.co.uk
www.share-aware.co.uk

Director of Savings
National Savings Bank
Boydstone Road
Glasgow
G58 1SB

Tel: (0141) 649 4555

The Director
Department of National Savings
Bonds and Stock Office
Preston New Road
Blackpool
FY3 9XR

Tel: (01253) 766151
www.nationalsavings.co.uk

The Director of Savings
Savings Certificate and SAYE
   Office
Milburngate House
Durham
DH99 1NS

Tel: (0191) 386 4900
www.nationalsavings.co.uk

The Building Societies Association
3 Savile Row
London
W1X 1AF

Tel: (020) 7437 0655
www.bsa.org.uk

Bank of England
Threadneedle Street
London
EC2R 8AH

Tel: (020) 7601 4444
www.bankofengland.co.uk

The Association of Investment
  Trust Companies
3rd Floor, Durrant House
8–13 Chiswell Street
London
EC1Y 4YY

Tel: (020) 7282 5555
www.iii.co.uk./aitc

The Securities and Futures
  Authority
25 The North Colonnade
Canary Wharf
London
E14 5HS

Tel: (020) 7676 1000
www.sfa.org.uk

The Panel on Take-overs and
  Mergers
PO Box 226
The Stock Exchange Building
Old Broad Street
London
EC2P 2JX

Tel: (020) 7382 9026

Association of Unit Trusts and
  Investment Funds
65 Kingsway
London
WC2B 6TD

Tel: (020) 7831 0898
www.investmentfunds.org.uk

Association of Private Client
  Investment Managers and
  Stockbrokers
112 Middlesex Street
London
E1 7HY

Tel: (020) 7247 7080
www.opcims.org

The Financial Services Authority
25 The North Colonnade
Canary Wharf
London
E14 5HS

Tel: (020) 7676 1000
www.sib.co.uk

4

MAJOR OVERSEAS MARKETS

WILLIAM BOURNE

Scudder Kemper Investments

4.1 INTRODUCTION

One of the earliest acts of the first Thatcher government, in October 1979, was to suspend exchange controls. Investing overseas, hitherto a cumbersome operation, suddenly became much easier, leading to a substantial growth in London's investment management and broking activities.

Since then, with the exception of a hiccough in 1990 because of the Gulf War, overseas investment has continued to grow rapidly. Figure 4.1 shows the total invested overseas by investors through insurance companies, pension funds and collective investment schemes. It can be seen that investors continue to increase their overseas assets despite the renaissance in the UK economy.

It is possible to distinguish two motives for this surge in overseas investment. One, which might be called the 'passive' reason – though this is not to decry it in any way – is the desire to further diversify the risk in a portfolio by reducing its dependency on one country's market alone. The other motive, the 'active' one, is quite simply the belief that overseas assets are going to do better than those in the UK.

4.2 OPPORTUNITIES OVERSEAS

The range of possibilities when investing overseas is wide, from the large, well developed markets of the US to the fledging entities of what used to be the Soviet Union and its satellite nations. Excluding the 'emerging markets' (for which see Chapter 5) the UK-based investor can divide the world into five main areas. The relative size of each of these markets within the 'global' stock market at the end of 1998 was as follows: North America 54 per cent; Japan 10 per cent; Continental Europe 21 per cent; the UK 10 per cent; and other markets 5 per cent.

It can be seen that the US market dominates in terms of size, though only ten years ago this title went to Japan. The percentage taken up by

Figure 4.1   Investment in overseas equities

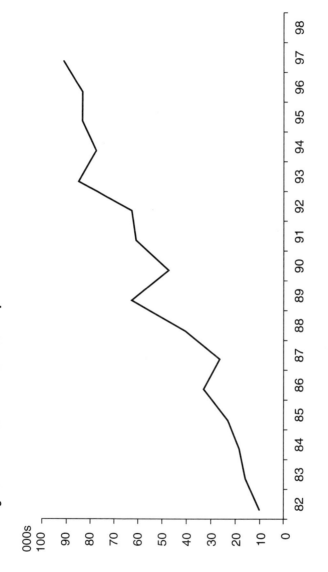

Source: Datastream

Continental Europe might seem surprisingly small, as it contains several economies of a size similar to the UK. The reason is that a larger proportion of companies in these countries remain in private hands, and are not quoted publicly on The Stock Market.

4.2.1 United States

The thin line in Figure 4.2 opposite shows the performance of the US stock market as measured by the Standard and Poors Composite Index. The thick line shows the performance of the US market in percentage terms with 100 as the base, adjusted for the sterling/dollar exchange rate, against the British market; it gives an accurate picture of what an investor would have gained (rising trend) or lost (falling trend) by investing in the US rather than the UK.

Until 1994 there was little to choose between the two markets, though the swings of up to 30 per cent during the period show how important it is to get one's timing right. The US then went through a period of out-performance, as investors were attracted by signs of renewed vitality. This has been particularly true in the new technology industries. More recently, the UK has succeeded in catching up.

There are in fact a number of exchanges in the US. In the case of the New York Stock Exchange (NYSE), companies quoted are generally large and to obtain a quotation they must have sound finances and a good record. The American Exchange and the over-the-counter market exist primarily for companies not qualified for the NYSE, but many large and good quality companies choose to remain on one or the other, finding the service perfectly adequate. The National Association of Securities Dealers Automated Quotations (NASDAQ) has also become an important market in the US, with a National Market and SmallCap Market. NASDAQ is the major method of over-the-counter trading, but also contains NYSE listed securities.

Apart from being the largest stock markets in the world, the US markets are probably the most sophisticated. Companies are closely analysed and many portfolios are run on an extremely rigorous mathematical basis. A great deal of company information is published and is readily available in printed form or on screens. Business is strictly regulated by the Securities and Exchange Commission. There are well developed options and futures markets, though these are principally designed for the institutional investor.

4.2.2 Continental Europe

In Figure 4.3 on p 85, the thin line shows the actual performance of the

Figure 4.2   United States

The US market

The US market relative to the UK market

----- FT/S&P WORLD UNITED STATES (US$) – PRICE INDEX WIUSAMS$

——— WIUSAMS$/WIUTDK$ (REBASED)

Source: *Datastream*

European markets, while the thick line tracks their performance relative to the UK.

The European stock markets performed extremely well in the mid-1980s, a result of their 'discovery' by international investors after a long period of somnolence. There then followed a period of under-performance as economic growth began to slow and, following the crash of 1987, international investors drew in their horns. Another sharp upward movement was precipitated by the fall of the Berlin Wall in November 1989 and the subsequent reappraisal of growth prospects for Europe. During the first half of the 1990s, lower economic growth has provided a background where European markets have struggled to match the UK. More recently, inspired by the launch of the euro, they have once again outperformed.

Stock markets in Europe have traditionally played a less important part in national life than in the UK or the US. Historically, companies have turned to the banks rather than to a country's stock exchange when looking for finance and this goes some way to explaining why their stock markets are smaller and less developed than elsewhere.

Although changes have occurred in the last ten years, and particularly in the last two years, the managers of European companies tend to place greater emphasis on the well-being of employees and customers than is the case in English speaking countries. Shareholders, therefore, come lower down the list of priority, with the result that they are treated less well than in some other markets and information is more difficult to obtain.

The main markets, in terms of size, are France and Germany, followed by the Netherlands and Switzerland. Among the Mediterranean countries, Italy and Spain figure largest though there are also bourses in Portugal, Greece and Turkey. All the Scandinavian countries are represented. Markets in the former Eastern Bloc are covered in Chapter 5.

4.2.3 Japan

Strong economic growth and financial deregulation created a substantial pool of liquidity in the mid-1980s. Much of this money found its way into the property market, though substantial sums were also invested in the stock market, giving rise to the now notorious 'bubble' of 1986 to 1989. The bubble finally burst when the authorities began to worry about asset inflation feeding through into more general price increases and, indeed, the stability of the whole financial system. The ensuing period of monetary retrenchment was followed by a sharp slowdown in the rate of economic activity: both of these factors lay behind the significant under-performance by the Japanese market between 1989 and 1997.

The Bank of Japan's efforts to stimulate the economy led to a recovery

Figure 4.3   Continental Europe

---- FT/S&P WORLD EUROPE EX UK – PRICE INDEX WIEXUK$
—— WIEXUK$/WIUTDK$ (REBASED)

Source: *Datastream*

Figure 4.4 Japan

FT/S&P WORLD JAPAN – PRICE INDEX WIJAPANS$
WIJAPANS$/WIUTDK$ (REBASED)

Source: *Datastream*

in the stock market in the second half of 1995, but renewed concerns over the future returned in 1997 and have yet to be fully allayed. The market is still standing at under half its level at the top of the bubble.

There are eight stock exchanges in Japan, although only the ones in Tokyo, Osaka and Nagoya handle large volumes of transactions. There are over 2,500 listed companies and these are split into three categories. The first category comprises nearly 1,300 large companies; the second, some 760 smaller companies; and the over-the-counter market, around 450 recently listed entities. In general, companies graduate from the over-the-counter market to the second category and then to the first category as their sales and profits reach the appropriate levels.

Japanese companies report business results every six months and the degree of information disclosed to investors is improving year by year, although sometimes falls short of standards experienced in the West.

An unusual feature of the Japanese stock market has been the presence of large 'cross shareholdings' in which one company will hold shares in a selection of other companies with which it has business or other relationships. In the past this has accounted for as much as 30 per cent of the market. There are some signs that some of these cross shareholdings are now being unwound.

The poor performance of Japanese pension fund managers in the early 1990s has spurred deregulation, so that foreign managers are gaining market share. This in turn has led to a shift in the way individual shares are appraised by fund managers, from which some companies have generally benefited.

4.2.4 Other Far Eastern markets

The performance of the Far Eastern markets in relation to the British market has been mixed, as shown in Figure 4.5 overleaf. Between 1986 and 1990 the record was dull, though this had much to do with the weakness in the US dollar which is the key currency for many of these markets. From 1991 onwards performance was much better, as investors began to recognise the potential in the region. This culminated in late 1993 when interest from America and Japan in particular drove markets to unsustainable levels. One of the side effects of this was that companies in the region were able to borrow money cheaply. When the US dollar rose, many companies found themselves unable to pay the interest on their US dollar debt and went bankrupt. Markets such as Thailand and Korea fell by as much as 80 per cent in 1997. Since then, supported by the strength of the US economy, they have made a partial recovery.

The Far Eastern markets include, by convention, Australia and New

Figure 4.5   Far East – excluding Japan

---- FT/S&P WORLD P/BASIN – PRICE INDEX WIPBXJ$/WIUTDK$
—— WIPBXJ$/WIUTDK$ (REBASED)

Source: *Datastream*

Zealand in the south, Hong Kong, Malaysia, Singapore and the smaller but fast growing areas such as Indonesia, Thailand, as well as Taiwan and Korea, and the Philippines. Increasingly China, with its own stock markets in Shanghai and Shenzhen, is attracting direct investment; India is expected to become a major market in the region. The smaller markets are covered more fully in Chapter 5.

While Australia and New Zealand are relatively mature economies, the rest of the area has seen rapid expansion in the last decade. These economies benefit from well-trained, low-cost labour forces and good connections with the huge US and Japanese consumer markets. However, the excessive, and in some cases unwise, expansion has led to a debt overhang. This final factor has been brought into sharp relief since Brazil's devaluation of the 'real' last year and the adverse impact this had on the region's economies.

While Australia and Hong Kong offer a broad range of investments, the other markets tend to consist of a limited number of blue chip stocks, particularly banks, and a large number of small stocks that are not so easily traded.

4.2.5 Emerging markets

In addition to these well established homes for international investors, there are the emerging markets such as Mexico, Turkey, or India. These are covered in Chapter 5.

4.3 CHOOSING A MARKET

4.3.1 Economic activity

It would seem common sense to argue that, since stock markets have something to do with the creation of wealth, choosing a market is a matter of picking the country with the best economic prospects. In the long term, this is generally true. However, it is not an infallible guide. For example, between 1975 and 1985, at a time when the German economy was growing substantially faster than that of the UK, the German stock market rose at an annualised rate of 10.4 per cent, while the British market went up by an annualised 15.6 per cent. Over a shorter-term horizon, it is generally true that the stock market of a country that is about to emerge from a recession is more likely to perform well than one where the economy is beginning to cool down.

4.3.2 Interest rates

Interest rates are important too, and these will generally shadow the rate of inflation. As a rule of thumb, a market where interest rates are falling should generally do better than one where interest rates are rising, as the cost of financing an equity investment will be falling at the same time as interest rates do.

4.3.3 Valuation

We now come to the vexed question of valuation. In the UK market, stocks can be evaluated against their earnings or their asset backing or their dividend yield, and the same thing can be done for individual stock markets. However, varying accounting standards in different countries, as well as the different roles stock markets are perceived to play, make international comparisons of this sort dubious. What may be useful is to look at each individual market against its own historical averages, but even here there are so many different measures that may be used that the results are often contradictory.

4.3.4 Currency

One of the most important considerations in investing overseas is that the investor is not only buying into the shares or bonds of a foreign country, but also its currency, and currencies can fluctuate substantially against one another. It is perfectly possible for the gains made by investing in one market in preference to another to be wiped out by adverse currency movements. For instance, between June 1991 and August 1992, the US market rose by around 12 per cent, far outstripping that of the UK, which fell by 5 per cent. However, during that period the dollar fell by over 20 per cent against sterling so that for UK-based investors the overall return from the US market would have been a fall of 9 per cent, in other words worse than if they had left their money at home. Hence it is absolutely vital to take the effects of likely movements in currencies into account.

To summarise, then, the major factors that should be considered when choosing where to invest are:

(1) the likely performance of the economy;
(2) the level of interest rates and likely changes in their direction;
(3) the valuation of stock markets; and
(4) the likely movements in the foreign exchange rate.

The correct choice of stock market involves a thorough command of these factors, judgement and, let it be said, a certain degree of luck.

No-one – not even the most experienced professional – expects to get it right all the time. If all this seems too intimidating, bear in mind that later in this chapter we discuss how to gain the advantages of investing overseas without having to make these choices.

4.4 THE MECHANICS OF INVESTING OVERSEAS

4.4.1 Direct investment

Despite the seemingly cumbersome arrangements for transferring stock, running a portfolio invested in British shares is not a particularly daunting task. Investing directly overseas can be different.

Consider, first, the information needed to make a decision about which shares to buy. Aside from the obvious language difficulties, companies in many overseas markets place little emphasis on their shareholders, so that even the annual accounts may yield significantly less information than would be the case for a British company. In addition, the accounts are likely to have been prepared under different accounting conventions, which further complicates analysis.

Then comes the question of buying, selling and holding stock. Stock may still be held in bearer form, so that the share certificates are the only evidence of title. In this case, dividends are not paid out automatically by the company, but have to be claimed by the shareholder. The same applies to capital issues. Hence the administrative work starts to build up and this can only be avoided by employing a custodian bank to hold the shares on the investors' behalf. At this stage the costs of owning shares begin to rise quite considerably. By extension, the whole process can be made much simpler by dealing through a British bank or broker who will look after the administration, but in this case a fee will be payable to the British company in addition to any local custodian or brokerage charges.

On top of this comes the question of local taxation which, even when a double taxation agreement is in operation, involves substantial extra work or administrative fees.

It is apparent, then, that investing directly in overseas assets is not an attractive route for most. It is therefore necessary to think about the various types of collective investment schemes which are available.

4.4.2 Collective investment schemes

A major advantage of any collective investment scheme run by a well resourced, professionally run investment management house is that the investor gets access to a broadly diversified pool of assets that are under continual review. However, in the arena of overseas investment, collective schemes funds offer further advantages.

Administration

The complexities of the mechanics of investing overseas have been outlined above; by investing through a collective investment scheme, the burden of all this administration is borne by the managers. Buying and selling overseas investments through a collective scheme is as simple as buying domestic funds.

Flexibility

The complexities surrounding the decision of which market to invest in were discussed earlier. The great advantage of a collective investment scheme is that it offers two different approaches to international investment – the global route and the country specialist.

Global funds

In general these funds will invest all around the world, changing their exposure to different markets as the managers see fit. The difficult decision about which markets to invest in is taken by the fund managers rather than the individual. The investor can therefore gain exposure to overseas markets with none of the agonising involved in the country allocation decision.

Specialist geographical funds

These funds are limited to investing in one specific area, generally one of those in **4.2** above. These are for investors who want to make their own decisions about country allocation, but want all the other advantages of collective schemes.

Whichever route is chosen, the international fund or the country specialist, the investor has a substantial array of vehicles to choose from. Most of the funds quoted will be general funds, in the sense that they will tend to invest in the larger stocks in each market. However, as in the UK, there are a number of specialist funds, invested in smaller companies, asset-backed stocks or particular sectors such as commodities.

The characteristics of each type of collective scheme – unit trust, open-ended investment company, offshore fund or investment trust – are discussed in Chapters 7 and 8. However, there are a few points to make about each of them in the context of international investment.

4.4.3 Unit trusts

Since their launch in the 1930s, unit trusts have proved to be the most accessible category of collective scheme for the overseas investor; most trusts tend to be generalist funds offering either particular regions or a wholly global portfolio (see Chapter 8).

4.4.4 Open-ended investment companies (OEICs)

These were launched in 1997 when new legislation came into effect. They have variously been described as a 'modern' form of unit trust and a 'unit trust in a corporate form'.

Like unit and investment trusts, OEICs offer investors a cost-effective means to invest on the world's stock markets. OEICs offer investors flexibility and simplicity while retaining the basic tax structure of unit trusts. 'Open-ended' simply means there is no maximum size to the OEIC. The funds expand and contract as investors buy and sell shares in it. 'Shares', in this context, are just like the units of a unit trust (see Chapter 8).

4.4.5 Offshore funds

These are broadly similar to unit trusts, except that income is received gross of tax. From the perspective of an overseas investor, the offshore fund sector tends to offer more specialist investment vehicles as well as the 'bread and butter' funds found elsewhere. For instance, one management house has no less than six funds specialising in different aspects of the US stock market.

One obstacle to an understanding of investment in offshore funds is that the fund may be valued in a currency that is neither the investor's own currency nor that in which the investments were originally denominated. For instance, the price of many offshore funds will be quoted in US dollars, even though the fund may have sterling-based investors and may itself be invested in the Tokyo stock market. A common mistake in this case would be to assume that, since the fund is denominated in US dollars, movements in the dollar will affect the value of the investments to the sterling-based investor. Not so; what affects the value of the investments in this case is the level of the stock market and the yen/sterling exchange rate – nothing else.

4.4.6 Investment trusts

The stock market value of an investment trust will usually be at a discount or, more rarely, a premium to the value of the underlying assets.

This discount to net asset value is a very useful indicator of investors' sentiment towards a particular stock market; the discount will tend to narrow as the market becomes more popular and conversely will widen as it falls from favour. For the contrarian investor who likes to invest in areas that are out of favour in the belief that sentiment will improve at some point, the level of the discount is a useful indicator; in other words the contrarian buys when the discount is large and sells when it narrows. The advantage of investment trusts is that the investor not only benefits from the rise in the value of the underlying assets but also from the narrowing discount to net asset value. For those who fancy their ability to pick the winners among global stock markets this is an attractively geared way of backing their judgement.

4.5 CONCLUSION

To summarise, investing overseas is most easily done through one or other of the collective schemes. Those looking to diversify their portfolios may feel attracted towards a global fund, where all the country allocation decisions are taken by the fund managers. Those going abroad because they feel that prospects are better than in the UK may well have more specific ideas and are more likely to be tempted by a fund specialising in a particular region or country. A key factor to remember is that returns on investments overseas can be significantly affected by fluctuations in exchange rates.

5

EMERGING MARKETS

DOUGLAS W ADAMS

Director, Templeton Investment Management Ltd

5.1 INTRODUCTION

Do you ever look at where things are made? If you do, it can hardly have escaped your attention that a large and growing number of products have their origins outside the major Western economies. Products manufactured in Asia or Latin America, but sold in Europe or North America, might include cheap children's toys – or sophisticated, state-of-the-art computer technology. Companies in many developing nations now compete successfully with the best in the world, combining skilled, but low cost, labour with up-to-date technology. In turn, these trends are opening up opportunities for investors to participate in the development process and spread of prosperity.

Are these opportunities only for professional investors or should anyone constructing a portfolio to meet long-term objectives include emerging markets in their range of possibilities? As anyone who reads the newspapers will know, emerging markets are volatile markets. Nevertheless, there are good reasons for the individual investor to include a degree of emerging market exposure in his or her portfolio. With young, ambitious populations the probabilities are that a number of emerging economies in Asia, Latin America and Southern and Eastern Europe will become economic powerhouses in the next 10 to 20 years.

5.2 WHAT ARE EMERGING MARKETS?

'Emerging markets' is the term commonly applied to financial markets in the developing nations of the world. This definition includes most of Asia, all of Central and South America, parts of Southern and Eastern Europe, and all of Africa. Not all countries covered by this definition possess equity markets, and some that do will not permit investment by foreigners. Prominent among emerging markets that have attracted substantial funds from Western investors in recent years are countries as diverse as Egypt, Morocco and Russia; and states more commonly associated with economic and technological advances such as Hong Kong, Singapore and Korea also often feature in emerging market portfolios.

5.3 WORLD OF CHANGE

Thoughts of developing nations often conjure images from television news bulletins of famines, civil wars, coups and deprivation. Problems do exist, but an exclusive focus on the problem areas blinds us to the more generalised, if less newsworthy, progress that most countries are making. A number of factors contribute to this progress. Improving standards of nutrition and education, the application of technology and the liberalisation of economies are judged by many as the main driving forces towards improvement.

Better nutrition

The world has never before enjoyed such an abundance of food. The food distribution challenge remains, but technologies are continually being developed to solve food shortages. For example, up to three billion people – mainly in Asia – rely on rice as their staple food. Improved rice culture has resulted in an increase in rice production over the last quarter-century which has outstripped Asia's population increase.

In November 1996, the World Food Summit in Rome was told that per capita food supplies in the developing world would rise from 2,500 calories in 1990/92 to more than 2,700 by 2010. Indeed, per capita daily calorie supply in the Near East/North Africa, East Asia and Latin America/Caribbean is expected to be near or above 3,000, close to developed world levels.

Improved healthcare

At the same time, the quality and availability of medical care shows substantial gains, even if it does lag the standards the UK enjoys. The number of doctors per 1,000 of population in Brazil rose from an average of 0.4 in 1950 to 1.5 in 1995 – a 275 per cent increase. In Turkey, over the same period, the number rose from 1.4 doctors per 100 to 3.1 – a 121 per cent rise.

Increased life expectancy

Putting better nutrition and healthcare together results in dramatic increases in life expectancy. Figures produced by the World Bank show that a child born in a lower-income country in 1960 had a life expectancy at birth of just 54 years. By 1993, this had grown to 69 years. Since the years from 16 to 65 tend to be the most economically productive, this increase in life expectancy boosts the economic potential of the developing nations. By contrast, in the developed economies, slowing population growth and an increase in the retired population will act as a damper on growth potential as we enter the 21st century.

More education

Learning and experience are further aspects of longer life spans. An individual finds it more worthwhile to learn skills the longer expected life is, and he or she also becomes much more productive through work experience. Educational standards have been rising in many of the developing nations. In 1940, adult literacy in China stood at just 8 per cent; by 1995, this proportion had risen to 73 per cent. Between 1960 and 1990, countries such as Jordan, Pakistan and Turkey more than doubled their adult literacy levels.

Technology transfer

Better standards of education give greater capacity to absorb and adapt new techniques and ideas – and as technology advances it becomes more transportable. Thus it is now commonplace for companies in emerging economies to apply the state-of-the-art techniques to their businesses. To take one notable example, the introduction of mobile phones has given emerging countries the opportunity to leapfrog past the obstacle of building up an infrastructure of land phone lines. Modern, reliable telephone links can be created almost overnight. Given that much of finance revolves around accurate and swift information exchange, such technological adoption is crucial to capital market development.

Faster growth

Taken together, these socio-economic changes have helped to boost growth in the developing nations as a group, leading to improved living standards for their populations. Annual growth in developing nations has been outstripping that of the developed economies over an extended period, and as shown in Figure 5.1 overleaf, the World Bank predicts that this outperformance will continue well into the next century.

However, this fast growth translates into an opportunity for investors only if there are accessible equity and fixed interest markets where transactions can be carried out cost effectively, preferably without intervening

Figure 5.1   Higher economic growth over the longer term – forecast growth in real GDP 1999–2009 (% per annum)

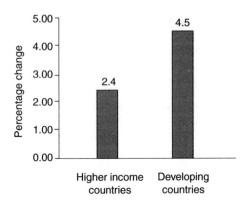

Source: *World Bank & Templeton*

taxes and exchange controls. Moreover, the extent to which shares or bonds represent good value for the future must be considered. If the enthusiasm of other investors has bid up the price of shares, then faster economic growth may already be discounted in the marketplace. In this sense emerging market investment has direct parallels with investment disciplines in the major markets.

Liberalisation

While many shares in emerging markets showed exceptional gains in the early 1990s, the events of the latter half of 1997 provided a rude awakening for those who thought the momentum of the Asian 'tiger' economies was unstoppable. Currency crises visited first Thailand and then its neighbours in the region in quick succession. Markets fell sharply. The crisis indicated that there are still fundamental problems at the heart of Asia's emerging markets – namely political cronyism, unwelcome government intervention and inadequate banking supervision.

It is certainly true that the 1990s trend towards economic liberalisation and privatisation provided a dramatic increase in the number, width and depth of those markets which are open. Governments in many developing nations are embracing investment by foreign portfolio investors as a means of attracting much needed capital with which to fund growth; experience has shown that such inflows speed up considerably following the introduction of open market policies.

Recent events indicate there is still some way to go before we see truly open markets in some of the Pacific Rim countries. Political cronyism is still rife in certain economies; removing such malign influences – indeed, removing the worst excesses of government control – often acts as a spur to growth in developing economies. Latin American countries have provided excellent examples in the past; now countries such as Korea are removing some of their barriers to foreign direct investment. Thus a virtuous circle develops with investment flows raising the sustainable growth rate, which in turn adds to the attractiveness of the country to further investment.

Volatility spells opportunity

The lesson of the 1990s for emerging markets investors is that sentiment, be that optimism or pessimism, can drive equity prices to levels far above, or far below, the instrinsic value of companies. In the wake of the Asian currency crisis, excess pessimism pervades many of the emerging markets, a stark contrast with the excess optimism that was prevalent throughout the early part of the decade. This volatility is both the danger and the opportunity of emerging markets. Astute investors prepared to sell at times of extreme optimism, but then to buy again when pessimism reigns, can reap handsome rewards from the long-term progress of developing countries.

Markets in context

One way of putting these developments in context is to compare the overall size of the emerging markets with those of the developed world. At the end of December 1998 the International Finance Corporation (IFC) calculated that emerging markets were capitalised at £1,139bn. This compares with their estimate of developed market capitalisation of £14,332bn, and a figure of £1,453bn for the London market alone.

Market catch-up

A striking example of the growth of emerging markets is given by the near 20 fold expansion of the total value of emerging market shares over the last 13 years. The December 1998 figure of £1,139bn contrasts with a figure of only £57bn in 1983. Put another way, in 1983 emerging markets as a group were only equivalent to around one-third of the total value of the UK market. At the end of December, they were capitalised at nearly 80 per cent of London – the world's third biggest equity market.

5.4 PERFORMANCE

In 1997, the newspapers were full of stories about the 'crisis' in Asian markets. Share prices plunged rapidly, and currencies lost a huge chunk of their value when compared with those of the developed nations. Then in 1998 the so-called contagion spread to Russia. Have emerging markets just been a good place to lose money?

As with most investment questions, the answer depends greatly on the time period the investor chose. The IFC, an arm of the World Bank, has been at the forefront of encouraging institutional investment in developing nations, and provides a series of indices which show the performance record of emerging markets individually and as a group. Of particular use are the series of investible indices tracking the performance of those markets and shares that are available to foreign investors. As Figure 5.2 shows, the IFC Investible Composite rose by 103 per cent in sterling terms in the period from its first calculation at the end of 1988 to December 1998. This compares with rises of 189 per cent for the FT All Share Index (an average of UK share prices) and 153 per cent for the FTA World Index (a measure of average share price movements worldwide) over the same period. But over 1997 and 1998 the IFC Investible Composite shows a drop of 34 per cent. Over the same period, the FT All Share Index was up 33 per cent.

Variation

Figures 5.3 and 5.4 show how much variation, both in terms of year-to-year movements and individual markets, is masked by the long-term,

Figure 5.2 Emerging markets, UK and World share index movements compared 1989–1998 (£)

Source: *Datastream*

Figure 5.3 Annual changes in share price indices 1988–98

Source: *Datastream*

Figure 5.4 Ten-year index price performance to December 1998 (£%)

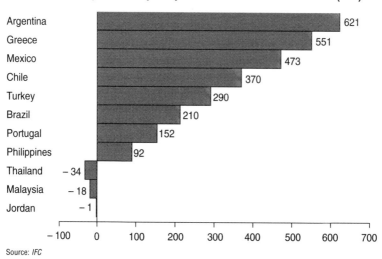

Source: *IFC*

aggregate data. For example, Argentina has performed remarkably well since the end of 1989 with a rise of 621 per cent, according to the IFC. That stands in stark contrast to Thailand, down by 34 per cent over the same period.

101

Table 5.1   Share price movements by country by year (£%)

	1990	1991	1992	1993	1994	1995	1996	1997	1998
Korea	-37.6	-13.2	28.0	23.8	9.5	-7.3	-44.4	-67.7	134.9
India	-0.8	22.1	51.9	21.5	0.3	-38.8	-11.1	10.0	-23.7
Philippines	-61.5	63.9	46.2	140.4	-16.3	-15.9	2.6	-60.0	13.6
Argentina	-47.0	412.6	-9.2	76.3	-30.2	-10.7	7.7	22.1	-28.1
Mexico	5.7	119.2	33.3	37.6	1.2	-50.4	6.0	54.8	-35.8
Greece	70.6	-16.7	-9.8	24.8	-6.3	9.2	-9.0	39.0	73.1
Turkey	-18.8	-39.9	-41.6	242.1	-45.8	-13.5	29.1	118.3	-54.1
UK	-14.3	15.1	14.8	23.4	-9.6	18.8	11.7	24.7	13.6

Source: *IFC & Datastream*

Big swings

Breaking down the longer-term picture into annual slices shows that the progress of individual markets is anything but smooth. Table 5.1 gives the year-by-year movements in sterling for some typical examples. There may be strong long-term returns, but the ups and downs can be dramatic in comparison to the developed markets.

Diversification gives stability

Another feature of emerging markets suggested by Table 5.1 is the low correlation between market movements. There is a tendency for emerging markets to move out of sync. Analysis of the correlation between these markets does confirm that their month-to-month movements are much more out of step than is the case for the developed markets. This is an extremely important attribute. As a consequence, a portfolio exposed to a wide range of emerging markets will exhibit far less volatility than a portfolio invested in one or two markets. In other words, in a diversified emerging market portfolio, losses in one area are likely to be offset by gains in another. This may not give the spectacular returns available when a portfolio is concentrated in a sharply rising market, but it does provide a much more stable route to long-term gains.

5.5 INDIVIDUAL MARKETS

As would be expected with such a diverse set of economies there is considerable variation among emerging markets in terms of size, whether measured by market capitalisation (total value of shares quoted on a market) or number of shares listed (see Table 5.2). India has by far the greatest number of shares quoted, 5,860, roughly seven times the next largest market, Egypt, which has 861. But the capitalisation of the Indian market is relatively modest at £65bn (end December 1998) – less than half that of Taiwan (£161bn), the largest emerging market in terms of value. Yet there were only 437 Taiwanese shares listed at the end of December 1998.

While the situation shows great improvement in recent years, the degree of openness of markets varies too. For example Chile, India and Korea still impose administrative or fiscal barriers of varying degrees of severity to foreign portfolio investors. There have been setbacks too; in 1998, the Malaysian authorities upset many international investors by introducing exchange controls, effectively freezing foreign investments in Malaysian shares.

Almost all markets showed steep declines. Only a handful of markets enjoyed rises, and for three of these – Korea, the Philippines and Thailand – the rises only partially restored the losses of 1997.

5.6 CONSTANT CHANGE

In the mid-1980s, when diversified emerging market funds first began to appear, it was commonplace for the portfolio to hold shares from as few as five or six countries, typically including Hong Kong and Singapore. Even then, portfolio managers would often include shares quoted on the major markets, where the choice could be justified by the companies' trading or business links with the developing world. Now as many as 25 to 30 countries can be represented in a diversified portfolio. This increase in diversity should help to lower the risk of global emerging market funds.

Changing attitudes

The sharp increase in interest in emerging markets by Western investors over the past decade, and the resulting flow of capital, provides a tempting example to governments of countries short of capital and where equity markets either do not exist, are rudimentary or where restrictions keep out foreign investors. It is hardly surprising therefore that a new wave of developing nations are now seeking ways in which they can overcome these hurdles to attract their share of this capital flow.

At the same time investment managers faced with the challenge of maintaining strong performance records strive to be first to invest in a new market which may yield undiscovered treasures in the form of

Table 5.2   Market statistics

	Market Capitalisation (December 1998) £m	Number of Issues (December 1998)	Five Year Total Return[1] (to December 1998) %	1998 Total Return[1] %
Latin America				
Argentina	28.1	130	−14.9	−24.6
Brazil	99.7	527	27.5	−28.3
Chile	32.1	277	−11.8	−25.8
Colombia	8.3	163	−27.1	−44.0
Mexico	56.8	194	−52.5	−36.5
Peru	7.2	257	12.3	−36.4
Venezuela	4.7	94	−18.1	−46.7
Total	236.9	1,642		
Asia				
China	143.3	853	−81.2	−50.0
Korea	70.9	748	−55.4	−127.0
Philippines	21.9	221	−65.2	12.2
Taiwan	161.1	437	−18.1	−15.8
India	65.2	5,860	−55.8	−19.9
Indonesia	13.7	287	−80.8	−26.1
Malaysia	61.0	736	−73.5	2.0
Pakistan	3.3	773	−73.3	−57.5
Sri Lanka	1.1	233	−53.8	−25.9
Thailand	21.6	418	−86.6	38.0
Total	563.1	10,566		
Europe, Middle East & Africa				
Czech Republic	7.5	261	−53.0	−5.7
Egypt	15.1	861	—	−25.6
Greece	49.5	244	204.3	99.4
Hungary	8.7	55	66.1	−8.2
Jordan	3.6	150	33.6	7.8
Morocco	9.7	53	—	33.6
Poland	12.7	198	−26.4	−9.1
Portugal	39.0	135	165.7	43.1
Russia	12.8	237	—	−83.7
South Africa	105.5	668	−25.9	−26.8
Turkey	20.8	277	−23.4	−50.8
Zimbabwe	0.8	67	−43.5	−56.0
Total	285.7	3,206		
Total emerging markets	1,086	15,414		

[1]IFCI Total Return Index
Source: *IFC, Datastream & Templeton*

undervalued equities. These mutually supportive forces will encourage an ever-growing list of new markets appearing in portfolios in the coming years.

New markets

In 1993 the potential of China held the focus, while in 1994 possibilities for investment in Russia and Vietnam began to emerge. More managers are now talking about the potential to be found in some African countries, largely because of the cheapness of shares, rather than the anticipation of an economic miracle. Kenya, Zimbabwe, Botswana and Ghana all probably fall into this category, while the transition to democracy in South Africa provides the possibility of investing in a relatively developed market. The Arab nations of northern Africa – Morocco, Tunisia and Egypt – all possess small equity markets which could become popular in time.

In Eastern Europe, Poland, Hungary and the Czech Republic have attracted most interest to date. Despite the crisis caused by the Russian debt default in 1998, equity markets are also developing in Russia and the Baltic States. And the privatisation process is moving at a whirlwind pace compared with that undergone in the UK. According to some estimates, more than 80 per cent of Russia's industrial workers now work in privatised or quasi-privatised firms. This gives Russia a smaller state-owned sector than many Western European economies.

Really, there is nothing new about investment in emerging markets. Last century, the United States was considered an emerging market. Less than 40 years ago, Japan was considered an emerging market. As these markets matured and developed, they were replaced by others. More than anything, it is the continuing potential for new markets to blossom that adds credibility to the view that emerging markets as an investment theme will endure well into the next century.

5.7 FACTORS TO CONSIDER

If you feel that you wish to take advantage of the opportunities available in emerging markets, how should you go about it?

5.7.1 Direct investment

Direct investment in emerging markets will not prove straightforward for the private individual or even for smaller institutions. Apart from Hong Kong, and perhaps Singapore and Mexico, it could prove difficult to find a private client stockbroker with the experience and inclination to deal directly in emerging markets. Thus direct dealing is restricted either to the purchase of those emerging market shares that are listed on developed markets or to those who initiate direct contact with a broker operating in the markets chosen. Then difficulties of time zone, language, currency, settlement, delivery of share certificates and cost of contact all arise. For example in Turkey settlement the day after dealing is required, hardly sufficient time for the paperwork to have reached the UK even by fax. Tracking direct investments would also prove difficult; coverage of individual shares in emerging markets is almost non-existent in the daily press, and even reporting of market movements is patchy. A final consideration is the risk inherent in investing in a single share in these new markets. If the markets themselves are volatile the movements at the level of individual shares can be extreme.

5.7.2 Funds

A wide range of funds suitable for the private investor now exists. These fall into a number of categories – closed-ended or open-ended, with global, regional and country-specific varieties.

Investment trusts

In the UK closed-ended funds are more usually known as investment trusts, and have a fixed number of shares in issue. This means that the fund manager has a given amount of assets to manage. If new investors buy shares in the trust the fund manager receives no additional assets to manage. Instead the share price rises reflect the buying pressure (see Chapter 7).

Unit trusts

Open-ended funds are typically unit trusts or the newly available open-ended investment companies (OEICs) Similar vehicles called Sicavs, usually registered in Luxembourg or Dublin, have appeared in recent years. As the name implies, these funds are open to new assets, and new buying of the fund results in new assets for the fund manager to look after. However, in contrast with investment trusts, buying pressure has no direct impact on the valuation of units (see Chapter 8).

57 Varieties

Global emerging market funds enjoy the freedom to invest in developing nations worldwide and so may move assets between countries as

conditions dictate. Regional funds are more constrained in their investment scope, and are limited to a particular geographical area of the
world, such as South East Asia or Latin America. Country funds limit
their exposure to a specific economy.

5.7.3 Open versus closed-ended

There is no right or wrong answer on which is the best route to take. It all
depends on circumstances. Broadly speaking, open-ended funds allow an
investor to purchase units which equate to a share of the net assets of the
fund, after initial charges. With most open-ended funds currently available in the UK no charge is made for the sale of units back to the
manager. Thus an investor in an open-ended fund knows that units may
be sold at any time at a price that is based on the value of the assets in the
trust.

Watch the discount

The price paid for shares in an investment trust depends on the balance
of supply and demand in the marketplace at any given time. Typically,
investment trusts trade at a price per share which is below the net assets
attributable to a share. This gap is termed 'discount to net asset value'.
The opposite phenomenon of a premium to net asset value is much less
common, although a few years ago the popularity of emerging market
investment trusts drove many on to a premium.

The Mexican crisis at the beginning of 1995 saw these premiums evap-
orate, illustrating the argument that investors who paid a premium run the
risk of facing a discount when they come to sell.

When investment trust shares are sold while trading at a discount to net
asset value, the return realised is below the underlying return on the
trust's assets. An investor paying £1.10 for shares with an underlying net
asset value of £1 and selling them later for £1.80, at a time when the net
asset value per share stands at £2, realises a profit of 63.6 per cent.
However, the assets in the trust have risen by 100 per cent over the same
period. An investor in an equivalent open-ended fund would have
achieved a return of around 95 per cent, even taking account of typical
initial charges. It is interesting to note that a number of emerging market
specialists offer both open and closed-ended versions of their funds, util-
ising the same investment team, disciplines and shares. When a premium
exists on a closed-ended fund and an open-ended alternative is available
it may prove beneficial for the investor to sell shares in the investment
trust and buy units in the open-ended fund. Of course the opposite can
also occur, giving a distinct advantage to investment trust purchasers in
depressed market conditions.

Long-term advantages

Proponents of closed-ended funds point out that in the case of volatile markets like those of the developing world, investment trusts possess a clear advantage for the long-term investor. Managers of a closed-ended fund do not have to worry that an inflow of new cash will appear at times of optimism, forcing them to buy shares that may have already risen to unattractive price levels from a long-term perspective. Nor do they face sudden calls for cash to meet the liquidations that often accompany a market setback, forcing them to sell shares that offer sound long-term prospects. Thus, it is argued that investment trust managers can take a more objective long-term view, buying and selling shares according to their own judgement, rather than finding that investment decisions are driven, at least in part, by the money flows that the fund experiences.

Micropal, the performance measurement service, provides comprehensive data on all the emerging markets funds available in the UK. An examination of these performance tables, an extract of which is shown in Table 5.3, suggests that for the short period during which both open and closed-ended emerging markets funds have co-existed no category of fund has a clear upper hand. Variations in performance driven by other factors remain more important.

Table 5.3   Global funds available in the UK: performance by type

Global Funds	5 year performance to December 1998	Type *
Templeton Emerging Markets Investment Trust	11.3%	CE
Genesis Emerging Markets Limited	–2.5%	CE
Foreign & Colonial Emerging Markets Investment Trust	–39.9%	CE
Beta Global Emerging Markets Investment Trust	–22.6%	CE
Fleming Emerging Markets Investment Trust	–35.5%	CE
City of London Emerging Markets Country Trust	–21.4%	OE
Invesco Global Emerging Markets	–44.8%	OE
Martin Currie Emerging Markets	–39.5%	OE
Gartmore Emerging Markets Fund	–37.3%	OE
IFCI Composite Index	–47.88%	–

* Open ended (OE) or closed ended (CE)

Source: *Standard & Poor's Micropal Emerging Markets Fund Monitor*

5.8 COUNTRY VERSUS GEOGRAPHICALLY DIVERSIFIED FUNDS

Among the emerging market funds available to UK investors, some have the freedom to invest in all the emerging markets of the world, some focus on particular regions such as South East Asia, or Latin America, while yet others concentrate on single countries. Generally the more specifically focused a fund, the more risky it will be.

Choosing a fund investing in the next market to enjoy popularity from domestic and international investors alike can give spectacular returns. But being sucked into a fund in a market that has already risen a long way can prove an expensive mistake. As illustrated by events in Mexico in 1995 – and even more dramatically by the recent events in South East Asia – falls of 50 per cent or more can occur rapidly in these markets, with little that the fund manager can do if the objective of the fund requires the assets to be invested in that country. For most investors a more diversified approach is appropriate.

Diversity equals safety

The main advantage of more widely spread funds is the safety that comes from diversification among economies with different structures, business environments, and political conditions. These differences mean that a change that affects one market adversely may have no effect, or even a beneficial impact, elsewhere. This is most applicable to those funds that have the freedom to invest in any emerging market in the world. While regional funds do have an advantage over individual country funds, there is a tendency for markets within regions to move in step, reflecting the structural similarities often found among neighbouring countries and a reflection of economic integration from strong trading links. This message was driven home to investors in Latin American funds in early 1995 when markets in Brazil and Argentina tumbled on the back of problems in Mexico.

5.9 CHOOSING A FUND MANAGER

For emerging markets the criteria for choosing a fund management group are no different from those that apply for choosing managers for the developed markets. First, does the manager's literature demonstrate a coherent strategy to the challenge of investing in emerging markets? Many different approaches exist – some focusing on individual shares, others on economic and political fundamentals, and yet others on a mixture of the two. A good manager will be able to articulate clearly the approach adopted. A poorer manager will be less capable of explaining how the task is carried out.

Resources

Secondly, can a manager show that the resources are available in terms of experience, people, technology and contacts to put the chosen strategy to work? Even professionals find good information on emerging market companies harder to find. Therefore if a manager professes a stock-by-stock approach then a global team will be required to carry out the necessary research.

Consistent success

Thirdly, can the manager demonstrate a consistent record of success in emerging markets? While performance in isolation provides an unreliable guide to the future, when examined in conjunction with other criteria it can provide greater insights. A good record but no clear strategy may just reflect good luck in the past which may not be repeatable in the future.

Diversify managers

Do not just look for one manager. Except for the smallest portfolios it makes sense to choose two or more managers with contrasting approaches. This adds to your overall diversification, as the pitfalls of one strategy are likely to be avoided by another.

5.10 TIMING

As with all equity investment there is no certain means of knowing the best time to invest.

Many who committed money to emerging markets in early 1994, following the strong performances in 1993, bitterly regretted their decision a year later. But to sell on short-term disappointments flies in the face of past experience of equity markets. All equity markets can be volatile in the short term, but the long-term rewards usually outstrip the returns available from other forms of investment and saving.

The arguments in favour of emerging markets rely on the long-term structural changes that are under way in the world economy. Patient investors who let these powerful trends work for them over an extended period of time are likely to reap the greatest benefits and, as in developed markets, regular investment through one of the many savings schemes linked to emerging market funds provides an excellent means of reducing the risk of committing funds at a short-term market peak.

5.11 CONCLUSION

Emerging economies will exert a major influence over the rest of our lives, with a strong probability that they will provide the most dynamic economic performance in terms of growth and progress in living standards. For investors they will provide the potential for strong long-term returns. However, the path will not be smooth and any investor in these markets must be prepared for the ups and downs.

Do not invest money that you may need in the short or medium-term in these markets, ie money you might want to call on in the next five to seven years to meet living and other expenses.

As a general rule, the younger or wealthier you are the greater the exposure you can afford to have in these markets, but it is probably wise to place an upper limit of 20 per cent of an equity portfolio in these markets. Also remember to include in your decision the exposure you may have to emerging markets via more generalist international unit or investment trusts.

Finally remember to update your thoughts on what markets are in the emerging category. Japan was an emerging market 25 years ago. Perhaps Mexico, South Korea and Turkey will count as developed markets in 2020, replaced by nations such as Peru, Cambodia and Ukraine in the truly emerging markets portfolios.

6

DERIVATIVES DE-MYSTIFIED

MALCOLM KEMP

Threadneedle Investment Managers Ltd

6.1 INTRODUCTION

The aim of this chapter is to set out what futures, options and swaps are, indicate how they are priced and give a few examples of when they are used. Derivatives enable asset management decisions to be undertaken cheaply and quickly. They offer fund managers the ability to tailor the risk/return profile of a fund in many different ways.

6.2 'SURELY DERIVATIVES ARE VERY RISKY?'

Derivatives have acquired a reputation for being risky, and have been blamed for some large losses, eg at Barings. However, this reputation is often misguided. The important thing is to consider the derivatives not in isolation, but *in conjunction with other assets in the fund.* Some derivatives will still add risk to the portfolio, but many can actually reduce the risk being run.

For example, a fund invested in equities might buy put options, which give the fund the right (but not the obligation) to sell the equities for a fixed floor, even if the equities have fallen further than this floor. These effectively provide insurance against large falls in the values of these equities. Viewed in isolation, they have speculative characteristics because they will rise in value very substantially if the market falls. Buying a put option in isolation is no more sensible than an individual buying insurance on a property he does not own. But viewed in conjunction with the rest of the portfolio the options make a lot more sense. In the above example, the rise in the value of the option compensates the fund for the fall in the value of the equities it owns, just like any sensible sort of insurance.

The key way to control any risks derivatives might introduce is to avoid *gearing.* It is gearing that could cause a modest market movement to lead to insolvency. It is gearing that is dangerous, not derivatives *per se.* This was vividly displayed by the collapse of Barings Bank in February 1995.

It had two large positions relating to the Japanese equity market which doubled up on each other, rather than cancelling out each other. This introduced massive gearing, which went badly wrong when the market moved adversely. However, it is important to bear in mind that gearing is not specific to derivatives. Dangerous gearing can be entered into by borrowing and investing in blue chips or gilts, without going anywhere near an option or a future.

6.3 WHAT IS A FUTURES CONTRACT, AND HOW DOES IT WORK?

Futures contracts are quick and efficient ways of increasing (or reducing) exposure to a particular market. There are many different exchanges on which they are traded, the largest three being the Chicago Mercantile Exchange (CME), the Chicago Board of Trade (CBoT) and the London Financial Futures and Options Exchange (LIFFE). Futures are based on or derived from (hence *derivatives*) an underlying asset. When futures began in 1848 at the CBoT, these underlying assets were agricultural produce as farmers were wanting to fix in advance a selling price for a specified quantity for a specified date in the future. More recently, however, these contracts have been eclipsed by financial futures in which the futures contract is linked to some underlying financial asset or variable, eg stock market indices, bonds, currencies or interest rates.

Perhaps the most important future for a UK investment manager is the FTSE futures contract traded on LIFFE. It is a contract based on the FTSE 100 share index of 100 leading UK equities. It is by far the most liquid futures contract relating to the UK equity market (indeed the amount of equity exposure traded using FTSE futures contracts usually exceeds the amount traded on the underlying stock market!). Similar contracts for other global equity markets are traded on other exchanges around the world.

The exposure to the equity market represented by one FTSE futures contract is £10 times the price paid. Thus with the FTSE around 6,400, the value of the market exposure represented by one futures contract would be around £64,000. This is the amount that would be lost by a buyer of one futures contract if the equity market fell to zero, the same as for an investor who bought actual stocks for £64,000 (in the proportions that make up the FTSE index). Similarly if the market doubled, any investor who had bought/sold one contract would gain/lose £64,000.

A *buyer* of one FTSE futures contract will therefore gain/lose £10 for every point that the FTSE 100 index moves above/below the price paid until the contract expires. At any point in time there are three separate futures contracts potentially tradable, with expiries in March, June,

September or December. Most of the trading actually takes place in the month with the nearest expiry, which is known as the *front month* contract.

Conversely a *seller* of one FTSE futures contract would lose/gain £10 for every point that the FTSE 100 index moved above/below the price received. It is possible to sell a future without holding the underlying stocks (indeed it is easier to do this than to short sell the stocks themselves), but it would of course be very risky to do this, since it introduces a form of gearing.

Every FTSE futures contract will have a buyer and seller. However, when a futures contract is effected, no cash or stocks are transferred between the two parties. Instead the futures contract behaves as if the buyer and the seller commit to buy/sell equities at expiry date. Perhaps a good analogy is the exchange of contracts prior to purchase of a property. Once contracts are exchanged the investor becomes exposed to the implications of owning the property (for example, if the house burns down, the investor will on completion pay a large sum to acquire a worthless asset, which is why it is important to insure a property from exchange of contract and not just from completion). Legal ownership however only transfers on completion.

In any sort of contract in which two parties commit to do something in the future each becomes exposed to the risk that the other will default on the contract. This is why a deposit is paid on exchange of contracts in a property transaction. Most of the complexities of futures arise from the need to introduce a procedure protecting either side from default of the other. Derivatives exchanges try to limit these exposures by use of a *central clearing house* and a *margining system*.

When a futures contract is entered into, both parties put up merely a returnable good faith deposit, called *initial margin*, to the clearing house. The current level of margin per contract is £3,000, but this figure can be increased in periods of high volatility. The clearing house for LIFFE is the London Clearing House, owned by several of the leading Clearing Banks. The clearing house then interposes itself between the two parties by replacing the original contract with two separate equal and opposite contracts, one between itself and the first party and one between itself and the second party. To avoid additional credit exposures arising as the FTSE index moves up or down, the contracts are *marked to market* at the end of each day, with any capital gain or loss being paid from or to the clearing house. These payments are called *variation margin*.

When the contract matures the initial margin is returned to each party. At expiry the FTSE future is *cash settled*, ie the seller transfers only the cash value of the shares rather than the shares themselves to the buyer. This means that the contract is legally classified as a *contract for differences*.

6.4 DEALING IN FUTURES AND STOCKS COMPARED

Futures contracts enable exposures to be bought and sold much more cheaply, quickly and efficiently than dealing in the underlying shares.

If FTSE futures did not exist, an institutional fund manager moving in and then subsequently out of the UK equity market would typically incur the following expenses:

(a) *on buying*
middle price to offer spread	0.2%
commission	0.2%
stamp duty	0.5%

(b) *on selling*
bid price to middle price	0.2%
commission	0.2%
Total	**1.3%**

Thus if FTSE were about 6400, it would need to move by nearly 83 points merely to compensate for the expenses incurred in such a 'round trip'.

In contrast, with FTSE futures, the bid-offer spread is around one index point, plus slightly less for the total round-trip commission. Also no stamp duty is payable. Hence for each £64,000 that is 'round-tripped', dealing in futures might cost roughly £20 compared with approximately £830 – a vast reduction in cost!

In addition, consider what would need to happen if the fund manager wished to change exposure quickly. With futures the trade could be done in a few minutes, with just one deal ticket. Effectively all the stocks would be dealt in at the same time. In contrast, the problems posed by dealing in 100 individual stocks at times of rapidly changing prices – plus the effort of booking, checking and settling all these trades, registering and perhaps claiming dividends, scrip issues etc – are obvious.

Moreover the required change in UK equity exposure might involve a compensating change in exposure to gilts or some specified overseas equity market(s). Appropriate futures contracts can also be used for the other side of such asset allocation switches.

6.5 PRICING FUTURES CONTRACTS

Investors who buy FTSE futures will make or lose money depending on market movements in much the same fashion as investors who buy actual stock. However, purchasers of the futures will be able to earn interest on the cash they do not need to use to invest in the market, although they will not receive the dividend yield that holding the shares would generate.

If the interest on cash is 6 per cent per annum and the dividend yield is 3 per cent per annum then the use of futures saves what is known as the *cost of carry* of:

$$6\% - 3\% = 3\% \text{ p.a.}$$

For FTSE futures with, say, three months before they expire, the cost of carry is 3 per cent divided by four, ie 0.75 per cent. So if FTSE were, say, 5,500 then the *fair value* of the futures contract, allowing for this cost of carry, would be 5,541. The futures contract will in general trade at a price which differs from this fair value, but not normally by very much, because otherwise arbitrageurs would become active bringing the actual price back closer to the contract's fair value.

6.6 WHAT IS AN OPTION?

Options are more versatile than futures contracts, but this also makes them more complicated.

There are two main types of options, called *calls* and *puts*. Again, it is possible to both buy and sell either sort of option – indeed for every buyer there must also be a seller of the relevant option.

A *buyer* of a call option has the *right*, but *not the obligation*, for a specified term to buy an agreed quantity of a particular asset at a stipulated price (from the option seller, otherwise known as the option *writer*). The stipulated price is called the *exercise* price or the *strike* price.

A *buyer* of a put option has the *right*, but *not the obligation*, for a specified term to sell an agreed quantity of a particular asset at a stipulated price.

An investor who buys an option, whether a call or a put, will not lose more than the option premium paid because he or she does not need to *exercise* the option if the asset price moves in the opposite direction from that anticipated. Potential profit from the option in isolation is virtually unlimited.

Conversely, an option writer will not make more profit than the option premium received, unless the option buyer behaves irrationally. Potential losses from the option in isolation can, however, be virtually unlimited. At first sight writing options would appear to be a very risky strategy. However, if the option is covered (see **6.2**) then losses from the written option are compensated for by profits in the stock used to cover the option. For example, if an investor holds stock and writes a call option on that stock then if the market rises a loss arises from the option, but it is counteracted by a gain on the stock held by the option writer. In effect the writer has foregone market upside (since the option buyer can buy the stocks off the writer at a fixed price even if the stocks rise above this level in value). In return, the option writer receives some premium income.

Two principal classes of options are recognised: so-called *American-style* options which can be exercised at any time up to the expiry date of the option, and so-called *European-style* options which can be exercised *only* at the expiry date. These terms no longer have any relationship to the geographic area to which the options relate or from which they originate.

6.7 PRICING OPTIONS CONTRACTS

Calculating a fair value for an option is a lot more difficult than calculating a fair value for a futures contract. The reason is that the value of an option depends in part on how likely it is for the option to be exercised. The price of an option also depends, inter alia, on the time to expiry, interest rates, volatility of the stock to which the option relates and the current stock price in relation to the exercise price of the option.

By far the most important tool used to value and price options is the *Black-Scholes option pricing formula*. This provides a theoretical fair value, C, for a European-style call option which depends on the sorts of factors described above. The formula is:

$$C = S.N(d_1) - X.\exp(-rT).N(d_2)$$

$$where: \quad d_1 = \frac{\ln(S/X) + (r + \sigma^2/2)T}{\sigma\sqrt{T}}$$

$$d_2 = d_1 - \sigma\sqrt{T}$$

S = current stock price
X = exercise price of option
T = time to expiry of option
r = risk-free interest rate (ie return on cash)
σ = standard deviation of stock price (measuring how volatile the stock is)
$\exp(x)$ = exponential function
$\ln(x)$ = natural logarithm function
$N(x)$ = cumulative probability density function for a standardised normal distribution (as might be expected, given the dependence on the probability of the option to be exercised)

Although these mathematical functions look complicated, they are all available within modern spreadsheet packages, such as Microsoft Excel. It is therefore very simple to calculate the Black-Scholes price within such a package, as long as suitable estimates of the parameters on which it depends are available, eg the rate of return available on risk-free investments and the volatility of the underlying stock price. The formula requires the stock not to be dividend paying, but there are relatively simple adjustments that can be made if the stock does provide dividends.

There is a similar formula for the fair value, P, of a European-style put option, but it can more easily be found using a relationship called put-call parity, ie:

$$S + P = C + X.\exp(-rT)$$

Put-call parity recognises the equivalence between buying a stock and a put now, and holding cash and buying a call now to be exercised at some specified future date. The ultimate *pay-off* from either strategy at expiry is the same, and therefore the two should also have the same value.

Although the Black-Scholes formula provides the basis for nearly all option pricing approaches, it is widely accepted within the market that it does not in isolation provide a complete explanation of actual market prices. For example, call options which are *out-of-the-money* (ie would not be exercised immediately, ie $S<X$) tend to trade at prices which require a higher volatility assumption (*implied volatility*) than call options which are at-the-money ($S=X$) or in-the-money ($S>X$). Also, the Black-Scholes formula only applies to European-style options and not to American-style options. For more complicated options it is nearly always necessary to modify the formula in some way, usually increasing the complexity of the mathematics involved. Indeed, derivative pricing experts are often jokingly called rocket scientists by others in the investment field, because of the high level of mathematical skills they often possess.

6.8 OVER-THE-COUNTER OPTIONS

Options traded on recognised exchanges are restricted to specified assets, strike prices and expiry dates. The sorts of assets on which options are available range from specific shares such as British Airways or market indices, such as FTSE. Usually there will be a range of strike prices and expiry dates available for any given asset, but most of the liquidity, ie dealing, would be concentrated in contracts which have the shortest period to expiry and have strike prices quite close to current market levels.

Options which are not traded on recognised exchanges are called *over-the-counter* – colloquially OTC. These permit much greater flexibility in contract design, including the ability to incorporate more complicated pay-off characteristics, and thus permit the option to be tailored to the precise requirements of the investor.

Often, options will be used purely as a way of implementing an investment view. However, option activity may be driven more by concerns over liabilities than assets. For example, a fund manager may launch a retail guaranteed equity bond which provides to the investor a guarantee of no capital loss, but also promises to give the investor a set percentage of any rise in the market over, say, a five-year period. The fund management house can then match this liability (and thus avoid the risk of not being able to provide the stated guarantee) by buying a suitable option from an investment bank.

6.9 WHAT IS A SWAP, AND HOW IS IT PRICED?

The most common equity derivatives are futures and options. The exposures bought and sold via equity derivatives often exceed those bought and sold via transactions in the underlying equities. However, even these volumes are relatively small compared to the volumes transacted in the swaps markets.

In a swap one party agrees to pay the other one sort of cash flow stream, receiving a different sort of cash flow stream in return. The most common sort of swap is a fixed for floating rate swap. In this contract, there will be some agreed principal sum, eg £100m. The first party will then agree to pay the interest receipts receivable were this sum to be invested in cash, which for large sums will vary up and down in line with what is known as LIBOR, the London Interbank Offered Rate. In return the second party will pay a fixed rate, eg 6 per cent per annum (ie £6m per annum) for the lifetime of the swap, which might be up to 25 years, say.

A corporation might for example be willing to enter into this sort of transaction in order to help it fix more precisely its likely borrowing costs. It might, for example, borrow money at today's variable interest rate, but avoid the risk of this interest rate rising substantially by swapping fixed payments in return for the floating rates it needs to service this debt. Fixed for floating rate swaps are also used extensively by building societies and the like if they are offering fixed rate mortgages to their customers (since they will generally need to pay floating rates to their depositors).

Practically any sort of cash flow can be swapped in this sort of fashion. For example, the swap could involve paying away the return achieved on the FTSE index in return for the (floating) return available from cash. By entering into such a swap, the investor would shed exposure to the UK equity market gaining exposure to cash instead, much like the result of selling a FTSE futures contract.

Not surprisingly, the fair price of such a swap can thus be calculated in a manner which is similar to that used for futures contracts. Swap contracts that contain *optionality*, ie some element of option-like behaviour, are more complicated to value and require techniques of the sort mentioned in **6.7**.

6.10 CONCLUSION

The difficulties of Barings, Sumitomo and Orange County amongst others have shown what can happen when the fundamental principles of trading in derivatives are forgotten by operators. However, when sensibly used, derivatives are a useful investment management tool, providing quick, cheap and efficient ways of shifting between different asset categories and managing risk exposures.

SOURCES OF FURTHER INFORMATION

Exchanges

The London International Financial Futures and Options Exchange (LIFFE)
Cannon Bridge
London EC4R 3XX.
Tel: (020) 7623 0444
Fax: (020) 7588 3624
Internet: http://www.liffe.com

Books

Options, Futures and Other Derivatives (3rd edn), John Hull, Prentice-Hall, 1997

Academic Papers

Actuaries and Derivatives, Malcolm Kemp, Institute of Actuaries, 1997

7

INVESTMENT TRUSTS

DAVID BALLANCE
Investment Director,
Threadneedle Investment Managers Ltd

7.1 INTRODUCTION

Collective investment media enable investors to pool their resources to create a common fund for investment by professional managers. The two great benefits of this collective approach to investment are (1) more efficient and economical investment management; and (2) greater security through the spreading of risk over a diverse range of investments.

To meet these needs, various different media, such as investment trusts, unit trusts, OEICs and offshore funds (see Chapter 8) and insurance bonds (see Chapter 14) have evolved from separate legal and financial origins, subject to varying regulation and tax treatment. The choice between the different media in practice may depend on the investor's convenience as much as the features of the collective media, which are increasingly given a 'level playing field' by regulations. Nevertheless there are still some marked differences in the ways these investments are marketed, priced and taxed, quite apart from the management of the underlying assets.

The most straightforward and flexible of these media is the investment trust, which is actually not really a trust, but simply a limited company in which investors buy shares and other securities so as to benefit indirectly from its assets and income. An investment trust is constrained by its authorised capital, which cannot readily be changed or repaid to shareholders, and the shares are generally bought and sold by investors on The Stock Exchange at market prices determined only by supply and demand.

7.2 HISTORICAL BACKGROUND

The first investment trust to be established in England was the Foreign and Colonial Government Trust, which was created as a trust in 1868 and in

1879, owing to doubts concerning the legality of its original structure, was reorganised as a public limited liability company under the Companies Act 1862. The original objective of this trust was, in the words of its initial prospectus, to provide '. . . the investor of moderate means the same advantage as the large capitalists in diminishing risk in foreign and colonial stocks by spreading the investment over a number of stocks'. By the early 20th century a number of other investment trust companies had been incorporated in England and Scotland and the investment trust had become firmly established in the UK as an investment medium. Some of these early trusts (including 'The Foreign and Colonial Investment Trust plc') still exist today despite two World Wars and many serious economic crises. During the last 100 years, investment trust companies have provided much new capital for UK businesses by underwriting or subscribing for public issues of securities and accepting private placings, thus giving important support to capital investment in the UK.

Investment trusts are probably the most flexible of the collective media, free to invest in any kind of assets, and the individual companies and the securities that they issue vary widely. In comparison with the other media, two distinctive characteristics are their ability to 'gear up' their sensitivity to the markets by borrowing, and the fact that the shares are generally priced by supply and demand in the market at significantly less than the value of the underlying assets of the investment trust. Both these factors tend to make investment trusts more sensitive to movements in the markets as a whole, while still spreading the specific risks of investments in individual stocks.

As explained in **7.7**, certain capital gains tax concessions are given to those investment trusts which have been approved by the Inland Revenue. In order to obtain approval the investment trust must, among other requirements, be resident for tax purposes in the UK and have its ordinary share capital listed on The Stock Exchange. This chapter deals primarily with investment trusts which have been so approved for tax purposes and which have been incorporated in the UK. Unapproved investment trusts can generally be treated like any other company.

7.3 RECENT DEVELOPMENTS

Investment trusts (ITs) constantly attract innovative uses and developments in the best traditions of the City. As well as around 400 existing investment trusts available in the stock market, a continual stream of new issues and additional tranches provides opportunities for both general and specialist investment of all kinds. Investment trusts have been particularly attractive to private investors in the form of personal equity plan holdings (PEPs), and are likely to remain available through ISAs.

The last two years have seen a stronger level of activity in venture capital trusts (VCTs). VCTs are not really typical of ITs generally, but merely happen to use the flexible form of an IT for a special purpose vehicle. A VCT, like any IT, is exempt from capital gains tax, so that VCTs themselves will be broadly tax neutral. However, in addition, investment in a VCT is free of income tax and capital gains tax, like an ISA; investors will receive income tax relief on subscriptions into new VCTs, and capital gains on other investments which would otherwise be chargeable to tax can be rolled over into a VCT investment within six months before or after realisation. It should always be realised that CGT rollover is a deferral, not a cancellation of the tax liability. The limit of £100,000 investment per annum is far more generous than for ISAs.

A VCT, like an IT, is a listed public company specially approved by the Inland Revenue, which must derive its income 'wholly or mainly' (in practice, at least 70 per cent) from securities; but which must also within three years of approval invest at least 70 per cent of its assets in 'qualifying holdings' in unquoted UK trading companies. At least 30 per cent of a VCT's investments overall must be in ordinary shares, with the balance in other share capital or long-term debt. A VCT may invest a maximum of £1m per year in any one trading company, which may not be larger than £11m immediately after the investment, and must not be controlled by the VCT or anyone else. No holding may exceed 15 per cent of the VCT. The detailed requirements for the trading companies are comparable to those for the Enterprise Investment Scheme, such as the requirement for the investment to be used in trading within 12 months.

All the VCT's investments must be new, ie initial subscription of shares or debt, and no securities of the trading company may be listed or quoted on the USM at the time (although listing on the AIM is allowed, as is subsequent admission to listing). Like an approved investment trust, a VCT must retain 15 per cent of its income, but it may also choose to distribute capital profits (see **7.7.1**).

The other area where there has been recent budget initiatives is that of housing investment trusts (HITs). However, the level of takeoff in HITs has been low, as evidenced by the pulling of the launch of the Saville's Property Investment Trust when only £25m was raised against hopes for around £40m.

7.4 LEGAL NATURE

7.4.1 Constitution

An investment trust is a limited liability company with a share capital, and is a legal entity separate from its shareholders or managers. In practice the trusts are often promoted and managed by fund management groups who run a number of investment trusts and other funds which, in some cases, own the management group. All trusts must now have a majority of non-executive directors, according to AITC guidelines. However, the shareholders are always entitled to vote to replace the management, and there has been much take-over activity in the industry.

Like any limited company, an investment trust company is constituted by the contract with its shareholders contained in its memorandum and articles of association. The memoranda of investment trusts usually contain wide powers to invest the company's funds in securities and property and to borrow, but, for tax reasons, commonly prohibit trading (as opposed to investing) in securities or property; and their articles of association normally contain a provision prohibiting the distribution of capital profits by way of dividend. However, approved status for tax purposes (see **7.7**) requires certain practical limitations on the exercise of these wide investment powers.

An investment trust, like any limited company, itself is not permitted to advertise its shares for sale except by reference to Listing Particulars, registered with the Registrar of Companies and complying with the Financial Services Act. However, managers will eagerly respond to enquiries, and increasingly advertise schemes to facilitate investment. Further advice and information are available from stockbrokers, through whom the shares are often bought, and from the Association of Investment Trust Companies (see 'Sources of further information' at the end of this chapter).

7.4.2 Investment trust securities

Investments are made by buying stocks, shares and warrants of the trusts. Apart from ordinary shares, a trust may issue debenture stock (secured by a charge on its assets), unsecured loan stock, preference shares or warrants. The holders of such securities are entitled to receive interest or preference dividends at the applicable rate before any dividends are paid to the ordinary shareholders. These securities may, in the long run, prove less profitable, but are more secure since, on a winding-up of the company, the ordinary shareholders are entitled only to any surplus assets remaining after payment of all other liabilities, including the repayment of principal and income due to holders of loan capital or preference shares. If an investment trust has a high proportion of its capital in the form of loan capital and preference shares, major fluctuations in the value of the underlying assets attributable to the holders of its equity share capital can result. This topic is discussed in more detail at **7.6.5**. (Debenture stocks, loan stocks and preference shares are discussed at **3.6**.)

Warrants are securities which give the holder the right (without obligation) to subscribe for shares subsequently on fixed terms: in the meantime the warrants are themselves listed investments whose market price will change rapidly according to the prices of the underlying shares, but in most cases without yielding an income. For example, suppose a warrant entitles the holder to subscribe for certain investment trust shares at 95 pence each. If the shares are currently worth £1, the warrant will trade at about 5 pence. In practice the majority of warrants will trade at a premium to their intrinsic value, because of time value. If the shares rise by 10 per cent to £1.10, the warrants should rise 200 per cent to 15 pence; conversely if the shares fall by 10 per cent to 90 pence, the warrants would be practically worthless. Warrants clearly offer a more volatile capital investment in the success of an investment trust than its ordinary shares (see also **3.7.2**).

7.4.3 Split capital trusts

As well as issuing all the usual company securities, investment trusts can also go further and, instead of ordinary shares, issue their capital split into different issues tailor-made for different kinds of investors.

In most ordinary companies, directors generally have considerable freedom as to how much dividend to distribute out of profits, and are only expected to manage their dividend policy to provide growing dividends indefinitely; such companies are not expected to be wound up, and shareholders' rights in a liquidation are largely academic. Investment trusts must distribute most of their income and none of their capital profits for tax reasons, although to some extent they can manage what proportion of profits are receivable as income.

However, some 60 split capital trusts are constituted with separate classes of shares which will be repaid (or at the least, the question will be put to a vote of shareholders) at a fixed date. Each class of share capital has specified entitlements to dividends in the meanwhile and to capital distributions, in a stated order of priority between the classes of shares, and the directors have very little discretion as to the application of whatever profits they make. While the total performance of the investment trust will always depend on the success of its investment managers, each class of shares will have relatively more or less predictable expectations, designed to be particularly valuable to certain kinds of investors. These benefits can make the total value of the trust's securities higher than if it simply issued one class of ordinary shares.

The earliest split capital trusts have capital shares, which provide no dividend income at all but the right at liquidation to all capital gains within the trust, and income shares, which distribute the entire trust's net income, but will be repaid at the liquidation date normally at their issue price. The prices of each share will reflect the demand from investors, taking account of the specified rights of *all* prior classes of shares and other securities. Thus, the income shares offer a very high running yield, suitable for ISAs or for trustees paying a widow's annuity, while the capital shares would attract a higher rate taxpayer approaching retirement.

7.4.4 Specialised split capital investment trust securities

Investment trusts are free to create any kind of securities for their investors, and the principle has been used to design shares with sophisticated characteristics, which require individual analysis of exactly what is offered and the security that will be obtained. These securities can be superbly efficient investments, but it is quite inadequate and highly dangerous merely to rely on the names of such specialised securities, and investors must consider the rights of both their own intended shares and all other securities which will have priority in any situation, together with current circumstances which change after the securities are issued. Some kinds of income shares have little or no capital entitlement, and other preference shares can have index-linked or other formula based income. Each class of security will have its own profile of risk and reward, ranging from a preferred stock many times covered by assets, to highly speculative zero coupon shares. The latter should not be confused with zero dividend preference shares or zero coupon debentures, which are actually very 'safe' (see below). Needless to say, the value of these securities will ultimately depend on the success of the managers' investment policy, but to very differing extents. The only real rule is that, inevitably, the sum of the rights of all classes of issued capital is equal to the total net capital and income of the trust. Thus, at the end of the queue on each distribution, one class of shares will have the most uncertain outcome, in effect securing all the prior entitlements; and naturally such risky securities will be priced to earn, on average, the highest expected rewards.

Amongst these more sophisticated securities are:

Zero dividend preference shares

This is a low risk investment suitable for financing future capital sums without income tax liability in the meanwhile, such as school fees. The risk can be assessed by measuring how many times the capital repayment is covered by net assets, or in other words how much the managers can lose without affecting the repayment at all.

Capital entitlements: a fixed capital return payable on liquidation.
Income: nil.

Income shares and annuity shares

It is essential to check exactly what type of share is being considered. These shares can be particularly appropriate for non-taxpayers, in ISAs, or for non-working spouses. In many cases, a gross redemption yield can be calculated and compared with that on the nearest equivalent gilt-edged securities, taking account of the different levels of risk.

Capital entitlements:

(1) the original split capital trusts repay a fixed amount on liquidation, and their income share price will fall towards this value as this date approaches; for example, traditional income shares that are issued at £1 and repaid at £1 would normally see their share price increase in the early years, as dividend growth increases the yield, before falling towards their final value in the latter years;
(2) some more recent issues are also entitled to part of any capital appreciation, after prior classes of shares are satisfied;
(3) a very different type, sometimes called annuity shares, have little capital entitlement which may be as low as 1p, or even less.

Income: these shares have exceptionally high running yields, benefiting from the income gearing probably by other classes of capital such as zero coupon shares and capital shares that do not rank for dividends.

Stepped preference shares

Another low risk security having priority over ordinary shares and most other classes, giving a known growing income and capital return if held to redemption (hence redemption yields can be calculated and compared with government securities).

Capital entitlements: a fixed capital return payable on liquidation.
Income: a predetermined dividend rising at a specified rate such as 5 per cent per annum.

Geared income shares

Otherwise known as highly geared ordinary shares, or income and residual capital shares. These shares are typically in structures with zero dividend preference shares or RPI-linked debentures. They are, effectively, a combination of income shares and capital shares and offer a high level of running yield and geared capital exposure.

7.5 CONDITIONS FOR PURCHASE

There are in general no limitations on the purchase of UK investment trust shares. Investors must of course satisfy any restrictions imposed by their own powers (eg as trustees), or any foreign laws to which they are subject. Investment trusts are normally a wider-range investment under the Trustee Investments Act, and collective investment media generally help to satisfy trustees' duty of diversification.

7.6 CHARACTERISTICS

All investment trusts have the same legal structure in common, but its flexibility gives an enormous range of very different investment vehicles, both as to the underlying investment management of the trust and the interests that investors can take. As well as traditional general trusts directly comparable with conservatively regulated unit trusts and insurance bonds, there are highly specialised issues tailor-made for particular purposes and suitable only for sophisticated or expertly advised investors of the appropriate type (see **7.4.4**).

7.6.1 Spread of risk and flexibility

An important feature of investment trust shares, like other collective investments, is the spread of risk which can be achieved by the investor. Investment trust shares represent an indirect interest in all the underlying assets of the trust, which can give the small investor a well balanced portfolio with a good spread of risk which would be too expensive and impracticable to obtain and manage by direct investment. But larger investors (personal or corporate) also invest through investment trusts in order to obtain professional or specialised investment management, currency management or gearing, and their attention to the trust's management of their interests may benefit all shareholders.

The wide investment powers of most investment trusts enable them, subject to the limitations acceptable for tax purposes, to follow a reasonably flexible investment policy. In response to changes in investment or fiscal conditions, they can adjust the emphasis in their portfolios on income or capital appreciation or on a particular sector of the market or geographical location. In addition, they are able, within limits, to invest in real property (although usually through the securities of listed property companies), in shares of unlisted companies and in other assets and, although they do not trade in securities themselves for tax reasons, they may establish dealing subsidiaries to take short-term positions in securities. Owing to SIB regulations, an authorised unit trust must necessarily have a less flexible investment policy than that of an investment trust.

The basic investment characteristics of any investment trust are stated in its prospectus and may be indicated in its name. However, since investment trusts are flexible vehicles and investment conditions are constantly changing, a better indication of an investment trust's current policy can be obtained from its latest report and accounts.

As well as its investment objectives and financial record, another vital characteristic of an investment trust is its size. A small investment trust may be able to out-perform a larger one by adopting a more flexible investment policy, but its shares could be less marketable than those of a bigger trust, with a greater spread between buying and selling prices.

7.6.2 Income and capital gains

The total returns from an investment are traditionally assessed as income and capital gains, but in an age where the marginal rates of tax on income and capital gains are similar the distinction is rather artificial, and the balance between the two can be deliberately adjusted (eg by selling securities cum- or ex-dividend). However, in general, dividend income is usually more predictable than capital performance, not least because it is often actively managed for consistency. Income and capital gains from investments are taxed differently and may be separately owned, so the balance between the two is very significant to many investors. Some markets, for example in the Far East and continental Europe, offer negligible dividend yields and correspondingly greater expectations of gains, but investment trusts may be chosen with a wide range of dividend policies.

As previously mentioned, the majority of warrants yield no income at all, which can be useful for instance to parents who would otherwise be liable to income tax on investments given to their children.

Most investors are free to adjust the 'income' they draw from their investments, either by reinvesting surplus net dividends, or by regularly selling shares to supplement the dividend yield. So far from being improvident, this is often a very sound strategy: up to £7,100 capital gains per year can be taken free of tax, in addition to the income tax allowances. Provided that the withdrawals do not exceed the capital gains (often profits retained within the trusts), the value of the investment will not be eroded. Note that if one sells discounted assets to realise a capital gain and provide a running income, then one can erode one's capital base markedly.

7.6.3 Investment overseas and currency management

Although most investment trusts adopt a flexible investment policy and are not rigidly committed to maintaining a particular proportion of their investments in any one geographical area, some of them specialise in one or more overseas areas in which they maintain special knowledge and investment expertise. These trusts provide a useful medium for overseas investment which often presents practical difficulties for direct investors.

Many trusts use foreign currency loans for overseas investment, so that the exposure of the trusts to the foreign exchange markets can be managed independently of the investments made in any country. At the same time the trust may be geared-up (see **7.6.5**), but whenever the managers choose to reduce the exposure of the trust to the market they can simply make a sterling deposit to remove the gearing.

For example, a foreign investment which gains by 20 per cent in local currency terms would still show a 20 per cent sterling loss if the exchange rate fell by a third. However, if the managers borrow the amount of the investment locally and the exchange rate falls, the liability to repay is reduced along with the assets. At the same time the trust's original capital remains intact, and could also be invested in any market.

Another, sometimes cheaper, way of hedging against exchange rate exposure is the 'currency swap' under which a UK investment trust swaps an amount in sterling with, say, a US company for an equivalent amount of US dollars. The US dollars received by the investment trust are used for portfolio investment. At the end of the agreed period the investment trust simply hands back the same amount of dollars to the US company in return for the sterling amount agreed at the outset. The risk of a default by the other party is limited to the possible exchange loss and attributable expenses, and both companies avoid the expenses of using a bank as intermediary.

The investment trust has always been a useful medium for overseas investment by UK residents because such investment is a difficult matter for most private investors, having regard to the distances involved, foreign market and settlement practices and the taxation and other problems which may arise in the overseas territories concerned. The average UK investor does not have sufficient resources to manage his UK investments effectively, let alone a portfolio of overseas investments.

7.6.4 Stock market price and underlying net asset value

An investment trust incorporated in the UK in general cannot usually purchase or redeem its own shares. Consequently, investment trust shareholders can normally only realise their investment by selling their shares through the stock market to other investors, or if the trust is wound up or taken over. The market prices of investment trust shares are dictated by supply and demand and for many years have generally stood at a discount to the value of their underlying net assets. These discounts and valuations are regularly published for most trusts. Investment trusts still often stand at a price in the stock market which is 15 or 25 per cent lower than the estimated amount per share which would be paid to shareholders on a liquidation of the company. The obvious explanation for these substantial discounts is a lack of demand for investment trust shares in the market. It is due, in part, to lack of publicity, competition from pension and insurance funds and unit trusts (whose managers are free to advertise their units for sale and to offer commissions to selling agents), and the fact that investment trust shares are often held by long-term investors. All these factors have contributed towards a comparatively low level of regular dealing activity in investment trust shares and so reduced their marketability. It also seems that as institutional fund management has become more sophisticated, it also seems that their appetite for investment trust shares has diminished.

To realise the profit inherent in the discount on net asset value, a number of investment trust companies have been reconstructed by their managers, taken over by other companies, placed in voluntary liquidation or 'unitised'. Unitisation is a scheme under which the shareholders pass a special resolution to wind up the investment trust and transfer its investments to an authorised unit trust in exchange for units of the unit trust. Subject to Inland Revenue clearance, unitisation does not of itself involve the investment trust shareholders in any liability to capital gains tax and on a subsequent disposal of units in the authorised unit trust, the acquisition cost of those units for capital gains tax purposes is the original acquisition cost of the shares in the investment trust from which the units arose. Following the unitisation, the former shareholders in the investment trust can sell their new units in the authorised unit trust at a price based on the underlying assets of the unit trust (see Chapter 8) and so the discount will have been effectively eliminated, although one needs to be aware of dealing costs and the bid/offer spreads.

The discount on net asset value has also been eliminated for some investment trust shareholders by take-over offers being made for their shares at prices near their underlying net asset value. Some of these take-over offers have been made by predator companies, while others have been made by institutions, such as pension funds, which see the acquisition of an investment trust company as an inexpensive means of acquiring a 'ready-made' investment portfolio and perhaps eliminating a competitor. However, a take-over, unlike a unitisation, may unexpectedly crystallise a liability to capital gains tax, though most will offer a tax efficient rollover.

If the discount is eliminated in one of these ways, or simply narrows as a result of increased market demand, it will be beneficial to holders who bought their shares at a discount and can sell at a price nearer to the net asset value. When investors come to sell their shares, so long as the discount is not larger than when they bought them, they should not suffer loss solely by reason of its existence, and in the meantime will have benefited from the income on the undiscounted or gross assets.

Another factor which will affect the stock market price of investment trust shares is the market-maker's turn, ie the difference between the higher offer price (at which the market-maker is prepared to sell to the investor) and the lower bid price (at which the market-maker is prepared to buy from the investor). The spread between the market-maker's bid and offer price will usually be wider in the case of shares of the smaller, less marketable trusts. It should be emphasised though that spreads are actually very narrow, and much narrower than bid/offer spreads on unit trusts.

This assumes that there is a sufficient market for the shares to enable them to be sold at all. In practice, a small investor in most of the larger investment trusts should not experience any difficulty in disposing of his or her shares at close to current market prices.

7.6.5 Gearing

In addition to its equity share capital, an investment trust may raise further capital by issuing debenture or loan stocks or preference shares and borrow money in sterling and foreign currencies. On a liquidation of the investment trust, holders of such stocks or preference shares and lenders of funds to the investment trust are entitled to repayment of fixed amounts of capital or principal from the assets of the trust in priority to equity shareholders. Only the surplus assets remaining, after discharge by the investment trust of all its other liabilities, are distributable to the equity shareholders. In effect, any increase or decrease in the value of the assets of the investment trust is primarily attributable to one or more classes of its equity share capital. An overall increase or decrease has a greater effect on the underlying value of its equity share capital in the case of a trust which has raised most of its capital in the form of loans or preference shares than in the case of a trust which has raised most of its capital by issues of equity shares. In UK securities terminology, if the proportion of a company's capital which has been raised in the form of loans and preference shares is large in relation to its equity capital, the company is described as 'highly geared' and, if small, the company's 'gearing' is said to be low; the US term is 'leverage'. Gearing levels of 10–15 per cent would normally be regarded as moderate for an investment trust. For conventionally structured trusts (ie excluding geared ordinary or capital shares in splits) gearing in excess of 30 per cent would be considered high.

The following examples illustrate the consequences of gearing; taxation and other factors have been ignored in the interests of simplicity.

Example 1: Ungeared trust

A new ungeared investment trust raises £1m by an issue of equity shares and invests the proceeds of the share issue in a portfolio of securities. If the value of the portfolio doubles to £2m, the assets of the trust attributable to the equity shareholders will increase 100 per cent. If the portfolio halves, the net value for ordinary shareholders will, likewise, decrease by 50 per cent.

Example 2: Geared trust

Suppose a new geared investment trust raises £1m by (a) issuing 500,000 preference shares at £1 each and (b) issuing equity shares at an aggregate price of £0.5m, and then invests the total proceeds of £1m in a portfolio of securities. If the portfolio doubles in value to £2m, on liquidation the investment trust will have to pay £0.5m to the preference shareholders; but, after this payment, the amount attributable to the trust's equity shares will have increased by 200 per cent from £0.5m to £1.5m. On the other hand, if the value of the portfolio halves, the preference shareholders will be repaid £0.5m, leaving nothing for the ordinary shareholders – a 100 per cent loss.

The ability of investment trusts to gear their portfolios in this manner is one of the principal differences between investment trusts and unit trusts. The latter have only very limited powers to borrow money without gearing up.

The examples given above illustrate the effect of gearing on the capital assets of an investment trust, but, if the lenders of money to an investment trust or its preference shareholders are entitled to payment of interest or dividends at a fixed rate, gearing will also have an effect on the income of the trust from its investments which is distributable to its equity shareholders. An increase (or decrease) in the income arising from a geared trust's investments will have a greater impact on the amount of income available for distribution to equity shareholders of the trust by way of dividend than will a similar fluctuation in the income of an ungeared trust.

Equity shareholders of investment trusts will benefit from investing in highly geared investment trusts when the assets in which those trusts have invested are rising in value, but they are at greater risk when such assets are falling in value. One of the more difficult tasks of a professional investment manager is to utilise gearing successfully. The investment manager must decide when to gear up the trust and when to undertake a rapid 'de-gearing' exercise by repaying borrowings or turning substantial portions of the investment portfolio into cash or assets which are not likely to fluctuate significantly in value.

7.7 TAXATION

7.7.1 Approval of investment trusts

This chapter deals with 'approved' investment trusts as opposed to 'unapproved' investment companies. Only approved investment trusts (and authorised unit trusts) attract the capital gains tax exemption outlined below. An approved investment trust is one which is not a 'close company' and which, in respect of an accounting period, has been approved by the Board of Inland Revenue. The Inland Revenue appears to have discretion to withhold approval, even in the case of an investment trust which would otherwise qualify, but it will approve a company that can show that:

(1) it is resident for taxation purposes in the UK;
(2) its income is derived wholly or mainly (which in practice means approximately 70 per cent or more) from shares or securities, or from eligible rental income (see **7.12**), or from any combination of the two;
(3) no holding in a company (other than another approved investment trust or a company which would qualify as such but for the fact that its shares are not listed as required by (4) below) represents more than 15 per cent by value of its investments;
(4) all its ordinary share capital is listed on The Stock Exchange;
(5) the distribution as dividend of capital profits on the sale of its investments is prohibited by its memorandum or articles of association; and
(6) not more than 15 per cent of its income from securities is retained unless legally required.

It is expressly provided that an increase in the value of a holding after it has been acquired will not result in an infringement of the 15 per cent limit referred to in (3) above. However, the holdings of an investment trust in its subsidiary companies are treated as a single holding for the purposes of this limit, as are its holdings in other companies which are members of the same group of companies. In addition, any loans made by the trust to its subsidiaries are treated as part of its investment in the subsidiaries for the purposes of ascertaining whether the limit has been infringed.

7.7.2 Approved investment trusts – capital gains

Investment trusts are corporations and their income is subject to corporation tax in the same manner and at the same rates as other corporations, but capital gains accruing to approved investment trusts are wholly exempt from capital gains tax in the hands of the trust. Thus active management of the trust's investments need not be constrained by tax on realising gains and the investor may only be subject to tax on disposing of his investment trust shares.

7.7.3 Approved investment trusts – income

The taxation of the trust's own income, and of the income and gains of investors in the trust, is exactly the same as for other limited companies (see Chapter 3). The corporation tax system is complicated and a detailed explanation of it is outside the scope of this handbook, but a brief summary may help.

Income

Franked investment income

This is income received by a trust in the form of dividends paid by a UK company. Franked investment income is not liable to corporation tax in the hands of the trust.

Franked investment income is so-called because up to 5 April 1999 when a UK company paid a dividend it was required to pay Advance Corporation Tax (ACT) to the Inland Revenue at the rate of 20/80ths of the net dividend. Thus when a company paid a dividend of £80 to a shareholder it paid ACT of £20 to the Revenue; the shareholder received a tax credit of £20. The trust itself was liable to pay ACT on its dividends to its own shareholders, but could offset this with ACT on dividends received.

The amount of the dividend plus the ACT was known as a 'franked payment'. In the hands of the company the ACT paid was treated as a repayment of the company's corporation tax bill.

The ACT system was abolished in respect of dividends paid on or after 6 April 1999. Companies no longer pay ACT when they pay a dividend; however, dividends still come with a notional tax credit but now at the rate of 10/90ths of the net dividend

Unfranked income

This is all other income (such as interest on gilt-edged securities, bank deposit interest and dividends paid by foreign companies). Interest paid by the trust and the fees paid to its investment managers are set primarily against unfranked income, reducing the amount liable to tax.

7.8 UNAPPROVED INVESTMENT COMPANIES

Unless an investment company has the status of an approved investment trust (see **7.7.1**), it is subject to ordinary forms of corporate taxation and will not qualify for the capital gains tax exemption mentioned in **7.7.2**. Thus both the investment income and capital gains made by such a company will be taxed, under the terms of the Finance Act 1987, at the corporation tax rate. Under the Taxes Act 1988, a close investment holding company does not qualify for the small companies' rate. In addition, if an investment company disposes of its assets and is then liquidated there is effectively a double capital gains tax charge, because (1) the company will be liable to corporation tax on capital gains realised by it on the disposal, and (2) its shareholders will be liable to capital gains tax for any capital gains realised by them on the disposal of their shares in the investment company, which will occur by reason of the distribution of cash proceeds to them in the liquidation. (Considerations affecting investment in a private investment company are discussed in **13.4**.)

Having regard to these disadvantages and to the fact that, so long as the investment company continues in existence, profits on the sale of investments may only be distributed to its shareholders by way of comparatively highly taxed dividends, the investment company has become unpopular as an investment medium. In fact, in order to mitigate this unsatisfactory taxation position, many unapproved investment companies have been 'unitised' (see **7.6.4**). The advantage of unitisation is that it defers the capital gains liability on the company shares until the ultimate disposal of the units issued on unitisation, which may be spread over several years to take full advantage of the annual CGT exemptions.

7.9 SUITABILITY

Investment trusts are a suitable investment medium for small and large investors who are resident in the UK for tax purposes, who wish to spread their investment risk and who do not have the expertise or the resources to make direct investments. However, the investor in investment trusts should be aware of the possible advantages and disadvantages which may result from the existence of the discount on net asset value (see **7.6.4**) and from the ability of investment trusts to gear their portfolios (see **7.6.5**). If the investor is unwilling to accept the risk involved for the sake of the possible greater rewards, the unit trust or open-ended investment company is probably a more suitable investment medium. On the other hand, investment trusts have frequently shown better long-term returns than unit trusts. Split capital trusts are highly suitable for the investors for whom they are designed, but more care must be taken accordingly.

7.10 MECHANICS

Investment trust shares may be bought in new issues or acquired on The Stock Exchange through stockbrokers, banks and other investment advisers. A number of stockbroking firms specialise in the investment trust sector and will be able to provide detailed information relating to individual trusts, including analyses of past performance, level of discount on underlying net asset value and investment policy. The Association of Investment Trust Companies freely offers excellent literature on investment trusts generally, and its members in particular. Information on individual trusts can be obtained from Extel cards (available in large public libraries), or directly from the managers, who may also offer shares for sale through 'savings schemes'.

Investment trust savings schemes are operated by managers to avoid some of the restrictions on marketing shares. Typically they offer lump sum, regular savings and dividend reinvestment options. The contributions are pooled by the managers and used to buy shares on The Stock Exchange, and the saving in transaction costs may reduce the investor's brokerage as low as 0.2 per cent, although some schemes provide for the payment of substantial commissions to intermediaries, the cost of which is ultimately borne by the investor.

Costs of both acquisition and disposal on The Stock Exchange will normally include stockbrokers' commission, which is subject to negotiation, but for a private investor is likely to be something between 1 and 1.65 per cent, depending on the extent of the service the client requires from the broker; there will usually be a minimum, perhaps £25, and a lower rate for large deals. On purchases, there will also be stamp duty at 0.5 per cent and the spread between bid and offered prices may be around 1.5 per cent, though it will usually be less on the freely traded shares of large companies. There is no initial charge payable to the managers, but further brokerage will be payable on final realisation of the shares by sale.

7.11 MAINTENANCE

Running costs vary from one investment trust to another, but management fees, often in the region of 0.5 per cent per annum on the value of the portfolio, are usually payable by the trust at half-yearly intervals in addition to its day-to-day operating expenses. New and converted specialist trusts, such as those involved in providing venture capital, often pay higher fees, perhaps 1.5 per cent. Economies can often be achieved in cases where the managers act as managers for several investment trusts and are therefore able to spread the burden of management and administrative expenses among a number of different trusts. These management fees and expenses are normally deductible from the trust's income for corporation tax purposes, whereas the management fee of a private portfolio manager generally has to be found out of the client's after-tax income. In the case of investment trusts, the level of management fees and the extent to which operating expenses may be charged to the trust are not controlled by any external regulation and generally trusts are lightly regulated without the expensive compliance arrangements required of unit trusts.

Like any other investment, holdings in investment trusts should be periodically reviewed by the investor or the adviser. Performance of the investment trust may be monitored by observing its quoted stock exchange price in the daily newspapers and the changes in its underlying net asset value, and by reading the half-yearly financial statements and annual directors' reports and audited accounts, which will be sent to registered shareholders and are generally available free on request. The annual report and accounts will contain detailed financial and other information relating to the trust and will usually include details of its investment portfolio as at the date of its balance sheet. The trust will also convene an annual general meeting of shareholders to adopt the annual report and accounts and to conduct other business. Registered shareholders may attend and vote on the resolutions proposed at these meetings or, if they do not wish to attend, they may appoint a proxy to vote on their behalf.

7.12 PREVIEW OF THE YEAR AHEAD AND CONCLUSION

Many of the themes that have been present over the last year are set to continue. In particular, while market prices of investment trust shares are below their underlying asset values, investors can take the opportunity to profit from this discount, either on a reconstruction, take-over or winding-up of the trust, or if rule changes or market conditions increase demand for (and so prices of) investment trusts. Recent examples of such actions would include the take-over of Lloyds Bank German IT by Gartmore, the liquidation of Govett American Smaller Companies IT, and the reconstruction of F&C German IT.

Predators continue to give every incentive for good performance to trust managers, who have started to respond with increased emphasis on advertising and developing retail demand through savings schemes and PEPs (ISAs from April 1999), combined with a greater emphasis on performance and providing enhanced shareholder value through structural change. The fact that an industry leader such as F&C has openly spoken about the likelihood of further consideration in the industry also underlines the likely durability of this trend. Against this, the freedom of investment trusts to issue innovative securities using sophisticated financial structures, and to invest with new techniques and instruments which are largely denied to other collective media, is of increasing importance as other differences are reduced. For example, because investment trusts do not have to contend with fluctuating capital flows, they are particularly suitable for index-matching investment policies: the first conversion of a trust into a fully indexed fund was not a success, but other trusts may do better. The flexibility of investment trusts in the hands of their professional managers will ensure they remain efficient and attractive investment vehicles for small and large investors alike.

USEFUL ADDRESSES

Association of Investment Trust
 Companies
8–13 Chiswell Street
London
EC1Y 4YY

Tel: (020) 7431 5222

SBC Warburg
1 Finsbury Avenue
London EC2M 2PP

(This firm does not deal directly with private investors, but publishes an annual *Private Investor Guide to Investment Trusts*, which includes a list of some suitable brokers.)

8

OEICS, UNIT TRUSTS AND OFFSHORE FUNDS

PETER GRIMMETT

Marketing Compliance Manager, Threadneedle Investment Managers Ltd

8.1 INTRODUCTION

Another form of collective investment medium (see Chapter 7) is that of unit trusts. A unit trust is a trust fund in which the investors hold direct beneficial interests. It is normally open-ended, meaning that units are created or redeemed at the current fair prices, and so the managers buy and sell units as required by investors (see **8.7**).

Obviously the honesty and competence of the managers of such trusts is of fundamental importance, and the constitution, management and marketing of trusts are all regulated in the UK, primarily under the Financial Services Act 1986. These powers are exercised by the Financial Services Authority (FSA) and currently a number of self-regulatory organisations with delegated powers over member firms. Only authorised persons may conduct investment business. The European Community Directive on Undertakings for Collective Investment in Transferable Securities (the UCITS Directive) requires all member states to assimilate their regulations for certain collective investment schemes, which may then be sold throughout the European Economic Area.

In 1997 a new form of authorised collective investment scheme was introduced into the UK – the open-ended investment company (OEIC). It is often described as a unit trust in corporate form, and whilst this is true, there are differences between the two products. In fact, the FSA OEIC regulations are very similar (and identical in some cases) to the unit trust regulations. The OEIC is considered to be a modern form of collective investment scheme (and a form that is very common in Europe) which provides more flexibility to the industry than previously available under unit trust regulations.

See **8.13** which outlines the key differences to unit trusts.

8.2 HISTORICAL BACKGROUND

Units in the first unit trust in the UK were offered to the public in April 1931 by the M&G Group, which still exists today as one of the leaders of the industry. Allied Investors Ltd, now Threadneedle Investment Services Ltd, followed in 1934 and remains one of the largest unit trust groups in the UK. The first trusts were 'fixed' trusts and offered virtually no flexibility in investment policy once the trust deed had been executed. Each new subscription was invested in the fixed portfolio and each unit was thus unchanged in its composition. Each unit was normally divided into sub-units for sale to the public.

The first 'flexible' trust (the type of trust which is marketed today) was not offered to the public until 1936. When the Prevention of Fraud (Investments) Act 1939 came into force, supervision of the new industry was made the responsibility of the (then) Board of Trade. Under that Act, revised and re-enacted as the Prevention of Fraud (Investments) Act 1958, the Department of Trade and Industry (DTI) laid down regulations for the conduct of unit trusts, supervised charges and 'authorised' unit trusts complying with its requirements until 1988. The power of authorisation for new unit trust schemes then passed from the DTI to the FSA.

The Open-Ended Investment Companies (Investment Companies with Variable Capital) Regulations 1996 (the 'ECA Regulations') came into force on 6 January 1997. The Regulations lay down the structural elements of the OEIC (essentially the formation, supervision and control, and the corporate code). The FSA added the flesh with the Financial Services (Open-Ended Investment Companies) Regulations 1997 which came into operation on 16 January 1997. These Regulations deal with the matters that an OEIC is required to comply with on an ongoing basis.

The first company to launch an OEIC was Global Asset Management in mid-1997. This was set up as an umbrella company but at the time had only one sub-fund (or spoke) when it was authorised. The next and arguably the first major OEIC to be launched in the UK was by Threadneedle in August 1997. Again it was set up in an umbrella format, but initially had 23 spokes making up the company. Threadneedle was also the first company to take advantage of regulations permitting unit trusts to be converted into OEICs and to market an OEIC into Europe.

8.3 AUTHORISATION

The main requirement for authorisation of a unit trust by the FSA is that a trust deed conforming with the FSA's regulations is executed between a company performing all management functions for the trust (the managers) and an independent trust corporation (the trustee) to hold the trust's investments and supervise the managers. Both the managers and the trustee must be incorporated under the law of, or of some part of, the UK or any other EU member state, must maintain a place of business in Great Britain and must be authorised persons to conduct investment business and so subject to the regulators' rules for conduct of business. The persons who are to be directors of a unit trust management company must be approved by the FSA. The trust deed and regulations must provide for, *inter alia*:

(1) managers' investment and borrowing powers and limits on investment of the trust's assets;
(2) determining the manner in which prices and yields are calculated and the obligation of managers to repurchase units at the 'bid' price;
(3) setting up a register of unitholders, with procedures for issuing certificates and dealing with transfers;
(4) remuneration of the managers and trustees;
(5) periodic audits of the trust and the issue of financial statements to unitholders, with reports by the managers, trustees and auditors;
(6) meetings of unitholders under certain circumstances.

Authorisation makes it possible for unit trust managers to advertise units for sale to the public and carries with it tax privileges for the trust. Here we deal only with unit trusts which have been authorised by the FSA; 'unit trust' here means an authorised unit trust unless otherwise indicated. (For discussion on unauthorised unit trusts, see **8.13**.)

Authorisation of OEICs runs along a very similar line and is created by virtue of the ECA Regulations. To market its shares to the public the OEIC must be authorised by the FSA. It is governed by its instrument of incorporation, rather than a trust deed.

8.4 HIGHLIGHTS OF THE PREVIOUS YEAR

Sales of unit trusts and OEICs in 1997, compared with the previous two years, were as follows:

	1996 *£m*	*1997* *£m*	*1998* *£m*
Industry sales	25,800	28,883	39,171
Industry repurchases	15,799	18,634	26,675
Net new investment	10,001	10,249	12,496

Source: AUTIF.

At 31 December 1998, the total funds invested in authorised collective investment schemes were £182.9bn (up from £157.7bn in 1997 and £131.9bn in 1996).

The number of authorised schemes was 1,739 compared to 1,680 in 1997 and 1,669 in 1996. There were 152 investment fund managers compared to 153 in 1997 and 161 in 1996. Unitholder accounts numbered 11.3 million (9.6 million in 1997 and 8.02 million in 1996).

UK Growth Funds dominated equity fund sales in 1998 even more so than 1997, with net total sales of over £2bn. However, gross sales of European Funds leapt 79 per cent to 2.8bn – the most significant change from 1997 (source: AUTIF).

8.5 PRICING OF UNITS

Since 1 July 1988, unit trust managers have been free to choose whether to deal on 'forward prices', ie at the next price to be calculated, or at prices already calculated and published, as had been the norm. Most management companies have availed themselves of this opportunity. With forward pricing, a buyer does not know exactly how many units he will receive, but he does know that he will deal at a fair, up-to-date price. If, on the other hand, a management company is dealing on historic prices and the value of a trust is believed to have changed by more than 2 per cent since the valuation on which the company is offering to deal, a new price must be calculated, and indeed a forward price must be given to any customer who requests it.

The bid and offer (or selling and buying) prices can be found in the newspapers with additional information available if the customer asks the management company for it.

The Financial Services Act 1986 became effective in 1988, superseding the Prevention of Fraud (Investments) Act 1958. As a result, much of the regulation of unit trusts, including authorisation, was transferred from the DTI to other bodies. The regulation of borrowing powers and permitted investment and the constitution of unit trusts is regulated by the FSA, but the management of trusts is regulated by the Investment Management Regulatory Organisation (IMRO) and the marketing by the Personal Investment Authority (PIA).

The pricing of shares in an OEIC is different, in that shares are single priced and the OEIC regulations generally express a preference to deal at a 'forward price'. Therefore there is one price at which an investor can buy or sell shares in an OEIC and he or she may not know that price until it is next calculated. The underlying mechanism in determining the price of a share is, however, similar to that of unit trusts.

A new concept is the dilution levy. In some instances the actual cost of the buying and selling a company's investments may be higher or lower than the mid-market value used in calculating the share price (eg due to dealing charges or through dealing at prices other than the mid-market price). Under certain circumstances this may have an adverse effect on shareholders' interest in the company. This is called dilution and to prevent this effect the directors/ACD (see **8.6** below) have the power to charge a dilution levy on the sale and/or redemption of shares. Any charge made is paid back into and becomes part of the company. The directors/ACD must declare under what circumstances a dilution levy may be charged in the prospectus.

8.6 LEGAL NATURE

A unit trust scheme is constituted by a trust deed which is made between the managers and the trustee. The managers are the promoters of the scheme and are subsequently responsible for the conduct of the investment and for administration. The trustee (usually one of the clearing banks or major insurance companies) is responsible for ensuring that the managers act in accordance with the provisions laid down in the trust deed. The trustee holds the trust's assets on trust for the unitholders. Regulations determine the content of the trust deed and other binding requirements, and both the trustee and the management company are subject to the IMRO Conduct of Business Rules.

The underlying securities are registered in the trustee's name or, if in bearer form, held in the custody of the trustee, which also holds any cash forming part of the fund. The trustee, as the legal owner of the underlying assets for the unitholders, receives on their behalf all income and other distributions made in respect of such assets.

The trust deed and regulations also lay down a formula for valuing the trust to determine the prices at which units may be sold to the public by the managers and at which units must be bought back by the managers from the public (see below). Additional units may be created to meet demand from the public or existing units may be cancelled as a result of the subsequent repurchase of units from the public. A unit trust is thus 'open-ended' and can expand or contract depending on whether there is a preponderance of buyers or sellers of its units.

Three prices are quoted for unit trusts. These are the 'offer' price, at which units are offered for sale to or subscription by the public, and the 'bid' price, at which the managers buy back units, and the cancellation price, at which the managers may arrange for units to be redeemed out of the trust's assets. These prices are, broadly speaking, ascertained in the following manner:

(1) the offer price is calculated by reference to the notional amount which would have to be paid to acquire the underlying assets held by the trust, to which are added the notional acquisition costs (such as brokers' commission and stamp duty) and the preliminary management charges (see **8.11.1**);

(2) the bid price is calculated by reference to the amount which would be received on a disposal of the assets held by the trust, from which are deducted the notional costs of the disposal, ie brokers' commission and contract stamp.

Investors must never be required to pay more for their units than the offer price as calculated under the trust deed, nor may unitholders on a sale of their units be paid less than the bid price as so calculated. When an investor buys units, the managers may either create them or sell units that they have previously repurchased and are holding in the manager's 'box'. The spread between the offered and bid prices can be between 8 and 11 per cent, but in practice most unit trust managers quote spreads for their own dealings in units between 4.5 and 6.5 per cent, which may be positioned anywhere between the maximum offered and minimum bid prices applicable on subscription for new units and cancellation of existing units.

Managers normally base their buying price for units in a particular trust on the full bid valuation if they are buying back more units than they are selling, since this is the price at which units must be cancelled. Conversely, if the managers are selling more units than they are buying, their selling price is normally based on the full offer price, at which units must be created.

A unit trust cannot 'gear' its portfolio by borrowings, either unsecured or secured on the trust's assets. The only circumstances in which borrowing is permitted are to anticipate known cash flows (such as dividends due).

The trust deed, which takes effect subject to any regulations under the Financial Services Act, may make provision for the trust to be terminated and also specifies circumstances in which the approval of unitholders at a general meeting needs to be sought. Such approval is required, among other things, for proposals to vary the provisions of the trust deed, to change the investment objectives of the trust or to amalgamate it with another trust. Unitholders' interests are thus protected despite the fact that no annual general meeting is held, since certain material changes affecting their interests may be effected only with their approval in general meeting.

As mentioned earlier, an OEIC is constituted under a form of company/corporate law as opposed to trust law for unit trusts. It is governed by its instrument of incorporation and its prospectus – the ECA and FSA Regulations lay down what is required or permitted to be disclosed in these two documents.

The two main parties in the OEIC are the directors (similar to a manager of a unit trust) and the depositary (similar to a trustee). Where there is only one director, it must be an authorised person (the 'authorised corporate director', or ACD). It is expected that most OEICs will be launched on this basis initially. The depositary has similar, but lighter, regulatory duties than a trustee, but maintains the essential requirement to have safe custody of the company's property and ensuring the company is managed in accordance with certain parts of the FSA regulations.

8.7 CONDITIONS FOR PURCHASE

Any individual, corporate body or trustee may acquire and hold unit trusts without any condition or restriction, subject to any limitation which may be imposed on its own investment powers.

Unit trusts are specifically mentioned as approved 'wider range' investments under the Trustee Investments Act 1961. Unit trusts whose portfolios consist exclusively of investments suitable for 'narrow range' investments under the same Act may themselves be included in the narrow range investments. Trustees should, however, satisfy themselves of their powers to invest in unit trusts by reference to their trust instrument.

Nearly all unit trust managers specify a minimum investment, usually in the range of £250–£2,000. Certain specialist funds have higher minima. These minima do not apply to monthly saving schemes, where amounts from £20 per month may be invested on a regular basis.

Since a unit trust is open-ended, there is no maximum holding, though a corporate or trustee unitholder may be restricted by his own investment limitations.

The position for OEICs is very similar.

Persons resident outside the UK may acquire and hold unit trust units, subject to the local exchange control rules in their country of residence or domicile. However, for reasons of taxation, it is usually preferable for such people to invest in 'offshore' funds.

8.8 CHARACTERISTICS

Unit trusts must invest the greater part of their portfolios in securities listed on recognised stock exchanges. Each manager, with the trustees' approval, will determine a list of 'eligible markets' for each trust. These will be markets which are considered to meet basic criteria of investor protection such as having regulatory authorities, high accounting standards and no restrictions on the repatriation of funds. Up to 10 per cent of the trust's property may be held in 'non-eligible markets'. Note that the determination of eligibility is not made by the FSA.

The investments of the majority of unit trusts are usually in equity shares.

Traditional authorised unit trusts may, in general, invest only in securities, although newer classes of unit trusts are now authorised to invest in other financial instruments, such as futures and options, warrants or property. These new schemes have separate regulations of investment and borrowing powers, and may have a separate tax regime. All trusts may use derivatives within the constraints of Efficient Portfolio Management for hedging purposes. With the exception of GFOFs (Geared Futures and Options Funds) all derivatives must be fully covered by cash, stock or other derivatives.

The specific investment characteristics of unit trusts will vary depending on the stated objective of any particular trust. However, all unit trusts share certain general characteristics.

At present, the current OEIC legislation permits only companies that comply with the UCITS Directive to be authorised. Those categories are securities companies, warrant companies, and umbrella companies consisting of securities or warrant companies.

8.8.1 General characteristics

Spread of risk

By acquiring an interest in a portion of all the investments in the underlying portfolio of a unit trust or OEIC, an investor can achieve a much wider spread of risk than could be achieved economically with limited resources. By spreading their investments across a large number of companies in a wide variety of industries in a number of different countries, investors can much reduce the risks inherent in a holding of shares in only one company or a small number of companies. The result is likely to be a much more even progression of capital and income growth. Regulations covering the maximum investment of a fund's assets in a single company or issue ensure that a wide spread of risk is achieved. In practice, funds usually hold something between 30 and 100 investments, considerably more than the required minimum.

Professional management

By committing investment funds to the purchase of a holding in a fund the investor is in effect delegating the day-to-day management of his or her portfolio to the scheme's managers. Virtually all management companies employ a team of investment specialists whose aim is to maximise capital and/or income performance, and who are given a wide discretion within the limitations imposed by the trust deed or instrument of incorporation to increase or decrease the scheme's liquidity or to switch investments as they consider appropriate. The advantage to the investor is that the investments are under the continuous supervision of people whose business it is to keep abreast of economic, political and corporate developments at home and abroad.

Simplicity and convenience

The sometimes tedious paperwork associated with owning a portfolio of securities is largely eliminated. Day-to-day decisions on such matters as rights and scrip issues, mergers and take-overs are all taken by the managers. Dividends are received by the trustee and distributions of the scheme's income are made, usually twice a year, to investors together with a report on the progress of their scheme during the preceding accounting period.

Marketability

In view of their open-ended nature, as a result of which units and shares can be created or cancelled to meet investors' requirements, unit trust units or OEIC shares can be regarded as an almost totally liquid investment, with none of the constraints on marketability sometimes encountered in connection with investment in some of the smaller listed companies. As a result of the pricing structure, referred to in **8.6**, purchases and sales of units or shares take place at prices which reflect the underlying value of the trust's assets.

8.8.2 Types of unit trust

While all unit trusts share the investment characteristics listed above, there are a very wide range of trusts which offer different investment objectives designed to suit different categories of investors. The main types are described below.

Balanced trusts

These invest in a portfolio which is usually composed of leading 'blue chip' shares with the aim of achieving a steady growth of both capital and income. These trusts are designed for the investor who wishes to invest in a wide spread of ordinary shares. They are suitable for the first-time investor in equities, who wishes to hold the units for longer term investment or saving.

Income trusts

These aim to achieve an above-average yield to the investor whose primary need is for a high and growing income. Normally, such trusts give a yield between 1.2 and 1.5 times that available on shares generally. These trusts are most suitable for retired people, widows, or others who depend on investment income. Such trusts may purchase convertible shares as a way of achieving their yield objectives.

Capital growth trusts

These are designed to seek maximum capital growth. The income from such trusts is usually low. These characteristics make them particularly suitable for those who want to build up a nest-egg.

Fixed interest trusts

These generally invest in a portfolio of government bonds, corporate bonds and convertible shares and may be either income or capital trusts. Such trusts may be suitable for those requiring a high income, although prospects for income growth are unlikely to be as good as in equity trusts.

Overseas trusts

These aim to provide the investor with an opportunity to invest through stock markets in other countries. Investment overseas is a particularly complex and difficult task for the private person, but can be rewarding in times when sterling is weak against other currencies or when economic conditions in a region overseas are particularly buoyant. The sharp depreciation of sterling in 1992 proved again the merits of investing in these trusts, as a hedge against devaluation.

Specialist trusts

Certain trusts, sometimes referred to as 'specialist trusts', are promoted to invest in particular sectors of the securities market (eg commodities or smaller companies). These trusts are suitable for the larger or more sophisticated investor who wishes to concentrate on a particular sector while still achieving a spread of risk. The specialist nature of such trusts means that the investor may be somewhat more at the whim of fashion; UK smaller companies' unit trusts, for example, after many years of above-average returns, markedly underperformed their more balanced counterparts from 1989 to 1991.

Accumulation trusts

Certain trusts within all the categories referred to above are structured and promoted on the basis that they will accumulate the net income within the trust rather than distribute it to unitholders. This income is nonetheless subject to taxation as if it had been received by unitholders.

'Tracker' trusts

Certain trusts are structured to imitate a stock market index and so achieve a performance matching that market. Because of their essentially passive nature, with investment managers taking fewer active decisions, such trusts normally have lower management charges. These trusts are also referred to as indexed trusts.

Open-ended investment companies (OEICs)

OEICs can also offer the same types of scheme outlined above. A key advantage, however, is that these funds can be made up of different classes of shares. For example, an umbrella company can be made up of several sub-funds, which in turn can have classes of shares such as net income, net accumulation, gross accumulation and even currency classes of shares. There could be an asset where, for example, the sub-fund is marketing in different countries and would like to market it in the currency of that country.

8.9 TAXATION

Authorised unit trusts (AUTs) and OEICs have their own taxation regime. They are treated as companies for tax purposes but with important differences. No liability to corporation tax arises on capital gains derived by the AUT or OEIC, the chargeable profits being limited to unfranked investment income less management expenses and charges on income. The rate of corporation tax levied on the profits is limited to 20 per cent.

Distributions by AUTs and OEICs are treated as dividends unless, under special circumstances (see below) they are treated as interest distributions. Distributions by way of dividend are treated in the same way as distributions by other UK companies, in that until 5 April 1999 advance corporation tax (ACT) at the rate of 25 per cent of the dividend paid had to be paid by the dividend payer. For individual unitholders in the AUT or shareholders in the OEIC resident in the UK, a tax credit was available on the dividend distribution equal to the amount of ACT which they could set off against their total income tax liability and, in appropriate cases, reclaim in cash. The tax credit satisfied the total tax liability of basic and lower rate taxpayers. Higher rate taxpayers were liable to an additional tax liability. On 6 April 1999, ACT was abolished and dividends can now be paid without the need to account for ACT to the Revenue. However, individual recipients of dividends continue to receive a tax credit which has been set initially as one-ninth of the amount of the dividend. This tax credit is sufficient to cover the liability of starter rate and basic rate taxpayers but is no longer repayable except for individuals holding their units or shares through a PEP or an ISA who may continue to receive repayment of tax credits until 2004. Higher rate taxpayers may still be liable to an additional tax liability.

The amount of distribution received by a unitholder or shareholder subject to corporation tax (and not dual resident) is separated into franked and unfranked components of the dividend. The unfranked component is deemed to be an annual payment received under deduction of income tax at the rate of 20 per cent and the franked component is treated as a dividend not subject to further tax liability. Whether unitholders or shareholders who are resident in countries other than the UK are entitled to payments from the Revenue of a proportion of the tax credit attaching to the dividend depends in general upon the existence and terms of any double tax convention between the UK and the territory of residence.

AUTs and OEICs which meet a qualifying investment test may make distributions by way of payments of interest rather than dividends. Such interest is paid under deduction of income tax at 20 per cent. The qualifying investment test is satisfied provided the market value of qualifying investments held by the AUT or OEIC exceed 60 per cent of the market value of all the investments held. Qualifying investments include money placed at interest, securities excluding shares in companies and shares in a building society. The tax deducted satisfies the tax liability of starter rate and basic rate taxpapers. Higher rate taxpayers may still be liable to an additional tax liability. In appropriate cases individual and corporate unitholders and shareholders may be able to obtain repayment of the income tax deducted. Non-resident unitholders and shareholders may be eligible for interest distributions to be made gross. When they are not paid gross, all or some of the income tax credit may be recoverable from the Inland Revenue. This depends upon the provisions of any tax convention or agreement which exists between the relevant country and the UK.

No taxation will be withheld from payment made to unitholders on redemption of units or shares. However, the redemption, sale or transfer of units may constitute a disposal (or part disposal) for the purposes of UK taxation of capital gains.

8.10 SUITABILITY

Unit trusts and OEICs are suitable for investors, large or small, whether trustees, corporations or private individuals who wish to invest in a portfolio of either general or specialist securities in the UK or overseas, but who do not wish, or are not investing sufficient sums, to run their own investments.

Because the income from and the value of all securities can fluctuate, investors should understand that collective investment schemes are risk investments. 'The value of the units as well as the income from them may go down as well as up' is the caveat which must appear in all collective investment schemes' advertisements and literature soliciting purchases. However, the fact that collective investment schemes cannot, generally, gear up, that present regulation ensures a reasonable level of diversification within the scheme, and the overseeing function of the trustee or depositary, considerably reduces the inherent risk of the investment.

8.11 MECHANICS AND MAINTENANCE

8.11.1 Mechanics

Unit trust units and OEIC shares may be acquired through any professional adviser (stockbroker, bank, accountant, solicitor or insurance broker). Many have departments specialising in advice on the selection of collective investment shares. There are also several firms which offer portfolio management and advisory services. If there is any doubt about the suitability of unit trusts or OEICs to the investor's needs, professional advice may be desirable in any case.

Alternatively, units or shares may be acquired directly from the managers on either telephoned or written instructions. The disposal of units and shares can be achieved in exactly the same way.

The names, addresses and telephone numbers of unit trust managers and OEICs are given in many leading newspapers, together with a list of the current prices of the schemes they manage. All managers supply more comprehensive information and copies of recent reports on particular funds on request.

The Association of Unit Trusts and Investment Funds can supply a comprehensive list of members and other general information about collective investment schemes on request. (See end of chapter for details.)

When units or shares are purchased, an initial charge is payable and is usually included in the price. There is no restriction on the initial charge, but the trust deed or instrument must contain a figure for the maximum permissible charge and all advertisements or literature must give details of the actual current charge. Initial charges are normally in the region of 3 to 6 per cent.

Most managers pay commission to accredited agents. This is borne by the managers from the permitted initial charge.

The investor receives a contract note giving details of the purchase and may subsequently receive a certificate showing the number of units or shares held. Payment of the proceeds of sale is normally made by the managers within a few days of their receiving the certificate signed on the reverse by the investor.

8.11.2 Maintenance

Annual management fees based on the trust's value are deducted by the managers normally from the scheme's income. As in the case of investment trusts, these fees are deductible from the trust's income for tax purposes. From the annual charge the managers must meet the costs of trustees' fees, audit fees, administration and investment management. The maximum permitted level of annual management fees must be laid down in the trust deed or instrument and the actual level charged set out in all advertisements and literature. If managers wish to increase the fees to a level not exceeding the maximum figure, holders must be given three months' notice in writing. Increases in the maximum figure must be approved by holders at an extraordinary meeting. Fees charged usually vary between 0.75 and 2 per cent per annum, although management charges for certain indexed funds may be as low as 0.5 per cent.

Certain other costs, including agents' fees for holding investments in safe custody overseas and the cost of collecting foreign dividends, may be charged to the scheme's income. These costs are usually small in relation to the total income.

The stamp duty and brokerage on the purchase and sale of underlying investments are borne by the scheme but are reflected in the pricing structure (see **8.6**).

Like any other investment, fund holdings should be periodically reviewed by the investor or his or her adviser. The investor should be able to monitor the performance of the managers by reading the half-yearly (or sometimes annual) reports which they are required to send. These reports should contain:

(1) a statement of the scheme's capital and income performance during the period, compared with appropriate indices;
(2) an assessment of portfolio changes during the period or any change in investment philosophy;
(3) the managers' view of the forthcoming period;
(4) a list of the current investment holdings;
(5) the figures for the income distribution; and
(6) a capital and income record.

8.12 OPEN-ENDED INVESTMENT COMPANIES

It is fair to say that OEICs are very similar beasts to unit trusts but due to the structure of the overarching legislation there are differences. Differences which are significant have been highlighted in the sections above (eg, single pricing, flexibility in classes of share, directors, and its legal structure).

Those used to the concept of unit trusts will recognise the many similar features (production of a prospectus, the investment and borrowing powers, income, report and accounts and other features listed above). Therefore, it is possible in most instances to read across to OEICs where the text refers to unit trusts.

Some of the terminology will have changed (eg shares rather than units, prospectus compared to scheme particulars, directors/ACD instead of manager and depositary for trustee) but the roles, although not identical, are in general very similar.

A further difference that should be noted is the requirement for an OEIC to hold annual general meetings of shareholders, in much the same way as a conventional company. Two essential elements of the AGM are that the directors must lay copies of the annual report before the company and that the auditors must be reappointed at each meeting. Other business that the company/ACD wishes to conduct with its shareholders may also be carried out at an AGM.

The tax treatment of an OEIC is identical to that of an authorised unit trust – see **8.9** above.

8.13 UNAUTHORISED UNIT TRUSTS

Unauthorised unit trusts are unit trusts which have not been authorised by the FSA (see **8.3**). Its income is liable to ordinary income tax at the basic rate (presently 23 per cent, falling to 22 per cent from 6 April 2000), the payment of which is reflected in distributions to the unitholders.

An unauthorised unit trust does not benefit from the capital gains tax exemption of authorised unit trusts. Capital gains tax is therefore payable in full, putting such a trust at a disadvantage in comparison with an authorised trust so far as capital gains tax is concerned, unless the unauthorised trust is an exempt trust.

8.14 EXEMPT UNIT TRUSTS

Exempt unit trusts are unit trusts designed for particular types of unitholders. While many such funds exist, their rationale was destroyed by the exemption of unit trusts from tax on chargeable gains in the Finance Act 1980. Exempt unit trusts may be in authorised or unauthorised form.

8.15 PREVIEW OF THE YEAR AHEAD

It is proposed that unit trust managers will be able to convert unit trusts into OEICs until 30 June 2000 and qualify for stamp duty and stamp duty reserve tax relief.

From 6 April 1999, a new tax efficient vehicle, the Individual Savings Account, replaced the Personal Equity Plan. Although the stocks and shares element is very similar, key differences include the ability to invest in a wider range of funds and the ability to designate a fund as 'CAT standard' if it complies with certain Treasury guidelines, for example on cost and access.

Following the successful introduction of the OEIC product rules in 1997, there is a chance that further developments proposing to extend the OEIC regime to include non-UCITS funds (most likely money market and fund of funds type schemes) may appear by the year end.

In the meantime investment fund managers can look forward to further debate on the ability to offer limited issue and limited redemption funds.

8.16 CONCLUSION

For the private investor who wishes to participate in the historically greater returns available from investment in the world's stock markets as compared to deposits or savings accounts, the unit trust and OEIC are ideal vehicles to mitigate some of the inherent risks. Prime examples include the role of the trustee/depositary who will protect the customer assets in the event of the manager's default, and the ability to gain the skill of an entire investment team of professionals for as little as £20 a month. Having decided on the vehicle the choice of manager and fund type, although initially daunting, should be enough to satisfy the requirements of almost every private investor.

If not, one can be sure that product development teams are already working on the next evolution in the market.

SOURCES OF FURTHER INFORMATION

Legislation

Capital Gains Tax Act 1979
Companies Act 1985
Finance Act 1980
Finance Act 1982
Finance Act 1984
Finance Act 1985
Finance Act 1986
Finance Act 1987
Finance Act 1988
Finance Act 1989
Finance Act 1990
Finance Act 1991
Finance (No1) Act 1992
Finance (No2) Act 1992
Finance Act 1993
Finance Act 1994
Finance Act 1995

Finance Act 1996
Finance Act 1997
Finance Act 1998
Financial Services Act 1986
Financial Services (Open-Ended
   Investment Companies)
   Regulations 1997
Financial Services (Regulated
   Schemes) Regulations 1991
Income and Corporation Taxes
   Act 1988
Open-Ended Investment
   Companies (Investment
   Companies with Variable
   Capital) Regulations 1996
Prevention of Fraud
   (Investments) Act 1958

Useful addresses

Association of Unit Trusts and
Investment Funds
65 Kingsway
London
WC2B 6TD

Tel: (020) 7831 0898

Association of Investment Trust
Companies
8–13 Chiswell Street
London
EC1Y 4YY

Tel: (020) 7588 5347

Department of Trade and Industry
Companies Division
10–18 Victoria Street
London
SW1H 0NN

Tel: (020) 7215 5000

The Association of Corporate
Trustees
43 Surrey Road
Bournemouth
BH4 9HR

Tel: (01202) 761112

Financial Services Authority
25 The North Colonnade
Canary Wharf
London
E14 5HS

Tel: (020) 7676 1000

9

REAL PROPERTY

GEOFFREY J ABBOTT
Dip FBA (Lon) FRICS
Head of Sales and Purchases Department
and Investment Consultant of Smiths Gore (Chartered Surveyors)

9.1 INTRODUCTION TO REAL PROPERTY

This chapter is a general introduction to the subject of real property and to Chapters 10 (dealing with residential property), 11 (agricultural land and woods) and 12 (commercial property). Readers should appreciate that the subjects covered are vast and complex. All matters referred to have been condensed and investors must take independent professional advice.

Real property is a legal interest in land and/or buildings of four principal types:

(1) residential;
(2) commercial;
(3) farmland;
(4) woodlands.

In the case of vacant farmland and woodland it may also include growing crops as well.

Investment in property falls into two main categories:

(1) Direct investment: by purchase of an interest in a property.
(2) Indirect investment: by purchase of units in property bonds and other unit linked schemes, or by the purchase of shares in a property company.

These chapters deal with direct investment.

Property is generally considered one of the most secure forms of investment as it is almost totally indestructible and immovable (it cannot be lost or stolen) and usually produces an income. However, an investment in property is complicated and a thorough understanding of all its implications is necessary to ensure optimum results are obtained from the investment selected.

Today, ownership of land and property is in many hands. The principal types of owner are:

(1) private individuals;
(2) trust funds;
(3) public and private investment and trading companies;
(4) institutions; and
(5) national and local government and various bodies under them.

Property owners or freeholders (superiors in Scotland) may have others under them with lesser interests in the whole or parts of their property. The owner of these lesser interests is normally either a lessee, a tenant or a licensee (vassels/feuers) depending on the nature of their interests. There can also be third party rights over property. These may vary from a right of the general public to use a footpath for instance, or a statutory undertaking to lay a water pipe or electricity on, under or over the owner's or lessee's land, or a personal right to cross another person's land.

An interest in property may satisfy three separate needs: enjoyment, investment and security. Enjoyment in its broadest sense might be considered as the actual use of that land, whether agricultural, a place to live, a place to manufacture, a place from which to extract minerals or a place of employment or entertainment. Enjoyment and investment are commonly combined, eg owner-occupiers of residential property rarely consider their home as an investment, although for the great majority it is the largest single investment that they will ever make.

Many forms of ownership of an interest subject to a letting do not entitle the investor to any direct enjoyment of the land but simply to participate in an agreed share of the income or produce obtained from it, usually in the form of a cash rent.

All readers must appreciate, however, that where investments are made for maximum financial gain the most important factor is timing. All markets are cyclical. Whatever the care in initial selection and subsequent management, if a purchase is made at the top of a market cycle short-term performance will inevitably be disappointing. Alternatively, almost all purchases made at the bottom of a cycle will ultimately perform well. Investment based on this strategy is known as counter-cyclical.

9.2 LEGAL, TAXATION AND COST FACTORS OF REAL PROPERTY

9.2.1 Legal

The legal root of English and Welsh property law is fundamentally different from that in Scotland. Whilst legislation is commonly drafted to give similar effects, it does not always do so in practice. Historically, the main purpose of property laws and legislation was to establish ground rules by which owners, landlords and tenants should behave to each other and their neighbours. However, recent legislation to protect the wider community's interests with planning and other legislation has tended to restrict the owner or tenant's right to do what he likes with his property. The body of law is substantial but its application to any individual property varies. An experienced property lawyer is therefore an essential member of any property investor's team.

9.2.2 Taxation

As with all forms of investment, owners of real estate are liable to pay revenue, capital gains and inheritance taxes in one way or another. The impact of these taxes on the owners of different types of property varies significantly and may determine the type of property invested in and even whether to choose property or non-property investments. Finally, business rates apply on occupation of most commercial property, and council tax on residential property.

The body of taxation law is again substantial, detailed and complex. An experienced property tax adviser should be consulted.

9.2.3 Costs

The purchase, ownership and the eventual sale of any interest in real estate will normally incur costs. When property is held for investment they will affect the net yield achieved. The level of costs will reflect the particular nature and circumstances of the property or portfolio held and will typically be in the form of acquisition, management or disposal costs.

Acquisition costs

The purchaser of any real estate should be prepared for costs of 2.5 to 4.5 per cent on top of the purchase price (costs associated with a lease may be substantially different). These costs are made up of 1 per cent stamp duty on properties having a value of £60,001 rising up to 2.5 per cent on properties worth more than £250,000 and 3.5 per cent on those worth more than £500,000. Additionally, 1 per cent should be allowed for agents' fees and 0.5 per cent for solicitors' fees. There may be an additional charge on the solicitors' account for search fees and VAT is payable on both agents' and solicitors' fees. The VAT status of many forms of property investment should also be checked out before an offer is made.

Investors should consider certain other additional costs, eg a structural survey on older buildings or a planning appraisal for potential development situations. The investment may also involve a mortgage or other form of borrowing and the associated valuation and commitment fees are normally paid by the borrower/purchaser.

Finally, the purchase of vacant farmland usually also involves the purchase of growing crops and the payment of tenant right. Professional fees for the valuation and negotiation of agreement on these will normally be in the 2.5 to 5 per cent range.

Management costs

Stocks and shares are essentially a passive investment, whereas most forms of property investment call for active management. Property management costs are very variable. Over the years most property will need to be repaired, insured, altered, re-let, improved or perhaps redeveloped. It is only by good management that the asset can maximise its rental and capital value in a changing marketplace.

Examples of typical management costs are:

(1) Fully let office on full repairing and insuring (FRI) lease – 2 to 3 per cent of gross rent.
(2) Small market town shop on standard repairing lease – 5 per cent of gross rent.
(3) Substantial arable farm on FRI lease – 7 per cent of gross rent.
(4) Complex traditional let estate – 10 per cent of gross rent.
(5) Short-term furnished residential letting – 20 per cent of gross rent.

Agents' property management fees are usually agreed at the outset, as a package to reflect the range of services needed, and paid out of rental income when received. Fees for farm and forestry management services depend on whether the agent is merely used on a consultancy basis or is responsible for the day-to-day running of a trading business. Where a surveyor is instructed to negotiate or advise on a rent review, lease renewal or re-letting fees range from 7.5 to 10 per cent of either the first year's rental obtained, or of the increase over the previous rent, depending on the circumstances of each case, plus VAT and expenses.

Disposal costs

The costs of selling are as variable as the types of property involved. Agents' fees vary from 1 per cent of the price achieved for a large commercial property investment up to 2.5 per cent for a smaller residential property, with the associated solicitors' fees normally in the 0.5 to 0.75 per cent range. VAT is also payable on professional fees.

Local advertising costs at the lower end of the residential markets are normally borne by the agent. National advertising and higher quality particulars, professionally printed, are usually met by the vendor, who also carries the cost of all advertising and printing for most other forms of property sale.

An owner may wish to dispose of just part of his property interest for a certain period. This would normally be dealt with by granting a lease, tenancy or licence. Agents' fees are typically up to 10 per cent of the first year's rent plus VAT and direct expenses, including marketing costs. Solicitors' fees depend on whether a standard lease/agreement is used or whether a document has to be specially drafted to meet the circumstances.

9.3 PROPERTY VALUATION

The diversity of property types and reasons for ownership produce a wide range of approaches to property valuations. The location, accessibility and setting of a property will always influence its value.

The capital value of a vacant house is an equation of demand and supply in the relevant market at the time. Reference to sales of comparable properties is the only guide. However, specific purchasers may pay a premium for a particular property for no better reason than that they want to live in it or it has a marriage value to their adjacent property. They are often referred to as 'special purchasers'.

In other sectors, such as sporting estates, the market seeks to quantify a purchaser's potential pleasure of ownership by relating value to past bag or catch records. Similarly the value of amenity woodlands is linked to the purchaser's anticipated pleasure in ownership. In commercial woodlands, however, the value is based on capitalisation of future income flows from timber sales, perhaps many decades ahead.

It is only in the markets for let properties that value is linked to the capitalisation of rent passing. Indeed in many sectors of the commercial property markets a well-let property is worth significantly more than its vacant equivalent.

In most commercial property markets the rental income is capitalised over a term of years or in perpetuity (depending on whether the property is leasehold or freehold) at an investment rate set by the market for comparable properties at the time. This rate will reflect the risks associated with that property (security of income, obsolescence of the building, economic factors and the cost/inconvenience of management). The capitalisation rate also reflects the expectation of future rental growth. Most forms of professional valuation today are covered by the *Royal Institution of Chartered Surveyors Appraisal and Valuation Manual* (the Red Book).

9.4 ROLE OF ADVISERS

Real property should never be acquired, sold or developed without the investor first obtaining competent professional advice. For most investors the advisers will comprise:

(1) A chartered surveyor: for knowledge of the relevant market, ability to appreciate and value potential properties, negotiating skills and finally ability to manage the property over the years to maximise its end value.
(2) A solicitor: with appropriate property experience to advise on legal matters generally, convey properties on purchase and sale and draw up leases and other legal documents throughout the life of the investment.
(3) A chartered accountant/financial adviser: to advise generally on funding/sources of capital and methods of minimising the impact of revenue and capital taxes over the years.

Dependent on the nature of property investments actually made, some investors may also require the services of other advisers from time to time. They might include architects, quantity surveyors, farm and/or forestry management consultants.

10

RESIDENTIAL PROPERTY

GEOFFREY J ABBOTT
Dip FBA (Lon) FRICS
Head of Sales and Purchases Department
and Investment Consultant of Smiths Gore (Chartered Surveyors)

10.1 HIGHLIGHTS OF THE PAST FEW YEARS

The housing recession, which set in in August 1988 in the south east and rippled around the whole country, has now relaxed its iron grip on the markets.

The recovery was uneven, but turnover of realistically priced houses has now recovered, although the threat of a manufacturing recession is affecting certain areas again. The Halifax National House Price Index currently stands at 239.0 as compared to 233.1 in 1989. However, this average represents only approximately 3.3 times average wages, as opposed to more than five times the national average wage in 1989.

10.2 THE ALTERNATIVES

10.2.1 Personal homes

The purchase of a home is probably the largest investment which the great majority of us make without ever considering it an investment. It is the only form of property investment where capital gains are normally tax free. The owner, if he or she has more than one home, may elect which is the 'principal residence' and may vary this from time to time subject to notifying the Inland Revenue. A person required to reside in employer-provided accommodation may acquire a house and enjoy capital gains tax exemption on it, provided he intends in due course to live in it.

The capital gains tax exemption usually applies to a house and up to one acre of grounds, but exceptions exist above and below this amount and professional advice should be sought.

The purchase of a home has long been considered the safest and soundest form of property investment. The purchaser enjoys absolute control over his or her investment and may obtain tax relief at 10 per cent for interest on existing mortgages up to £30,000 until April 2000. Funds for purchase are traditionally obtained on mortgage from building societies and insurance companies or the major clearing banks who entered this field in 1981.

Houses are normally sold by private treaty, but investment or let houses, and mortgage repossessions, are sometimes sold by auction. Factors to consider on house purchase include:

(1) style, location and potential planning factors;
(2) structural condition;
(3) availability of main services (gas, water, electricity, telephone, drainage);
(4) the local rate of council tax.

The length and cost of journeying to work is an increasingly important factor. Unmodernised houses may be eligible for local council improvement grants.

However, the most important question is whether you and your family actually wish to live in the house. First and foremost it is to be your home.

Insurance of property should usually be on the estimated cost of replacement (equivalent reinstatement cost), which may bear little direct relationship to the market value of the property. It should normally be index-linked to increase the sum insured in line with inflation of building costs between periodic reviews.

10.2.2 Let houses and flats

Let houses and flats are occupied by tenants and produce a rental income. They are often referred to as 'investment' houses or flats and most postwar legislation was viewed as favouring tenants. As a result the market shrank dramatically though legislation in the 1980s to restore the market has had some effect.

Rent Acts

Many let houses and flats are covered by the old Rent Acts (commonly referred to as 'regulated tenancies') under which the tenant has security and the rent is fixed from time to time by the Rent Officer (an official of the local authority) at a 'fair rent' level which is generally well below market levels. Increases set by the Rent Officer may only be phased in over a period of years and will be influenced by the new Rent Acts (Maximum Fair Rents) Order 1999.

Protected shorthold tenancies (one to five years)

Under the Housing Act 1980, protected shorthold tenancies were introduced for new lettings of more than one year but less than five years, under which the landlord can regain possession upon expiry, provided certain conditions are fulfilled. Whilst the initial rent may be agreed between the parties, the tenant may apply to have the rent fixed by the Rent Officer at any time.

Assured and assured shorthold tenancies

These were introduced under the Housing Act 1988 for new lettings after 15 January 1989 at market rents, subject to a right of appeal to the Rent Assessment Committee who will look to comparable market lettings in the area. Both give the landlord greater rights to possession at the end of the term, but in the case of assured shorthold tenancies the landlord or his successors have the right to a court order for possession.

Corporate tenants

Corporate tenants are excluded from the security of tenure provisions of all the Acts, though tenancies predating 15 January 1989 are subject to the rent officer's assessment of a fair rent. Care must be taken to ensure that all sublettings to company employees are genuine, as 'sham' arrangements may result in a secure sub-tenancy.

Long leasehold houses (over 21 years)

Houses or flats let on long leases were common, particularly in the major cities. Under the Leasehold Reform Act 1967 the lessees of the majority were granted the right to enfranchise or purchase their freeholds.

Under the Leasehold Reform, Housing and Urban Development Act 1993 these rights of enfranchisement, subject to a number of conditions and exceptions, were extended to higher value leaseholders previously excluded from the 1967 Act.

General

In the case of old regulated tenancies, a 100 per cent or more increase in capital value can be released if vacant possession is gained.

Let houses and flats are considered a safe and secure form of investment if the location is selected carefully, management standards are high and the investor understands the nature of the tenancy. Subject to the inevitable political risk of a change in legislation reversing the more favourable 1980s legislation (is the new Maximum Fair Rents Order a portent?), let houses and flats are worthy of consideration.

10.2.3 Blocks of flats

The investment considerations for blocks of flats are similar to those for let houses and flats. However, the market in blocks of flats has tended to be determined by their 'break-up' value rather than by the income produced. This break-up value arises through an investor being able to acquire a complete block of flats at a figure which will enable him subsequently to dispose of the flats either to the occupying tenants or with vacant possession, if obtained, and so realise an overall capital gain.

In the late 1980s the competition for blocks of flats having a break-up value was dramatic. However, it is a high risk form of investment, as there is no guarantee of obtaining vacant possession. Recently tenants have formed their own associations to try to control their landlords' operations, and the political risks and social problems for an investor operating in this market are considerable.

The situation is confused by the fact that tenants of flats were granted under the Landlord and Tenant Act 1987, a right of first refusal if the landlord decided to sell his interest.

Further, the Leasehold Reform, Housing and Urban Development Act 1993 gave tenants, subject to complex rules and criteria, the right to initiate either the purchase of the freehold of their block of flats or an extension of their leases.

There have also been a number of highly publicised abuses of the rules by certain landlords and further restrictive legislation seems inevitable.

10.2.4 Holiday homes and time sharing

With increasing leisure time, the demand for holiday homes in the UK (which vary from a site on which to park a caravan to a substantial secondary house) has increased considerably. The value of these properties is very much related to the personal choice of the purchaser, who is greatly affected by the ease of access to and from the major conurbations and the environment when he gets there. They can be good investments, with the added advantage that they can provide holiday accommodation for the family as well.

Holiday homes may also be purchased abroad. Specialist advice needs to be taken on such matters as local exchange control, the mechanics of purchase and availability of services. Good agents and lawyers are even more essential abroad than in the UK.

Partly as a result of this, a new concept of property ownership known as 'time sharing' became popular in the late 1980s. In essence, this provides for the investor to acquire an interest for a stated period (a week or a

167

month) in each year in perpetuity or for a period of years. It effectively widens the spectrum of investment to encompass the smaller investor who can secure holiday accommodation with the added potential of capital growth.

It has sometimes been associated with questionable sales techniques and even fraud, but it is an interesting concept for those who have limited funds which would otherwise be insufficient to purchase a holiday home. If the owner does not wish to use the accommodation each year, the property can often be exchanged if the location is in a major resort.

The method of sale varies, some properties being sold freehold and others on long leaseholds. An annual service payment is payable by the owner, together with the cost of electricity, water and other services used during a vacation. There are a number of companies specialising in this market who advertise nationally.

Holiday homes can be a sound investment but location is critical. If abroad, there are many possible pitfalls, not the least of which can be guaranteeing sound title.

10.3 PREVIEW OF THE YEAR AHEAD

Memories of the recession in the housing markets and the horrors of 'negative equity' have receded, although the markets remain sensitive to interest rates and employment security.

Currently the market is expected to move ahead by an average of 8 per cent over the next year, notwithstanding the withdrawal of mortgage interest tax relief. Some economic commentators suggestions that interest rates would have to be raised to contain the inflationary effects of rising house values proved to be correct when they were increased in September 1999. However, it is not yet clear whether this indicates a reversed trend upwards for future months.

11

AGRICULTURAL LAND, WOODLANDS AND MISCELLANEOUS

GEOFFREY J ABBOTT
Dip FBA (Lon) FRICS
Head of Sales and Purchases Department
and Investment Consultant of Smiths Gore (Chartered Surveyors)

11.1 INTRODUCTION

The last two decades have been a period of dramatic change for the land using industries, in perceptions of desirable land uses generally and in the pressures on rural land of our predominantly urban population. Since 1939, pressure to increase self-sufficiency in both agricultural and forest products had led to significant changes in crop and livestock selection/husbandry and the rapid incorporation of modern technology into the rural industries.

Since the 1980s, the domestic Green lobby and 'conservation interests' have become increasingly significant, overlaid by international concerns such as damage to the ozone layer and global warming. The issues underlying these pressures for change are complex. Yet the great mass of our urban population has little direct contact with the countryside; the problems in the countryside are often seen in oversimplistic terms.

Currently, as concerns about BSE decline, the theoretical implications of Genetically Modified Organisms (GMOs) 'escaping' are causing increasing concern and the market for expensive, organically grown produce is growing.

Few yet acknowledge that the achievement of these green objectives will ultimately have a dramatic effect on the life-styles and work practices of our urban populations. The majority of gasses which attack the ozone layer and cause acid rain emanate from urban chimneys, heating systems and exhaust pipes. Similarly much of the pollution in our rivers is the result of discharges from urban factories and sewage works.

The countryside is about diversity. An investment primarily in one form of land use will often directly or indirectly involve other land uses as well. Houses and woods are an integral part of farmland and all often overlay mineral deposits and are the natural habitat of the sportsman's quarry.

Throughout this chapter we seek to indicate typical cash yields on the various forms of land use but obviously many of the benefits of owning country property, which influence its value, do not come in the form of annual income.

Many purchasers of a vacant farm also get a nice house to live in and perhaps an interesting shoot as well; development possibilities (whether in the form of houses, leisure uses or mineral workings) or favourable capital or inheritance tax treatment in the future earn no income today; the surrender of the tenancy of a house or farm in due course can release significant latent capital value; and the mere ownership of a certain stretch of countryside can give the owner great personal satisfaction.

It is these factors and the post-war investment track record of country property which explain the historically relatively low initial yield typically earned on most forms of investment in land.

In the context of agricultural support, the much maligned Common Agricultural Policy in Europe used to be about price support, but is now increasingly about subsidising conservation objectives.

The countryside is also covered by an ancient web of footpaths and bridleways which historically served the practical needs of local communities. In their present form they are not ideal for the recreational purposes they primarily serve today. The threatened imposition of ill-considered legislation to additionally grant a 'right to roam' over 'open land' to the general public can only be divisive – whereas an overall rationalisation would be welcomed by both landowners and farmers.

11.2 AGRICULTURAL LAND

11.2.1 Background

Usable agricultural land in Great Britain totals approximately 45,000,000 acres of which about 66 per cent is owner/occupied or vacant, and 33 per cent is subject to secure Agricultural Holdings Act (AHA) tenancies. They form two very separate markets with significant valuation and yield differences for otherwise physically similar properties. Within these overall totals there is an enormous diversity of soil types, topography, climate and physical location to which individual farmers apply their financial resources and technical/managerial skills. The result is the diverse range of land uses and end products still found in the countryside today.

Table 11.1 Approximate distribution of soil grades and land uses

Soil Grade	England Percentage	England Acres 000s	Wales Percentage	Wales Acres 000s	Scotland Percentage	Scotland Acres 000s	Great Britain Percentage	Great Britain Acres 000s	Principal Farming/ Forestry Uses	Principal Alternative Uses
I	3.3	806	0.2	8	0.3	49	1.9	863	Intensive arable cropping eg bulbs, vegetables, roots & cereals. No forestry.	Coarse fishing in drainage channels and lowly valued pheasant shooting. Principally 'dull' flatland but greater potential on poorer Grade II land out of Fens and similar areas
II	16.7	4,083	2.3	96	2.3	383	10.2	4,562	Arable cropping/intensive grassland eg cereals with roots and/or dairy cows. Limited forestry.	
III	54.0	13,203	17.5	729	13.6	2,175	36.1	16,107	Extensive arable cropping, rotational grassland eg cereals, oilseed rape & beans or grass leys for dairy cows, beef, sheep. Hardwood forestry mainly.	Pheasant/partridge shooting/roe deer stalking. Game fishing if suitable rivers/ streams. Limited B&B, pony trekking etc.
IV	15.7	3,838	44.2	1,842	10.2	1,631	16.4	7,311	Permanent grassland/rough grazing eg beef and sheep rearing with limited dairying & cereals. Commercial softwood forestry.	Grouse shooting, Red deer stalking on open hill. Roe deer stalking in softwood plantations. Game fishing where suitable water.
V	10.3	2,518	35.8	1,491	73.5	11,775	35.4	15,784	Rough grazings often with rock outcrops, eg principally summer grazing with hardy sheep breeds & hill cattle. Limited softwood forestry.	Extensive B&B, pony trekking, hill walking, rock climbing etc.
TOTAL	100	24,448	100	4,166	100	16,013	100	44,627		

Note: MAFF Grades for England and Wales with Scottish equivalent.

Investors are strongly recommended initially to reflect quietly on Table 11.1 on p 171. Whatever the financial resources and skills investors bring to bear on the property they buy, its many physical and climatic characteristics will rule the uses to which it is suited. Field scale bulb growing is only economic on the better soils and hardwood trees simply will not survive on solid rock at high altitudes. Finally, a good livestock farmer is seldom a good arable farmer and *vice versa*.

Within both the vacant and let (often referred to as 'investment') land markets there are therefore many sub-markets within which properties suited to different principal agricultural uses are grouped.

Investors should also appreciate that a farmer runs a business. Like any other business, the actual financial results on any individual farm, however well the farming system is suited to the property, will reflect the farmer's managerial/technical skills and commercial judgements. As reflected in the rental market, the profit potential of a good farm is significantly greater than a poor farm. However, managerial skills on the individual farm remain critical to that unit's actual profitability. There will always be examples of poor farmers on the best land going out of business and good farmers on the poorest land making good money.

All investors should make a firm policy of regularly sitting down with their advisers to review whether this property or that one should still be owned or sold or perhaps passed down to the next generation. As part of these regular reviews, the potential of all land for higher value alternative uses should also be considered together with actions which might help to ensure its eventual release.

Could that droughty field cover potentially valuable gravel deposits, or might the field by the village be developed in 20 years' time? If the answer is yes, consideration should then be given of whether you will need that money in due course or whether it would make more sense to pass the land down to the next generation at purely agricultural value. Finally, a well-screened site is more likely to receive planning consent in due course than a prominent one out in the open. Should a belt of trees be planted now?

11.2.2 Highlights of the previous year

After a period of strong profits and rental/land value growth, the land markets entered a period of uncertainty following the General Election in May 1997 with the reduction in demand being matched by the fall in supply. During the past year the combined effects of the strong pound and reduced product prices have decimated farming profits. At the same time, values in the alternative markets soared to new heights, not withstanding a serious crisis of confidence in the important Pacific Rim Region, Russia and, more recently, Brazil.

In the investment or let farmland market supply to the open market fell from almost 36,000 acres in 1996 to just under 20,000 acres in 1997 and just over 11,000 acres in 1998. Average gross yields moved out from 3.8 per cent gross on the rents passing which equate to around 4.25 per cent gross on Arbitrators Award levels of rent.

In the vacant farming market, supply also fell and the value of land in unfashionable locations declined slightly, particularly in the live-stock/grassland areas. However, numerous sales by Smiths Gore demonstrated that reasonable quality arable land in sought after areas has held up very well. Indeed, the number of offers for recent sales in Norfolk and North Lincolnshire shows that demand considerably exceeds supply.

11.2.3 Vacant possession land

As vacant farmland now represents over two-thirds of all farmland in Great Britain it is obviously the principal land market. By definition it is freehold land offered for sale with vacant possession or available for the purchaser to physically occupy. Over the years between 1 and 2 per cent is offered for sale on average each year in packages from five acres of bareland to 5,000 acres fully equipped with houses and buildings. However, offerings in recent years have been well below both these his-toric levels and demand.

The principal buyers of most commercial farmland today are farmers who buy the land to farm, though many others buy from time to time for various reasons. The market for particularly attractive stretches of coun-tryside with high quality houses or for Scottish sporting estates is dominated by the wealthy, and in some cases the international wealthy, for reasons unlinked to the income which they may be able to earn from ownership of the property. In the case of land overlying potentially valu-able minerals or which may be developed over in the future, the more imaginative investors or mineral operators and developers will normally compete to purchase.

Vacant possession land has been a very satisfactory investment since the Second World War, but values have fluctuated over the years and timing, as in all investment, has been a major factor for the most successful.

Given the diversity of the markets and understandable regional variations over time, reliable statistics about past land value trends are very difficult – and potentially dangerous if used for short-term comparisons. The only series which stretches back over the whole of the post-war period is the Oxford Institute/Savills series but it is based on averaging vacant land sales *at auction*. It can therefore make no allowance for properties withdrawn 'in the room' and subsequently sold privately. Further, it probably disproportionately reflects grassland value trends as auction is

Table 11.2 Average vacant land values at auction

	With Possession £/acre		With Possession £/acre
1951	88	75	539
52	76	76	734
53	73	77	991
54	75	78	1,327
55	80	79	1,769
56	78	1980	1,726
57	73	81	1,729
58	85	82	1,844
59	101	83	2,082
1960	123	84	1,978
61	124	85	1,935
62	134	86	1,697
63	168	87	2,001
64	214	88	2,178
65	235	89	2,654
66	242	1990	2,568
67	258	91	2,431
68	280	92	2,202
69	299	93	2,208
1970	245	94	2,333
71	262	95	2,484
72	596	96	3,560
73	757	97	3,263
74	636	98	2,934

a more common method of sale in the livestock areas. It remains, however, the best guide to value trends over time and is set out in Table 11.2.

When selecting in which part of the country to buy, private investors are understandably usually influenced by their background. As a general rule, investors in straight farmland should seek to acquire the best land in the chosen area, because history shows that given a competent level of farm management, the best land generates the greatest profits over the years.

Further, outside of the wholly commercial areas of farming such as the Fens, farmland with an attractive appearance has always tended to sell for a premium value. As conservation considerations become more influential, the land markets are increasingly reflecting the conservation value of otherwise well-farmed land. Enhancing the wildlife value of a property, by well-planned hardwood tree planting, pond maintenance and sensitive management of ancient pastures, should be an on-going management consideration of all investors.

Table 11.3 Typical monetary benefits of farm ownership per acre

	Intensive Arable	Extensive Arable	Dairy (inc. Quota)	Livestock Rearing	Hill Farming (inc. Sheep Quota)
Land Value, say	£4,250	£3,000	£5,500	£2,250	£1,000
Working Capital, say	550	450	1,300	550	450
TOTAL CAPITAL	£4,800	£3,450	£6,800	£2,800	£1,450
Net Profit, say (inc. rental value)	£400	£250	£415	£100	£100
Annual Return, say	8.33%	7.25%	6.10%	3.57%	6.90%

Source: *Smiths Gore Farm Management (1997)*

In recent years an increasing level of grants and subsidies has been available for conservation policies, which are often based on the poorer quality soils. Increasing levels of such reliable 'high quality' income from government sources may well seriously distort the value of such inherently poor soils in the future.

CAP reform has also established the form of agricultural support for the future — away from encouraging ever increasing output per acre and towards fixed payments per acre cropped or breeding livestock maintained, with currently 10 per cent of arable land being Set Aside.

Remembering what was said earlier about the importance of management to the actual financial results (see **11.2.1**), and that some of the benefits of owning vacant farmland do not come in the form of cash income, the monetary benefits for a well run unit may be expected typically to work out as shown in Table 11.3.

These overall yields, being an amalgam of the secure return to the investor as landowner (in the form of rental value of around 50 per cent of the net profit) and the higher risk return to him as a trading farmer, reflect the fact that farming has passed through a profitable phase. Also the vacant value of the farm is typically 200 per cent or more of its let land value.

There are many options open to investors for the management of vacant farms or land and they should take professional advice. Investors may manage a farm personally, farm in partnership with another farmer or they may have a contractual or profit-sharing arrangement with another farmer. Following the passing of the Agricultural Tenancies Act 1995, land previously 'let' on these complex arrangements is increasingly being let on new Farm Business Tenancies structured to suit the circumstances of the individuals.

The method chosen will depend on the investor's income requirement, managerial ability and capital situation. The choice will affect the amount of farming capital required, the level of return obtained, and the extent of involvement in the day-to-day running of the investment.

'Intensively housed livestock' is a specialist form of farming and is restricted mainly to house pigs, poultry (chickens and turkeys), veal, barley beef and salmon or trout. These enterprises are usually capital-intensive in buildings and equipment and are restricted to small acreages (2 to 20 acres). As any pig farmer will cornfirm at the present time, the investment can be speculative in a very volatile market.

11.2.4 Let or investment land

'Let' or 'investment' land comprises about 33 per cent of the total usable agricultural acreage of Great Britain, having declined from around 90 per cent at the turn of the century. Most land is let under the old Agricultural Holdings Acts (AHA lettings) to a tenant who pays a rent and the investor may therefore not be able to live on the property or farm it.

Traditionally, let land was worth two-thirds or more of its value with vacant possession. However, in the post-war period, most legislation affecting the landlord/tenant relationship was seen as favouring the latter, and taxation policy has tended to favour the owner-occupier. As a result, AHA lettings are now generally worth only half of the land's vacant value.

From September 1995 all new lettings of farms (not being succession tenancies under the old Agricultural Holdings Act) are in the form of Farm Business Tenancies (FBTs) covered by the new Agricultural Tenancies Act. Subject to the length of the tenancy granted, the value differential between vacant and let land should be less, although this market is still relatively untested.

Investment opportunities vary from single let farms to large residential estates; from 10 acres up to 5,000 acres or more.

AHA lettings are technically annual tenancies but which actually give security for life, indeed often with rights of succession, subject to certain rules, for up to two further generations.

The tenancy agreement must be examined by a professional adviser, since it forms the basis for all matters affecting the investment in the future.

Rent levels vary. Rents fixed under the old Agricultural Holdings Acts may be 50 per cent below the rents obtainable from FBT lettings. Examples of sitting tenant AHA rents per acre compared to FBT rents might be:

(1) for well-equipped Grade I or II soil arable farms in the Fens: £90 as opposed to £180 or more;
(2) for well-equipped Grade II or III soil arable farms (not Fens) and well-equipped dairy farms; £60 as opposed to up to £120; and
(3) for poorer land or poorly equipped farms: £40 as opposed to £80.

Three yearly rent reviews on AHA lettings had been showing between 7 and 10 per cent compound annual growth, although the recent sharp decline in farming profitability will restrict rental growth in the immediate future.

Under most AHA tenancy agreements the landlord is responsible for insuring and for a major part of the cost of repairs to the houses and buildings though full repairing and insuring tenancies were common from the early 1970s.

Most AHA let land is owned by private families as part of substantial estates passed down through the generations, or is held by traditional institutions such as the Crown, the Church and numerous colleges and charities, most of whom buy for the long term.

Tenanted land may be one-third of the total stock of farmland in Great Britain but, because of this ownership pattern, only represents a very small part of the total farmland market each year. Supply to the market obviously varies but last year only 11,000 acres passed through the open market as compared to 36,000 acres in 1996. This is only about a fifth of what was typical in the 1970s.

Currently, buyers of let farms are a broadly based group comprising tenants buying in their farms, private investors, family trusts, certain charities, both traditional and financial institutions and some foreign investors.

Management is customarily undertaken by professional firms of chartered surveyors, with land agency departments, or by resident agents on larger estates.

Investors should be aware that there is no fixed relationship between gross and net yields. A typical gross yield today of 4.25 per cent on the rents passing might net back on a full repairing and insuring let farm to 3.75 per cent, whereas on a traditional landlord repairing and insuring let estate it might be under 3 per cent in the short term. However, that let estate may well have latent potential to be released by active management which may compensate for the lower initial net yield. Each investment opportunity must be viewed on its own merits.

11.2.5 Redundant farm buildings

The last Government's White Paper 'Rural England – A Nation

Committed to a Living Countryside' pointed out that only 1.3 per cent of those living in the countryside now actually earn a living off the land. However, 31 per cent of manufacturing and 25 per cent of service sector employment (and an even higher proportion of business start-ups) are based in the countryside.

Consequently, more and more planning authorities are viewing sympathetically well thought out schemes with good access for business-related re-use proposals for redundant farm buildings. They can be an attractive diversification for farm owners.

11.2.6 Finance

The basic rule for investors in farmland is that they should have the majority of the funds available in cash. Except in special circumstances farmland investments should not be made on the back of borrowed money. The initial gross return to a typical investment in a let farm is currently only 4.1 per cent. Investment in a similar vacant farm is typically twice as high so the return on investment in land (being the rental value of that land) is currently 2 per cent. A significant proportion of the purchase price therefore borrowed at say 7.5 per cent cannot be funded by the farm.

Within the agricultural industry, facilities for short-term borrowings of working capital are commonly provided by the clearing banks. Merchants' credit can also be taken but, when allowance is made for the discounts which may be lost, it can prove very expensive. Medium-term finance for machinery purchases, etc may also be provided by the clearing banks and various finance/leasing houses.

Long-term finance to the industry has traditionally been provided by the Agricultural Mortgage Corporation and the Scottish Agricultural Securities Corporation, with all the main clearing banks participating more recently. Subject to the borrower's ability to service the loan, up to two-thirds of the agricultural value of a farm can usually be borrowed at competitive rates which may be variable or fixed and be for up to 40 years. Interest is normally tax allowable and repayment of principal is commonly by way of linked life policies.

11.2.7 Preview of the year ahead

With historically low inflation, lower food reserves around the world, very volatile product prices and a stronger sterling, the agricultural industry faces an uncertain future – along with most of manufacturing industry.

The excessive levels of demand of a year or two ago for commercial farmland have thinned and values look set to plateau for the time being. However, demand for residential amenity farms remains strong and values may well rise in this sector.

Whilst the fall in farm profitability might indicate a greater fall in land values than have been seen, the alternative investment markets have gone on to new peaks – making farmland look increasingly realistically priced.

11.3 WOODLANDS

11.3.1 Background

Woodlands cover just over 5 million acres or about 10 per cent of the surface area of Great Britain. This compares with between 20 to 30 per cent in most EU countries. Ninety per cent of UK timber consumption is imported, at a cost of £7.2bn in 1990. Annual timber production in Great Britain grew from about 3.5 million cubic metres in 1980 to 5.35 million cubic metres at the end of the decade and nearer 10 million cubic metres around the Millennium. Consumption is also rising.

Of the national forest, some 25 per cent is made up of hardwoods (often referred to as deciduous woodlands) and 75 per cent is made up of softwoods (often referred to as coniferous or evergreen – but note the deciduous larch). Woodlands and forests take three principal forms.

Amenity and sporting woods and copses

These are normally found in lowland Great Britain in the form of hardwood mixtures. They are usually relatively small and can be politically sensitive locally, often being covered by Tree Preservation Orders. Whilst individual trees may be substantial and of significant value, these woods have little to do with commercial timber production. However, they can provide great enjoyment and satisfaction to the buyer.

Larger blocks of hardwoods

Typically found in lowland Britain, they can have a significant value but day-to-day management is often influenced by sporting and conservation considerations. Originally they formed parts of larger estates and can prove a very worthwhile investment.

Commercial softwood plantations and forests

These are commonly found in the higher rainfall areas of the country, principally in the south west, the hills of Wales, the north of England and Scotland, with other pockets such as the Breckland Sands around Thetford on the Norfolk/Suffolk borders and the New Forest in Hampshire. Being based on fast-growing trees well suited to both the pulp industry and the sawwood market, they are the backbone of commercial forestry. Conifers grow in western Britain almost twice as fast as in Scandinavia, Russia and most of North America, thus providing shorter rotations and a long-term competitive advantage.

Of the national forest approximately 40 per cent is owned by the Forestry Commission and 60 per cent by private investors/estates. The Forestry Commission was established in 1919 to encourage private owners to restore the productivity of their 3 million acres of woodland ravaged by fellings during the First World War and to create a State Forest of 1.75 million acres. The Commission's current estate is just over 2 million acres and principally made up of softwoods. As part of the wider privatisation programme of the last Government, the Forestry Commission had a target of selling 250,000 acres, or just over 10 per cent of its forestry portfolio, by the end of the decade. This policy was revised by the new Labour government, but its effect is unclear.

The privately owned forest is more balanced overall between hardwoods and softwoods. The former tends to be owned by farmers and estate owners in lowland Britain. Much of the latter is in the hills having often been established by investors during the 1960s, 1970s and 1980s, with substantial incomes from other sources motivated by tax planning considerations available at the time.

Forestry planting still attracts substantial grants though forestry costs can no longer be offset against other income. The ownership of woods also has other valuable advantages:

(1) income from productive woodlands is tax free;
(2) assets comprising forestry business qualify for 100 per cent relief from inheritance tax after two years' ownership;
(3) the land element can attract capital gains tax rollover relief.

Investment in woodlands is essentially about investing in relatively low value land with a growing crop on it, the rotation life of which may typically range from 40 years for some fast-growing conifers to 100 or 200 years for slower growing hardwoods. Normally, the first 20 years or more are about outgoings to establish the crop and manage it through to production age. From the commencement of thinnings, income may be expected to pick up from humble beginnings every five years for softwoods and ten years for hardwoods through to the bulk of the income from the felling of the final crop. A softwood crop planted today may be expected to show an internal rate of return of around 5 per cent per annum over the life of the crop.

Alternatively an investor may acquire an established plantation already in production and obtain a tax-free income. Such a wood is typically valued on the basis of a discounting of the expected net income stream in the 5 to 7 per cent range.

The underlying economic argument for investing in forestry is that the world has been consuming its forests at well in excess of sustainable growth rates for many decades. A significant shortfall of timber is therefore likely in the future. However, as much of the world's timber reserves are in the Third World and the old Communist Europe, which is primarily concerned with short-term economic survival, the supply of timber on to the world markets may continue at in excess of growth rates. However conservationists in the US were able to halt felling over a large area in 1992 to protect the habitat of the Spotted Owl. This directly affected the supply and price of timber in 1992–93.

11.3.2 Market trends

Demand for attractive amenity woods and established commercial woodlands with a positive cash flow remains strong with the value of the former underwritten by various conservation bodies. Similarly well-roaded areas of good softwoods in production and close to markets are highly sought after, with plantations in the 'golden triangle' in south Scotland achieving premium prices.

However poorer areas of softwoods in isolated areas, with poor access or younger plantations many years away from production, are heavily discounted.

11.4 MISCELLANEOUS LAND USES

11.4.1 Accommodation land

'Accommodation land' refers to small areas within a farm or estate which do not naturally fit in with the main land uses. They are often held for alternative use at a later date or as grazing land for conservation purposes (for instance a small area of permanent grassland). The expression can also be taken to mean those small areas of farmland which come up for sale from time to time, typically on the edge of a village or town.

Because of the limited acreage, accommodation land often appeals to the smaller investor with limited funds available, although it is usually more expensive to buy per acre than normal farmland. For the investor prepared to take on the problems of management and supervision they can sometimes generate a significant income from pony grazing. A portfolio of such units can give outstanding performance over the years if planning consent for an alternative high value use (eg residential development) is granted on parts.

Accommodation land with vacant possession is sometimes held unused, but more often let on short-term arrangements.

Grazing for ponies and horses is normally done on a per head per week payment basis and often generates a premium income. Horses are however choosy grazers and pasture deterioration usually results from horse grazing over the years.

On specialist dairy/beef farms, other people's sheep are often bought in 'on tack' during the winter months to tidy up the pastures. Payment is usually on a per head per week basis.

11.4.2 Sporting rights

Sporting rights normally form an integral part of any land sale and usually form only a minor element of capital value within the overall transaction. However, on Scottish sporting estates they are often the main constituent of value, assessed by past records of the bag or catch. In such cases ease of access will be a significant factor.

Sporting rights may be divided into three main categories:

(1) fishing – game and coarse;
(2) shooting – driven and rough;
(3) stalking – red and roe deer.

Sporting rights in England and Wales can be a legal estate and are on occasions reserved out of the sale of agricultural land and woods. In Scotland, only salmon fishing rights can form a separate legal estate. They may therefore be acquired separately from the land for personal use or letting, and timesharing of stretches of well-known fishing rivers has become common. Since 1 April 1989 VAT has been payable on that element of the value of a land sale which relates to the value of the sporting facility. However a transaction will normally only become taxable where a sporting income or value is separately identifiable. There is a further concession that farm tenants will only be expected to pay VAT on the sporting element of their tenancy agreements if it is greater than 5 per cent of total rent.

Fishing

Salmon fishing

Capital values of salmon fishing vary enormously according to location and river reputation but can range up to £8,000 a fish or more. Sea trout are considerably less valuable. Rents can range from £50 to £500 per rod per day. Pollution and salmon disease can have a devastating effect on both rental and capital values and the affect on English and Welsh rivers of the recent restrictions on spring catches remains an open question. Salmon fisheries cannot be created artificially, and are principally associated with rivers in Scotland and parts of Wales and the West Country.

Trout fishing

This can be on freshwater chalk streams in the south (which command the highest rates and prices), on other rivers generally or on artificial or natural lakes or reservoirs. Demand has been high with rents almost matching salmon river rates on the very best chalk streams. There is evidence of some over-supply of man-made trout lakes in certain areas.

Coarse fishing

Coarse fishing normally occurs in standing or slower-flowing waters in middle England and East Anglia which are usually rented by angling associations or smaller syndicates. Prices and rents vary greatly but old ponds close to large centres of population may provide a surprisingly large income.

Shooting

Shooting rights are, subject to economic conditions, readily lettable to a growing number of field sports enthusiasts. Shoots vary from a well-organised grouse moor in Scotland or the north with accommodation, through to substantial pheasant or partridge shoots in the south or east, perhaps let by the day with beaters and a cordon bleu lunch, down to a rough shoot over a small farm enjoyed informally by friends. Sporting rents vary from significant sums on the very best shoots to a minor additional income to the farm of £1 or £2 per acre. Charges for the best pheasant shoots, mainly in the south, lie in the £17.50 to £28 per bird range, with the best grouse moors in the north and Scotland ranging up to £100 per brace.

Deer stalking

Red, Fallow, Roe, Sika and Muntjac deer are the quarry, though Red and Roe deer are the principal species. In the UK, Red deer stalking on the open heather hills of the Highlands of Scotland is the most well-known and the most highly valued at a cost of up to £320 per stag. Roe deer stalking is traditionally more highly valued on mainland Europe, but commercial lettings in suitable locations are becoming increasingly popular in the UK at between £200 and £450 per buck.

The build up of Roe deer numbers throughout the woods of Great Britain has resulted in professional stalkers shooting from high seats for vermin control purposes and the value of the carcasses. Red deer are also controlled in this way in the Thetford Forest in East Anglia. However, in the south west Red deer, and in the New Forest Fallow deer, have traditionally been controlled by hunting with hounds.

Sporting generally

Sound game, vermin and habitat management practices can enhance the holding capacity and sporting qualities of a property but they cannot change the nature of it. For instance, grouse will only survive on a well-managed heather moor in the hills of the north or Scotland which benefits from peace, quiet and vermin control. The once famous Langholm Lodge in Dumfriesshire has just been closed after a period of five years during which the then Harrier population was allowed to develop and exterminate the grouse population.

Corporate entertaining has increasingly influenced rental levels on the best sporting estates over the last 20 years but the quality of service they demand is also high. Commercial lettings of sporting rights are seldom therefore profitable in their own right but more a means of subsidising the owner's hobby.

The purchase of quality sporting rights, as a separate investment, is normally only for the very wealthy investor who can afford an often substantial capital payment, perhaps millions of pounds, with the prospect of significant annual outgoings. The less wealthy must therefore limit their ambitions to more humble rough shooting, a gun on a syndicate shoot or the purchase of a time share on a suitable river. For most investors, sporting rights will be an indirect benefit of the purchase of a farm, wood or estate.

Market trends

With increasing wealth, leisure time and transport facilities, demand for sporting rights has been increasing steadily. Capital performance has generally been very satisfactory with the market for the very best becoming international. However, they are about enjoying expensive hobbies and are threatened by the combination of the high sterling and the increasingly powerful anti-blood sports lobby.

11.4.3 Stud farms and training establishments

Stud farms

Subject to planning, agricultural land may be developed for the breeding of thoroughbred bloodstock, riding horses or ponies. The demand has been increasing with over two million people now members of the various horse societies. For stud farms in the most favoured locations, such as Newmarket, Lambourn and Malton, demand is usually relatively strong, although values are lower in locations further from the recognised breeding centres where the main stallions stand. The centre of the national bloodstock industry is Newmarket where the National Stud and Tattersalls Sale Paddocks, which have a worldwide reputation, are both based. Stud farms in the favoured areas command a substantial premium over VP farmland.

The environment of a good stud farm is of great importance if the young stock are to grow and develop properly. The type of soil, particularly to facilitate the building of bone, is critical and the best are to be found on free draining chalk soils. A stud farm typically varies in size from 50 to 250 acres and may be a private stud (where the owner maintains his own animals only) or a public stud (where one or more stallions are kept and the mares visit during the covering season and often the foaling season as well). Stables must be of high standard with special boxes and facilities for covering and foaling purposes. The cost of putting up post and rail fencing is high because of the need for small paddocks and double fences.

To establish a stud farm can take up to 20 years for the hedges and shelter belts to mature. Good quality residential accommodation at the stud will be required for the stud groom and other employees: for a medium-sized stud a minimum of five to six houses might be required.

Stud farms usually change hands by private treaty in a limited and highly specialised market. Purchasers will usually be closely connected with the bloodstock industry. It is exceptional for stud farms to be bought as an investment on a tenanted basis.

Training establishments or yards

At various centres in the country, but particularly at Newmarket, Lambourn and Malton, there are established training facilities with extensive gallops and all weather tracks. Training yards usually comprise a trainer's house together with a number of cottages and hostels for stable lads; a minimum of 15 boxes with tack, feed and hay stores; and often special open and covered exercising areas. Business rates are payable on both stud farms and training yards.

Market trends

The specialised markets for both stud farms and training yards expanded throughout most of the 1980s with the best being in a truly international market. However, the recession hit the racing industry hard. Most owners of studs are men of substantial wealth who weathered the troubles, but many owners of training yards were not similarly endowed and many had increased their facilities during the late 1980s. The fall in values and the number of horses in training hurt them badly.

In the last few years there has been a useful increase in both the number of mares covered and two-years-olds going into training, but the decision last year of the Maktoum family to move many of their two-year-olds to France has shaken confidence.

11.4.4 Mineral bearing land

All minerals other than oil, gold, silver and coal usually belong to the freehold owner of land but may have been reserved to a predecessor in title. On acquisition, purchasers should always check that the mineral rights are included. The principal minerals are coal, sand, gravel, silica sand (glass), iron-stone, clay (brickmaking or china), limestone and in certain areas other special deposits (tin, copper, etc). With limited exceptions all coal belongs to The Coal Authority and oil/gas deposits to the government.

Strict planning regulation affects mineral excavation and specified areas are designated in most County Plans. Virtually no excavation is permitted on land classified as Grade I or II. Geological maps indicate the approximate location of minerals and resistivity surveys and test borings can establish mineral deposit patterns, depths and volumes. Development is usually carried out through a sale or lease to one of the principal operating companies.

The sale of mineral-bearing land incurs capital gains tax on chargeable gains. Profits from the commercial operation of mineral workings are liable to income tax (or corporation tax), with capital allowances (including a depletion allowance of, in general, 50 per cent of the royalty rate of the minerals) available for certain expenditure. Mineral royalties are taxed, broadly, as one-half as income and the other half as capital.

Tipping, fishing, boating and water skiing rights may be reserved and provide high levels of income and reversionary asset value on completion of excavation. The 'hole in the ground' was often worth more than the original land. However, with the evolving principle that 'the polluter shall pay', and the new rate of tipping tax on landfill sites of £10 per tonne (rising by £1 per tonne per annum through to 2004 at least) of degradable materials this situation may be changing.

The end value of restored land is currently uncertain, and any hint of noxious materials on site could result in a negative value.

Minerals are a speculative investment if the land is purchased by an investor other than a mineral operator with mineral exploitation specifically in view. However, some farmland can produce high yields from unexpected mineral excavation. High prices should not be paid merely to hold a speculative 'mineral bank'.

11.4.5 Public leisure/entertainment, retail land uses and commercial uses for redundant farm buildings

Like most subsidiary forms of land use, these categories are all relatively marginal to the whole but potentially significant profit centres on individual properties in the right locations. The managerial skills required are, however, very different from those of a farmer or forester and, if management of the main activity is not to suffer, they are best treated as a separate activity. Their common characteristic is that they are intended to appeal to the general public. They come in three main categories, though they often overlap with each other.

The passive leisure land uses

The obvious examples are leased golf courses, caravan and camping sites and mobile home parks – though the higher the standard of the site and more extensive the facilities (a shop for instance) the less managerially passive they become.

These properties are usually located at or near seaside areas or in areas of scenic beauty. Mobile home parks may be for permanent (all year round) occupation in certain areas specified by local councils. Planning controls are stringent on all large-scale parks or sites. Special facilities are required under the Caravan Sites and Control of Development Act 1960 including washing and toilet facilities, electricity and roads. The Mobile Homes Act 1975 confers on caravan home owners a limited security of tenure. Planning permission is almost always required and not easy to get in areas viewed as being of high landscape value.

An investment of this type can be lucrative but is high risk, demanding considerable pre-acquisition investigation. The Caravan Club provides information on sites and the pitfalls associated with them. Fashions change and the weather greatly affects the income from holiday parks, particularly in coastal areas, where serious storms can result in large losses.

The active leisure entertainment land uses

These are typically golf courses, wildlife parks, pleasure gardens, theme parks, riding schools/pony trekking centres and grand houses open to the public. Planning permission is required for wildlife parks, pleasure gardens, golf courses and riding schools. Location is of paramount importance since it is essential to be close to urban populations with good road access. Initial development costs are high. It is probable that future legislation and higher design and maintenance standards will further aggravate the position. For country houses it is specially important to check the building status for planning purposes, since 'listed' buildings are graded under the Town and Country Planning Act 1971 and the Town and Country Planning (Scotland) Act 1972, which impose varying degrees of responsibility on the owner, including the need to obtain listed building consent for demolition, improvements or even minor alterations.

Houses having historic and amenity value are frequently opened to the public as a trading venture, enabling the owner to continue to live in the family home. The trading venture is intended to support the upkeep of the property and its general environment. Other large houses have been acquired for institutional purposes, such as research centres, out of town offices, training centres and health farms.

The problems with marketing wildlife parks, and more recently golf courses, demonstrate that an investment of this kind is highly speculative in all but the prime locations. It is more often seen as a means to an end by existing owners rather than as the reason for a purchase.

Retail land uses

Farm shops and garden centres are the obvious examples. Farm shops are usually ancillary to farm businesses; they enable the farmer to obtain better prices than he would on the wholesale market by cutting out the middleman. However, EC hygiene regulations are becoming even more restrictive.

Garden centres are normally run by individuals or small companies, but in a few cases they are larger enterprises with multiple sites. Planning consent is required.

The location of both farm shops and garden centres is important, the best sites being on main roads and close to large centres of population. The increase in leisure has stimulated the popularity of these enterprises, supplying requisites to the keen gardener and also to consumers increasingly interested in fresh farm produce, especially for the deep freeze. The 'pick your own' method of sale at certain seasons can be successful and at farms where it is in operation good car parking facilities are essential. However, economic success proved illusory for many and this sector has declined.

Enterprises of this kind can be a valuable source of additional income and capital if correctly developed out of a farm unit (which is usually owner/occupied) but they are seldom sold as investments.

USEFUL ADDRESSES

Country Landowners Association
16 Belgrave Square
London
SW1X 8PQ

Tel: (020) 7235 0511

Department of the Environment,
Transport and the Regions
Eland House
Bressenden Place
London
SW1E 5DU

Tel: (020) 7890 3000

Agricultural Mortgage
Corporation PLC
AMC House
Chanty Street
Andover, Hampshire
SP10 1DD

Tel: (01264) 334344

Ministry of Agriculture, Fisheries
and Food
Whitehall Place
London
SW1A 2HH

Tel: (020) 7270 3000

Agricultural Development and
Advisory Service (ADAS)
Oxford Spires Business Park
The Boulevard
Kidlington
Oxon OX5 1NZ

Tel: (01865) 842742

Royal Institution of Chartered
Surveyors (RICS)
12 Great George Street
London
SW1P 3AD

Tel: (020) 7222 7000

Incorporated Society of Valuers
and Auctioneers
3 Cadogan Gate
London
SW1X 0AS

Tel: (020) 7235 2282

Environment Agency
Kingfisher House
Goldhay Way
Orton Goldhay
Peterborough
PE2 0ZR

Tel: (01733) 371811

National Association of Estate
  Agents
21 Jury Street
Warwick
CV34 4EH

Tel: (01926) 496800

Forestry Commission
231 Corstorphine Road
Edinburgh
EH12 7AT

Tel: (0131) 334 0303

Royal Institution of Chartered
  Surveyors (Scottish Branch)
7–9 Manor Place
Edinburgh
EH3 7DN

Tel: (0131) 225 7078

Scottish Office of Agriculture and
  Fisheries Department
Pentland House
47 Robb's Loan
Edinburgh
EH14 1TY

Tel: (0131) 556 8400

Caravan Club
East Grinstead House
East Grinstead
West Sussex
RH19 1UA

Tel: (01342) 326944

Food From Britain
301–344 Market Towers
New Covent Garden Market
London
SW8 5NQ

Tel: (020) 7720 2144

Rural Development Commission
141 Castle Street
Salisbury
Wiltshire
SP1 3TP

Tel: (01722) 336255

12

COMMERCIAL PROPERTY

ANDREW BULL

ARICS, Partner in Jones Lang LaSalle

12.1 INTRODUCTION

Review of 1998

1998 was a year of two distinct halves. The first half saw the property market buoyed by strong economic growth. However, following on from the economic crisis caused by the turmoil in the Asian and emerging market economies, confidence among consumers and business was dented. Notwithstanding this, because of the action taken by the Bank of England in cutting interest rates from 7 per cent to 5.25 per cent, confidence is now being restored.

Despite the global economic turmoil in the second half of 1998 and the Government's increases in stamp duty, institutional net investment in UK land and property totalled a record £4.5bn. Net investment in the first quarter of 1998 was at £1.31bn, surpassing the previous best of £1.26bn in the first quarter of 1998. Over 1998, property represented around 7.5 per cent of total net investment, up from 3 per cent in 1997.

The 1998 IPD Annual Index reported total returns for standing investments at 11.8 per cent, down from 16.8 per cent in 1997. Rental growth was 7.3 per cent, although this was not fully reflected in capital values which rose by 4.6 per cent. Trading and development contributed positively to returns, adding 0.4 per cent to returns and bringing them up to 12.2 per cent.

The IPD Monthly Index showed that there was a downward trend in the second half of the year following fears about the economy. Retail experienced the sharpest slowdown in the Monthly Index, finishing the year as the Index's poorest performer. However, the Annual Index recorded retail returns of 11.6 per cent only, trailing industrials on 13.2 per cent, mainly because of the Annual Index's inclusion of large shopping centres. IPD's figures show polarisation in the shopping centre market with larger centres returning an average of 16.5 per cent in 1998, around 5 per cent over smaller centres.

The retail sector was the best performing sector in 1997, buoyed by windfall payments, low base rates and significant increases in disposable income. However, last year the sector was hit by a fall in consumer confidence, a slowdown in earnings growth and the introduction of tax self-assessment which further reduced the level of disposable income in the sector. Although consumer confidence has remained weak in recent months, the reduction in base rates is already starting to have a positive effect on the housing market, which should feed through into retail spending and in turn benefit the sector.

Office rental growth of 7.3 per cent led the other sectors, although yields moving out in the second half of 1998 damped returns to 11.6 per cent. Performance of the office sector has picked up recently and the latest figures from IPD show that it was the best performing sector in February. The sector is likely to continue to benefit from the low levels of supply partly caused by the reluctance of developers to invest in speculative schemes. The recent improvement of business confidence shown through a number of trade surveys will also help the sector.

The industrial sector was the best performing sector on the IPD index last year and is forecast to benefit in the short term from a recovery in manufacturing output because of a possible fall in the value of sterling, combined with an improvement in the health of the economies of the UK's trading partners. Industrial property has benefited from its high income nature and, with borrowing rates where they are at the moment, this is likely to result in investor interest in the sector remaining strong throughout 1999.

Merrill Lynch's survey of property fund managers shows that the property sector is returning to favour, with buyers outnumbering sellers for the first time in ten months. Merrill Lynch's equities analysts have also noted signs of more positive tenant and investment demand. In particular, the outlook for secondary property has improved with lower interest rates. Commerzbank believes that capital growth in 1999 may offset the impact of the Budget's stamp duty rise.

February 1999's IPD Monthly Index reported property returns continuing to slow to 11.2 per cent for the 12 months to February. Between the sectors, offices – in particular London offices – led the sectors, benefiting from an upturn in rental growth with a year-on-year return of 12.2 per cent. Retail and industrial returns benefited from a positive yield shift to provide year-on-year returns of 9.9 per cent and 12.7 per cent respectively.

12.1.1 Types of investors

Property investments appeal to different types of investors dependent

Figure 12.1 Property, equity and gilt yields 1972–98

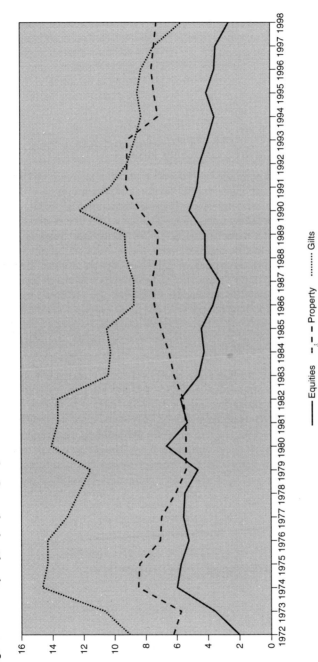

Equities ——— Property – – – Gilts ·········

Source: *Hiller Parker, Datastream*

upon an investor's requirement for income or capital growth, and the level of risk the investor will accept. Properties can be subdivided according to location, type and size. Small industrial units and multi-million pound office investments are unlikely to be of interest to the same investor. Risk-averse investors such as insurance companies and pension funds will prefer to invest in 'prime' properties in established locations let to blue chip tenants on long full repairing and insuring leases. A factor of considerable importance to these investors is the security of rental income and capital gain. Other investors will, however, be prepared to accept a higher level of risk by purchasing 'secondary' properties if the return is considered to be sufficiently attractive.

The purchase of a commercial property involves the giving up of a capital sum now in exchange for future returns which can be either the benefits of owner-occupation, income flow and/or capital gain. Underlying any property investment decision will be the option of alternative investments, namely stocks, shares, cash, unit trusts and even works of art. In selecting an investment, the investor will seek the highest real rate of return on capital invested but, depending upon the object of the investment, may 'trade off' a reduced rate of return in consideration for increased liquidity or security of income. An investor's tax status will also be an important factor.

12.1.2 Property valuation

In its simplest form, the basis of property valuation is the capitalisation of rental income of a property over a term of years or in perpetuity (depending on whether the property is leasehold or freehold) at an investment rate of return which reflects all the elements of risk associated with that property (security of income, obsolescence of the building, economic factors and the cost/inconvenience of management). The capitalisation rate chosen to value the property will also reflect the expectation of future rental growth and consequently tends to be significantly lower than the yields available from fixed-interest securities. This phenomenon (also illustrated by the dividend yield of equities) is known as the 'reverse yield gap' and since the 1970s has varied between about 1 and 8 per cent.

12.2 TYPES OF COMMERCIAL PROPERTY

Direct investment in commercial property falls mainly into the following categories:

(1) retail including supermarkets and retail warehouses;
(2) offices including town centre, out of town and campus;

(3) industrial including factories, warehouses, hi-tech and trade centres

and, to a much lesser degree:

(4) farmland and forestry;
(5) leisure.

Most investors with a significant long-term investment portfolio aim to hold the majority of the investments balanced between the retail, office and industrial categories, where there is a well-defined investment market.

12.2.1 Purchase of commercial property

Due to the large amounts of capital required for the purchase of even the smallest commercial property, the commercial property investment market is, like the equity market, generally confined to UK and foreign insurance companies, pension fund and property companies, together with a number of wealthy private individuals or family trusts. UK insurance companies and pension funds began investing in commercial property in the mid-1950s, broadening their asset bases beyond the equities and government securities which had hitherto formed their principal media for investment. UK pension fund investment reached a peak as a percentage of their assets in 1979 and significant net new investment was not then seen until the late 1980s.

During 1997, many institutions restructured their portfolios. Purchases of property increased from 6.6 per cent last year to 11.8 per cent of the total, at the end of 1997. This figure was almost matched by 10.3 per cent of sales.

Figure 12.2 shows rental value growth accelerating during 1997 in aggregate as the market recovered. It is, however, clear from other market evidence that a high degree of polarisation still exists, both between prime and secondary property, and particularly in 1997 between large floorplate and other properties.

12.2.2 Lease of commercial property

During the 1980s commercial buildings were generally leased for a term of 25 years with five-yearly rent reviews to the property's current open market rental value. During the early 1990s the supply/demand balance has been so radically altered that the market is one in which tenants' desires are paramount. There has been marked owner reluctance to grant shorter leases but the trend to shorter leases and the granting of tenants' options to determine leases continues. At the same time increased incentives by way of cash payments and rent-free periods have resulted in

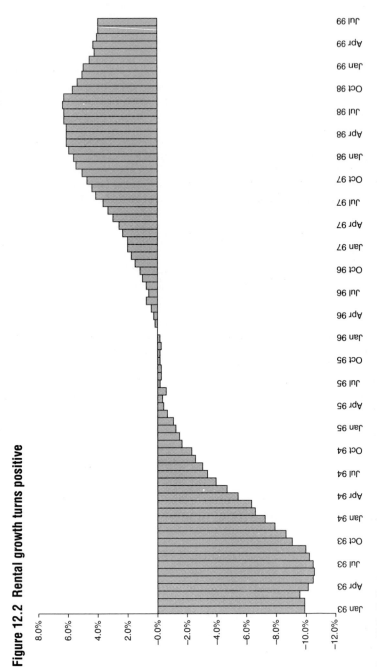

Figure 12.2 Rental growth turns positive

Source: *IPD Monthly Digest*

reduced returns to landlords. Under the terms of what is known as a 'full repairing and insuring' lease, the occupational tenant is responsible for (or for at least the cost of) carrying out all repairs to and insurance of the property. Whilst the day-to-day management of a commercial property investment is of vital importance in terms of maintaining the performance of the investment, and in particular in achieving the best possible rent on review, in the case of a letting of an entire building (as opposed to one which is in multiple occupation) the process is essentially one of collecting the rent and checking that the repairs and insurance are in place. In multi-occupied buildings the repairs and insurance are carried out by the landlord, or the landlord's managing agents, with the costs being recovered from the tenants. An investment in commercial property has historically been regarded as a passive investment, with the day-to-day and portfolio management responsibilities being undertaken by a firm of managing agents.

12.2.3 Rent reviews

Investments in commercial property provide regular opportunities for increasing the income obtained from the property through rent reviews. Since the Second World War the time period between rent reviews has altered. Formerly leases were granted with a period of 21 years between rent reviews, but latterly this decreased to 14 years, then to seven years and is currently five years. Generally, rent reviews result in the rent increasing to the then open market rental value of the property and most institutional leases provide for the rent review to be on an upwards only basis. As mentioned earlier, oversupply and reduced tenant demand resulted in rents falling, increased incentives and shorter lease terms. However, leases granted with terms long enough to have five-yearly rent review provisions have on the whole continued to include upward only rent reviews.

12.2.4 Rental growth

As can be seen from the Figures 12.3 and 12.4 on pp 198 and 199 showing rental growth in the three major investment sectors throughout the decade of the 1980s, and also the mean asking yield for the three sectors through the same time period, the rate of rental growth has varied enormously from a peak of about 30 per cent per annum to an actual decline in rental terms. At the same time, yields have altered by as much as 25 per cent.

Figure 12.3 Rental growth by sector 1973–98

Source: IPD, JLW FM Strategy

Figure 12.4 Property yields by sector 1972–98

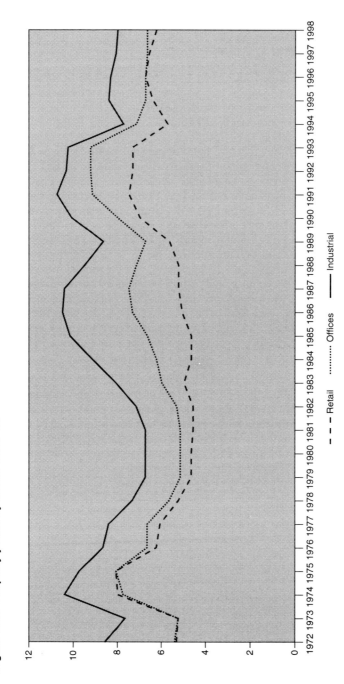

- – – Retail   .... Offices   ——— Industrial

Source: Hillier Parker.

12.3 SHOPS

12.3.1 General

Historically, three factors have affected the rental and capital value of shops: location, location and location. Due to the fact that the quality of the location can readily be ascertained, shops have been regarded as one of the most secure forms of commercial property investment. In the past, principal high street locations were rarely subject to major change, except when a town centre redevelopment scheme or a new shopping centre was planned, when it was usually possible to predict the effect that these new centres would have on the existing shopping patterns has been significant. The provision of sufficient and accessible car parking and an attractive environment will ensure that retail parks and out of town centres continue to prosper, although future out of town schemes will be limited by current planning regulations which now support town centre regeneration. The retailing sector is undergoing significant change, with many retailers repositioning in the market, restyling their outlets and merchandise, and taking over competitors. In addition there was dramatic growth in 'speciality' retailing where a number of retailers have been successful in targeting specific markets and responding quickly to changes in consumer demand. Hence the more established chains experienced greater competition for prime pitches in the high street.

A large number of the best shop units in the UK are now owned by the institutions, although a proportion are still owned and occupied by the major retailing organisations. In recent years rental growth has been considerable throughout the retail sector. There has been keen competition to make further investment in this category, whilst the availability of suitable investments is extremely limited in relation to the amount of investment money available.

In the property investment market, shops are categorised as prime, secondary and tertiary.

12.3.2 Prime

Prime shops are those situated in the best trading locations along the principal high streets in the larger towns where major multiple retailers, such as Boots, W H Smith and Marks & Spencer, are to be found. The rental income obtainable from shop units within these locations varies enormously depending on the importance of the particular town.

12.3.3 Secondary

Secondary shops are shops either on the fringes of the best trading positions within the larger towns or in the best shopping positions in the smaller towns. Due to the shortage of prime shop units now available for commercial investment, the institutional demand for this type of property has grown in recent years. Since the prospects for rental growth in these locations have proved more erratic than those in prime locations, investors expect a higher yield.

12.3.4 Tertiary

Tertiary shops are shops on the fringes of the secondary trading positions and shops in neighbourhood shopping parades, including 'the corner shop'. There is a negligible demand from multiple tenants for representation in these locations. Therefore, covenant strength is poorer and the management load heavier. Consequently, demand for these properties derives principally from private investors. This market is usually very active with sales of all sizes taking place by private treaty or auction.

12.3.5 Out of town shopping

Out of town shopping has evolved through the recognition of the car-borne shopper and may generally be divided into food and non-food retailing. The main DIY specialists (Sainsbury's Homebase, W H Smith Do-It-All and B & Q) are often found grouped together and require units of 35,000–50,000 square ft. Out of town food retailers now include most of the major food chains. Good surface car parking and main road prominence are essential criteria.

Out of town shopping often provides a combination of retailing and leisure facilities for the consumer including cinema, ten pin bowling, restaurants, a night club and sports facilities.

12.4 OFFICES

12.4.1 General

In the early 1970s many provincial towns, as well as central London, became seriously over-supplied with office accommodation and rents either remained level or fell. This started to happen again to a lesser extent in the early 1990s. A factor in the demand/supply imbalance is the lengthy period from planning to completion of a development.

The quality of an office building is of greater importance than that of a shop unit. Occupational tenants are setting ever higher standards, requiring good quality finishes, modern lifts, central heating, adequate car parking facilities, the abilty to accommodate a growing range of sophisticated office equipment (notably computers, word processors and communications equipment) and, particularly in central London, double-glazing and air conditioning. The costs of maintaining offices, especially the mechanical services, the unified business rates, and the cost of refurbishing the accommodation, mean that the tenant and investor are subjected to high outgoings. These have increased as a direct result of technological changes having shortened the lifetime of buildings and services.

The most expensive office locations in the UK have historically been the West End and City of London. Since the tenant will be responsible for all outgoings under the terms of his lease, the actual cost of occupation will probably be double the cost of the rent alone. Due to the security and perceived prospects for long-term rental growth offered by buildings within the West End and City of London, there has been a strong institutional demand for investments. Increasingly, foreign investors as well as UK investors have been active in this market although recent over supply and falling rents in both the City and West End have resulted in more fluctuation and uncertainty in value, leading to reduced investment activity and caution amongst investors.

The other principal office areas in London follow a similar but less expensive pattern to that of the City and West End, although in the late 1980s an upswing in demand coupled with relatively restricted supply resulted in these locations experiencing dramatic growth in rents. Outside London, rents vary from centre to centre, with the towns immediately to the west of London along the M4 corridor being the highest outside London.

12.4.2 Conclusion

Offices form the backbone of most commercial property investment portfolios because of the amount of money involved and the past performance of rental growth on rent review. They are likely to remain a dominant feature of institutional portfolios and the preferred areas are those in central London and certain selected provincial centres. However, it is becoming necessary to spend large capital sums more frequently to maintain the quality of the investment. Over many years the cost of central London office occupancy and the inconvenience of commuting have encouraged companies to move their operations to suburban and provincial locations.

12.5 INDUSTRIAL

12.5.1 General investment: factories and warehouses

The declining importance in Great Britain of the industrial and manu-facturing sectors, the volatility of the economy and the relatively short economic life of industrial buildings have resulted in investors requiring higher yields for factories and warehouse premises than for shops and offices. In this context, institutional investors tend to prefer warehouse buildings, as opposed to factories, due to the fact that these tend to be less specialised and therefore require fewer remedial works when a tenant vacates the premises. Industrial processes also tend to have a more destructive effect on the actual fabric of the property.

12.5.2 Location criteria

Although the uses of factories and warehouses are different, both in prac-tical and in legislative terms, it is convenient to categorise them together, since the locational and investment criteria are similar. The most desirable investments in this category are situated on well-located industrial estates, close to major conurbations and motorway access points or the national airports. It is interesting to note that proximity to rail services is not an important criterion in the UK, being less important than a good supply of labour and good estate services for the factory owner.

12.5.3 Institutional criteria

The insurance companies and pension funds have developed certain cri-teria which they look for in modern industrial and warehouse buildings. These criteria relate to clear working height, floor loading capacity, the presence of sprinklers, the proportion of office space to warehouse space within the unit, the number of loading doors, the presence of a concreted hard standing in front of the unit and adequate car parking. Whilst these institutional criteria are often in excess of the criteria required by occupi-ers, investors would be wise to purchase units meeting institutional criteria, since they will find a wider market in which to sell the property in the future.

12.5.4 Yields

Yields available on prime industrial and warehouse investments are higher than those on prime shops and offices. Rental growth experienced over the late 1970s was, generally, very satisfactory but became static in the early and mid-1980s during the economic recession, and improved again in the late 1980s. Investment in modern industrial and warehouse buildings is a more recent trend than investment in offices and shops but now forms around 25 per cent of a typical portfolio. Opportunities do exist for non-institutional investment where very high yields can be obtained from obsolescent or poorly located properties, but these carry commensurate risk.

12.6 HI-TECH

Whilst many areas of traditional manufacturing industry were affected by the economic recession, the hi-technology field experienced considerable growth. This resulted in a new direction in the design and use of industrial buildings with tenants becoming increasingly discerning as to their preferences in building design and working environment. The most radical change has been the introduction of the building which comprises a two- or three-storey structure designed to permit the interchangeability of functions such as offices, research and development, laboratories or industrial. An out of town location, extensive car parking and land-scaping with imaginative and functional finishes both internally and externally create a high quality corporate image. The first and still largest business park in the UK is Stockley Park off the M4 very close to Heathrow airport. Both back office and headquarters type functions are now moving to such business parks.

12.7 AGRICULTURE

Having experienced growth in popularity with institutional investors, at one point forming in excess of 5 per cent of some investment portfolios, farmland and forestry have been increasingly less popular as a result of falling values and the perception of a continued fall in values. In addition, investors have begun to appreciate that in many instances the economic support or tax benefits of these investments have been and are likely to be subject to political tinkering, thus dramatically altering the value of many investments at a stroke.

Smaller, more picturesque farms, especially those with attractive houses have, however, become increasingly attractive and prices have continued to rise for successful businessmen desirous of changing their place of domicile and lifestyle (see also Chapter 11).

12.8 LEISURE

Investments in the 'leisure industry' include hotels, marinas, golf courses, sports centres and entertainment facilities. The growing demand for leisure facilities, both home-based and from tourists, is resulting in increasing investment in this field. It is, however, regarded as an investment in management expertise rather than in the property which the particular leisure activity occupies, and great caution is therefore necessary. Quite often an investor's return will be geared to the operator's turnover or profitability rather than to the premises' rental value, which can sometimes be very difficult to determine.

Whilst the returns from leisure industry investments, in terms of capital gains, can be substantial for the astute investor, the risks are considerable and such investments are not recommended to small investors.

13

BUSINESS VENTURES (WITHOUT PARTICIPATION IN MANAGEMENT)

MIKE WILKES
Pannell Kerr Forster, Chartered Accountants

13.1 INTRODUCTION

There are always people with experience and no money looking for people with money and no experience. The former sometimes have the money and the latter have had the experience. That is not to say that, in general terms, such arrangements should always be avoided. There are plenty of good ideas which need financing and the rewards to the investor can be substantial, but such investments call for faith in someone else's judgement, nerves of steel and an instinct for gambling. Many ventures have turned out well after being (sometimes more than once) on the verge of disaster. Those who do not like walking along the edge of a precipice should keep to gentler paths.

Individuals seeking after finance will often paint the picture of their prospects in rosy colours, not through dishonesty but because of enthusiasm, and such enthusiasm should always be discounted. Unfortunately it is often highly contagious, so that impersonal, dispassionate, professional advice is essential. The pitfalls should be considered every bit as carefully as the opportunities. It is easier to lose money than to make it; but money is seldom to be made without accepting an element of chance.

In some cases money, once put into a venture, is effectively locked in, come what may. At best it may be possible to withdraw it only at considerable cost. On the other hand, by good judgement and good luck (and any successful venture requires both), there are fortunes to be made. The essential feature of the investments considered in this chapter is that the investor relies wholly on the expertise of someone else – company director, active partner, racehorse trainer and so on – and will probably be involved in matters of which he or she is ignorant or, at least, inexperienced.

It must never be forgotten that taxation will make inroads into both income and capital gains, and, in this respect, professional advice should always be taken. There may be alternative ways of making investments so that, with this in mind, every scheme requires careful expert consideration. Equally, if losses are incurred, steps should be taken to see that the maximum tax advantage is obtained. The advice of an accountant or a solicitor or probably both can be invaluable, not only in dealing with legal and financial problems that are puzzling the prospective investor but often also in pointing out problems of which the layman may be totally unaware. The effects of taxation are touched on in the following sections, but complex problems can arise which it is impossible to deal with briefly. In every case the solution will depend upon the individual facts.

1981 saw the introduction of the 'Business Start-up Scheme' intended for the encouragement of investment in companies starting new businesses. Provided that the investment complied with the numerous, rigorous and complex provisions set out in no less than 16 sections of and two Schedules to the Finance Act 1981, the amount invested could be deducted from the income of investors in computing their income tax liabilities.

The scheme was superseded by the 'Business Expansion Scheme' which, while similar in concept, was more generous in amount, wider in its application and subject to even more complicated legal rules. The scheme was, in many cases, viewed as a tax-saving vehicle rather than a way to take a stake in new ventures and came to an end on 31 December 1993. The 1994 Finance Act introduced a new investment incentive scheme, the Enterprise Investment Scheme, which replaced the Business Expansion Scheme and the 1995 Finance Act provided for the approval of Venture Capital Trusts (VCTs), yet another investment incentive vehicle. Further refinements were included in FA 1997 and F(No 2)A 1997 and there were 45 pages of amending legislation in the Finance (No 2) Bill 1998. Although the avoidance of tax is the inducement to make such investments, the legislation includes a number of anti-avoidance provisions.

The view is sometimes held that professional advice is an expensive luxury which can be dispensed with. Nothing could be further from the truth. If it seems expensive it is because the mass of all-pervading legislation of recent years has made it dangerous to take any steps in commerce (or indeed in much else) without considering the application of statute law, statutory instruments and regulations. Professional advice taken at the outset often avoids difficulties and disputes at a later stage which may well prove far more expensive in legal costs.

13.2 THE CURRENT BUSINESS CLIMATE

Although smaller private companies were most affected by the recession, it must be hoped that the apparent upturn in the economy, and the various tax incentive schemes which have been introduced, will help to encourage the creation and expansion of new small businesses. Property values are at last beginning to move upwards again, although experience has shown that we should be wary of 'false dawns'. Despite recent problems, Lloyd's finally appears to have started to address and resolve some of its major difficulties and some may consider that it is a more viable proposition now that corporate underwriting is a reality. As always however the potential profits are likely to diminish, in line with the reduction in personal risk, and certainly for the foreseeable future it seems likely that Lloyd's will still have to rely on individuals who are prepared to put their personal assets at stake.

13.3 MINORITY HOLDINGS IN PRIVATE COMPANIES

13.3.1 Introduction

It was for many years a feature of company law that a private company was one which restricted the transfer of its shares and any company which did not do so was a public company. Under the Companies Act 1980 (a statute enacted largely as a move towards European uniformity) this distinction was swept away and although the words 'public' and 'private' are retained, their meanings are now quite different. A public company is defined in the Companies Act 1985 (a consolidating Act bringing together the provisions of the Companies Acts of 1948, 1967, 1976, 1980 and 1981), and any company not within that definition will be a private company. The principal distinction is that a public company (denoted at the end of its name by the letters 'plc' or by the words 'public limited company') must have an authorised and allotted minimum share capital which is at present £50,000 but which may be altered by Statutory Instrument by the Secretary of State. At least one-quarter of that allotted share capital of a public company must be paid up before it can commence business. No such minimum capital requirements exist in relation to private companies. A company need no longer restrict the transfer of its shares to be a private company under the new Act. References in this part of the chapter to 'private companies' are intended, generally, to refer to the smaller family company where control rests in the hands of a few shareholders who are probably the directors or related to the directors. As regards the transfer of shares see **13.3.4**.

A minority holding in a private company may be acquired in a number of ways: it may be inherited; it may be bought from an existing shareholder; it may arise when a company is newly formed to undertake the starting of a business venture; or it may arise on the allotment of shares by a company taking over an existing company or undertaking.

A minority holding is, for the purpose of this chapter, any holding of shares or other securities which does not give the holder control of the company, and thus includes a holding of non-voting shares or debentures. Assuming that a company has shares of one class only, of which each has one vote, a holding of less than 50 per cent is a minority holding. However, in some companies there are different classes of shares and shares of one class only, for example, might carry a vote, the others carrying no vote or giving the right to vote on certain specified matters only. In other companies there may be one class of shares carrying one vote each and another class of which the shares carry a hundred votes each, so that a holding, in nominal value, of more than half the company's issued capital does not necessarily carry control. Careful scrutiny of the company's capital structure is vital before making an investment in a private company.

13.3.2 Powers of the minority

At general meetings of a company, a vote is first taken by a show of hands (subject to anything in the articles of association), giving each member personally present one vote regardless of the size of his or her holding. Under common law any one member may demand a poll, the votes then being counted, normally on the basis of one for each share held. The articles may include a requirement that a poll must be demanded by more than one member, but such a requirement is limited by s 373 of the Companies Act 1985 so that, except for certain purposes, an article is void if it requires the demand for a poll to be made by more than five members, or the holders of more than one-tenth of the voting rights, or the holders of more than one-tenth of the paid-up capital entitled to vote.

When a poll is held, each member has (in the absence of any contrary provision in the articles) one vote for each share held. Thus on a poll, one member holding 60 per cent of the issued shares will be able to outvote a dozen members holding the other 40 per cent between them.

An ordinary resolution requires a simple majority of members voting, so that a minority shareholder cannot, in the face of determined opposition, prevent its being passed. However, a special or extraordinary resolution, which is necessary for certain fundamental decisions, requires a majority of three-quarters of members voting, so that on a poll, where each share carries a vote, the holder of 40 per cent of the issued shares, although a minority shareholder, could block such a resolution. An extraordinary resolution is required for, among other things, winding up a company that cannot, by reason of its liabilities, continue in business, and the articles of the company may require such a resolution for various other purposes. A special resolution is necessary for, *inter alia*:

(1) the alteration of a company's objects (although, in that case, the holders of not less than 15 per cent of the issued share capital may apply to the court to have the alteration cancelled);
(2) the alteration of a company's articles;
(3) the change of a company's name (subject to the approval of the Department of Trade and Industry);
(4) a reduction of capital (subject to the approval of the court);
(5) the re-registration of a public company as private or a private company as public under the 1985 Act;
(6) the re-registration of an unlimited company as limited; and
(7) the winding-up of a company voluntarily.

In addition to considering the effective powers of the majority, it must be remembered that the day-to-day running of the company's business is in the hands of the directors. As a last resort, majority shareholders can remove and appoint directors; minority shareholders cannot. In this connection it is important to note that most companies' articles of association preclude the payment of a dividend in excess of that recommended by the directors. If, therefore, the directors feel it is desirable for any reason to retain the profits, or the bulk of the profits, within the company rather than distribute them by way of dividend, minority shareholders may find that they are not receiving a satisfactory return on their investments and, even with the assistance of the majority shareholders, there may be little they can effectively do about it.

Arising out of the matters discussed in the previous paragraph, it will be appreciated that the majority could deal with the affairs of a company in a way which might be to the detriment of the interests of the minority, particularly where the minority controls 25 per cent or less of the voting power. The law, however, provides protection for an oppressed minority in two ways. First, the minority may petition the court to wind up the company on the ground that it is just and equitable to do so. This is, in many cases, an unsatisfactory course to pursue since the assets will be sold at their break-up value, the goodwill will disappear and the minority will not have achieved its object, namely that the company should continue to operate but that its interests should be safeguarded. Secondly, the minority may petition the court for relief under s 459 of the Companies Act 1985.

Protection under the 1948 Act was provided where the court was of the opinion that the company's affairs were being conducted in a manner oppressive to some part of the members (including the petitioner) and that to wind up the company would unfairly prejudice that part of the members although the facts would justify winding-up on the grounds that to wind up would be just and equitable. The court, on being so persuaded, could make any order which it thought fit. There is a considerable body of authority about what constitutes oppression for this purpose.

Under s 459 of the Companies Act 1985, protection is afforded by the court if it is satisfied that the conduct of the company's affairs is 'unfairly prejudicial to the interests' of some part of the members. A petition may also be brought under this provision based on 'any actual or proposed act or omission' of the company. The meaning of 'unfairly prejudicial' is not defined and awaits judicial interpretation.

13.3.3 Liability for uncalled capital

The essential feature of a limited company is that the liability of its shareholders is limited to the capital they put in or agree to put in, and no further demands can be made on them by the company or its creditors except where shares are issued which are not fully paid. The holder of such shares may be called upon by the company to pay up the unpaid balance, and failure to pay on a call may result in forfeiture of the shares. Any holder of partly paid shares must therefore always bear in mind that a contingent liability attaches to them. If the additional capital is required for development of the business, it will probably be all to the good. It sometimes happens though, that it is needed because the company is in difficulties and may amount to throwing good money after bad.

13.3.4 Transfer of shares

Difficulties may arise in connection with the disposal of a minority holding of shares in a private company. One of the hallmarks of a private company under the Companies Act 1948 was that it restricted transfers of its shares, and if the articles did not so provide, it was not a private company. The usual form, following reg 3 of Table A in Pt II of Sched 1 to the Companies Act 1948, provided that 'the directors may, in their absolute discretion and without assigning any reason therefore, decline to register any transfer of any share, whether or not it is a fully paid share.' It follows that, in such cases, the board must approve the proposed new shareholder and, where the articles are in the form set out above, the court will not inquire into the directors' reasons for refusing to register a transfer if none are given. Thus, whatever the value of the shares might be in terms of the assets and liabilities disclosed in the company's balance sheet, it may well be difficult to find a purchaser at anything approaching that value. The Companies Act 1948, s 28, which made restrictions on transfers essential for a private company, was repealed by the Companies Act 1985. There is nothing to prevent a private company from imposing such a restriction in its articles and in the case of any company whose articles already include it, it will remain in force unless the articles are amended. The articles of any company in which it is proposed to invest should therefore be examined with this point in view. The new Table A (under the Companies Act 1985), which sets out a suggested form 8 for the articles of association of a company, does not include any provisions relating to the refusal of directors to register a transfer of fully paid shares, but it is not unusual to see an express provision to that effect included in the articles of association of private companies.

Dealing with shares in a private company is often also restricted by a provision in the articles that a member wishing to dispose of his shares must first offer them to the other members at their fair value which is frequently determined in the absence of agreement between the intending seller and the directors, by the auditors, or an independent chartered accountant. The articles should therefore be examined with this in mind and also with a view to discovering whether, on death, a member's shares may pass to his or her personal representatives to be dealt with according to the will. In addition minority shareholders who are employees might be required under the articles of association to transfer their shares on ceasing to be employed by the company in question.

13.3.5 Loans

An investor may prefer to put money into a company by way of loan rather than by purchasing shares. A loan may be charged on all or any of the company's assets or its uncalled capital, or may be on a debenture, secured or unsecured. The nature of a debenture is difficult to define and Lindley J said in *British India Steam Navigation Co v IRC* (1881) 7 QBD 165, at p 172, '. . . what the correct meaning of "debenture" is I do not know. I do not find anywhere any precise definition of it'.

It is always necessary to proceed with caution when lending to a company. Its memorandum and articles should be inspected to ensure that the borrowing is *intra vires*, and the terms of any loan or debenture must be clearly set out and agreed. Independent professional advice is essential. In particular, where the lender is the settlor in relation to a settlement of which the trustees or a beneficiary are participators of the company, quite unexpected income tax liabilities may arise under s 677 of the Income and Corporation Taxes Act 1988 when the loan is repaid.

Money invested in a company by way of loan will normally entitle the lender to interest at a fixed rate. If the company fails investors should not, if adequately secured, be out of pocket: if the company prospers they will receive their interest regularly, and in due course the loan will be repaid, but they will not share in the prosperity of the undertaking.

13.3.6 Taxation

Two applications of taxation must be borne in mind. First, prior to 6 April 1999, when a dividend was received, a 'tax credit' was given equal in amount to the income tax at the rate of 20 per cent which would have been payable on the aggregate of the dividend and the tax credit. The company became liable to pay advance corporation tax (ACT) on the dividend at a rate of 20 per cent on the aggregate, such ACT ranking as a credit against the company's corporation tax liability. However, with effect from 6 April 1999, ACT was abolished, and the tax credit available to investors was reduced to 10 per cent. Higher rate taxpayers will be given relief for the tax credit, and the total of the net dividend and the notional tax credit will be taxed at a special rate of 32.5 per cent. Basic rate taxpayers will have no further tax liability.

Secondly, if and when shares are disposed of and a chargeable gain results, capital gains tax may become payable. The Finance Act 1988 changed the base date from 1965 to 1982 which favoured many long-term investors, but that Finance Act also unified the rates of tax on income and capital gains so that the maximum rate of capital gains tax increased from 30 to 40 per cent.

Incidentally, a notional capital gain may arise where assets are given away or disposed of for consideration which is less than their full open market value. A person who makes such a gift or sale at an undervalue is treated as if he or she had received full market value. However, it may be possible for gains arising on such transactions to be deferred or 'held over'. The Finance Act 1989 abolished the general right to hold over gains on gifts, but the hold over provisions continue to apply to gifts of business property (and shares in unquoted trading companies generally fall within this category).

The tax payable on a capital gain arising from the sale of shares on 5 April 1999 will normally be computed as follows:

Sale proceeds	x
Less incidental costs of disposal	x
	x
Less cost/31 March 1982 value	x
Less Indexation up to the amount of the gain (adjustment for inflation based on the increase in the RPI from acquisition to 5 April 1998)	x
Less capital losses on other transactions in the year	x
Less £6,800 annual exemption – £7,100 from 6 April 1999 (unless utilised against other gains)	
Less capital losses brought forward (if any)	?
Net gains taxed at either 20%, 23% or 40% (20% or 40% from 6 April 1999)	x

Indexation relief ceased on 6 April 1998, and is replaced with taper relief. This has the effect of reducing the chargeable gain by a fixed percentage, according to the number of years the investment has been held. The maximum relief is 75 per cent for business assets and 40 per cent for non-business assets, and becomes available when the asset has been held for ten complete tax years, after 5 April 1998. However, a 'bonus' year will be given for assets which were held on 16 March 1998.

13.3.7 Losses

Looking on the gloomy side, it is possible that a loss may arise on the sale of shares in a private company, or on its liquidation. Such a loss may arise because investors cannot recoup their original investment, but even where they do get their money back, an allowable loss could still have arisen for disposals made prior to 6 April 1995 because of indexation (ie the adjustment made to reflect inflation and calculated as a percentage of the allowable cost reflecting the increase in the RPI during the period in which the investment has been held).

A major change was included in the 1994 Finance Act, which limited the amount of indexation relief which could be claimed for disposals made after 29 November 1993. The initial text of the Bill provided that, for such disposals, indexation relief could only be used to reduce chargeable gains to nil and would not be available to create, or increase, an allowable capital loss.

However, following representations, the Chancellor tabled an amendment to the Finance Bill (now incorporated in the Finance Act 1994) which provided for transitional relief for individuals, and trustees of settlements made before 30 November 1993. For losses realised on disposals made during the period from 30 November 1993 to 5 April 1995, indexation relief was available up to a maximum of £10,000. This indexation relief had first be used to reduce the net chargeable gains for 1993–94 to the level of the taxpayer's annual exempt amount of £5,800. Any unused indexation losses could be carried forward and used, with any indexation losses on disposals during 1994–95, to reduce chargeable gains for 1994–95. Any such indexation losses which could not be used during 1994–95 were not available to carry forward to 1995–96 and later years.

Example 1 – disposals prior to 30 November 1993

An individual invests £10,000 in December 1989. On 14 June 1993 he sells for £11,000. However, the RPI has increased by 18 per cent between 1989 and 1993. Before indexation he has a gain of £1,000 but after taking this into account he has an allowable capital loss of £800.

Example 2 – disposals between 30 November 1993 and 5 April 1995

The circumstances are similar to those in Example 1, but the sale takes place on 31 March 1994. Assuming the RPI has increased by 20 per cent between 1989 and 1994, there is an indexation loss of £1,000. This indexation loss can be set off against other gains arising for 1993–94, which are in excess of the annual exemption of £5,800. Any balance can be carried forward for use in 1994–95. If this cannot be utilised in 1994–95, no relief can be carried forward to 1995–96 and subsequent years. This example also assumes that other indexation losses arising during the period 30 November 1993 to 5 April 1995, when added to this indexation loss, do not exceed £10,000.

Example 3 – disposals after 5 April 1995

The circumstances are similar to those of Example 1, but the sale takes place on 6 December 1996. In this case the indexation relief is limited to the amount of the unindexed gain, ie £1,000, and no capital loss is created.

Reinvestment relief

Reinvestment relief was first introduced in the March 1993 budget as a relief for entrepreneurs on the selling of their own business. It was only given real substance in the 1994 Finance Act when the relief was extended for disposals made after 29 November 1993, and became available for *any* capital gain where the gain was reinvested in shares in a qualifying unquoted company. The 1995 Finance Act contained further extensions to the relief so that it was available for gains reinvested in Enterprise Investment Schemes and Venture Capital Trusts.

Example

Wendy sells her shares in SAL Ltd in December 1996, for £20,000. She originally purchased the shares in January 1985 for £5,000. In May 1996 Wendy invested £10,000 in ordinary shares in a Venture Capital Trust. Wendy's capital gains tax position would be as follows:

	£	£
Proceeds		20,000
Less:		
Cost	5,000	
Indexation relief (say)	3,000	
		8,000
Net gain		12,000
Less reinvestment relief		(10,000)
Net chargeable gain		£2,000

> If Wendy was a higher rate taxpayer, her combined income tax and capital gains tax relief could amount to 60 per cent (20 per cent income tax relief for the investment in the venture capital trust, and 40 per cent deferral of capital gains tax).

Reinvestment relief was abolished from 6 April 1998, but was partially replaced by EIS and VCT deferral relief which is incorporated in the rules for each of these investments.

Capital losses are not normally available to be set against an individual's income, although they do attract capital gains tax relief. However, where individuals have subscribed for ordinary shares in a qualifying trading company and incur an allowable loss on disposing of the shares, they may claim relief from income tax instead of capital gains tax. This provision is to be found in s 574 of the Income and Corporation Taxes Act 1988. Note that this relief applies only where taxpayers have subscribed for the shares and not where they had bought them from another shareholder, unless that other is his or her spouse, and acquired the shares by subscription. It applies only to ordinary share capital and stock and the company must be a 'qualifying trading company' in the terms of the definition provided by the section, that is to say:

(1) it must exist wholly or mainly for the purpose of carrying on a trade (other than dealing in shares, securities, land or commodity futures);
(2) it must be resident in the UK from its incorporation until the date on which the shares or stock are disposed of; and
(3) none of its shares or stock must have been quoted on a recognised stock exchange at any time since 12 months before the date on which the shares or stock were issued.

The relief will be given if the loss results from a sale at arm's length for full consideration, a distribution on a winding-up, or a claim that the value has become negligible giving rise to a deemed disposal. Partial claims are not allowed and if the loss exceeds income for the year of claim the excess may either be carried forward or set off against capital gains. Information may be obtained from the Small Firms Service of the Department of Trade and Industry.

13.3.8 Loans

Until relatively recently, professional advisers normally recommended that a person making a loan to a private company should do so on terms which made the loan a debt on a security. This is because such loans constitute an asset for capital gains tax purposes whereas normal loans are outside the scope of capital gains tax (which is fine until the investor seeks relief for a capital loss). As a general principle, losses are available to offset capital gains only if they arise from assets which are chargeable assets for capital gains purposes.

As already stated, as a general principle, a debt on a security does constitute an asset for capital gains tax purposes. This definition is itself obscure.

There is a further problem that even where a loan constitutes a debt on a security, relief may be withheld on the basis that the security is a 'qualifying corporate bond' (in this particular context, a qualifying corporate bond is one where the investor does not qualify for an allowable loss for capital gains tax purposes). It is possible to ensure that a debt on a security does not fall within the definition of a QCB, but it is necessary for the loan to have certain qualities and in particular the loan should normally contain provisions under which it may be converted into ordinary shares or preference shares. Professional advice is essential here.

Loans which are not debts on a security or QCBs

Even where a debt does not fall within the category considered above, it may in certain circumstances entitle the lender to relief as a capital loss if it becomes irrecoverable. The conditions which render the loan a qualifying loan for this purpose are in s 253 of the Taxation of Chargeable Gains Act 1992. These are as follows:

(1) The money lent must be used by the borrower wholly for the purposes of a trade carried on by him or her or for the setting-up of a trade subsequently carried on by him or her.

(2) The borrower must be resident in the UK. The Act does not say at what point the borrower must be so resident and neither does it require the business to be carried on here.

(3) The debt must not be a debt on a security. If it is it will fall within the provisions referred to previously.

13.3.9 Relief for financing costs

Interest paid on a loan to an individual is eligible for tax relief only if the money borrowed is used for certain purposes. These include the acquisition of an interest in a close company or in a partnership. In the case of a close company it must be used for the purchase of ordinary shares in a trading or estate company, or for the making of a loan to such a company to be used wholly and exclusively for the company's business. Individuals will be entitled to the relief if: (1) they hold not less than 5 per cent of the company's ordinary share capital; or (2) they hold some part thereof, however small, and have in the period between the application of the loan and the payment of the interest been personally engaged in the conduct of the business in the case of a partnership, and 'worked for the greater part of his time in the actual management or conduct of the company', in the case of a company. During the same period he or she must not have recovered any capital from the company or partnership. For details of the complex provisions regarding this tax relief reference must be made to ss 360 and 362 of the Income and Corporation Taxes Act 1988.

13.3.10 Conclusion

It will be appreciated that many problems may arise in connection with company law and tax law. The latter in particular has become a matter of great complexity and specialist advice should always be taken. When all the legal hurdles are overcome, the sky's the limit and, if all goes well, the end result may be that the company 'goes public' or is taken over by a public company, leaving the shareholder with readily realisable shares in a company which may be or become a household name.

13.4 PRIVATE INVESTMENT COMPANIES

The first part of this chapter is concerned primarily with trading companies, but much of what has been said applies equally to private investment companies. These are companies which do not carry on a trade but invest, usually either in real property or in stock, shares and similar securities, and receive rents, dividends and interest. The line between property investment and property dealing companies is a difficult one to draw and presents a problem which the courts have often been called upon to solve. The question is essentially one of intention, but it is not always easy to decide how the available evidence (which may be scanty) should be interpreted. Some of the differences between dealing or trading companies on the one hand and investment companies on the other are dealt with below.

First, when a property is disposed of at a gain, the gain in the hands of a dealing company is part of its trading profit and is taxed at the appropriate rate of corporation tax. Where the disposal is made by an investment company, the gain may be a chargeable gain as defined for capital gains tax purposes and taxed as such. Secondly, an investment company is charged to corporation tax *prima facie* on the full amount of its income and must make a management expenses claim by virtue of which a deduction is allowed for the cost of management. Management expenses (nowhere defined in the legislation) are usually less than the expenses allowable against trading profits. Thirdly, an investment company, if it is a 'close investment-holding company', is less favourably treated than a trading company as regards distributions.

Because of provisions contained in the 1989 Finance Act, the company is generally ineligible for the small companies corporation tax rate. This means that it has to pay tax on its profits at the full 30 per cent rate rather than at 20 per cent. Furthermore, restrictions may apply to repayment claims for tax deemed to be withheld from dividends declared by the company.

In general the capital gains tax treatment of gains and losses arising on shares and loans to private trading companies applies equally to shares and loans involving private investment companies. However, there is one important difference: it is not possible to claim income tax relief under the Income and Corporation Taxes Act 1988, s 574 as described in **13.3.7**.

A further disadvantage which attaches to an investment company (or indeed to any company which makes chargeable gains) is that a double tax liability may arise on capital gains. On the sale of an asset by the company, tax becomes payable (as explained above) on the chargeable gain. That net gain increases the company's assets and hence the value of the member's shares in it. On a disposal of those shares a further chargeable gain may arise.

A private investment company has larger funds at its disposal than each individual shareholder and may thereby take advantage of opportunities not presented to the smaller investor. Furthermore, the minimum commission charged by a stockbroker may add disproportionately to the cost of investments of the smaller investor. Both these advantages, however, attach to any method by which small investors join together. So long as the basic agreement governing the project is carefully drawn up and fully understood by all those co-operating, a joint co-operative investment scheme may avoid the drawbacks of a private investment company while at the same time possessing many of the advantages. The taxation of unapproved investment companies (whether private or public) and their shareholders is discussed at **7.7**.

13.5 ENTERPRISE INVESTMENT SCHEME

13.5.1 Introduction

In his budget in November 1993, the Chancellor announced a new investment incentive scheme, intended to provide a 'targeted incentive' for new equity investment in unquoted trading companies, and to encourage outside investors to introduce new finance and expertise. The Business Expansion Scheme (BES), introduced by the Finance Act 1983, came to an end on 31 December 1993, and was replaced with the Enterprise Investment Scheme (EIS), with effect from 1 January 1994. There are numerous and complex conditions which must be satisfied in relation to the investor, the trade, and the investment. Although many of the rules included in the provisions were common to both the EIS and its predecessor, the BES, there are some important differences.

For shares issued by a qualified unquoted trading company relief is given to investors at the lower rate of 20 per cent on the amount subscribed for the shares in the year of assessment in which the shares are issued or the income tax payable, if lower. Tax reliefs, which are expressed in terms of tax, double taxation credits and tax deducted at source from annual payments, are ignored for this purpose.

In addition to income tax relief, an individual may claim capital gains tax deferral relief in respect of any other capital gain which is reinvested in an EIS during the period beginning one year prior and ending three years after the disposal which creates the capital gain. The maximum investment which may attract relief for 1998–99 and future years is £150,000 per annum (£100,000 for 1997–98 and earlier years). These limits apply to husband and wife separately. It is also possible to carry back up to half of an amount invested by an individual between 6 April and 5 October in any year to the previous tax year, subject to a maximum of £25,000 (£15,000 for 1997–98 and earlier years). However, the relief carried back must not take the individual over the limit for the previous year.

Unlike reinvestment relief, which applied prior to 6 April 1998, the CGT deferral relief contained within the EIS legislation does not require that an EIS income tax claim must also be made. The income tax relief and the CGT relief can be claimed independently, and either can be claimed without the other. Only individuals are able to claim both income tax and CGT deferral relief, as trustees are only able to claim CGT relief.

Provided that the shares have been held for at least five years, the shares are exempt from capital gains tax on disposal. Unlike investments in the BES however, a loss on the shares' disposal both before or after the five-year period has elapsed may still attract income tax or capital gains tax relief.

There is no maximum amount of money which a company can raise in a particular tax year under the EIS. Prior to 6 April 1998 this was limited to £5m. In addition, participation is restricted to companies with gross assets of less than £15m before an investment, and no more than £16m after it.

It must be borne in mind that one of the conditions for the granting of this relief is that the company must, throughout the relevant period (see **13.5.4**), be unquoted. This means that the company's shares or securities must not be dealt in on either The Stock Exchange or USM. Although a company's shares may be dealt in on the AIM, this will not in itself disqualify it, but it is probable that the £15m gross assets test will rule out many AIM companies.

If, at the end of the five-year period, the company is still unquoted, investors may find themselves effectively locked in. If there is no quotation and investors cannot find a purchaser for their shares they can realise their investment only if the company either disposes of its assets and winds up or sells its undertaking to a quoted company, so that its shareholders finish up with either quoted shares or cash. The directors may, however, be reluctant to accept the loss of directorships which would follow a winding-up and might well follow a take-over.

It must also be remembered that the EIS was introduced to encourage the investment of risk capital and that that is exactly what such an investment is. Tax benefits may follow an investment under the scheme but there is no certainty that the investment will be successful. Companies in commercial enterprises often have difficulty in producing a prospectus which is of much use to the prospective investor. Projections, by directors, of future profits should be read with caution. The cost of such professional reports as are required for a public flotation will often be prohibitive for new, small and possibly speculative enterprises.

13.5.2 Tax relief available

If all the conditions set out in **13.5.3** are complied with, a claim for relief may be made. It must be accompanied by a certificate from the company (authorised by the Inspector of Taxes) to the effect that it has, at all necessary times, complied with the conditions set out in **13.5.4**. The claim may be made at any time after the company has carried on the qualifying trade or activity for four months and must be made not later than two years after the end of the year of assessment in which the shares were issued. If the four-month period expires after the end of that year, it must be made within two years after the end of that period.

If a claim is allowed before the end of the qualifying period (see **13.5.4**) and any subsequent event results in a contravention of any of the conditions, the relief will be withdrawn. If the company fails to carry on the trade for four months by reason of a winding-up or dissolution for *bona fide* commercial reasons and not as part of a tax-saving scheme, the claim will not fail for that reason. Provision is made in the legislation requiring that information leading to a loss of relief must be sent to the Revenue.

In practice, a claim would normally be included in the claim to relief page of the self-assessment tax return. A claim is only permissible if you have already received the appropriate certificate, but it is not necessary to submit this with the return. It should however be kept safely in case it is necessary to provide it at a future date.

Example of EIS income tax relief

Malcolm's total gross income for 1998–99 is £40,000. He inherits £50,000 during the year, which he decides to invest in a qualifying EIS company. All his taxable income comes from an employment.

Malcolm's income tax position for 1998–99 is:

	£
Total income	40,000
Less personal allowance	4,195
Taxable income	35,805
Tax thereon:	
£4,300 at 20%	860
£22,800 at 23%	5,244
£8,705 at 40%	3,482
	9,586
Less EIS relief – lower of	
(a) £50,000 × 20% = £10,000 or,	
(b) £9,586	(9,586)
Tax payable	Nil

13.5.3 Individuals eligible for relief

For individuals to be entitled to the relief under the BES they had to be resident and ordinarily resident in the UK at the time of issue. This requirement does not apply to investors in the EIS, and relief is available for non-residents if they are liable to UK income tax. There is a further relaxation in that an investor can become a paid director, without forfeiting entitlement to relief under the EIS. This is, however, subject to the proviso that the individual was not connected with the company or its trade prior to the issue of the EIS shares.

The words 'connected with' are given a very wide meaning. An individual is connected with a company if he or she:

(1) or an associate (defined below) is an employee of the company or of its partner, or is him- or herself its partner or is a paid director of the company or of a company which is in partnership with it;

(2) possesses (directly or indirectly) or is entitled to acquire more than 30 per cent of the company's issued ordinary share capital, loan

capital and issued share capital, voting rights or such rights as would entitle him or her to more than 30 per cent of the assets available to equity holders on a winding-up;

(3) has power to secure that the company's affairs are conducted in accordance with his or her wishes by means of the holding of shares or the possession of voting power of that or another company or by virtue of any power in the articles or other document regulating that or any other company; or

(4) is a party to a reciprocal arrangement under which some other person subscribes for shares in a company with which the individual (or any other individual who is a party to the arrangement) is connected.

For the purposes of (1) above, 'associate' means:

(1) the individual's husband or wife, parent or remoter forebear, child or remoter issue or any partner;

(2) a trustee of any settlement in relation to which the settlor is or was the individual or any of the persons mentioned in (1) (other than a partner), whether living or dead; or

(3) where the individual is interested in any shares or obligations of the company which are (with certain exceptions) subject to a trust or form part of a deceased's estate, any other person interested therein. It may, in this connection, be difficult to ascertain who is an associate and who is not.

The shares must be held in a qualifying company for at least five years and any income tax relief claimed will be clawed back if shares are disposed of within the five-year period.

However although income tax relief may not be available, or withdrawn because the investor is treated as connected, CGT deferral relief may still be due.

13.5.4 Qualifying companies

Two expressions used in connection with the qualification of a company require explanation.

(1) *The 'relevant period'.* In relation to 'qualifying companies' and 'qualifying trades' this means the period of three years beginning with the issue of the shares or, if the company was not at the time of such issue carrying on a qualifying trade, the period of three years from the commencement of such a trade.

(2) *A 'qualifying subsidiary'.* This means a subsidiary company which is not less than 70 per cent (90 per cent prior to 17 March 1998) owned and controlled by the parent company, no arrangements

being in existence by virtue of which it could cease to be so owned and controlled. That condition must be satisfied until the end of the 'relevant period' unless there is an earlier winding-up or dissolution for *bona fide* commercial reasons which is not part of a tax-avoidance arrangement and on which the subsidiary's net assets are distributed not more than three years after the commencement of the winding-up. Prior to FA 1997 the subsidiary had to exist wholly or substantially to carry on qualifying activities or be a 'dormant' company, ie one which had no corporation tax profits and did not include the making of investments as part of its business. Following FA 1997, this rule was relaxed and the business of the group as a whole is now considered. Relief is not now denied unless the non-qualifying activities form a substantial part of the whole group's activities.

The conditions to be complied with by the company are as follows:

(1) It must, throughout the 'relevant period', be an unquoted company which must exist wholly or 'substantially wholly' for the purpose of carrying on wholly or mainly in the UK one or more 'qualifying trades' (see **13.5.5**) or must carry on a business which consists wholly of either:
   (a) holding shares or securities of, or making loans to, one or more 'qualifying subsidiaries'; or
   (b) both (a) *and* the carrying on wholly or mainly in the UK of one or more 'qualifying trades'.
(2) The company's share capital must not, at any time in the 'relevant period', include any issued shares that are not fully paid up.
(3) The company must not, at any time in the relevant period, control (whether alone or with any connected person) another company or have a 51 per cent subsidiary or be controlled by another company (whether alone or with a connected person) or be a 51 per cent subsidiary nor must any arrangements be in existence at any time during the relevant period which could bring the company within any of the prohibited situations. An exception is made, however, for companies having subsidiaries which are themselves qualifying companies under (1) above.
(4) The original rules provided that a company's interest in land could not exceed one-half of its total assets. This condition was however removed with effect from 29 November 1994, under the provisions of the Finance Act 1995.

Another significant change from the BES rules is that qualifying companies can now include foreign companies. Provided that they trade in the United Kingdom, they will not be required to be incorporated or resident in the United Kingdom.

13.5.5 Qualifying trades

Some guidance was given by the Revenue, in a Statement of Practice dated 12 September 1986, of what, in their view, is meant by carrying on a trade 'wholly or mainly in the United Kingdom' referred to in **13.5.4**. Each case is determined on its facts including the 'totality of the activities of the trade'. Thus, regard is had to such factors as the location of capital assets, and the places where purchasing, manufacturing, selling and other things are done. The carrying on of some activities outside the UK does not disqualify the company if, in the Revenue's words, 'over one-half of the aggregate of these activities takes place within the country'. The phrase 'over one-half' suggests that some precise measurement must be possible. The Statement of Practice goes on to say that a company would not be excluded from relief solely because its output is exported, or its raw materials imported, or storage or marketing facilities exist overseas.

A 'qualifying trade' is one which does not to any substantial extent comprise:

(1) dealing in commodities, shares, securities, land or futures;
(2) dealing in goods otherwise than in an ordinary trade of wholesale or retail distribution;
(3) banking, insurance, moneylending, debt-factoring, hire-purchase financing or other financial activities;
(4) leasing (except for short term), chartering or ships;
(5) receiving royalties or licence fees;
(6) providing legal or accountancy services;
(7) oil extraction activities; or
(8) providing services of the nature of those set out in (1) to (7) for a trade carried on by any person who controls the trade carried on by the company.

A trade under (5) above is not disqualified if the company carrying on the trade is engaged, throughout the relevant period, in the production of films or in research and development and if all royalties and licence fees received by it in that period are for films produced by it, or of sound recordings or other products arising from such films or from research and development.

In addition to the restrictions listed above, the Finance (No 2) Bill included further exclusions of the types of activity that will qualify from 17 March 1998. These are:

- property development;
- farming or market gardening;
- holding, managing or occupying woodlands or any other forestry activities, or timber production;
- operating or managing, or managing property used as, hotels or comparable establishments;

- operating or managing, or managing property used as, nursing or residential care homes.

The trade must be carried on on a commercial basis and with a view to realising profits. It must have been carried on by the company for four months before the relief will be allowed and, if not carried on at the time of the issue, must be begun within two years thereafter.

13.5.6 Qualifying investments

For the investment to qualify for relief it must itself comply with a number of conditions:

(1) it must be made by the individual on his or her own behalf;
(2) the shares must be taken by subscription and not by purchase from an existing shareholder;
(3) the shares must be new ordinary shares which, throughout the five years from the date of issue, carry no present or future preferential rights to dividends, assets on a winding-up, or to redemption; and
(4) the shares must be issued for the purpose of raising money for a qualifying trade or activity carried on, or to be carried on, by the company.

The 1995 Finance Act contained provisions which relaxed the rules for shares issued after 28 November 1994 to allow relief to individuals, even where they are involved in the control of another company carrying on a similar trade.

Although the investment must be made by an individual, to qualify for relief, it may be made through an approved investment fund. Particulars regarding some of such funds are obtainable from the British Venture Capital Association.

13.5.7 Withdrawal of relief

Relief for investment in an EIS will be clawed back if an investor disposes of the shares within a period of five years, unless the disposal arises because the company has gone into liquidation. In these circumstances further income tax or capital gains tax relief may be due to the investor. Where the investor receives no payment as a result of the liquidation, the net amount of his investment may qualify as a capital loss.

The comments set out above should be taken as a guide only. They do not cover every detail of the proposed legislation but should help in identifying most of the difficulties to be faced in crossing this morass of regulations.

13.5.8 Venture capital trusts (VCTs)

In his 1993 budget the Chancellor announced proposals to create a new relief for investment in venture capital trusts. This announcement was followed by a consultative document, and the 1995 Finance Act contained provisions introducing the relief with effect from 6 April 1995.

VCTs are companies which are similar to investment trusts and to obtain approval they must meet a number of conditions, in particular:

(1) the ordinary share capital of a VCT must have been quoted on The Stock Exchange;
(2) the VCT must not retain more than 15 per cent of the income that it has derived from shares or securities;
(3) the income received by the VCT must have been derived wholly or mainly from shares or securities;
(4) the value of investments held by the VCT must consist of at least 70 per cent of qualifying shares or securities;
(5) at least 30 per cent of the value of a VCT's qualifying holdings must be made up of ordinary shares;
(6) the value of a VCT's holding in any one company must not exceed 15 per cent of its total investments.

It may be possible for a VCT to be granted provisional approval provided that the 70 per cent, and 30 per cent conditions mentioned in (4) and (5) above will be met within three years, and the other conditions in the current or next accounting period. This provisional approval will be withdrawn if the VCT fails to meet the conditions within these time periods.

The Finance Act included changes to the rules, which govern the types of company in which VCTs may invest, and these were brought into line with those applicable for EIS relief with effect from 17 March 1998.

Further rules were also introduced for VCTs, for accounting periods ending after 1 July 1997, although not in respect of funds raised by the issue of shares before 2 July 1997. These were:

(1) guaranteed loans and securities cannot qualify as part of the fixed proportion of qualifying investments which a VCT must hold; and
(2) VCTs must ensure that ordinary non-preferential shares represent a minimum of 10 per cent of their total investment in a company.

13.5.9 Qualifying holdings

These must consist of holdings in unquoted companies which exist wholly or mainly for the purpose of carrying on a qualifying trade in the United Kingdom. For these purposes a qualifying trade is as defined for the EIS, and the gross assets of the unquoted company must not exceed £16m, immediately prior to the VCT's investment.

Income tax relief

Relief can be claimed by resident individuals aged 18 or over, and is available in two different ways.

First income tax relief at the rate of 20 per cent is given for amounts subscribed for new ordinary shares in the VCT, although the amount subscribed in any one year must not exceed £100,000. The relief is withdrawn unless the shares are held for at least five years.

In addition, dividends from ordinary shares held in VCTs are exempt from income tax, to the extent that the value of the shares acquired each year does not exceed £100,000.

Capital gains tax

Where investments in VCTs have qualified for income tax relief, disposals after five years are exempt from capital gains tax.

Capital gains deferral relief is also available for investments in VCTs, provided that the VCT shares for which the individual subscribes are issued during a period beginning 12 months before, and ending 12 months after, the date of disposal of the asset creating the capital gain which is to be deferred.

In common with investments in the EIS the deferred gain may be reinstated if the investor disposes of the shares, other than to his or her spouse, or ceases to be resident in the United Kingdom within five years of the issue of the VCT shares.

The relief is also withdrawn if the company ceases to be a qualifying VCT within three years of the issue of the shares, or within three years of the commencement of trading, if later, or the investor ceases to qualify for the 20 per cent income tax relief.

13.6 DORMANT PARTNERSHIPS

13.6.1 Introduction

It is not unusual for a person commencing a trade to find him- or herself short of capital. In such circumstances an investor who is persuaded of the trade's potential viability may be prepared to put up the capital but not want to play any active part in the carrying on of the business. The investor is then a 'dormant' or 'sleeping' partner. Since partners are generally entitled to take part in the running of the business, this arrangement must be the subject of a special agreement.

Unless the business name consists of the names of all the partners, it must comply with the provisions of the Business Names Act 1985. This Act governs names which may and may not be used for business purposes and how and where they must be disclosed. A register of such names was formerly maintained but was closed in February 1982.

13.6.2 Loan creditors

It is important to distinguish dormant partners from loan creditors. If the investors receive a fixed rate of interest on their investment they are probably not partners at all. Under s 2 of the Partnership Act 1890 the receipt of a share of the profits is *prima facie* evidence of partnership, although the receipt of such a share or of interest at a rate varying with the profits does not of itself make the lender a partner. This apparent contradiction was explained by North J, in *Davis v Davis* [1894] 1 Ch 393, and it appears from his judgment that the Act means that all the relevant facts must be taken together, no special weight being attached to the sharing of profits. It is difficult to see how the Act could be intended to mean that, although, in fairness to North J, it is equally difficult to see that it could be intended to mean anything else either. In the majority of cases there is (and there certainly should be) a written agreement making the position clear. If the agreement so declares, and the name of the dormant partner is included in the firm's name, there is little doubt of the existence of a partnership.

13.6.3 Rights and liabilities

Once it is established that the 'investor' (to use a neutral term) is a dormant partner and not merely a loan creditor, certain rights arise. For example, he or she is entitled to inspect and take a copy of the firm's accounts and, in the absence of any agreement to the contrary, to investigate their contents.

A dormant partner is, generally, personally liable for the firm's debts even if the creditors were unaware of the partnership at the time when the debts arose. This liability extends to the whole of the partner's personal fortune. Such an arrangement can therefore carry considerable personal risk, although this can be curtailed by the formation of a 'limited partnership'.

Under the Limited Partnerships Act 1907 it is possible for partners to limit their liability to the amount contributed by them to the partnership at its inception, although there must always be at least one partner whose liability is unlimited. Limited partners may not receive back any of their capital so long as the partnership continues, and if any of it is returned to them, their liability up to the amount of their original contribution will remain. They are, of course, entitled to draw out their share of the firm's profits.

Limited partners must always be dormant partners. Should they take any active part in the running of the business, the limitation of their liability is lost, and it will then extend to the whole of the partnership's debts and to the full extent of their personal assets.

The law relating to dormant partnerships is liberally sprinkled with traps for the unwary, and the law relating to limited partnerships is particularly unsatisfactory. No partnership of any sort should be entered into without taking legal advice, and although the law does not require a partnership agreement to be reduced to writing, it is always desirable that it should be. Whatever the relations may have been at the outset, it is only too easy for the partner entering too readily into informal arrangements to find the whole of his or her personal estate at risk in respect of liabilities which the partner played no part in incurring. It is when things start to go wrong that dissensions occur, and by then it may be too late to correct matters which should have been dealt with at the outset.

13.6.4 Taxation

A trading partnership, like any other trader, is normally assessed to tax on the basis of the profits of the trading year ending during the tax year of assessment. For example, if the accounts are taken to 31 December, the profits for the year ended 31 December 1998 form the basis of the assessment for the tax year 1998–99. This general rule is subject to various complications relating to the opening years, the closing years, changes in partnership treated as a cessation, and losses. Having determined the amount of the assessment for, say 1998–99, that amount is apportioned among the partners in accordance with their profit-sharing arrangements for that fiscal year.

Earned income is defined in s 833(4)(c) of the Income and Corporation Taxes Act 1988 as income which is 'derived by the individual from the carrying on or exercise by him of his trade . . ., in the case of a partnership, as a partner personally acting therein'. Any partnership income not falling within that definition is investment income. Since a dormant partner (whether with limited liability or not) does not, by definition, act personally in the business, it must follow that any income derived from the partnership will be investment income. This will be of significance in relation to retirement pension schemes.

13.7 MEMBERSHIP OF LLOYD'S

13.7.1 Introduction

Some 300 years ago Edward Lloyd opened a coffee-house in the City which proved to be a popular meeting place for men with an interest in shipping. In 1692 he moved to larger premises on the corner of Lombard Street and Abchurch Lane, where the financial quarter had become well-established, which soon became known as a centre where ship-owners could take insurance cover. With the increasing size of ships and value of cargoes, the size of the risks grew and individual underwriters were obliged to join in syndicates, so creating the system which still functions today. Lloyd's itself, as in its coffee-house days, does no more than provide accommodation and facilities for the underwriters; it is not, and never has been, an insurer. Lloyd's was incorporated by Act of Parliament in 1871, and that and later Acts regulate the fundamental rules and authorise the making of byelaws by the members. An Act of 1911 authorised the underwriting of non-marine risks, regularising what had already become well-established practice.

Lloyd's of London published a business plan on 29 April 1993, which set out proposals intended to improve the profitability of Lloyd's by increasing capacity, cutting costs and capping losses arising prior to the 1986 account. However, the most fundamental proposal was to allow corporate membership of Lloyd's from the 1994 account. This introduced the concept of limited liability for the first time in the history of Lloyd's.

Members of Lloyd's (called 'Names') are grouped into syndicates and share in the syndicates' profits or losses. As regards losses, each member of a syndicate is liable only for his or her agreed share (unlike a partnership loss where each partner is jointly and separately liable for all losses) but at present that liability extends to the whole of a Name's assets. Generally, Names take no part in managing the affairs of their syndicate. They are thus entirely in the hands of their Underwriting Agent (see **13.7.2**).

Income and gains received by Names comprise:

(1) investment income and capital gains on deposits and reserve funds (see **13.7.2**);
(2) investment income and capital gains on premiums received and invested by the syndicate; and
(3) underwriting profits (excess of premiums over claims) if any.

It must not be overlooked that both capital and underwriting losses may also arise. Figures are produced three years in arrears.

Following a series of unprecedented disasters, further problems surfaced in 1991 with claims of fraud and mismanagement, and some syndicates remained open until the Reconstruction and Renewal plan was finally agreed, since they were unable to reinsure to close. Names suffered unprecedented losses.

Despite the drop in membership from the late 1980s, many Names increased their premium limits for 1996 and including corporate members the capacity of the market was over £11bn. Many non-corporate members, however, no longer have the readily realisable wealth formerly relied on (see **13.7.2**) and rely instead on bank guarantees secured against property.

It is suggested that much of the malaise stemmed from the Lloyd's Act 1982 which ruled that brokers could no longer own agencies managing syndicates. The intention of this was to prevent conflicts of interest but it probably resulted in brokers moving business elsewhere.

Certainly the problems of Lloyd's were considered. As well as many resignations there was much litigation and constant bad news which tended to scare off potential members. During 1996 Lloyd's announced details of a Reconstruction and Renewal plan, which involved the creation of a reinsurance company, Equitas, to reinsure 1992 and prior year liabilities. This gave Names an opportunity to end the uncertainty about past liabilities, and allow those who wished to leave Lloyd's, to do so.

Whilst it may be possible to reduce the element of risk by taking out high level stop loss insurance policies and entering into members' agency pooling arrangements (MAPAs), one cannot avoid the fact that under the present regime an individual Name accepts unlimited personal liability.

13.7.2 Application for individual membership

Aspiring members must satisfy Lloyd's that they are suitable to join their number. They must be sponsored by the existing Names, one of whom must be a director, employee or partner of the prospective Name's intended Members' Agent. The application form is posted in the Underwriting Room and the applicant is then interviewed by a sub-committee. The sub-committee, whatever other questions it may ask, always asks whether applicants clearly understand that they will be trading with unlimited liability. The liability is not limited to the wealth shown (see below) nor to the amount of the deposit (see below). In the event of a substantial claim arising, the whole of the applicant's personal estate is at risk.

It is generally recommended that members should spread their risk among a number of syndicates. Membership of one syndicate only may mean a heavy financial loss in the event of a major disaster. MAPAs, which were first introduced on 1 January 1994, allows its members to take a smaller share in a wider range of syndicates, and thus help to reduce the exposure of each Name.

At an early stage, and certainly before election, applicants must investigate the syndicate or syndicates which they hope to join. Assistance in the choice of syndicate may be obtained from a Members' Underwriting Agent (not the same as a Managing Agent, although they may be so in practice). The policy for investing syndicate funds and the likely premium income will be explained by the syndicate's Underwriting Agent (see below) and the result of the last seven 'closed years' will be made available. A 'closed year' is one in respect of which the underwriting account has been closed by reinsuring any outstanding liabilities, usually at the end of the third year. The applicant should also enquire about the establishment of personal reserves, transfer to the Special Reserve Fund, and the form of accounts.

Applications for membership must be approved by the Committee, who apply a means test to the applicant's readily realisable assets which include Stock Exchange securities, life policies at their surrender values, reversionary interests and real property but not the applicant's principal residence. Gold (up to 30 per cent of the total), which must be held by an approved bank in the form of bullion or coins, is valued at 70 per cent of market value. Such things as shares in private companies, jewellery and antiques are not included. An applicant needs to show that he has readily realisable assets worth £250,000.

Where the applicant's wealth comprises items not readily realisable but is in other respects satisfactory, the Committee will accept, in whole or in part, a guarantee or letter of credit from an approved bank, as collateral for which the principal residence may be included. The object of the means test is to ensure that as far as possible, funds will be available at short notice to meet a claim, however large it may be. A booklet entitled 'Membership: the Issues' is obtainable from Lloyd's and sets out all the information which an applicant should know.

13.7.3 Conditions of individual membership

The Members' Underwriting Agent controls the underwriting affairs of the underwriting members of his agency. The agent maintains the accounts and records and deals with taxation, reserves, investments and other day-to- day matters as well as watching the statistics which give a guide to current trends. It is also the agent's duty to ensure that the rules laid down by the Committee of Lloyd's are complied with. Every underwriting member enters into an agreement with the agent which sets out the terms and conditions on which the agent acts, including salary or fee and rate of commission.

Every individual underwriting member is required to deposit with the Corporation of Lloyd's approved investments or cash which the Corporation holds as trustee. The Lloyd's deposit must be maintained at a minimum of £25,000. For further details enquiries should be made to the deposits department at Lloyd's. The investing of the deposit may be delegated to the Underwriting Agent or may, within the Committee's rules, be dealt with by the member. The income arising on investments deposited remains the income of the member.

A member's premium limit is the maximum premium income which may be underwritten by him or her in any one year. It is allocated to the syndicate and is then divided among the members in proportions agreed in consultation with the agent. The limit may be increased or decreased according to the deposit's market value and may be raised if additional amounts are deposited and evidence of sufficient means is produced. If the limit is exceeded the member is normally be required increase the deposit.

An entrance fee is payable in cash on election and varies according to the category of membership. Entrance fees are not deductible from profits for tax purposes. An annual contribution to Lloyd's Central Fund is also required. The Fund was set up in 1926 for the protection of policyholders in the event of the inability of a member to meet his or her liabilities out of his or her syndicate's trust funds, deposit, reserves and personal assets. The reserve is the amount which, under the Rules, has to be set aside each year to meet the estimated cost of winding up the Name's underwriting accounts.

13.7.4 Taxation

The special provisions covering the taxation of the income of underwriters are in ss 450–457 of the Income and Corporation Taxes Act 1988, as amended by FAs 1993–1995. This changed the way in which Lloyd's Names were taxed from the 1994 underwriting account. The 1995 account profits will not be assessed for 1995–96, but in 1998–99, the year of distribution. In normal circumstances this change would have created a three-year period for which no syndicate profits were assessable (1994–95 to 1996–97). However, as a result of the Reconstruction and Renewal arrangements many Names were entitled to debt credits which were assessable for 1996–97. Briefly, the effect of the current legislation for underwriting years from the 1994 underwriting account is as follows.

Underwriting profits are assessed on the basis of the profits distributed during the year of assessment. Thus the profits of the underwriting year ending 31 December 1995 are assessed for the fiscal year 1998–99.

Underwriting profits are profits or gains arising from underwriting business or from assets forming part of a premium trust fund, and income arising from personal reserves and the Lloyd's deposit. However, capital gains arising from personal Lloyd's funds and deposits are not treated as part of Lloyd's trading income, and are added to other personal capital gains arising during the tax year.

A premium paid for reinsurance is deductible as an expense. Losses of an underwriting business are allowed against other income of the year of assessment in which they are incurred, or alternatively against that of the previous year if the underwriter was carrying on an underwriting business in that year. They cannot, however, be carried forward against general income of a later year but can be set against future underwriting profits, which includes personal Lloyd's income from the Lloyd's Deposit and Personal Reserves.

For many years it was possible for Names to transfer part of their underwriting profits into a Special Reserve Fund. The object of this fund was to provide a source of money which could be called on in years in which a loss arose. However the old style Special Reserve Fund was quite limited, in that only a maximum of £7,000 could be transferred each year and tax relief was only available at a rate equal to the difference between the basic rate and the higher rate of tax.

A new type of Special Reserve Fund was introduced with effect from the 1992 account, although any existing old style special reserves could be transferred to the new reserve fund. Transfers to the fund will qualify for both basic rate and higher rate relief, and it will be possible to transfer 50 per cent of Lloyd's profits into the reserve each year, providing that the value of the funds held in the reserve does not exceed 50 per cent of the Name's overall premium limit. Any income or gains arising from assets held in the reserve are exempt from income tax and capital gains tax.

Withdrawals from the reserve will be made to fund losses, cash calls, or on resignation or death. This will be treated as underwriting income of the Name at the time of withdrawal. The tax calculation will be based on the actual value of the withdrawal rather than the 'book values' of the assets comprising the withdrawal. In effect the increase in the value of the fund attributable to income and gains will not be taxed as it arises, but on withdrawal.

13.8 INVESTMENT IN ANOTHER'S EXPERTISE

The first difficulty in making an investment of this kind lies in discovering the innovator whose expertise is to be given financial backing. The innovator seeking capital has many avenues open. Investors may consult the National Research Development Corporation, the Council for Small Industries in Rural Areas, Investors in Industry Group plc (formerly known as the Industrial and Commercial Finance Corporation) or the Small Business Capital Fund. Alternatively they may look for capital through their bank or a merchant bank, through local accountants, solicitors or insurance brokers, through the Rotary Club or the Round Table, through the local branch of the British Institute of Management or through the Small Firms Council of the Confederation of British Industry. The prospective investor can approach any of these agencies to inquire whether they know of any worthwhile ideas for which backing is sought.

Once the innovator has been located, the venture's prospects must be carefully examined, not only by the investor's accountant but also by an expert in the technical field where appropriate. Inquiry should be made as to how much of the investor's own capital is being put into the venture. If they have little they cannot be expected to put much in, but their intentions in this respect indicate their real confidence in the venture. Plans should be carefully prepared and the amount required should be meticulously calculated, all contingencies being taken into account. The information required includes particulars of the product or process, with technical explanations and specifications of patents, if any. Its advantages over existing products or processes must be explained and the costs of development detailed, together with reasoned estimates of future sales. Mere hopes based on speculation will not do.

In general terms, an investor may back another's expertise by means of a private company, a partnership or a loan. A loan will probably be the least attractive method for two reasons. First, adequate security is unlikely to be available. Secondly, the income is limited to interest at a fixed rate, thus denying the lender any participation in profits should the venture prove an outstanding success – the greatest attraction of this type of investment. For private companies and partnerships, it is necessary to determine the appropriate proportionate interests of the investor who is putting in capital and the expert who is putting in expertise. Both may be of equal importance: indeed both are essential, but 50:50 holdings can mean deadlock and are better avoided if possible. This immediately gives rise to a problem which needs professional advice and probably tough negotiating.

Some of the legal aspects of the arrangement (including any liability for taxation on profits or gains arising) are dealt with in general terms earlier in this chapter. As has already been stressed, every case will present individual problems, and both commercial and professional advice should always be sought. Adequate financial and administrative control is essential for investors, and they will usually be wise to insist on their own accountant auditing the books and their representative keeping a close eye on the running of the business.

13.9 RACEHORSES

13.9.1 Introduction

Investing in racehorses is not for the faint-hearted. The rules regulating racing in this country are made by the Jockey Club from whom detailed information may be obtained. Anyone proposing to invest in a racehorse is presumably already well-acquainted with the turf and will know something about horses. Investment may be either in horses in training or in stallions. (Investment in stud farms and training establishments is discussed at **11.4.3**.)

The increase in the cost of buying and running a horse led to an expansion of syndicated ownership regulated (for horses in training) by the Jockey Club 'rules of racing'. New syndicates are, however, no longer accepted by the Jockey Club and where a horse is owned jointly it must now be by way of a legally enforceable partnership of which each member is registered as an owner. The number of partners is restricted (as it was for syndicate members) to 12. The partnership agreement (which should be drawn up with legal advice) must be registered with the Jockey Club. All partners are jointly and severally liable for entrance fees, stakes, forfeits and jockey's fees. That is to say that any one of them may be held individually liable for the full amount and will then have to recover the due amounts from the other partners.

It is recommended by the Jockey Club that anyone proposing to become a part-owner by way of a partnership should contact them before taking any steps in the matter. The rules governing joint-ownership are complex and the Jockey Club would prefer to advise at the outset rather than unscramble an arrangement that contravenes the rules.

An interest in a racehorse may be bought through the medium of a limited company but it must be realised that the investor is then buying a share in the company and not a share in a horse. There are a number of public limited companies engaged in these activities.

13.9.2 Stallions

As well as investments in horses in training, investments may be made in syndicated stallions. In this case there are no rules of the sort set out for horses in training – *ad hoc* arrangements are made in each case. A stallion may stand at stud until it is 20 years old, but the value of a nomination falls as it approaches that age. A stallion will give about 150 services each season, covering each mare three or four times. Stud fees at present range generally up to about 2,000 guineas, although that figure may be greatly exceeded in special cases.

In a typical syndicate there will be 40 shares, most of which will be held by shareholders with one share each. The agreement usually provides for a committee, including the major shareholder or shareholders, to be set up. The committee will be empowered to decide all matters relating to the management of the stallion and the affairs of the syndicate as agent for the shareholders, although its powers regarding the stallion's disposal are usually limited. Generally each shareholder is entitled to one nomination per share for the season. The maximum number of nominations for the season is fixed, and in so far as it exceeds the number available to shareholders, the excess may be sold and the proceeds set against expenses which are borne *pro rata* by the shareholders. The agreement usually provides that the committee must approve mares to be served by the stallion and that a barren mare must also be approved by a veterinary surgeon. A veterinary surgeon will examine any maiden mare before service. Restrictions are usually placed on the disposal of shares and nominations, but it may happen that during the season in question the shareholder has no mare suitable for nomination and in such a case the nomination will be sold.

13.9.3 Taxation

Income tax

It was held in *Benson v Counsell* (1942) 24 TC 178 that receipts from the sale of nominations were receipts of annual income chargeable to income tax under Schedule D Case VI, although they were not trading receipts within Case I. This decision was based on the fact that the taxpayer had not bought the rights to nomination sold: what he had bought was an interest in the horse. The sale of the rights merely realised the horse's reproductive faculties and it thus became an income-producing asset. In 1915 the Earl of Derby unsuccessfully contended that a stallion at stud was 'plant' for the purposes of capital allowances (see *Derby (Earl) v Aylmer* [1915] 3 KB 374).

Capital gains tax

The sale of a share in the horse, whether it is a horse in training or a stallion, does *not* give rise to a taxable gain, since s 45(1) of the Taxation of Chargeable Gains Act 1992 takes out of the charge to capital gains tax any gain accruing on the disposal of, or of an interest in, an asset which is tangible, movable property and a wasting asset. There is no doubt that a horse is tangible and movable, nor that it is a wasting asset (ie one with a predictable life not exceeding 50 years).

13.10 BACKING PLAYS

It is possible that, somewhere, a playwright has just written a play that will take London by storm and play for years to packed houses. It is, on present showing, most unlikely. It is estimated that only one show in seven put on in the West End will be successful which suggests that somewhere along the line there is a failure to foresee what the public will and will not like. In past years flops have included *Stop the World I Want to Get Off*, *Exclusive*, *Metropolis*, *Sherlock Holmes*, *Someone Like You*, *Look Look*, *Dean*, *Barnardo*, *Can-Can*, *Fire Angel*, *King*, *Top People*, *Y*, *Ziegfeld*, *Troubadour*, *Bus Stop*, *Bernadette*, *My Lovely . . . Shayna Madel*, *Rick's Bar Casablanca* and *Children of Eden*. Together they have lost millions. The last one, alone, is said to have lost £2.5m.

This is not the place to consider the reasons for this failure rate but those tempted to put money into a play should realise that their chance of making anything out of it is slim. It is statistically more probable that money put in will be lost without tax relief. This is the ideal investment for those who enjoy losing money.

Those who put up the money for a theatrical production – the 'angels' – normally split the profits with the management: the angels usually take 60 per cent and the management 40 per cent, although the proportions are a matter for agreement. The agreement usually also provides for an 'overcall', ie a liability on the part of the angels to put up additional capital should it prove necessary. Before the profits are divided between angels and management there has to be deducted such of the fees and expenses of management as may be specified in the agreement. The agreement should be carefully scrutinised by an adviser familiar with these matters to ensure that the angel is getting his or her fair share.

Anyone determined to risk this gamble against heavy odds should first become familiar with the track records of various producers. Eager investors should then attempt to force their money on one who seems successful. If a producer makes the approach, consider why his usual sources of finance are not available. There is no central exchange through which investments can be made although assistance may be obtained from the Society of West End Theatre. Whilst not arranging investments itself, the Society will give advice and maintains a list of prospective backers. Since backers will normally have no opportunity even to read the play they are simply betting on the producer's wisdom.

The cost of mounting a play varies enormously. A large-scale musical can cost millions to stage, and with production and running costs at their present levels a show has to run for a considerable time before the production costs are covered and anything is paid out. If the production is successful the investor will receive an agreed share of the net profits which will, first, recoup the costs and, thereafter, constitute income for tax purposes.

As a variant of the traditional method of financing, advantage may be taken of the provisions of s 574 of the Income and Corporation Taxes Act 1988 which enables losses on unquoted shares in certain trading companies to be set off against a taxpayer's income. The resulting loss is thus, to some extent, cushioned by income tax relief.

13.11 OPTIONS ON BOOKS

An investor with sufficient faith in a little-known author may back that faith by purchasing an option, exercisable usually for one year, to develop the book into a film or play. A little-known author is suggested as, in the case of a best-seller writer, the option is likely (if it is available at all) to be extremely expensive. It is, of course, much less expensive to buy such an option than it would be to buy the copyright outright.

Once the option is purchased it will become necessary to write or procure a script from the book and then to persuade a film company or theatrical producer to take it up. The time involved in these activities may necessitate the purchase of another year's option.

Would-be purchasers should consult a firm of literary agents for further advice. A list of agents is published in the *Writers' and Artists' Yearbook*.

13.12 PREVIEW OF THE YEAR AHEAD

Interest rates have continued to drop, although the unexpected rise in September 1999 has caused speculation that further rises may occur, despite a 36-year low record inflation rate. Stock market prices have continued to rise despite many forecasters claiming that they are over-valued. Property values have stabilised and seem to be in an upward trend.

The Labour Government seems anxious to encourage investment in venture capital, but restrictions in the types of eligible activities mean that there is still a considerable measure of risk involved.

Lloyd's have again produced profits for the 1995 account, although at a lower level than for 1994. It seems likely that a profit position will continue for 1996 and 1997, but there is no guarantee that this trend will continue in future years.

USEFUL ADDRESSES

Registrar of Companies/Registrar of
  Limited Partnerships
Companies Registration Office
Companies House
Crown Way
Cardiff
CF4 3UZ

Tel: (029) 2038 8588

Lloyd's of London
Lime Street
London
EC3M 7AH

Tel: (020) 7623 7100

National Research Development
  Corporation
101 Newington Causeway
London
SE1 6BU

Tel: (020) 7403 6666

Rural Development Commission
141 Castle Street
Salisbury
Wiltshire
SP1 3TP

Tel: (01722) 336255

Investors in Industry Group plc
91 Waterloo Road
London
SE1 8XP

Tel: (020) 7928 3131

British Venture Capital Association
Essex House
12–13 Essex Street
London
WC2R 3AA

Tel: (020) 7240 3846

Development Capital Group Limited
21 Moorfield
London
EC2P 2HT

Tel: (020) 7588 2721

Department of Trade and Industry
  Small Firms Service
To obtain address of nearest
  centre, dial 100 and ask the
  operator for Freefone
  Enterprise

British Institute of Management
3rd Floor
2 Savoy Court
Strand
London
WC2R 0EZ

Tel: (020) 7497 0580

Confederation of British Industry
Centrepoint
103 New Oxford Street
London
WC1A 1DU

Tel: (020) 7379 7400

Jockey Club
42 Portman Square
London
W1H 0EN

Tel: (020) 7486 4921

Society of West End Theatre & West
  End Theatre Managers Ltd
Bedford Chambers
The Piazza
Covent Garden
London
WC2E 8HQ

Tel: (020) 7836 0971

14

LIFE ASSURANCE

VINCE JERRARD LLB, ACII

Legal Director, Allied Dunbar Assurance plc

14.1 INTRODUCTION

Assurance contracts may be divided into three broad types, according to the nature of the primary benefits provided:

(1) life assurance policies (including single premium bonds) pay out a lump sum on death or on the expiration of a specified period;

(2) purchased life annuities pay periodic sums as long as the annuitant is alive;

(3) pension contracts provide pensions and other benefits and are available through one's work or occupation.

Within each of these categories there are further subdivisions. Pension contracts are dealt with in Chapter 15.

14.2 HIGHLIGHTS OF THE PREVIOUS YEAR

14.2.1 Life assurance business

In recent years life assurance business has benefited from a buoyant stock market, a recovery in the housing market and relatively low building society interest rates. The problems of personal pension mis-selling in the late 1980s continue to attract publicity as the companies continue with the review of these sales. The pensions market has been further damaged by the uncertainty surrounding the Government's proposals over the new 'stakeholder' pensions.

The 'restructuring' of the industry continues with more mergers, acquisitions and de-mutualisations. A further reduction in the number of active life companies is expected in future years.

14.2.2 Individual savings accounts (ISAs)

These are a new type of tax-favoured savings vehicle, introduced in April 1999. It is too early to tell whether the ISA will be a success, but the product's complexity is a disadvantage. In launching the ISA, the Government has created the 'CAT mark', a standard which a product can achieve through being clear and through carrying low charges. In effect, this is a 'control' over product design, a development which is likely to continue in the future with stakeholder pensions.

One matter which is of concern is whether the charging structures imposed on the industry will enable it to offer proper, high quality advice in respect of these products.

The scheme will run for a minimum of ten years, and UK-resident individuals aged 18 or over are able to invest up to £5,000 per annum (£7,000 in 1999–2000). There are three investment areas – equities, life assurance and cash deposits – each of which will allow savings to grow free of income and capital gains taxes. In addition, a 10 per cent tax credit will be paid by the Revenue on any dividends from UK shares and unit trusts until 5 April 2004.

Life policy investment within the ISA is limited to £1,000 per annum and cash deposits will have the same limit (save in year 1999–2000 when it is possible to invest £3,000 in cash). Life funds backing ISA policies benefit from a 10 per cent tax credit on UK equity dividends for five years commencing in April 1999.

While equity and cash investment have enjoyed participation in tax-favoured products in recent years (PEPs and TESSAs respectively), life assurance has been disadvantaged in comparison. The ISA is an important opportunity for the life industry. The rest of this chapter deals with non-ISA life policies.

14.3 LIFE ASSURANCE POLICIES

14.3.1 Legal nature

Life assurance policies are contracts between the individual policyholders and the life insurance company. The general principle underlying life assurance policies is that the insurance company is the collecting house of pooled risks and investments of policyholders and offers benefits directly to them based on personal contracts.

The life company maintains the underlying investment funds in its own right but, depending on the policy's nature, undertakes to pay the policyholder either a specified sum, a sum which is increased periodically out of the company's profits, or one which varies with the value of part of the underlying fund.

An important characteristic of the life assurance policy as an investment is that it does not produce an income, as such, but is essentially a medium- to long-term accumulator. The income and capital gains of the underlying funds accrue to and are taxed in the hands of the insurance company, but the benefit is passed on, to a greater or lesser extent, in the growth in value of the policy. Many types of policy, however, allow regular or irregular encashment of part of the policy (withdrawal plans or encashment of bonuses) to serve as 'income', if required (but see 'Withdrawal plans and policy loans' at **14.3.4** and also **14.3.6** concerning part surrender of single premium policies).

14.3.2 Pre-conditions

To take out a life assurance policy an *insurable interest* in the life to be assured must exist, ie a pecuniary interest that would be adversely affected by the death of the life assured. At the time the policy is taken out, the policyholder must have an insurable interest in the life assured commensurate with the sum assured. Individuals have an unlimited insurable interest in their own and their spouses' lives.

Usually, where life assurance is taken out as an investment, the contract is applied for and held by a person on his or her own or spouse's life, or on their joint lives, for his or her own personal benefit or for their joint benefit. Policies can, however, be the subject of gifts, in which case they are generally written in trust for the benefit of the beneficiaries (see **14.3.7**). They can also be assigned, by way of gift, or for value, or as security for a debt (eg as collateral security for a house mortgage or an overdraft).

14.3.3 Divisions and types

Endowment, whole of life and term assurances

All life policies provide life cover – a sum or sums assured payable on death. Most policies, other than temporary assurances, also provide investment benefits – sums payable on surrender or maturity. Life policies may be divided into endowment, whole of life and term policies, depending on the emphasis that is placed on savings or on protection (life cover):

(1) An endowment policy, which has a high savings element, is one under which the benefits are payable at the end of a predetermined period (the endowment period) or on death, if earlier.

(2) A whole of life policy is one under which the benefits are in general payable on death, whenever it occurs.

(3) A term policy is a temporary assurance, the sum assured being payable on death within a specified period only.

Both endowment and whole of life policies may be surrendered (ie cashed in) prematurely for a cash lump sum, the size of which depends on the contract's nature. Term assurances generally do not have an investment element as far as the individual is concerned, and so rarely have any surrender or cash-in value.

With profit, without profit and unit-linked policies

Within the endowment and whole of life categories, life policies can be of different types, depending on the way in which the sums payable by the company are determined:

(1) *With profit* contracts are policies under which a minimum sum is guaranteed to be paid by the life company, augmented from time to time by bonuses declared by the company according to its profits. These bonuses may be reversionary (bonuses added to the sum assured, either yearly or triennially) or terminal (bonuses declared at the end of the policy as an increment to the final payment). Reversionary bonuses may be simple or compound: simple bonuses are based only on the sum assured, while compound bonuses are based on the sum assured plus previous bonuses. Reversionary bonuses are usually expressed as a percentage of the sum assured or of the sum assured as increased by previous bonuses. Under a with profit endowment policy the individual receives at maturity the minimum sum assured plus the bonuses, reversionary and terminal.

A development in recent years has been the creation of what are called 'unitised with profits' policies. These are with profits business but are structured to give the appearance of unit linking, particularly in terms of the policy charging structure. Frequently, unitised with profits business offers a 'smoothed' growth, often with a guaranteed minimum rate, but the guarantee may only apply to maturity and death values and not to earlier surrenders.

(2) *Without profit* contracts are policies under which the life company guarantees to pay an absolute sum and invests the premiums in such a way as to produce that sum, bearing any shortfall in the return or retaining any profit in excess of the guaranteed return.

(3) Under *unit-linked* policies the life company maintains a number of underlying funds, which are divided, for accounting purposes only, into 'units'. The company undertakes to pay to the policyholder an amount equal to the greater of the guaranteed sum and the value of the units allocated to the policy. The underlying fund might consist of

specific types of investment media often with a choice of geographical spread (such as property, equities, unit trusts, investment trusts, government securities, local authority and bank loans or deposits, or building society deposits) or the fund may consist of a combination of some or all of these ('managed' or 'mixed' funds). Out of every premium a proportion is allocated to the purchase of units which are credited to the policy. The movement in value of the underlying fund is directly reflected in the price of the units allocated to the policy and hence in the value of the policy benefits. Many types of policies give the policyholder the right to transfer his or her policy link from fund to fund at his option, by way of a simple procedure at low cost (eg a policy that is linked to an equity fund may be switched to become linked to fixed interest securities or bank deposits).

A life company generally has full investment freedom of the type of investments it chooses, subject only to the investments being a suitable 'match' for its liabilities. In the case of unit-linked policies the Insurance Company Regulations only permit linkage to certain types of assets, such as those listed in (3) above.

If the contract is one under which a guaranteed minimum or guaranteed absolute amount is provided, investors know that they will get at least that sum. At the same time, in the case of with profit policies, the investor has the advantage of having the guaranteed minimum augmented from time to time by reversionary and terminal bonuses, or, in unit-linked contracts, augmented by the movement of the value of the underlying fund (capital growth plus reinvested income).

Regular premium and single premium policies

A further broad division of life policies (of all types) depends on how premiums are payable:

(1) regular premium policies (also known as annual premium policies) are those under which premiums are payable annually, half-yearly, quarterly or monthly, either throughout the policy's duration or for a limited premium-paying period of time; and

(2) single premium policies are purchased by way of one single premium or lump sum (although such policies can usually accept further investment at any time).

Qualifying and non-qualifying policies

A brief introduction to qualifying and non-qualifying policies is given at **14.3.6**. The distinction between the two types of policy is important because their proceeds are treated differently for tax purposes in the hands of the policyholder.

14.3.4 Characteristics of regular premium policies

Investment and protection

All endowment and whole of life policies have an investment or savings element as well as a life insurance protection element. The extent to which the policy is slanted towards investment depends on the policy's nature and duration and the relationship between the premiums payable, the age of the life assured and the extent of the life cover provided.

In general, policies that have a low sum assured relative to the premiums payable over the policy life have a high savings or investment element, and conversely, high sums assured relative to the premiums payable mean that the policy is tilted more towards life assurance cover than towards investment. In considering life policies as investments, temporary or term assurances will be excluded, as these generally do not have a surrender value and benefits are payable only on death. They are usually taken out purely for life cover protection, to provide for one's family or to cover a prospective liability such as inheritance tax.

The type of policy that individuals should take out generally depends on their circumstances and objectives, weighing up not only the required degree of investment relative to protection but also the required degree of certainty of result relative to the potential for increased gain.

In general, the incidence of inflation and the conservatism of companies in guaranteeing a long-term return has meant that without profit policies have tended to provide a relatively poor rate of return compared with with profit and unit-linked policies.

A with profit policy gives the prospect of sharing in the company's investment performance where this exceeds that needed to meet the guarantee – but the need to satisfy the guarantee may still lead the company to a more conservative investment strategy.

With no guaranteed investment return a unit linked policy could be viewed as a little more risky but may also offer the prospect of better fund performance.

Withdrawal plans and policy loans

In the past, a feature of many regular premium policies with a high investment content was the facility, after a period of years, to operate withdrawal plans, under which the premium was reduced to a nominal amount, eg £1 per annum and regular or irregular sums could be taken from the policy by way of partial surrender to serve as an income, leaving the balance to accumulate. This withdrawal facility was challenged by the Revenue and withdrawn from qualifying policies issued on or after 25 February 1988. Policies issued before that date may continue as qualifying policies despite the presence of such an option. Substantially the same result may be achieved by taking out a series of smaller policies and cashing in individual policies from time to time while continuing the remainder and it may be possible to take withdrawals from a policy provided it has not suffered such a large premium reduction as was previously allowed. Many policies also give the policyholder the right to borrow from the insurance company at a beneficial rate of interest on the security of the policy.

14.3.5 Characteristics of single premium policies

In the main, the relevant single premium policies for investment purposes consist of single premium 'bonds' which are whole of life assurance policies. For many years these have been, in the main, unit-linked policies often marketed as property bonds, managed bonds, equity bonds, etc by reference to the initial underlying fund to which the policy was linked. There are also single premium endowment policies, but these are less significant.

In recent years, there has been considerable business written as with profit bonds. Although these did not generally incorporate the usual guarantees on future values, they did prove to be attractive in a time of recession and stock market uncertainty.

The main investment characteristic of single premium unit-linked bonds is the high allocation of the premium to investment in the underlying fund, with relatively low life cover. Virtually the entire premium is allocated to 'units', save only for the initial management charges, resulting, in effect, in the investment of most of the premium in the chosen fund. Most companies offer a wide choice of unit funds for the bond linkage.

Subsequently, at no cost or for a small administrative charge, policyholders may switch their investment to one or more of the other funds and are thereby entitled to select a fund which reflects their own view of market conditions. Switching does not amount to a realisation for tax purposes, which is an important investment advantage.

The income produced by the underlying fund is reinvested, net of tax and annual charges, in the fund. A bond, therefore, serves as an automatic income accumulator as well as giving the investor the benefit of the capital growth from the fund, less a deduction for the insurance company's tax on capital gains.

At various times in recent years, market conditions have also made guaranteed income bonds very attractive for both life companies and investors. They may be structured as single policies paying annual amounts as a spendable 'income' by way of part surrender; or may be a combination of policies, some providing the annual 'income' and one providing the investment return at the end of the investment period, usually five years. The Revenue has challenged the efficiency of some of these arrangements, contending that the annual payments are actually Schedule D Case III income and not part surrenders of capital but FA 1997 confirmed the position to be that which it was thought to be by the industry.

A case decided (on the hearing of a preliminary matter) in the middle of 1994 raised the question of how much life assurance protection a single premium bond had to provide for it to qualify as a life assurance policy. At first instance the judge decided that a policy providing a death benefit equal only to the surrender value at the time of death was not a life assurance contract.

An appeal against this decision in 1996 reversed it and restored the previous industry understanding.

Withdrawals

Most unit-linked single premium bonds allow the investor the right to make regular or irregular withdrawals by way of partial surrender to serve as an income. The same result can be achieved by splitting the investment into a number of smaller policies and encashing individual policies in full from time to time. As these policies are not qualifying contracts they are not affected by the Revenue's attack on withdrawal plans referred to in **14.3.4** but see the section 'Withdrawals' in **14.3.6** below.

Ease of encashment

One of the most important characteristics of single premium bonds is the ease of encashment: there are few formalities other than production of the policy, a surrender form and proof of title. In the case of property bonds, some companies reserve the right, in exceptional circumstances, to defer encashment for a period so as to protect the general body of policyholders by avoiding forced sales of property.

14.3.6 Taxation

Taxation of the life company

The Revenue's review of life company taxation, announced in the 1989 budget, resulted in a statement by the Treasury in December 1989 and other changes announced in the 1990 budget. Legislation was included in the Finance Acts 1989 and 1990 to give effect to these changes. In the main, they took effect from January 1990.

The proposals were less radical than some of those originally canvassed and built on the existing 'I-E' (income-expenses) framework. The following is a very brief outline of an extremely complex tax regime.

The life company's management expenses are deducted from the investment income and capital gains of the life fund and the net amount is subjected to tax in the life company's hands at a rate of 23 per cent in respect of the policyholders' share of profits (20 per cent in respect of the policyholder's share of investment return corresponding to savings income, to reflect personal taxation) and 31 per cent (30 per cent from April 1999) in respect of profits attributable to shareholders in the case of a proprietary company. However, the expenses associated with the acquisition of new business are spread over a period of seven years.

As life companies are generally able to defer realisations of assets for a long period, they usually pass on this benefit in the form of a lower rate of deduction for tax on capital gains from the funds. This is especially true of unit-linked policies.

Previously, deferring capital gains had been achieved by investing life funds in units trusts. Much of the investment management could be achieved through the unit trust company selling its underlying assets, these being free of tax from capital gains. However, current rules (with transitional reliefs) charging tax on unrealised gains in life company holdings of unit trusts are promoting more direct investment by life company funds.

Taxation of the policyholder

Qualifying and non-qualifying policies

The income tax treatment of a life policy in the hands of the policyholder depends on whether the policy is a qualifying or a non-qualifying policy. Policy provisions in standard form are usually sent to the Revenue by the life company for confirmation of compliance with the qualifying rules ('pre-certification'). Generally (although the rules do vary for different types of policy) a qualifying policy is one where the premium-paying period is ten years or more and where the premiums payable in any period of 12 months do not exceed more than twice the premiums payable in any other period of 12 months or $\frac{1}{8}$ of the premiums payable over ten years. In the case of a whole of life policy, the sum assured payable on death must not be less than 75 per cent of the premiums payable until age 75; and in the case of an endowment policy, the sum assured payable on death must not be less than 75 per cent of the premiums payable during the term of the policy, but for endowments this percentage is reduced by 2 per cent for each year by which the age of the life assured, at commencement, exceeds 55. Taxation of company-owned policies is considered later.

Qualifying policies

Tax relief on the premiums   In the case of a qualifying policy issued before 14 March 1984, policyholders are eligible for tax relief on the premiums if the policy is written on their or their spouse's lives, if either of them pays the premiums, and if the person paying is resident in the UK for tax purposes. The current rate of tax relief on premiums paid is $12\frac{1}{2}$ per cent. If eligible, the premiums may generally be paid to the life company net of the tax relief and the company will obtain the difference from the Inland Revenue. Tax relief is allowed to the policyholder to the extent to which the total gross premiums paid by him in the year do not exceed £1,500 or, if greater, $\frac{1}{6}$ of his taxable income after deducting charges on income but before deducting personal reliefs. Tax relief will not be available if a person other than the life assured or his or her spouse (such as an assignee) pays the premiums.

No life assurance premium relief is available for policies issued for contracts made after 13 March 1984. For these purposes a policy issued on or before 13 March 1984 is treated as being issued after that date if the benefits it secures are increased or its term extended (either by variation or by the exercise of an option built into the contract) after that date.

Policies intact   While the policies are held intact there is no tax charge to the policyholder.

Tax-free proceeds if kept up for minimum period   If a qualifying endowment policy has been maintained for at least three-quarters of its term or ten years, whichever is shorter, and has not been made paid-up within that period, the entire proceeds will be free of income tax in the hands of the policyholder. For a whole of life policy the appropriate period is ten years. If, however, a qualifying policy is surrendered or made paid-up within these periods, the profit ultimately made on realising the policy (whether by cashing in, death, maturity or assignment for value) is potentially subject to the higher rate of tax – but not the basic rate – as with non-qualifying policies (see below).

Capital gains tax   No chargeable gain arises on the disposal of either qualifying or non-qualifying policies (note that surrender and payment of the sum assured under the policy are treated as 'disposals' for these purposes) where the disposal is by the original beneficial owner or by an assignee who gave no consideration for the policy (eg received the policy by way of gift).

On the other hand, if an assignee realises a profit on a policy (or an interest under it) that he or she not being the original beneficial owner, acquired for value, it is liable to capital gains tax in the same way as other chargeable assets.

To deal with the trade in second-hand policies (which were taxed under the then more favourable capital gains tax regime), anti-avoidance legislation was introduced in 1983 so that, broadly speaking, post-26 June 1982 policies remain in the same income tax regime despite being assigned for money or money's worth. Such policies may give a potential liability to both income and capital gains tax although the Taxation of Chargeable Gains Act 1992, s 37 prevents a double tax charge arising.

Person liable for the tax charge   See below.

Non-qualifying policies

Tax relief on the premiums   No life assurance premium relief is allowed on premiums paid under non-qualifying policies whether issued before or after 14 March 1984.

Policies intact   As with qualifying policies, while the policies are intact there is no tax charge on the policyholder.

Termination   On final termination of a non-qualifying policy, on death, cashing in, maturity, or sale, the only income tax charge, if any, is to higher rate income tax but not basic rate. To determine whether a charge arises, the gain – basically, the excess of the cash surrender value over the premium paid – is divided by the number of years the policy has been held ('top slicing'). Any previous withdrawals are also taken into account. This slice is then added to the taxpayer's other income for the year (after reliefs and mortgage interest). If the slice, then treated as the upper part of the individual's income, puts the investor in the higher rate bracket, the average rate of tax on the slice at the higher rate less the basic rate is applied to the whole gain. If the slice does not attract the higher rate of tax, the gain is, similarly, free of tax. Note that the benefit of top slicing does not apply for the purposes of the higher personal allowances given to those aged over 65 years.

Note also that it is only the income in the year of encashment that is relevant. If no chargeable events occur during other years, the individual's income, no matter how high in those years, is irrelevant. Thus, bonds or other non-qualifying policies can be realised tax-effectively in a year when the policyholder's other income is relatively low (eg after retirement).

Example 1 – no income tax charge

A basic rate taxpayer whose income after personal reliefs is £1,000 below the higher rate threshold cashes in a single premium bond, held for eight years, for a total gain of £5,000. This gain is divided by eight to produce a 'slice' of £625. The slice, when added to other income, still does not take the investor into the higher rate of tax. No tax is payable on the gain of £5,000.

Example 2 – income tax on the gain

> If the slice (£625 in the above example), treated as the upper part of the tax-payer's income, falls wholly in the higher rate band of 40 per cent, then the gain of £5,000 will be subject to income tax at the rate of 17 per cent (ie £850) being the difference between the relevant higher rate (40 per cent) and the basic rate of 23 per cent (tax year 1999–2000).

Note that, on death, the gain which may be liable to tax is calculated, broadly speaking, as the cash surrender value immediately before death plus previous relevant capital payments under the policy, less the premiums paid. In this way the 'mortality profit' made under the policy at that time is not taxed as part of the chargeable gain.

Withdrawals   Annual tax-free withdrawals or partial surrenders of up to 5 per cent of the premiums paid are permitted up to a total amount equal to the premium or premiums paid. Unused allowances are carried forward. If more than the 5 per cent annual allowance is taken a chargeable excess occurs. The excess becomes liable to the higher rate of tax (but is not liable to the basic rate) if, when added to the taxpayer's other income, it falls into the higher rate.

The 'top-slicing' procedure referred to above applies with some modifications: the first chargeable excess is divided by the number of years since commencement; subsequent excesses are divided by the number of years since the previous excess. The amounts withdrawn are taken into account in computing the gain or loss on final cashing in: the final gain or loss is equal to the cash surrender value, plus previous withdrawals, less the premium or premiums paid, less excesses previously brought into charge.

Example

> Original investment in a bond of £5,000. The bondholder takes withdrawals of 6 per cent per annum for nine years and cashes in the bond after ten years for £8,000. The final gain on cashing in is £8,000 + £2,700 (ie 9 × 6% × £5,000) – £5,000 – £450 (ie 9 × 1% × £5,000) = £5,250. The 'slice' is therefore £5,250 ÷ 10 = £525. This slice is added to the investor's other income in the year of cashing in to determine if any tax liability exists on the slice and, if so, the rate of charge, after deducting the basic rate. The net rate of charge, if any, on the slice is then applied to the gain of £5,250.

Personal portfolio bonds are single premium policies, usually written offshore, which enable the investor's benefits to be closely linked to a portfolio of assets personal to the investor. The Finance Act 1998 introduced a new tax charge on such policies by deeming a gain of 15 per cent of the total premiums paid to the end of each policy year and previous deemed policy gains. This charge was not imposed in respect of any policy year ending before 6 April 1999. This provision does not apply to 'managed portfolio bonds', which give the investor access only to generally available, pooled assets.

Person liable The person liable for the tax charge is the policyholder if the policy is held beneficially, or the individual for whose debt the policy is held as security. Thus, if a policy is assigned by a parent to his or her child by way of a gift and the latter encashes it after attaining majority, the liability, if any, is the child's regardless of the donor's income and is determined by the child's income at the time of encashment.

Where a policy that is held in trust is cashed in, any chargeable gain is treated as income of the settlor and the tax is his or her liability, although the settlor can recover from the trustees any tax liable in this way. If a policy, previously held in trust, has been assigned to the beneficiary in execution of that trust and is subsequently encashed, any gain forms part of the beneficiary's income and is taxed accordingly.

The Finance Act 1998 contained provisions to counter what were known as 'dead settlor trusts', through which it was possible to avoid tax on life policy gains realised after the settlor's death. The new rules result in tax being charged on the trustees (or perhaps the beneficiaries) where the trust's settlor is dead (or not resident in the UK) at the chargeable event. The new rules do not apply where the settlor had died before 17 March 1998 and the policy was effected before that date.

Timing Where the taxable event is the death of the life assured or the maturity, total encashment or sale of the policy, the gain is treated as arising at the date of that event. In contrast, however, withdrawals from policies are treated as happening at the end of the policy year in which they take place. For example, if a policy was effected on 1 June, a withdrawal in February 1999 will be treated as taking place on 31 May 1999 and so will be part of the 1999–2000 tax computation for the policyholder and not the computation for 1998–99, the year in which it actually occurred.

14.3.7 Suitability

Life assurance policies are different from the normal run of investments in that they are capital assets that do not produce income as such. All income and capital gains produced by the underlying fund of investments accrue to the life company, while the policyholder receives the benefit in the form of an increase in value of the policy: the net income and gains after tax are taken into account in the value of the units or bonus additions, as the case may be. For this reason, life assurance policies are a very useful means of obtaining capital growth and accumulating income for medium- to long-term investment if immediate income is not required. This can be particularly important for higher rate taxpayers and various types of trust.

Both regular premium and single premium policies (qualifying or non-qualifying) also have the advantage that while they are held intact, the policyholder has no administrative burdens or tax returns to render, as the income and gains are the company's responsibility.

The new ISA life policies should be able to offer attractive returns, although investment is limited to £1,000 per annum (see **14.2.2**).

The medium- and long-term investor

Both single and regular premium policies are ideally suited to the medium- or longer-term investor seeking an institutionally managed investment. Life companies have considerable investment freedom and with profits policies reflect the results of investment across a wide spread of assets. Unit-linked policies offer a choice of property, equity, fixed interest, managed and many other types of unit funds, as well as the ability to switch investments between funds as market conditions change. Indeed, the keynote of most unit-linked policies these days is choice and flexibility to meet changing circumstances, so as to maximise the potential growth and protect the real value of the investment against inflation, particularly over the longer term; while with profit policies offer the relative stability of participation in the company's profits. For the individual who wants a direct link to a managed fund of commercial properties there are few investments comparable with a property bond, or a policy linked to a property fund, or a managed fund with a property content.

Qualifying policies issued pre-14 March 1984 may have the added attraction of tax relief on the premiums – something not available to other comparable forms of investment – as well as freedom from tax on the proceeds if maintained for the required period. The ability of companies to defer realisations and thus make deductions for capital gains liabilities at a rate lower than the life company rate on chargeable gains has been a continuing advantage (but see **14.3.6** for more recent changes to unit trusts held by life companies).

Beneficiaries

Life policies are suitable investments for individuals seeking personal investment benefits for themselves or their spouses, or for making gifts to beneficiaries. Since policies are automatic income accumulators, they represent useful investments as gifts for children or for children's own capital. As gifts of policies do not cause chargeable events, a higher rate taxpaying spouse can give a policy to a basic rate (or non-taxpaying) partner before encashment. In this way, any gain otherwise taxable may avoid being taxed by virtue of the new independent taxation regime introduced in April 1990 which no longer aggregates the investment income of married couples. Policies can also be taken out by trustees as investments of the trust, provided the power is given in the trust instrument to invest in non-income-producing property and provided an insurable interest exists, eg a policy on the life of a beneficiary for the ultimate benefit of that beneficiary.

A donor wishing to take out a policy for the benefit of children or other beneficiaries can do so at the outset by completing a standard trust form produced by the life company at the time of application. Trusts can range from very simple forms for the benefit of named beneficiaries absolutely (under the Married Women's Property Acts or corresponding legislation in Scotland and Northern Ireland, for spouse or children) to more elaborate forms, such as children's accumulation trusts and trusts where the settlor reserves a right to apply the benefits amongst a class of beneficiaries which may even include the settlor (although to be efficient for inheritance tax purposes the settlor should be excluded from any personal benefit). Similarly, it is relatively simple to make a gift of an existing policy by assigning it to a beneficiary or to trustees for a beneficiary.

The tax considerations described in **14.3.6** should, of course, be taken into account, as well as the taxpayer's potential income and tax position at the time of prospective encashment (as it is that time that is primarily relevant, not any time during the currency of the policy).

Companies

Companies have frequently found it useful to invest surplus funds in life policies, particularly where providing for a future liability or the replacement of an asset in the future. An insurable interest in the life of the assured must exist. In the past, the only tax consequence of such an investment has been that applicable to a close company in the case of a single premium bond or the premature encashment of a qualifying policy, but the Finance Act 1989 contained new provisions so that, broadly speaking, all policies owned by companies (and those assigned to secure a company debt or held on trusts created by a company) are treated, in effect, as non-qualifying policies and taxable as Schedule D Case VI income. In this case no credit is given for tax deducted in the life company's funds and no top-slicing is granted.

The new rules apply to policies effected on or after 14 March 1989 and those altered after that date so as to increase the benefits secured or extend the term.

A measure of relief is given in cases where a qualifying endowment policy is used to secure a debt incurred by the company in purchasing land to be occupied by it for the purposes of its trade (or in constructing, extending or improving buildings occupied for that purpose). In such cases, and subject to certain conditions, only the excess policy proceeds over the amount of the debt is taxable as a policy gain.

14.3.8 Charges

In the case of with profit and without profit policies, the company's charges are implicit in the premium rate for the sum assured. In the case of unit-linked policies, the company's charges consist of a proportion of each premium and charges inside the unit funds. For example, in the case of single premium bonds, typically an initial charge of 5 per cent of the premium is made. This is followed by annual charges in the order of 1.25 per cent of the value of the fund (although this does vary from company to company) deducted from the fund, either monthly or with the same frequency as the fund valuations. These charges cover items such as the company's expenses and profit margins. Such annual charges can become quite significant where the policy has achieved a high value. For this reason some companies have adopted the approach of using a policy charge which is designed to ensure that each policy contributes a fair amount to the company's expenses, irrespective of the policy's size. In such cases any annual management charge deducted from the funds is reallocated to the policy.

Switching a unit-linked policy between funds can usually be done for a small administrative charge that is far lower than the equivalent cost of switching other investments.

14.3.9 Mechanics

Life assurance policies are generally taken out through the intervention of an intermediary such as an insurance broker or salesman of the life assurance company, or a solicitor, accountant or estate agent acting as agent, or directly with the life company itself. The intermediary, although often the policyholder's agent, is generally paid a commission by the life company itself, although some insurance brokers charge the client fees (which are offset against their commission) for the work involved in preparing reports and undertaking financial planning for the client entailing the use of life assurance policies. The Financial Services Act 1986 introduced the concept of polarisation to the industry. This seeks to make clear to consumers whether they are dealing with a representative of one company or a broker who will survey the market on the client's behalf.

14.3.10 **Maintenance**

Policies can be held in the individual's own name (usually in the case of policies held for the individual's personal benefit) or by trustees. As long as the policy is not cashed in there are no tax returns and no paperwork. It is only where excessive tax relief is taken on qualifying premiums or gains arise on the happening of a chargeable event (eg a single premium policy that is encashed or a qualifying policy encashed prematurely) that tax considerations arise. It is perhaps largely because of the ease of administration that many individuals with personal share portfolios take advantage of share exchange schemes introduced by life companies enabling them to exchange their shares for single premium bonds at reduced dealing costs.

Holders of unit-linked policies may receive annual fund reports, though the level of useful information provided varies between companies. Because the investment performances of unit-linked single premium bonds are directly related to the underlying funds, it is advisable to review the performance of the respective funds regularly with a view to switching between funds. This can be done with relative ease and at a low cost but for the majority of investors a carefully selected managed fund satisfies the requirements for a large proportion of their investment.

14.4 PURCHASED LIFE ANNUITIES

14.4.1 Legal nature

There are two broad types of purchased life annuities:

(1) Immediate annuities are contracts under which, in consideration of a lump sum paid to the life company, the company undertakes to pay an annuity to the annuitant for life, or for some other term, the rate of the annual annuity depending on the age and sex of the annuitant and on the yields prevailing for fixed interest investments at the time.
(2) Deferred annuities are similar to immediate annuities except that the annuity commences at a future date.

Both annuity contracts are direct contracts with the life company. Some annuity contracts provide for a guaranteed minimum number of payments; some allow the contract to be surrendered for a cash sum that takes into account the growth in the purchase consideration and any annuity payments that have already been made. Other types of annuity contract allow for a cash sum, representing the balance of the original purchase consideration, to be paid on death.

14.4.2 Pre-conditions

There are generally no pre-conditions to investment in purchased life annuities. The purchaser of the annuity is generally the annuitant him- or herself or someone else who wishes to provide for annual payments to the annuitant.

14.4.3 Characteristics

An annuity contract represents a fixed interest investment providing either regular annual payments for the life of the annuitant (lifetime annuities) or for a fixed period (temporary annuities). These payments represent a partial return of capital plus a rate of interest on the investment. In the case of deferred annuity contracts the initial purchase consideration is accumulated at a fixed rate of interest before the annuity commences. Frequently, deferred annuity contracts are purchased with the object of taking advantage of income accumulation before the annuity commencement date and of cashing in the contract before that time (these are commonly known as 'growth bonds'). In general the life company fixes the rate of the annuity in advance, although cash surrender values may be related to yields on government securities at the time of cashing in. The actual investment yield earned by the life company is irrelevant to annuitants, as they enjoy a guaranteed benefit.

In the past, two separate purchased annuity contracts were sometimes combined. For example, a temporary immediate annuity for a limited period was combined with a deferred lifetime annuity. This combination, known as a 'guaranteed income bond' (more frequently now written as a cluster of endowment policies), had as its object the provision of a short-term 'income' in the form of the temporary annuity, with the cashing in of the deferred annuity before the annuity commencement date to provide the return of 'capital'. The contracts were so structured that the cash-in value of the deferred annuity generally equals the total purchase price of the two contracts. The tax consequences of this combination have to be closely watched, especially for higher rate taxpayers (see **14.4.4**). Another combination is that of an immediate lifetime annuity, to provide an income for life, and a deferred annuity that can be commenced at a later stage to augment the income or, if the additional income is not taken, to pay a lump sum on death.

Investment and interest rates are such that, at present, annuities do not appear to offer very good value for money, a particular concern in the pensions market where part of the pension benefit is, generally, required to be taken in the form of an annuity.

14.4.4 Taxation

The life company

In the past, annuities paid represented charges on the income from investments held by the life company for its general annuity business. To the extent, therefore, that the annuities paid equalled or exceeded the interest earned by the company, the interest did not bear tax, and could be passed on to the annuitants gross (although then subject to taxation in the hands of the annuitant).

The Finance Act 1991, however, made the taxation of general annuity business much the same as ordinary life assurance for accounting periods beginning after 31 December 1991 with a generally detrimental effect on purchased life annuities.

The annuitant

Annuities paid are divided into capital content and income content, according to actuarial tables prescribed by the Inland Revenue. For example, if a man aged 70 purchased an annuity of £1,800 per annum payable half-yearly in arrear for a consideration of £10,000, £900 of the annuity might be regarded as capital with the balance of £900 being treated as income for tax purposes. In other words, every annuity is deemed to be partly a return of the original capital invested plus a yield or interest element. The interest element of each annuity payment received by the annuitant is treated as unearned income, although since the abolition of the investment income surcharge for individuals by the Finance Act 1984 this is not currently a significant disadvantage.

Despite this treatment of payments as part capital and part income, the Revenue appear to regard annuities as substantially a right to income so that they cannot be transferred between spouses to take advantage of independent taxation.

In the past, if an annuity contract was encashed or assigned for value, or any capital sum paid on death, any profit made by the annuitant over and above the purchase price of the annuity, unlike single premium bonds, was subject to basic rate tax (as the company would not have paid tax on the income of its general annuity business) and higher rates if applicable. However, as part of the change to the company's tax position, the 1991 Finance Act also brought the chargeable event regime for annuities into line with that for life policies, eg by not charging gains to basic rate income tax.

Higher rate tax is charged in much the same manner as on single premium policies. In other words, the gain element is 'top-sliced' by the number of years the annuity contract has been in existence, and the resulting slice is added to the taxpayer's other income in the year of encashment to determine whether the higher rate of tax is applicable. The rate on the slice (less the basic rate) then applies to the entire gain. In calculating the amount of the gain the capital element of any annuities paid prior to encashment (but not the interest element) is included as part of the gain.

14.4.5 Suitability

Immediate life annuities are suitable for investors who wish to purchase a continuing income for the rest of their lives by way of a lump sum. Deferred annuities are a means of providing an income to start at a future date, or of accumulating a lump sum with a view to encashment at a future time when other income may be sufficiently low to offset the tax disadvantages of encashment.

14.4.6 Mechanics

Like other life contracts annuities may be purchased through an intermediary or from a life company direct.

14.4.7 Maintenance

As far as immediate annuities are concerned, annual tax returns and tax payments are necessary in respect of the interest element of the annuities. In the case of deferred contracts, no maintenance is required while the annuity contract is intact and not paying an annuity, since the income is income of the life company and not the annuitant. On cashing-in, tax returns are necessary and tax may be payable.

14.5 PREVIEW OF THE YEAR AHEAD

With confidence returning to investors and consumers the prospects for the industry in 1999 look better than has been the case for some years.

The rate of change in the industry shows no signs of abating with developments like the introduction of the ISA, but the decision not to proceed with the proposed new life policy regime is welcome.

Although all would subscribe to the need for client protection, there is a view that the current regime has gone too far by elongating the sales process while failing to deliver to consumers relevant, useful and succinct information on which to base their decisions.

14.6 CONCLUSION

Life policies remain a very simple way of making lump sum or regular investment, although they are best used for medium- to long-term savings.

They act as 'income accumulators' and the life company deals with all tax liabilities while the plan is maintained in force. Withdrawals can often be taken to provide the policyholder with a spendable 'income' and these too can often be taken very simply and with little paperwork. This makes policies easy to administer from the policyholder's viewpoint and they are attractive to many people as a result.

As a pooled investment, they offer a spread of risk normally unobtainable by individual investors, including exposure to the commercial property market. Inexpensive switching between the company's funds, the built-in life cover and the prospect of tax-free proceeds are also attractive benefits of investment through life policies.

The recent tax changes, which have increased liabilities on the industry, have already led to many contracts being repriced, but reduced tax rates applying to policyholder income and gains should provide some level of compensation for this.

The introduction of ISA life policies in April 1999 has enabled the industry to offer tax-favoured life products for the first time in many years – an opportunity it will be eager to embrace, not only in terms of sales volumes but also from the point of view of further rehabilitating its reputation after the pensions mis-selling problems of the late 1980s.

USEFUL ADDRESSES

Association of British Insurers
51 Gresham Street
London
EC2V 7HQ

Tel: (020) 7600 3333

National Association of Pension
Funds
12–18 Grosvenor Gardens
London
SW1W 0DH

Tel: (020) 7730 0585

Inland Revenue Public Enquiry
Room
West Wing
Somerset House
Strand
London
WC2R 1LB

Tel: (020) 7438 6420

Society of Pension Consultants
Ludgate House
Ludgate Circus
London
EC4A 2AB

Tel: (020) 7353 1688/9

Pension Schemes Office
York House
PO Box 62
Castle Meadow Road
Nottingham
NG2 1BG

Tel: (0115) 974 0000

PIA (Personal Investment
  Authority)
(Address and helpline number as
for FSA, below)

FSA (Financial Services
  Authority)
25 The North Colonnade
Canary Wharf
London
E14 5HS

Tel: (020) 7676 1000

IFA Association
12–13 Henrietta Street
Covent Garden
London
WC2E 8LH

Tel: (020) 7240 7878

Life Insurance Association
Citadel House
Station Approach
Chorleywood
Rickmansworth
Herts
WD3 5PF

Tel: (01923) 285333

Pensions Management Institute
PMI House
4–10 Artillery Lane
London
E1 7LS

Tel: (020) 7247 1452

15

PENSION CONTRACTS

STUART REYNOLDS LLB,
Director, Legal Department, Allied Dunbar Assurance plc

15.1 INTRODUCTION

Pension schemes in the UK can be divided, broadly, into three classifications: the State scheme; personal pension arrangements; and occupational schemes.

Approved pensions schemes have many of the constituents of the perfect investment: tax relief on contributions, largely tax-free growth, the prospect of a tax-free lump sum and a wide choice of underlying investments in large pooled funds to spread the risk. The major disadvantage is the need to purchase an annuity (taxed) at retirement. Recent changes have removed some of the problems which this can cause.

Not surprisingly, these benefits are carefully guarded by the appropriate authorities through a considerable number of rules and restrictions. This chapter summarises the main benefits and the conditions for their enjoyment.

15.2 HIGHLIGHTS OF THE PREVIOUS YEAR

The last year was an eventful one for the pensions industry. The Government announced its proposals for the future of pension provision and the bad publicity surrounding the mis-selling of personal pensions continued. However, there were also some subtle changes, stemming largely from trends that have been present for many years, which are likely to prove more fundamental over the longer term.

First, the effects of long-term economic changes are beginning to be felt. Most commentators have for some time been predicting that for the foreseeable future we are entering an environment of both low inflation and low interest rates. The possible introduction at some stage of the euro, and the current level of modest inflation and a sustained period of growth, have reinforced this view.

One side effect of this otherwise positive economic outlook has been a revision downwards in the long-term assumptions for investment growth in pension funds. The Personal Investment Authority has responded to this by significantly reducing the rates used for projections of future pension funds. The changes, which take effect from July 1999, reduce the upper rate for projections from 12 to 9 per cent and the lower rate from 6 to 5 per cent. Over 25 years the effect on the final projected funds is a significant reduction. These are, of course, simply a projection of what might happen – the pension funds will grow in line with actual investment returns and are not affected by the changes to the rates used by insurance companies in their illustrations.

For investors the message is clear: to be sure of an adequate pension at retirement, contributions will need to increase significantly if the economic forecasts turn out to be correct. A similar message will be felt, over time, by employers running final salary occupational schemes who will face increased contributions for the future.

A second side effect of the changed economic picture has been that during the year, long-term interest rates continue to decline. Annuity rates are now at historically low levels as insurance companies have reduced their rates to reflect the lower yields on the assets held to back the annuity payments. This has caused an immediate drop in the retirement income for those retiring now. It has also made the ability to defer annuity purchase under a personal pension plan more attractive. Some commentators are now actively calling, with some force, for the requirement to purchase an annuity from an insurance company to be dropped altogether.

Annuity rates also fell because of improved mortality experience. Medical advances, healthier lifestyles and fewer smokers mean that people are living longer, increasing the costs of paying annuities, which are guaranteed for life. Recent studies by the Institute of Actuaries have revealed that life expectancy is improving dramatically, particularly for males, and that the pace of improvement is, if anything, accelerating. The chances of today's 20-year-olds living for much longer than the traditional three score years and ten are significantly greater than just ten or twenty years ago.

The combined effect of improved mortality and low interest rates has meant that policies sold in the 1970s and early 1980s which had annuity rate guarantees are now proving very attractive for investors. The guaranteed rates offered by these policies are often higher than current annuity rates. However, whilst this has meant that investors with these policies have benefited, the insurance companies have had to set aside significant reserves to pay for the increased sots of providing the guarantees. This has generated some controversy and, in the case of some

Equitable Life policyholders, a legal dispute as to how these costs are to be borne.

For pensioners retiring now, today's low annuity rates mean that it is often too late to contribute more to their pensions – their choice may be restricted to accepting a low pension or, if they can, deferring the purchase of annuity. Annuity deferral, or income withdrawal, may be attractive for some but it is not without its risks. The fact that the level of income is not guaranteed for life is something that must be taken into account. Annuity deferral may only be suitable for investors with larger pension funds who are able to accept a relatively high level of risk.

It is clear that 20-year-olds starting a pension today need to set realistic levels of regular contributions and maintain these throughout their working lives; this is likely to be the only strategy to achieve a reasonable level of retirement provision. For everyone else, now is the time to review existing pension arrangements to ensure that they will be adequate. A delay in starting or in increasing contributions at or to a realistic level is likely to prove costly.

The industry made good progress in resolving mis-selling cases with most of the major firms achieving their targets for completion of Phase 1 of the Pensions Review. Phase 2 of the review is now well underway, having been heralded by a hard-hitting TV advertising campaign led by the Financial Services Authority. The campaign trod a dangerous line – although it is to be applauded as a means to encourage investors to ask for cases to be reviewed, it risked giving the impression that the scale of mis-selling is much greater than it is. When the dust has finally settled on the Review, the final reckoning will reveal that the overwhelming majority of personal pensions were correctly sold and represented good advice. If the fear of potential mis-selling deters investors from making adequate pension provision, the real social costs of the Review may prove to be very significant indeed.

Against this background, the Government's proposals for pension reform in its Green Paper (see **15.8** below) have a tough task if they are to meet the stated objective of increasing retirement provision. The changes, although not due to take effect until at least April 2001, are likely to have a considerable effect on UK pensions, both through the introduction of stakeholder pensions and changes to the state pension scheme. The Green Paper proposals have been the subject of a wide-ranging consultation, which will continue for some months to come yet.

In the interim period there is considerable uncertainty about the exact form the final proposals will take. Both the industry and the regulators have been concerned about the prospect of 'planning blight' if investors deferred decisions to start new plans or make increases before April 2001. Although care is still needed to select a plan that is suitable, the industry has responded with a wide range of options for investors who may wish to transfer to a stakeholder pension when these become available. Delaying the start of a pension can significantly reduce the final pension fund. The Government will need to avoid extending the planning blight period by finalising its proposals as quickly as it can. Equally, investors should not be put off from starting contributions now and should ask their advisors for information about the options available to them when choosing a pension plan.

15.3 THE STATE PENSION SCHEME

The benefit the State provides to those in retirement falls into two main parts: the basic retirement pension and a supplementary earnings related pension (SERPS). Everyone is entitled to the basic retirement pension payable at State Retirement Age, subject to payment of the necessary National Insurance contributions. For an individual whose earnings have been at the national average level throughout their working life, the State will provide a basic pension of approximately one-third of the final earnings level.

The State Retirement Age is currently 65 for males and 60 for females. The State Retirement Age will be equalised in the future at 65 for both males and females. This will apply to women retiring after 6 April 2010 with a sliding scale for women retiring over the previous ten years. For women whose dates of birth are on or after 6 April 1955 the common State Retirement Age of 65 will apply. Women born before 6 April 1950 will benefit from the current age of 60. For those women with dates of birth

Table 15.1 New State Retirement Ages for women

Date of Birth		Pension age (years/months)	New pension date
Before 6 April 1950		60/0	–
6 April –	5 May 1950	60/1	6 May 2010
6 May 1950 –	5 June 1950	60/2	6 July 2010
6 June 1950 –	5 July 1950	60/3	6 September 2010
6 July 1950 –	5 August 1950	60/4	6 November 2010
6 August 1950 –	5 September 1950	60/5	6 January 2011
6 September 1950 –	5 October 1950	60/6	6 March 2011
6 March 1951 –	5 April 1951	61/0	6 March 2012
6 March 1952 –	5 April 1952	62/0	6 March 2014
6 March 1953 –	5 April 1953	63/0	6 March 2016
6 March 1954 –	5 April 1954	64/0	6 March 2018
6 March 1955 –	5 April 1955	65/0	6 March 2020
6 April 1955 and after		65/0	–

between those dates the sliding scale applies. For each month (or part of a month) that a woman's date of birth is after 6 April 1950, her retirement date will be deferred by one month.

SERPS was introduced in April 1978 to provide an additional State pension based on earnings (within certain limits) rather than the flat benefit provided by the retirement pension. SERPS also provides a widow's benefit if a husband dies after retirement and also, in certain circumstances, if he dies before retirement. SERPS is funded by the higher rate National Insurance contributions payable by both employers and employees. The self-employed do not contribute towards, or benefit from, SERPS.

In recent years the State pension scheme has come under pressure by increases in life expectancy and larger numbers of retired people in the population. These concerns led the Government to reduce the benefits under SERPS so that only those reaching State pension age in the years 1998 and 1999 will receive the original maximum benefits. Those reaching State Retirement Age in or after the year 2010 will receive a pension of only 20 per cent of their earnings (within certain limits) instead of the 25 per cent originally intended, and the relevant earnings to be taken into account will be the average of lifetime earnings and not the best 20 years' of earnings, as was the original rule for SERPS. A sliding scale will operate for those retiring in the years 2000 to 2009.

15.4 CONTRACTING-IN AND CONTRACTING-OUT

Those who are participating in SERPS (ie employees earning more than the lower threshold for standard rate National Insurance contributions) are said to be 'contracted-in' to SERPS. Since SERPS was introduced it has been possible to opt-out of the scheme (referred to as 'contracting-out').

Until 6 April 1988, this 'contracting-out' was only possible through an employer-sponsored occupational pension scheme which guaranteed to provide a broadly equivalent level of benefits to the SERPS benefits being lost. Since 6 April 1988, employers have been able to offer contracting-out on a 'money purchase' basis without having to provide the guarantee previously required. In both cases National Insurance contributions are reduced for both the employer and employee but with the loss of SERPS benefits.

However, this change still left the decision whether to offer contracted-out status firmly in the employer's hands. Further changes which took effect on 1 July 1988 gave the individual employee the right to contract out of SERPS on an individual basis, without his or her employer's consent. The personal pension plans which enable this are also money-purchase arrangements.

Contracting-out through personal pension plans involves the payment of 'protected rights contributions' to the relevant pension contract. The contributions are identified separately from any other contributions paid and create a 'protected rights fund'; it is the 'protected rights benefits' paid out of this fund at retirement which replace the SERPS benefits lost through the decision to contract out. The Pensions Act 1995 introduces a system of age-related contracting-out rebates which applies for the tax year 1997–98 and onwards.

Contracting-out via a personal pension plan is an annual decision and the individual can contract back into SERPS for the purposes of future benefits.

In general, contracting-out will be of benefit to younger employees but may not match the likely SERPS entitlement for some older people and for those on lower earnings.

15.5 TYPES OF PENSION CONTRACTS

There are two main types of pension contract in the context of life assurance investment:

(1) Personal pension plans for the self-employed and individuals who are not in pensionable employment take the form of deferred annuity contracts between the individual and the life company directly and are purchased by single or regular premiums.

(2) Occupational pension schemes take the form of contracts between the trustees of the scheme (set up by the employer) and the insurance company (in the case of an insured scheme) and provide benefits for employees as a group or on an individual earmarked basis. Controlling directors of director-controlled companies other than investment companies are also eligible for occupational pension schemes.

Since April 1988 individuals have been able to opt out of their occupational pension scheme and provide for their own benefit via a personal pension plan. It is often not advisable to do this if the occupational pension scheme is a good one. Alternatively they will be able to top-up the pension provided by their occupational scheme by making Additional Voluntary Contributions to that scheme or by effecting a free-standing AVC (FSAVC) plan with a pension provider of their choice.

15.6 CHARACTERISTICS OF PENSION CONTRACTS

As with life assurance policies there is a wide variety of types of investment. Companies offer with profit contracts with a level of guaranteed benefits but the right to participate in profits and unit-linked contracts with a wide choice of unit funds and the ability to switch between funds to provide growth on top of any guaranteed benefits. A further development has been a series of guaranteed equity funds, where investors can benefit from the performance of an index, usually the FTSE 100 Index, but are protected from stock market falls.

An attractive option for some employers is to split their pension investment between an insurance company and other investment media by what is known as a 'self-administered scheme'. One of the attractions of such an arrangement is the facility of investing part of the pension fund in the employing company itself either by loans or equity investment (see **15.7.6**).

An attraction of all pension contracts is that the income and capital growth produced by the investment of the premiums accumulate on a gross basis, because pension funds are not generally subject to UK income tax or capital gains tax, although from 2 July 1997 approved pension schemes are no longer able to reclaim the tax credits against the dividends from UK equities.

As the contracts provide essentially for retirement annuities and pensions, they cannot generally be surrendered for a cash consideration: benefits must take the form of pensions (part of which can be commuted on retirement) and life cover (including a return of the premiums with reasonable interest, which in the case of unit-linked contracts means the growth in value of the units). An important feature of many of these contracts is the 'open market option' at retirement, enabling the annuitant to use the accumulated fund to purchase an annuity or pension from any other company offering a higher rate. Although funds invested in these contracts generally remain 'locked in' until retirement, the availability of loans, on commercial terms, to companies taking out pension schemes or to individual members of these schemes can overcome this limitation (see **15.7.6**).

15.7 ELIGIBILITY, TAXATION, CONTRIBUTION LIMITS AND BENEFITS

15.7.1 The life company

The income and gains attributable to the life company's pension liabilities are effectively free of UK tax, and it is thus able to pass on to its policyholders the entire gross increase in value of the assets and income, after deduction of its charges, without any deduction for UK tax. However, from 2 July 1997 the life company is unable to reclaim the tax credits against the dividends from UK equities.

15.7.2 Personal pension plans

Eligibility

You will be eligible to make contributions to a personal pension plan (PPP) if you are in receipt of 'relevant earnings'. This means either earnings from non-pensionable employments, or from businesses, professions, partnerships, etc. Generally, you are not eligible if you belong to a pension scheme operated by your employer, but you are eligible if it provides only a sum assured payable on your death while in the employer's service. Controlling directors of investment companies are not eligible for any form of PPP in respect of earnings from such a company nor are certain other controlling directors who are in receipt of benefits from their employer's occupational scheme.

Tax relief on premiums and limits

If you have relevant earnings, and pay either single or annual premiums to a PPP within the limits mentioned below, you enjoy full tax relief on those premiums in the relevant years. However, an 'earnings cap' applies so that contributions to a PPP will only be possible in respect of earnings up to £90,600 for the 1999–2000 tax year (previously £87,600 for the 1998–99 tax year). The legislation provides that this figure will be increased in future years in line with the RPI (although this did not apply for the tax year 1993–94).

Employees can pay premiums net of basic rate and any higher rate relief is claimed through the PAYE coding. The 20 per cent lower rate band does not affect the rate at which employees can deduct basic rate tax. The self-employed must make contributions gross, and claim relief through their annual tax return, a separate claim or, in some cases, by a reduction in subsequent payments on account under the self-assessment system.

The annual limit for contributions to PPPs is 17.5 per cent of your 'net relevant earnings'. This means relevant earnings from your non-pensionable employment or business, etc, less certain deductions such as expenses, trading losses and capital allowances. The limits for older tax-payers are currently as shown below.

An amount not exceeding 5 per cent of your net relevant earnings can be used to provide a lump sum payable from the PPP in the event of your death before age 75. Premiums used to provide this life cover must be included as part of the contributions you are permitted to pay to your PPP.

Age at beginning of year of assessment	%
36–45	20.0
46–50	25.0
51–55	30.0
56–60	35.0
61 and over	40.0

Contributions may be paid to a PPP and a s 226 contract (see **15.7.4**) at the same time but the contribution limits apply to the 'aggregate' of contributions to the two plans (although the 'aggregation' is not always straightforward and paying contributions to both a PPP and a s 226 con-tract can restrict the overall contribution possible in some cases, particularly where contributions are above the earnings cap).

If your employer pays contributions to your PPP, these too must be taken as part of the maximum contribution which can be made to your plan. Employer's contributions are not treated as the employee's income. Protected rights contributions paid to your PPP to enable you to contract out of SERPS can be paid in addition to the maximum permissible contribution calculated as the appropriate percentage of your net relevant earnings.

Years for which relief is granted

Generally, relief is given against net relevant earnings of the tax year in which the contributions are paid. However, you can elect to have any premium you pay treated for tax purposes as if it has been paid during the preceding tax year, or, if you had no relevant earnings in that year, for the premium to be relieved against earnings in the tax year before that; ie there is a 'carry-back' period of one or two years.

To the extent that premiums paid in any year fall short of the permitted maximum of net relevant earnings, it is possible to 'carry forward' the shortfall on unused relief for up to six years and use the shortfall (on a first-in first-out basis) to obtain relief against a premium paid in a subsequent year, to the extent that that premium exceeds the maximum percentage limit of net relevant earnings for the year in which it is paid. The amount of relief which is available in any year as a result of the carry back and carry forward provisions is restricted to the amount of net relevant earnings for that year.

Benefits payable and age at which they may be taken

The PPP scheme established by the pension provider can allow the individual to make more than one contract (or arrangement) under it. The advantages of this are that, as benefits from an arrangement can, generally, be taken only once if they are to include a cash lump sum, multiple arrangements can give the opportunity to take benefits in stages.

Your pension may start being paid at any age between 50 and 75. It is not necessary for you actually to retire before the annuity can commence. In certain occupations the Revenue allow an annuity to start earlier than the age of 50 (eg jockeys, motor racing drivers, cricketers, etc).

It is no longer necessary to purchase an annuity when benefits from a personal pension are taken. The annuity purchase can be deferred until age 75. Until then, or the date when the annuity is purchased if earlier, income withdrawals are taken up to a limit broadly equal to the amount of the single life annuity which could have been taken. The amount of income withdrawals has to be reviewed every three years and the withdrawals are taxable in the same way as annuity payments.

Should your PPP incorporate a sum assured, on your premature death the lump sum would be paid and this can be arranged to be free of inheritance tax by writing it in trust where the PPP scheme itself is not set up under trust. The whole of any annuity payable either to you, your spouse or your dependants will be treated and taxed as income (and not, as is the case with purchased life annuities, partly as income and partly as a return of capital – see **14.3.4**). The annuity is taxed under Schedule E and subject to the PAYE system.

A lump sum may be taken from the PPP, between the ages of 50 and 75, up to a maximum of 25 per cent of the fund then being used to provide you with retirement benefits.

You are permitted, instead of taking the annuity from the life company with whom you hold the contract, to utilise the fund built up for your annuity to purchase an annuity from any other company, thus obtaining the best terms then available ('open market option'). If your PPP is provided by an organisation which is not a life assurance company, your pension (and life assurance) must be provided by a life company.

15.7.3 Contracting-out via a PPP

Scheme certificates

If a PPP has an 'appropriate scheme certificate' from the Occupational Pensions Board it will be able to receive protected rights contributions (and may be funded by them entirely) and so enable the individual employee to contract out of SERPS. A PPP which receives only protected rights contributions (a 'PPP(PRO)') can be effected by an employee who is a member of a contracted-in occupational scheme but wishes to contract out on an individual basis.

Contributions

Protected rights contributions consist of a National Insurance rebate. For the tax years 1999–2000, 2000–01 and 2001–02, the rebates are age related and vary between 3.8 and 9 per cent of the individual employee's band earnings (the earnings between the upper and lower earnings limits). Both employer and employee continue to pay full National Insurance but the rebate is paid by the DSS to the individual's plan after the end of the relevant tax year.

(From April 1993 to April 1997 a system of flat-rate rebates operated with an incentive of 1 per cent of band earnings payable for those over 30.)

The protected rights pension must commence between State pension age and the age of 75. From 6 April 1996 males will be able to take their protected rights pensions at age 60 in the same way as females. It must increase at 3 per cent per annum or the rate of the RPI, whichever is lower, and must not discriminate between males and females, married or single people in terms of the annuity rates offered. No lump sum benefit can be taken from the protected rights fund.

A protected rights pension must continue for the benefit of a widow/ widower or dependant on the individual's death, at a rate not less than one-half of the individual's pension. On death before retirement age the protected rights fund can be paid to the deceased's estate or nominees but no life assurance sum assured can be included in the protected rights benefits.

15.7.4 Retirement annuity contracts (s 226 contracts)

In many ways s 226 contracts were similar to the new PPPs but there are some key differences, eg no employer's contributions; contributions paid gross and the tax reclaimed; no facility for an employee to contract out through a s 226 contract and no general entitlement to take benefits before the age of 60. One important way in which a s 226 contract could be more favourable than a PPP was in providing a cash commutation equal to three times the annual annuity payable after the cash had been taken. This figure is often more than the 25 per cent of the fund available as a lump sum under a PPP. (Contracts entered into on or after 21 March 1987 are subject to a maximum cash lump sum of £150,000 per contract.) The earnings cap does not apply to s 226 contracts and the contribution limits are also different from those which apply to PPPs.

No new s 226 contracts could be entered into after 30 June 1988 but contracts in existence by that date can continue much as before. Contributions can continue to be paid to such contracts and regular contributions can be increased in the future.

Note that, although many s 226 contracts contain an open market option to allow the annuity to be purchased from a life company other than the one with whom the pension plan has been effected, exercising such an option after 30 June 1988 has the effect of transferring the policy proceeds to a new PPP (unless the policyholder has a second s 226 contract already in existence with that other life company). Thus, in the absence of another s 226 contract, the benefits will be paid out of a PPP with the resulting less favourable calculation of the maximum cash lump sum compared to the s 226 contract.

15.7.5 Occupational schemes

These are schemes provided by an employer for the benefit of some or all of his employees but they are not available to directors of investment companies. To be effective, the scheme should be approved by the Pension Scheme Office (PSO) which is a branch of the Inland Revenue.

'Approval' will prevent contributions paid by the employer being taxed in the employees' hands as a benefit in kind. 'Exempt approval' gives the additional benefits of the gross roll-up in the fund and tax relief for the employee in respect of regular contributions he makes to the scheme. Exempt approval also means that the employer's contributions are deductible business expenses without relying on the normal rules for deductibility applying to Schedule D income. In most cases approval is given under the PSO's discretionary powers which are extremely wide-ranging.

It is not possible for an employer to make membership of an occupational scheme (other than one providing death in service benefits only) compulsory. Employees are able to opt out of their employer's scheme and so become eligible to effect their own PPP, independent of the employer. In general, leaving an occupational scheme is unlikely to be wise except where its benefits are extremely poor; expert advice should be sought if this is contemplated.

Contributions

The employer must make some contribution to the scheme although the employee may indirectly provide the necessary funds by agreeing to a reduction in salary — 'a salary sacrifice'. Contributions by the employer to an exempt approved scheme are deductible business expenses, although relief on non-regular contributions may be deferred by being spread over a maximum of five years. The employee may make personal contributions of up to 15 per cent of his or her remuneration. Personal contributions attract tax relief at the highest rate paid by the individual.

Unlike PPPs there are no specific limits on the amount of contributions which may be made to an occupational scheme; instead (subject to the various 'income capping' rules referred to below) the controls operate on the level of benefits which is allowed. If a scheme becomes 'overfunded' (ie where the scheme has more capital than is necessary to meet its prospective liabilities), payment of further contributions may be restricted or capital may have to be returned to the employer. If a refund is made to the employer it is taxable at a special rate of 40 per cent.

Benefits and limits

The benefits that can be provided by an approved occupational scheme are regulated by a series of Inland Revenue limits. These limits have been restricted over the years including important changes announced in the 1987 and 1989 budgets. Each generation of limits has in general been preserved or 'grandfathered' for those who were members of existing schemes at the time of the budget when the changes were announced. Other changes, the majority of them relatively minor, have also been made at other times. Details of the earlier limits can be found in previous editions of this work and in the *Allied Dunbar Pensions Handbook*. The limits which apply to members joining new schemes are summarised below.

The Inland Revenue limits are based on a percentage of the individual's 'final remuneration'. This must be calculated in one of the two ways permitted by the PSO, namely:

(1) the remuneration in any of the five years preceding retirement, leaving service or death (as applicable) together with the average of any bonuses, commissions, etc averaged over at least three consecutive years ending with the year in question; or
(2) the highest average of the total earnings over any period of three consecutive years during the last ten years of service.

Certain items are excluded from the calculation, such as share option and share incentive gains and golden handshakes, and some controlling directors have to use the second definition of final remuneration. There is also a maximum amount of earnings that can be taken into account and this is £90,600 for the 1999–2000 tax year (previously £87,600 for the 1998–99 tax year). This figure should increase in future years in line with the RPI (although indexation did not apply for the 1993–94 tax year).

Within this framework, an individual can accrue a pension at the rate of one-thirtieth of final remuneration for each year of service with his employer up to a maximum of two-thirds final remuneration. To achieve this it is necessary to achieve 20 years of service.

The benefits can be taken on retirement between age 50 and 75. The benefits must be in the form of a pension but part of the pension can be commuted for a tax-free lump sum. The maximum lump sum is three-eightieths of final remuneration for each year of service or 2.25 times the pension available before commutation, if greater. The maximum lump sum, again available after 20 years of service, is one and a half times final salary.

It is also possible to incorporate widows' and dependants' benefits, including a lump sum of up to four times salary, together with a refund of personal contributions, which can be paid free of tax.

Company directors

In general, the same rules apply to 'controlling' directors as to any individual in an occupational pension scheme. However, because a director of a family company is in a rather different position from an ordinary employee, the Revenue have imposed some limitations on directors with at least 20 per cent control, eg the measurement of final salary is more stringent than for non-controlling directors. Directors with 20 per cent control and members of families controlling more than 50 per cent of the company are not eligible to join a company's approved pension scheme if it is an investment company.

15.7.6 Loans and self-investment

The use of pensions in connection with loans made to the pension plan-holder or occupational scheme member helps to reduce one of the disadvantages of pension schemes, ie capital invested in the fund is 'locked-in' until retirement.

Typically, a lender who makes an interest-only loan might expect the individual to repay the capital out of any lump sum entitlement from the pension. Such lump sums will not be assigned to the lender as security for the loan but, for example where the loan is for house purchase, the mortgage over the property, assigned life assurance protection and the existence of the pension cash entitlement will usually satisfy the lender's requirements.

It is important that the pension contracts remain independent of the loan arrangements and that effecting the pension does not guarantee the availability of the loan. The pension must not be taken out to obtain the loan as the pensions legislation requires the pension scheme to be solely for the purpose of obtaining retirement benefits.

Another approach to 'unlocking' some of the pension fund is for the fund to be invested, in part, in shares of the employer company, in making the loans to the company or in purchasing premises from which the company trades.

There are restrictions on the availability and amount of loans that can be made to the employer company under the Social Security Act 1990. In addition, Inland Revenue rules have also restricted this type of 'self-investment'. Loans are limited, for the first two years of a scheme's existence, to 25 per cent of the fund's value excluding transfer values, followed by a limit of 50 per cent of the fund.

The other approaches, which are also subject to restrictions, are usually only available to self-administered schemes in which the trustees have wide powers of investment compared to 'insured schemes' where the investment is usually confined to a policy issued by the insurance company concerned.

15.7.7 Contracting-out via an occupational scheme

As already mentioned, it is possible to use money-purchase schemes to contract out of SERPS.

A contracted-out money purchase (COMP) scheme will receive protected rights contributions as is the case with a PPP. However, from April 1997 a COMP will receive the payments partly in the form of monthly direct flat-rate payments from the employer and partly in the form of age-related payments from the DSS as with a PPP. The total rebates from all sources range between 2.2 per cent and 9 per cent for the tax years 1999–2000, 2000–01 and 2001–02.

With a COMP, the Inland Revenue's limits on maximum benefits apply to the aggregate of the protected rights and non-protected rights benefits; a contracted-in occupational scheme member may obtain the maximum benefits from the occupational scheme, in addition to the protected rights benefits, from a PPP(PRO) effected to contract out of SERPS. The age-related incentive payable from April 1993 did not apply to a COMP.

Protected rights benefits from a COMP can be taken at age 60 by both males and females.

15.7.8 Unapproved occupational schemes

These may be established by employers to provide benefits greater than those otherwise allowable. In this way, for example, benefits in excess of two-thirds of final salary can be provided and top-up pensions can be given to employees with short service or those who are subject to 'income capping'.

There are none of the special tax benefits normally received by approved pension schemes and employer contributions will only obtain relief under the normal business expenditure rules, but lump sums can be paid free of tax from funded schemes. However, such schemes do retain certain tax benefits including, in some cases, the ability to roll up income at the basic rate of tax rather than at the special rate of tax applicable to some trusts. In appropriate cases this can result in a saving of tax where the employee is a higher rate taxpayer, as is likely to be the case. In addition, prior to 6 April 1998, realised capital gains were taxed at the basic rate (23 per cent for the tax year 1997–98) but are now taxed at the rate of 34 per cent applicable to all trusts. Until 30 November 1994 it was also possible to set up offshore schemes with enhanced taxation benefits. Although the employee is subject to tax on payments into the scheme (whether set up offshore or not), it was also possible to arrange for a degree of tax-free growth and freedom from tax on lump sum benefits. This is no longer possible as the Finance Act 1994 imposed a new tax charge on schemes set up to avoid tax in this way. The new rules apply to all schemes set up after the 1994 November budget and existing schemes which are varied after that date.

15.7.9 Free-standing AVC schemes

Since October 1987, all occupational scheme members are entitled to top-up their pensions by making contributions to a separate pension scheme of their own. Such a 'Free-Standing' Additional Voluntary Contribution (FSAVC) scheme may not be commuted for a cash lump sum and must be aggregated with the occupational scheme to determine the maximum permitted benefits. The overriding limit on personal contributions, 15 per cent of salary (capped where appropriate), remains.

Although regulated by the occupational pension scheme tax legislation, FSAVC schemes also have similarities to PPPs in that they are individual arrangements independent of the individual's employer. The maximum limits on benefits and contributions are, however, those applicable to occupational schemes (see above). An employee's contributions to such schemes must be paid net of tax relief at the basic rate.

As long as contributions to the FSAVC do not exceed £2,400 per annum, the employer need have no involvement in an employee joining an FSAVC scheme. Even where the contributions exceed £2,400, the employer's involvement at the outset is restricted to providing sufficient information to allow the maximum contribution which can be paid to be calculated by the FSAVC provider. In some cases the funds built up in the FSAVC together with the benefits from the employer's scheme may exceed the Inland Revenue limits. Where a scheme is overfunded in this way any over-provision is returned to the scheme member subject to a tax charge. This charge also applies to AVC schemes established in-house by employers.

15.8 WELFARE REFORM

At the end of 1998, the Government published its proposal on Welfare Reform. This took the form of a consultation paper entitled 'A New Contract for Welfare: Partnership in Pensions'. The need for reform is set out starkly in the introduction to the paper. The Government's view is that the 'current system – public and private – will not guarantee a decent income in retirement for everyone. On the contrary, it risks leaving up to a third of future pensioners facing poverty'. The reforms are wide-ranging and will, when they come into force, affect many of the areas covered in this chapter. What follows is a brief summary of some of the main proposals, although it should be borne in mind that they are subject to further consultation and will inevitably change over the coming months.

The basic state pension will be retained and, coupled with the new 'minimum income guarantee', will provide a basic retirement income for all. As now, the state pension will be increased in line with price inflation each year.

The State Earnings Related Pension Scheme (SERPS) will be replaced by a new 'State Second Pension' (SSP). The SSP will primarily be targeted at low earners (ie those earning less than £9,000 per year). Those earning less than £9,000, but more than the lower earnings limit, will receive an SSP of roughly double the amount that SERPS pays to a person on the same earnings. Those off work who are caring for young children or disabled relatives, or who are ill or disabled themselves are likely to be allocated 'credits' towards the SSP. These changes are likely to come into effect at the earliest in April 2000.

For middle earners, primarily those earning between £9,000 and £18,500, the Government intends to introduce a new 'stakeholder' pension scheme. The new plan may also benefit higher earners too. Stakeholder pensions are intended to be 'secure', 'low cost' and 'flexible'. Security will be achieved by setting up schemes under trust with independent trustees who, it is intended, will protect the interests of scheme members. The low cost element is intended to be achieved by requiring those employers who do not offer an occupational scheme to provide access to a stakeholder pension scheme and collect contributions by deductions from their employees' salaries. In this way, it is hoped that advertising and administrative costs will be lower. Stakeholder pension schemes will have a simple charging structure, probably with a set maximum level of charges. Flexibility will be achieved by ensuring that there will be no penalties for stopping or restarting contributions and allowing scheme members who stop working to contribute, with tax relief, for a period of five years.

The tax advantages of stakeholder pension schemes will be similar to personal pensions, in other words tax relief on contributions and a tax-free lump sum of up to one quarter of the fund. Contributions to the scheme are, however, likely to be limited to a fixed sum of £3,600 per year or 100 per cent of earnings, if lower.

15.9 SUITABILITY

Personal pension plans and occupational pension schemes provide highly tax-efficient benefits. In consequence they are suitable for and extremely attractive as investments for those with earned income who wish to provide for personal cash and income during retirement and protection for their wives and families during their working lives. Because the premiums are deductible for tax purposes from earned income, the effective cost is relatively low, while the tax-free growth inside the pension fund enables substantial accumulation of funds for pension benefits. The emerging benefits, in the form of tax-free cash commutation and pensions, receive beneficial tax treatment. However, the fact that pension benefits can only be taken after certain ages tends to make such schemes suitable only for those prepared to take a long-term view.

15.10 PREVIEW OF THE YEAR AHEAD

Making predictions for the year ahead is seldom easy. However, over the next year it is already clear that the pensions scene will be dominated by the Government's Welfare Reform proposals.

Experience from similar reform programmes in other parts of the world shows that we are likely to be in for a prolonged period of 'reform by press release'. While the Government's intentions may be clear, there remains a vast amount of detail which has still to be resolved. These 'details', some of which are fairly fundamental, are likely to emerge piecemeal over the coming months. The Government has already announced that it plans a series of further consultation exercises and industry pundits will be keen to seize upon the next snippet of information. In some cases this will take the form of formal proposals from the Government. In others it will be the result of speculation – informed or otherwise.

The essential areas which have still to be resolved centre on the form that stakeholder pension schemes will take. Some crucial questions remain unanswered. Will stakeholder pension schemes be available to the self-employed? The Government hopes to extend them to the self-employed but has not decided how this will be done. Will it possible to have a stakeholder pension and a personal pension at the same time? At the time of writing, the current proposals suggest that this will not be possible, but this has been criticised by some commentators. How will tax relief be given on stakeholder pension schemes? Will this be through a 'pensions relief at source' system, such as that for personal pensions, or by other means? What is the relationship between stakeholder pension schemes and the Treasury's proposals for a 'pooled personal investment' (PPI) vehicle? The concept of PPIs was announced separately by the Treasury, but they appear to be intended to be similar to the DSS stakeholder proposals without the independent trustee structure.

One further question will be whether the problems with annuities can be satisfactorily resolved. Forcing investors to purchase annuities, as they must do at age 75 even where they have elected to defer annuity purchase to the latest date, creates problems for insurance companies and investors alike. Solving this problem will, on its own, be a difficult task.

The current level of uncertainty must be swiftly addressed if confusion and genuine planning blight are not to prevail. The position for investors and advisors alike is unsatisfactory while the uncertainty remains. Deferring the start of a pension comes with a near guaranteed cost in the form of a lower pension fund at retirement. This goes against the main thrust of the Government's proposals which is that those who can afford to save for their retirement do so.

The Government has recognised that investors need better information about the choices available to them. The Green Paper proposals included plans for better information on schemes, including the development of telephone information lines and better annual statements. The premise is that this will enable investors to 'see for themselves if they should save more for retirement'. In practice, it is doubtful whether the provision of information alone will be sufficient to encourage more people to save.

The Government has specifically rejected more compulsion in the pensions system. If it wants to meet its objective of delivering rising incomes to the majority of pensioners, it needs to ensure that stakeholder pensions are both attractive and accessible to investors. In turn, this means that it will need to reflect the need for investors to have individual advice when it sets the charging basis for stakeholder pension schemes. One thing the proposals will not do is make pensions any simpler. Nothing short of the wholesale sweeping away of the existing system would have achieved that and the Government has rejected that option too. The need for advice has never been greater with even more choices available to investors. The lower charges envisaged in the stakeholder environment, although a laudable aim in itself, may prove costly if it is made more difficult for pension firms to provide proper advice tailored to individual circumstances.

The Government's Green Paper summed it up: 'Pensions are all about security. We all want to be able to retire on a decent income, and as we live longer and healthier lives, we want to be able to save more, so we can make the most of our retirement.' In practice, for most people this means that they will need to save more from a younger age to provide for a retirement which may be longer than ever before.

15.11 CONCLUSION

The tax-deductibility of premiums, largely tax-free growth and prospects of a tax-free lump sum make pensions an extremely attractive investment.

There are, of course, some restrictions (lack of access to the fund until a minimum age, ability to take only a proportion as a lump sum, limits on the investment permitted, etc) but these do not detract from the investment benefit of pensions where the pension is effected for the right reasons, ie as long-term planning for retirement.

USEFUL ADDRESSES

See end of Chapter 14.

16

COMMODITIES

MARTIN SQUIRES

Rudolf Wolff & Co Ltd

This chapter is aimed as an introduction to the commodity markets and a brief review and forecast of markets themselves. The areas covered are:

(1) Introduction to commodities.
(2) Types of commodities: physical and futures markets.
(3) Characteristics of commodities.
(4) Methods to participate in the markets: cash, futures, options and managed funds.
(5) Recent market performance and outlook for the year ahead.

16.1 INTRODUCTION TO COMMODITIES: WHAT THEY ARE

The commodity markers had their origins in the Industrial expansion of the 19th century. Industrialisation led to a rapid growth in demand for basic commodities, which created increased price volatility as supplies became more dependent on the arrival of shipments from abroad. This price volatility meant more efficient means were needed to price and allocate commodities. The early commodity markets therefore enabled traders to buy and sell contracts for physical commodities, on the basis of today's prices for delivery in the future.

Today's commodities exchanges still provide this service, although they have generally evolved to provide more of a pricing mechanism, where traders buy and sell the right to a commodity (a future), than trading the physical commodity. That said, the commodity exchanges are still backed by physical delivery and if a futures contract becomes prompt, then it is the physical commodity that has to be delivered or taken up.

The prime reason for the markets is still to provide a means whereby trade users can fix the price at which they sell or buy their raw material commodities in the future. For fabricators using commodities, this means that the price of their finished goods can be determined before being produced, by locking-in (hedging) the cost of the commodities needed to produce the finished goods. Likewise a producer can plan in advance whether it is profitable to continue producing the commodity in the period ahead. If the future price is above the full cost of production, the producer can sell futures against forward production and guarantee a profit for the period ahead.

Today's commodity markets are very sophisticated and form an integral part of the world financial markets where banks, producers, consumers, merchants and investors are all participants.

This chapter largely deals with the concepts of the commodity markets with insight into those commodities that can be bought and sold through, or are regulated by, the London Clearing House, The London Metal Exchange, The London Commodity Exchange, and London International Financial Futures Exchange.

16.2 TYPES OF COMMODITIES

16.2.1 Softs and metals

The raw material commodities can be sub-divided into two categories: soft commodities and metals.

The term 'soft commodities' loosely describes all non-metallic commodities: cocoa, coffee, sugar, rubber, grain, potatoes, wool, edible oil, nuts, etc. The London Commodity Exchange was merged with LIFFE and is Europe's primary soft commodity exchange, operating markets in coffee, cocoa, sugar, the BIFFEX Freight Index and UK domestic agriculture markets.

The London Metal Exchange (LME) is the centre for trade in the main non-ferrous base metal futures such as aluminium, copper, zinc, lead, nickel, tin and aluminium alloy. The London Bullion Market Association (LBMA) looks after the interests of London's bullion markets. The bullion markets are physical markets and not futures markets.

The London Clearing House (LCH) deals with the clearing and settlement of the futures markets. Membership of LCH guarantees the fulfilment of the contract to both buyer and seller, thus avoiding the need for both buyer and seller to be concerned with each other's financial health. In effect, the LCH becomes the counterparty to each trade that its members carry out with other members.

16.2.2 Physical and futures

The commodity markets can be broken down into 'physical' and 'futures'. The physical markets deal with trading of the actual commodity and would normally result in the physical exchange of a commodity. A futures contract deals with commodities that are traded for delivery at a pre-defined future date and in the majority of cases the commodity is not expected to be delivered. As a futures contract is a tradable contract, it is generally liquidated before the contract becomes prompt. This means that the contract is cancelled by a corresponding and opposite contract, which means the trader's net position is square and that any difference in buying and selling prices is settled in cash.

By buying or selling in the futures market against a physical position, hedgers are able to safeguard themselves against the risk that the value of their unsold goods will depreciate through a fall in price or, alternatively, against the risk that pre-booked forward sales will show a loss if the commodity price rises.

Example

A merchant, who has taken delivery of 25 tonnes of copper, but has not secured a buyer for the metal, is exposed to the risk of copper prices falling. To offset this risk (exposure), he can sell (hedge) one futures contract, the basis being the price at which he bought the physical metal. Upon finding a buyer for the physical metal, he then buys back his futures contract on the basis of the price at which he sells his physical metal. This means that while he holds the 25 tonnes of copper in stock, he is not vulnerable to a fall in the copper price, as any fall in the price is offset by a profit on his futures contract, and vice versa.

This mechanism for hedging risk works when the futures markets are liquid, that is when there are sufficient buyers and sellers to make a two-way market.

Market liquidity is increased by the existence of speculators. The speculator buys or sells a commodity on the expectation of making a profit. By taking the opposite view in the market to the hedger, the speculator takes on the unwanted risk that the hedger wants to avoid.

Investment in physical markets is complicated by having to pay the full cash cost of the commodity, the warehouse and insurance costs, etc. Metals have the advantage over soft commodities in that they are generally less bulky and are not perishable.

Investing in futures avoids many of the disadvantages of physical commodity investing. The speculator can avoid taking physical delivery of the commodity as long as the future contract is closed before the contract becomes prompt. By dealing in futures, the speculator is able to trade soft commodities as easily as metals, without the worry of the commodity perishing, or the more expensive storage costs.

16.2.3 Financial futures

The third category of futures is the financial futures, which regards money as another commodity. Financial futures grew rapidly in the 1980s and have enabled traders to use their money more flexibly by trading and hedging interest rates, bonds and stock market indices in the same way they would trade other raw material commodities.

These financial futures contracts are structured, regulated and cleared just like the raw material commodities and provide opportunities for investment managers, financial treasurers and traders seeking profit opportunities.

Interest rate market contracts are the most important of the financial futures. These range from short-dated three-month papers to long maturity government bonds and are denominated in most of the world's major trading currencies. The major contracts are traded in three time zones, providing around-the-clock access.

Stock index contracts are also well established and becoming increasingly popular, as are the option derivatives on the stocks. In addition to speculation, these products enable investors and fund managers to hedge their portfolio rapidly or to gain immediate access to the market (see **16.3–16.5**).

16.3 CHARACTERISTICS OF COMMODITIES

Commodity markets are sophisticated, internationally traded and price movements are often volatile. It is these characteristics which provide many attractive trading opportunities.

16.3.1 International markets

The word 'commodity' is defined in an economic sense as 'an exchangeable unit of economic wealth'. In most cases these units of economic wealth are internationally recognised and therefore have a real value, which is recognised and traded internationally. This widespread need for the commodities also means the markets are liquid and have high turnover as each commodity often passes through many traders'/industrialists' hands before being consumed. The liquidity, high volume and interest in these commodities means that in most cases it is possible to trade large volumes fairly quickly without disrupting the balance in the market.

16.3.2 Frequent opportunities

The prices of commodities continuously fluctuate as buying and selling pressure shifts. The driving forces for prices in the long term are the supply and demand fundamentals. In the short term the markets may move in the opposite direction to that suggested by the fundamental factors. This divergence provides further opportunities for trading. In the futures markets, because the prompt date is a date in the future, the contract can be sold short. This means that the trader can sell the contract before buying it back at a later date. Therefore, even if traders expect prices to fall, they can still trade and profit from a falling market. This second dimension to the futures market is not available to most private investors in equities. However, the futures markets can at times be very volatile, and the investor directly involved in a commodity will need to follow the market closely and is best advised to seek the guidance of an established broker and investment adviser.

16.3.3 Real assets

Raw material commodities are real assets with intrinsic values. This means that they could always be sold for cash and in the long term they are a good potential hedge against inflation or currency depreciation.

16.4 METHODS OF PARTICIPATION IN THE COMMODITY MARKETS

There are many opportunities for investors to participate in the commodity markets and a host of investment vehicles that can be used to do so. The following deals with the more direct approaches of investing in commodities and commodity futures.

16.4.1 Physical (cash) metals

Possibly the least speculative means of getting involved in the metals is to buy physical metal. Once bought, investors pay insurance and warehousing costs, but because payment has been made in full and there is no

---

gearing involved on the initial capital investment, they do not have to pay additional margin payments.

The time to buy cash metals is when prices have fallen considerably below the costs of metal production, which in theory should eventually lead to production cutbacks at plants that are no longer economically viable. This brings about a change in the supply and demand balance of the metal.

It should be made clear that an oversupply situation in the metal markets can last for a number of years, so this type of investment should be seen as a long-term investment strategy.

In addition, it should be realised that world production costs also fluctuate; in times of falling metal prices, producers attempt to cut production costs in an effort to remain economically profitable.

The long-term cyclical nature of commodity prices is inherent in the markets, as high prices encourage additional production and less consumption, for example through the emergence of substitutes. Consequently, a market which has a balanced supply and demand could become one with oversupply. This leads to lower prices. Conversely, in a period of low prices, consumption increases and production decreases, which eventually leads to a drawdown in stocks and higher prices as demand for metal outstrips supply. These cycles mean that the further prices diverge from the world production costs, the more likely there is a change in the direction of the price trend. These factors influence the market over the long term and may take a few years to change the direction of a commodities price.

16.4.2 Cash and carry

The cash and carry is a risk-free way of trading in commodities, for a known return on funds employed. In addition, a cash and carry sometimes provides opportunities for a capital gain.

This method of trading takes advantage of markets where forward prices are at a premium to cash (spot) prices. This premium is known as a 'contango'. In normal (contango) market conditions, the futures price is above the cash price. The exception to this occurs when there is a physical shortage of the commodity for nearby delivery; when this occurs, forward prices trade at a discount to the cash price. The discount is known as a backwardation. Normally the contango reflects the cost of storage, insurance, and the opportunity cost of tying up money while holding the physical commodity. In other words, the contango reflects the interest payments lost by not having the money in the bank, plus the cost of insurance, plus the cost of storage.

A cash and carry is a trade involving the purchase of a commodity for immediate delivery and simultaneously selling an equal amount of the commodity for a future delivery date. In a contango market, this means you are buying at a lower price and selling at a higher price. The difference is the gross profit. Occasionally, while the investor is holding a cash and carry, a shortage in the commodity occurs and the market's contango narrows or even turns into a backwardation. In this case holders of the cash and carry can sell their cash commodity and simultaneously buy back their future position, thereby making a capital gain. Contangos are limited to the cost of capital, storage costs and insurance, whilst backwardations have no natural limits. In recent years, market regulators, in particular the LME, have imposed backwardation limits to ensure orderly market trade conditions, that is to prevent market aberrations/manipulations.

16.4.3 Futures

The basic commodity traded on the exchanges is the outright futures contract. This provides the investor with a high-risk vehicle to trade commodities and requires the services of a futures broker. The buying or selling of a futures contract by an investor/speculator involves them taking a view on whether prices are set to rise or fall during the period of the futures contract. At any time during the life of the futures contract, the contract can be closed-out by making a corresponding and opposite trade.

For example, if an investor buys one March 2000 Cocoa then to close out his or her position he or she needs to sell one March 2000 Cocoa before the March 2000 Cocoa contract becomes due. If on 4 January he or she sells one LME three months copper, with a prompt date of 4 April, then when he or she closes the contract he or she needs to buy one lot of LME copper on the basis of the three months' price and then adjust the contract to the (prompt) date of his or her original short position – in this case 4 April.

Because dealing in futures is for forward delivery, only a proportion of the value of the contract is initially required as payment. This initial payment, known as initial margin, is normally around 10 per cent of the value of the full contract. Therefore, an investment in £100,000 worth of copper will only require an initial outlay of £10,000. This means that the funds the investor initially commits are geared at 10 per cent.

Your risk, however, is on the full £100,000 value of the commodity; therefore a 10 per cent move in the price of the commodity against the investor would mean a 100 per cent loss on his or her initial funds. Should the value of the commodity move against the investor, then he or she would be required immediately to provide funds equal to the open position loss of his or her futures contract. This difference is called 'variation margin' and is paid in addition to the initial margin. Both initial and variation margins are used by the broker as collateral against any difference in the current market value of the contract and the starting value of the contract when the investor initiated the trade.

It is this gearing and the need for variation margin payment which gives commodity markets their high-risk reputation. Of course, it is the ability to make 100 per cent on the investor's funds with only a 10 per cent movement in price which makes the market attractive to speculators.

16.4.4 Options

A less risky way to invest in the commodities is to buy options. An option is a traded contract which gives the buyer the right, but not the obligation, to buy a futures commodity at a specific price (strike price) at a predetermined date in the future. The risk is limited to the initial payment that the buyer has to pay for the option, which is known as the 'premium'. The advantage of trading options is that for a predetermined cost there is the potential for a significant gain. This premium can be traded, as it is calculated on the basis of the underlying future's current market price, volatility and the time until option is declared. Therefore, should the option become profitable, the holder of an option can at any time prior to the declaration of the option lock in a profit by one of the following means:

(1) trading a futures contract against the option position;
(2) selling the option and making a profit out of the difference between the premium paid to buy the option and the premium collected when sold;
(3) waiting until option declaration and notifying the broker that the holder intends to declare the option, in which case the option position is converted into a futures position at the strike price of the option. The investor then has to close the futures contract to take the profit, by establishing an equal and opposite futures position.

If the futures price moves in the opposite direction to the option, then the option holder allows the option to expire and the loss is limited to the initial premium paid.

There are numerous types of options and, by combining various types, the investor can produce option strategies which provide different opportunities.

The basic options are call and put options. A call option gives the buyer the right to buy a futures contract and a put option gives the buyer the right to sell a futures contract, but not the obligation (see also **6.6**).

A grantor (uncovered seller) of an option takes on unlimited risk, as by selling the option he or she gives the buyer of the option the right, but not the obligation, to take up a futures contract at a predetermined price on a predetermined date in the future. Option grantors are traditionally the trade (consumers and producers), who use options as a means of raising cash. Investment fund managers and risk seekers also grant options, but option granting is a high risk activity, whereas option buying will provide an investor with a highly leveraged position with a limited liability.

16.4.5 Managed funds

Investing in commodities through managed funds provides the ideal vehicle for investors to get exposure to the risk/rewards that the futures markets offer, but do not have the time, inclination or expertise to follow and trade the markets.

The types of funds on offer vary dependent on the level of risk/reward. Some offer a guarantee that at least the initial sum will be returned after a pre-set period, but this guarantee means that the fund is relatively lowly geared and therefore less risky than a highly geared fund where the initial investment is at risk.

Essentially there are two types of funds that invest in commodity futures, options and derivatives. The traditional type of funds are the Unauthorised Collective Investment Schemes, which pool investors' money so that the investment benefits from a diversified portfolio investing in futures and options. These funds are generally registered offshore and are open-ended funds, which work on a unit allocation basis (see also **8.13**).

The second category of funds is the Futures and Options Funds (FOFs) and the Geared Futures and Options Funds (GFOFs). These funds work in a similar fashion to the Authorised Unit Trusts, which traditionally were not allowed to invest in futures. At the time of writing these new funds have not been widely developed.

Funds generally operate on the basis that the fund manages the money it raises by investing the money with a number of Commodity Trading Advisors (CTAs). This enables the fund managers to select the best performing CTAs and as market conditions change, the allocation of money with each CTA can be optimised. The fund manager monitors the returns from the CTAs and handles the fund's administration and risk management.

Normally the only cost to the investor will be standard brokerage charges plus a small management fee of between 1 and 3 per cent and an incentive fee, which is assessed on the performance of the fund. This fee generally averages around 15 to 20 per cent of the increase in value of the fund in an agreed accounting period.

Commodity funds generally have full jurisdiction over the money invested with them, although some funds specialise in certain market segments and have pre-set risk management principles.

The performance of all funds relies heavily on fund managers' judgement and how accurately they anticipate the markets.

In selecting a fund manager, the investor needs to see how the manager has performed in the past. Although this by no means guarantees future performance, it does give some insight into how skilled the manager and the operation is.

The traditional funds are registered overseas to provide tax incentives for investors. Generally, the minimum investment into this traditional type of funds is around £10,000. The advantage of managed funds is that they provide individual investors and institutions with access to a market which is growing rapidly in volume and which provides numerous opportunities for investors to diversify their investment portfolio.

16.5 REVIEW AND OUTLOOK FOR COMMODITIES IN 1999–2000

Table 16.1 Changes in commodity values between 1997 and 1999

	End 1997	End 1998	End Q1 1999	% Fall 1997 to Q1 1999
Copper ($)	1,760	1,493	1,393	−21
Aluminium ($)	1,563	1,241	1,235	−21
Nickel ($)	6,120	4,110	4,830	−21
Zinc ($)	1,127	933	1,005	−11
Lead ($)	566	474	509	−10
Tin ($)	5,370	5,175	5,250	−2
Coffee ($)	1,702	1,815	1,530	−10
Sugar ($)	309	240	204	−34
Dow Jones	7679	9217	9822	28

16.5.1 **Financial markets**

The past couple of years have been a roller-coaster ride for all financial markets. The ride began in the summer of 1997 with the devaluation of the Thai Bhat. This triggered a chain reaction throughout Asia, as the global investment community scrambled to de-invest and place their funds into safer European and US investment vehicles. The simple reason for the switch out of ASEAN was the growing fear of debt defaults, following several years of over investment (ie creation of surplus capacity) and diminishing returns. This in turn exacerbated Asian debt defaults, resulting in mass bankruptcies, mounting unemployment and destruction of consumer wealth/spending power. These Tiger nations had for the past decade experienced rapid, near on double-digit economic growth, which was predicted to continue through into the new millennium. Nobody foresaw an end to the Asian miracle and invested in new capacity in anticipation of continued robust growth. As their financial markets collapsed, demand fell, plunging ASEAN into recession, creating global commodity surpluses as excess capacity which had been brought on line in anticipation of continued robust growth in Asia became redundant.

The ASEAN financial crisis then spread throughout the emerging world as bankers looked to retrench and cut their exposure in all newly industrialised economies, fearing debt contagion as global commodity prices declined. Reduced exports, hence shrinking commodity revenues, further exacerbated the plight of the developing economies, as their ability to repay foreign debt was heavily dependent on these revenues and the semi-fabricated goods they produced.

The next economy to fall was Russia's, triggering the collapse in the Rouble's value from 6 Roubles to 24 against the dollar in little under a month during the autumn of 1998. This discomfort then spread almost to the US's back door as Brazil looked set to catch Asian 'Flu, as the emerging market debt crisis has become known. Over this period, the Dow Jones came under increasing downward pressure as talk of an overdue correction swirled in the market, intensified by the near collapse of the highly (over-)leveraged LTCM hedge fund. These events led the tightening of global money supply and speculation that a global recession may be on the cards.

Crisis was averted as the Fed took action, easing rates and by so doing rekindling the strength in the US stock markets and their economy, which was entering its seventh year of expansion. The Dow Jones began 1998 at 6560; by the end of the year it had reached a high of 7679 and is currently threatening to accelerate through around 11000 to 12000. The ability of the Dow, and for that matter the major European bourses too, to sustain their upward momentum in the face of slowing global growth principally lies in the lack of secure and alternative investment vehicles for the money exiting the debt-ridden emerging economies. Contributing to this surge of investment was the wealth of money generated by US pension contributions, all underpinned by market uncertainty and the global deflationary environment.

Stability is slowly returning to these savaged emerging economies, which is beginning now to attract investment. Whilst US inflation remains contained and economic growth remains suppressed in Japan and Asia, the Dow Jones's strength is expected to be sustained in the coming months. Towards the latter stages of 1999, inflation is expected to creep back into the US economy, rekindled by the rebound in commodity prices and wages pressures. Oil prices have nearly doubled in value since the beginning of 1999 and other commodities too are strengthening. This, in conjunction with the shifting of the risk/reward profile back in favour of Japan and Asia, is likely to lead to a stalling of the Dow's rally and even trigger the long heralded correction of the US stock markets. A major retracement in US equity prices would also more than likely take the puff out of the US's ballooning economy.

Early signs are already evident that the market perceives that there is limited downside risk in Asia after two years of decline, as some investors have begun to return. At the time of writing, the Nikkei has risen by 27 per cent in 1999 to 17300 and is expected to climb further, although this is not to say that, for now, the Dow Jones cannot extend its rally.

16.5.2 Metal market review

Base metal prices have not been immune to the collapse in Asian demand, exacerbated by the over investment in production capacity. Investment in new mine/smelter capacity had been evident throughout the early to mid-1990s, as new operations looked to benefit from the forecasted continued robust growth in Asia. Lofty metal prices and the potential high returns that could be obtained through investing in new, low-cost operations in the developing world economies also stimulated and encouraged this investment.

With a 20–50 per cent contraction in demand in parts of Asia, which, including Japan, accounted for 35 per cent of western world metal consumption, metal surpluses rose as this new production came on stream – a trend evident throughout the world of commodities, as metal, softs and energy products (such as oil) fell and were trading at historical lows in early 1999.

The inability/reluctance of producers to react quickly to the downturn in consumer demand, exacerbated by end user de-stocking, contributed to the global market price weakness and a mounting glut of supply. With falling profits and mounting losses, high-cost producers by late 1998 begun to face reality and idle high cost capacity. The realisation that their cost reduction programmes would not be sufficient to make marginal operations efficient forced the issue of closures, because of the cost of capital required to reduce their cash costs, in the face of ever declining commodity prices.

This perceived change in sentiment, spurred on by aggressive cuts by oil producers, fuelled speculation that significant cuts by metal producers would be realised. This triggered a wave of metal buying, which lifted prices as metals followed the lead of the oil price.

The uncertainty over future global demand growth has not been completely eased, but with resource equities strengthening and a semblance of a recovery in ASEAN economic activity, a wind of change is beginning to sweep through the commodities markets. Investment funds underweight in mining/resource equities have increased their exposure in this area, having shied away from the sector during the past couple of years. This change is underpinning the turnaround in metal futures, but there is still one crucial element missing from the equation in order to sustain the rally. That is consumer forward buying and restocking. There are tentative signs that this is also returning, but further production cuts will be required to convince consumers to join in. The worm is turning, but has not yet come up for air.

Metal market outlook

The prospect for metal prices is improving. After two years of decline the tide has begun to turn. The resource equities look to be providing the lead once again, as they did ahead of the turnaround in the base metals in late 1993. Then the resource stocks led the base metals by some 12 months. These stocks have been strengthening since the tail end of 1998, and this has already begun to feed through to the base metals. The lead-time has been shorter this time, which is mainly attributed to the rising involvement of the investment funds in commodities, which have already been well established in the equity markets for several years. The road to recovery is unlikely to be smooth, but in the light of metals prices performance this year to date, there is a perception that the lows have been seen and that an up cycle is developing.

Copper outlook

A market surplus is forecast for this year and next, though these have been downgraded in recent months, in light of the realised and anticipated production cuts. A global demand recovery is by no means certain, but equally the fear of a global recession has receded. The US economy is likely to remain the cornerstone of global growth in 1999, barring a collapse in their stock market, with Chinese copper demand also expected to underpin consumption over the next 12 months. China is embarking on a massive infrastructure spending programme, which entails the expansion of their electricity grid. The resultant increased demand for copper cable is expected to offset the weakness in other Chinese sectors and foreign investment, as a result of the collapse in South East Asia's economies. Global copper concentrate is in short supply, compared with smelting capacity, which is reflected in lower concentrate treatment charges being sought, and obtained, by smelters. This, coupled with scrap tightness, is expected to lead to a rise in Chinese refined copper imports this year, as they seek to build stock ahead of their infrastructure plans. Rising Chinese imports, signs of improving demand growth prospects in South East Asia and production cuts are reducing the world's predicted metal surplus. The resultant affect of this improving outlook for copper is likely to trigger increased consumer restocking and, therefore, higher prices.

Aluminium

The price of aluminium has turned dramatically in line with the general performance in the base metals, in spite of large surpluses and little evidence of producers looking to more idle capacity. In 1999, a 500,000 tonne western world metal surplus is foreseen. This, coupled with some 450,000 tonnes of idle capacity and a predicted surplus for 2000, is expected to limit aluminium's upside potential. Contrary to market expectations, some production cuts were realised in early 1999 which, coupled with the relatively low levels of consumer stocks, led to a rise in aluminium price predictions. Japanese port stocks, which had doubled in the 12 months following the Thai Bhat devaluation, have once again fallen to levels seen prior to the Asian crisis (a trend evident throughout the emerging world). This has been attributed more to a slashing in imports over the past 12 months, rather than a recovery in Japanese or Asian demand. Nevertheless, having drawn upon their inventory excess and with imports stabilising (even showing signs of rising), the upside is believed to offer the greater potential. Japan may not be out of recession yet, but as with the rest of Asia the worst is felt to be over. European confidence remains low, but with interest rates declining, the right steps are being taken to foster a recovery. A sustained recovery may be some way off, with the high level of producer forward selling expected to lurk above the market, but even in spite of this a return to 1999's $1,158/tonne low is thought unlikely. The large build up of consignment stock, estimated at 600,000 tonnes, encouraged by a healthy contango on the LME, is not seen as restrictive to aluminium's initial upside potential. This material is believed to be tightly held in financing deals and by merchants, who having accumulated this metal during the downturn, are unlikely to offer this material back to the market until the LME spreads tighten significantly and/or higher prices are realised. The risks to the downside remain, as Asia's recovery is not set in stone, and Europe's and Japan's economies remain in poor shape: set this against significant surpluses forecast for this year and next, aluminium has its work cut out to recovery. To end on a positive note, much of this news is already in the price and as recent market performance has shown, aluminium has the capability of treading this road to recovery and is expected to do so.

Nickel

Production disruptions and voluntary capacity closures and cuts have seen a predicted surplus for 1999 recede, with a small deficit now foreseen. By December 1998 the nickel price had fallen by 50 per cent, from a $8,320/tonne peak two years earlier. The collapse in stainless steel demand, which accounts for 65 per cent of global nickel demand, as construction projects were either delayed or cancelled, principally in Asia, saw the western supply/demand balance swing into a significant surplus. This demand weakness and the threat of new, low-cost supply coming onstream compound the metals decline. As said, the outlook has improved, but there is still the threat that the new, low-cost laterite production could see the market balance swing into oversupply. Current market consensus is not optimistic on the production capabilities of these new projects and have consequently taken a conservative view on their output levels over the next couple of years. This view has been enhanced by the delays in commission that these projects have and are experiencing. Their costs are not expected to be as low as initial estimates, but still lower than the current western average, and should they meet their production targets, prices are likely to correct this year's strength. There are several other laterite projects at the feasibility stage, the implementation of which will be influenced by the success of the current three Australian operations. The psychological impact of this possible massive expansion in nickel supply is expected to limit nickel's upside potential, with prices thought unlikely to return to the levels seen in the first half of this decade, ie in excess of $8,000 per tonne. Another swing factor is the level of exports from Russia; in recent years these have stabilised at around 200,000 tonnes (20 per cent of western world demand). Despite their high costs, Norilsk, Russia's principal producer, has managed to raise production. The massive devaluation of the Rouble in August has shielded Norilsk from the low nickel price: however, this year exports are expected to fall because of Norilsk's modernisation programme, which will restrict output during the first half of 1999. In conclusion, nickel has the potential to extend its recent gains in line with the improvement in the global economic outlook, but is likely to see these gains impaired should the new laterite producers beat consensus expectations. Such a scenario would ultimately lead to a further rationalisation of nickel production. Therefore, the nickel price recovery is expected to continue, but the path is likely to be rocky and fraught with danger.

Zinc

Zinc has in recent years been promoted as a belle of the metals market, but since the ill-fated short play by the Chinese in 1997, compounded by the Asian crisis, the metal has struggled. The past six months have seen a turnaround in the metal's fortune, and capacity closures and upgrades in global demand figures have seen a small surplus diminish. Nevertheless, despite the decline in available metal stocks and the speculative interest that helped lift the price back above $1,000 early in 1999, several factors are still restricting the upside potential. The principal fear is China's export potential, which was brought home in 1997 when exports more than doubled as they sought to metal their excessive forward sale commitments. In 1998, exports fell back as stockpiles were replenished, but still at levels ahead of previous years. This, coupled with new mine and idled capacity coming onstream throughout this year and in 2000, is expected to ease the concentrate tightness and suppress the metals upside. Concentrate treatment charges are therefore expected to strengthen after the past couple of years' decline. Century, at 500,000 tonnes, is the largest of these new mines, but mine capacity is not the only area of expansion, as additional smelter tonnage is being brought on too, though at a slower rate. This said, the upside offers the greatest potential, and with low consumer inventory and signs of a sustained improvement in Asia (or limited downside), forward buying and downstream restocking is likely to underpin further price gains. Bring into this equation the growing concern over the Millennium technology bug, available metal stocks are expected to tighten, hence further buoying prices into the new Millennium.

16.5.3 Soft commodities review and outlook

Coffee

The high level of the Brazilian crop in 1998 pressured prices during the second and third quarters of last year. Subsequently problems with the weather in Central America and Columbia reduced the production prospects for that area. This culminated in Hurricane Mitch, the worst storm for many years, which caused substantial damage to the area. As a result prices steadied at 3 per cent, and physical differentials improved by the close 1998.

Demand was expected to fall significantly in the last quarter of 1998 following the forecasts of economic depression. In the event the situation was not as bad as had been planned for, and the roasting industry had to step up its rate of buying between November and January.

The devaluation in Brazil and the resultant increase in exports have dominated this year. Prices have fallen by 13 per cent in the first quarter of 1999 and are continuing to come under pressure in the second. Production in Central America has been revised upwards as the effects of the hurricane were less than estimated on the current coffee crop. Damaged infrastructure (roads, bridges etc) has been repaired, with overseas aid, much quicker than originally thought possible. This has lead to a late increase in the flow of coffee from that area which has also depressed prices.

For the remainder of 1999 the fundamental situation will be dominated by Brazil again. After last year's heavy crop, production in 1999 will be much reduced, possibly by as much as 30 per cent. Increases elsewhere will offset part of this loss, but the overall prospect is for prices to recover from current levels.

Sugar

Since the beginning of the year, sugar prices have lost 50 per cent of their value. Prospects of another large surplus, and the continuing economic problems in the Far East and Russia, are affecting demand, which is taking its toll on prices. The single most bearish factor was the prospect of a crop in the region of 18.5m tonnes out of Brazil, and the devaluation of the Brazilian Real in early January. This saw the Brazilian millers embark on an aggressive round of pricing in the No 11 contract. Sugar fell to a 13-year low and is likely to remain depressed through to the third quarter of 1999, as there is a prospect of large deliveries being made against the No 11 July contract. Until some tangible evidence can be seen of producers cutting back on production, the market will have trouble sustaining any major rally.

The depressed state of the market, particularly toward the end of April, has sparked some interest from end users, but not in sufficient quantity to change the overall bearish sentiment. In view of the low current price, sugar is expected to see an extended period on consolidation around the 4.00–4.50 cents per lb.

Cocoa

In the latter part of 1998 revisions emerged on the level of demand, and the previously forecast deficit began to erode, but even in September a deficit of 150,000 was forecast. But the collapse of Russian demand and the upward revision in production from the Ivory Coast began to pressure prices.

The market then gradually developed into one of the strongest bear trends for many years, as prices declined by some 40 per cent. Investment funds took advantage of the situation to build up one of the biggest short positions ever seen. This, coupled with another record crop from the Ivory Coast and a slump in world consumption for cocoa products, saw prices fall steadily, with little interruption in the trend from September 1998 through to May 1999.

The market has remained under pressure, as manufacturers have reduced the amount of cover that they carry on their books. Buying has switched to a hand-to-mouth basis, reducing the need to hold huge amounts of stock.

Cocoa prices are expected to remain under pressure until the investment funds reverse positions and feel that the time is right to buy cocoa. Shipper defaults and losses on the futures markets have cast a further negative cloud over the market, suggesting further market weakness.

17

GOLD AND OTHER VALUABLES

JOHN MYERS AND HELEN BAIRD

Solon Consultants

17.1 INTRODUCTION

17.1.1 A long-term hedge in precious metals

Traditionally, investors have looked upon precious metals and other valuables as a long-term hedge against political or economic chaos. When inflation has soared, when currencies have weakened, when stock markets have plummeted, precious metals have gained in attraction; historically, the greater the fear, the higher the price rises. Gold is the archetypal precious metal, once sought for its allure and its rarity, and its habit of reasserting its worth when ephemeral standards fail.

Many still regard gold as intrinsically valuable, internationally acceptable and negotiable. For these reasons, it maintains a historical image as the ultimate form of money, a store of wealth unaffected by wars and political turmoil. However, recent events have tarnished that image. Hedging, with the help of futures, options, gold mining shares, physical holdings and indices, has damped oscillations. Also, exchange controls have weakened. That has made it easier for wealthy people who dread war and local hyperinflation to shift into dollars, euros or Swiss francs, instead of gold. Political crises across the world have therefore had little impact on the bullion market of late. The Gulf conflict, the breakup of the former Soviet Union, and successive Balkan conflicts only marginally affected the price.

Could a central bank still run wild and cause unbridled inflation? Perhaps; but what protects savings is a government that wants to protect them. Any government can allow inflation, as Russia did in recent years, to finance state activity by creating new money. It can do so, unless gold reserve requirements are so stiff that no human can determine economic policy – only gold can. Few democracies in the late 1990s would accept this constraint.

Those who nonetheless want a return to the gold standard do not trust governments. However, most people are not as pessimistic about the motives, capabilities and skills of the money managers. In practice, nations no longer settle balance of payments' deficits with gold, and gold no longer backs currencies. Nor are countries and trading blocs willing to let the ebb and flow of their gold supply determine economic activity and the fate of their people. Admittedly, in times of calamity, gold is always likely to be a safe and valued haven. Otherwise, gold will remain something to use in jewellery and dental work, and an ingredient of coins in collectors' hands.

Nevertheless, the interplays of demand and supply in bullion markets remain complex. Unlike other commodities, dream and doubt, more than industrial utility, have often driven demand. Increasingly, the actions of the 'official sector' govern supply and prices more than the efforts of producers. (Central banks are responsible for gold's role as a quasi-monetary standard and, for the moment, control almost one-quarter of the supply.) Yet, with enthusiasts, gold holds its reputation, perhaps sullied, as a long-term insurance against the collapse of economies, markets and currencies. Bullion 'bugs' still state confidently that the metal will sustain, or even increase, its value in times of great uncertainty.

Maynard Keynes dismissed the metal as 'a barbarous relic'. Others insist that 'something that has been a store of value for 5,000 years will not go out of fashion'. They also point to the physical characteristics of bullion bars, wafers or coins. The metal is largely immune to the effects of weather, moisture, oxidation or sea water, and to the corrosive effects of most acids and alkalis. Gold hoarders go on believing that their holdings will endure, and offset any severe downturn in portfolios of stocks and shares during a monetary or political crisis. Furthermore, prices of gold and platinum are usually expressed in US dollars. The bugs therefore see these metals as a hedge against sharp falls in non-dollar currency markets.

For a few financial planners, the strength of the case persists. They still recommend wealthy investors to keep perhaps 5–10 per cent of their assets in precious metals. Some intrepid souls, with cash to spare, continue to hold 10–15 per cent of their wealth in gold. The truly enchanted are even bolder. In 1997, Robert F Hague disclosed his fiscal conservatism to the New York Times. The retired American investment banker keeps 90 per cent of his portfolio in gold bullion, coins, unit funds and individual equities. Hague told the journalist: 'I've felt for many, many years that we're going to have to use gold to straighten out our financial system. The reason the economy and the market look so good is the excess of credit and debt. It's all false. There will come a time when we recognise gold as the ultimate money.'

Others disagree. Experts point to the negligible annual return produced by gold bullion or coins – an average of just 0.46 per cent from 1991–96.

Investors have also been critical of the gold bugs, especially in America. Investing in commodities such as gold and silver 'is not for most average investors,' says Thomas O'Hara, chairman of the US National Association of Investors Corporation. 'Gold is very risky; it provides no regular income, such as occurs from investing in common stocks,' he says. Metal prices are 'volatile and subject to manipulation from speculators'. Investing in gold or silver is 'primarily for very wealthy individuals'. Others should perhaps be careful not to become gold's fool.

Most investors should 'stay away' from gold, agrees John Markese, executive director of the American Association of Individual Investors in Chicago. If a person 'just has to buy some gold', then owning shares in a broadly based natural-resources mutual fund is probably the safest route. Nevertheless, the gold component 'should not be more than 10 percent of the value of the investor's mutual-fund portfolio,' he says.

From a positive standpoint, gold has unique properties – superior electrical conductivity, ductility and malleability. Gold is also beautiful. These qualities are timeless, and are the reasons that gold provides a long-term store of value. The importance of gold as a 'safe haven' has diminished in recent years; however, the possibility of world political turmoil, even if small, makes some investment in gold or gold mining shares seem prudent.

Silver and platinum have also become respectable vehicles for investment. Admittedly, they are riskier than gold. The prime use of silver, for example, is as an industrial material, with at least a chance that its price will fall during a recession. Platinum is an alternative, but prices are highly volatile. Its popularity has depended largely on its use in automotive catalytic converters that, with technical developments, now require decreasing amounts of the metal. Nevertheless, worldwide demand has risen, boosted at the margin by low-cost platinum jewellery sales in Japan, and by the US mint's introduction of a platinum bullion coin.

In principle, buying gold and platinum should help to even out the volatility of an investment portfolio. The historical evidence is that prices of precious metals, like gold, have oscillated spectacularly on occasion. They are not investments for the nervous or the needy. Records show that, in times of low inflation – for example the 1990s – shares, bonds and unit trusts substantially out-perform gold and other precious metals.

On balance, the unpredictability of prices makes precious metals unsuitable investments for individuals with limited capital. Nor are these commodities wise purchases for investors who might require liquid funds in a personal emergency, or a reliable flow of income from their savings.

17.1.2 Development of the gold market

In this century, gold has recorded five major price rises in world markets. Its history, of course, is as a coinage metal and a measurement of national wealth. In 1934, as part of America's 'New Deal', the bullion price was upgraded and fixed in US dollar terms at $35 per ounce. This lasted for 40 years until President Nixon severed gold's links with the dollar. On the open market, bullion then reached $200 per ounce, mainly because of petrodollar inflation and weak central banking strategies.

In the inflationary 1970s, investors rushed to convert paper money into gold. The price of an ounce of gold rose to $825, the last big surge in the bullion price. It then dropped to $300 an ounce in mid-1982, only to rally again, reaching $500 per ounce in June 1983. Since 1987, gold has fallen back. In 1991 the dollar price averaged $362.26, down 6 per cent on 1990, and declined further to a six-year low of $336 in April 1992. This was despite the Gulf War, turmoil in South Africa, and the collapse of the Soviet Union.

By March 1993, gold had tumbled yet again, and was fixed at a seven-year low of $326, with the most pessimistic predicting still lower prices. Against their expectations, gold recovered to show a strong price performance in 1993, which it sustained during the 1994 bull market in commodities. For gold, 1994 and 1995 were years of consolidation with prices remaining within a steady $370–395 trading range. This left the average dollar price for 1995 at 7 per cent above its 1993 average, the first increase of substance since 1990.

Throughout this period, new buyers entered the market on a large scale. For the first time, China surpassed the US as the world's largest buyer, importing 350 tonnes (10 per cent of world output) in 1992, when China lifted exchange rate controls on semi-official currency swap markets. China's dollar depreciated by 30 per cent and, within days, Hong Kong's gold outlets reported an upsurge of 20 per cent in demand from Chinese customers.

Chinese consumption grew by 130 per cent in 1994 as wages increased and people sought a hedge against inflation rates, which rose to a post-1949 high. Demand remained high throughout 1995, due to the lifting of exchange rate controls, the rapid depreciation of China's currency, and a traditional cultural affinity for gold. The market grew at this time in other South East Asian countries, where many people bought gold partly as a guard against economic, financial and geopolitical uncertainties. Purchases in South East Asia rose to about one-third of the world's annual gold consumption. Steady sales of gold occurred in Thailand, Taiwan, Singapore, Malaysia and South Korea.

In 1996, the World Gold Council reported a fall of 4 per cent in gold sales across the world's principal markets. The main factor was a sharp drop in Japan, and to a lesser extent in China and Europe. According to the Council's annual study, sales in Japan in 1996 dropped 40 per cent from 1995 to a seven-year low, because of 'continued consumer caution'. In Taiwan, another important market, gold sales dropped 23 per cent because of an economic downturn and record joblessness. In Europe, buying of the precious metal was down by 6 per cent, because of 'weaker investment demand'.

Strong investment and jewellery demand triggered a 9 per cent increase in gold sales across the World Gold Council's 21 key markets in 1997. However, in Asia, the financial crisis caused overall gold demand in the region to fall by 10 per cent, and in South East Asia by 26 per cent. Thai demand declined by 71 per cent. Financial problems in Japan led to a 44 per cent drop in jewellery demand in 1997. Nevertheless, the prevailing instability in financial institutions there led some Japanese to buy gold in other forms. Investment demand increased by 2 per cent in 1997, and by 38 per cent in the final quarter.

Concerns remain about the Japanese market. When news breaks of terrorist gas attacks and failures of financial institutions, the economy suffers, and local industrial demand for gold falls. Conversely, these uncertainties can prompt the Japanese to buy gold for security. However, this did not happen in 1997 on any large scale, and distress selling increased local supplies.

In other parts of Asia the trend was more positive. For example, in India buying gold rose 6 per cent to a record level of 500 tonnes in 1996, and by a further 45 per cent in 1997. Turkey, the Gulf States, and Taiwan likewise recorded significant increases in demand in 1997.

Supported by strong jewellery and investment demand, US sales also rose by 6 per cent to a record 350 tonnes in 1996, and then by 9 per cent in 1997. This was the result of high demand in all sectors but particularly for bullion coins, sales of which increased by 207 per cent in 1997.

On world markets, gold prices fluctuated around $350 an ounce in 1996. In 1997 the price fell below $300 an ounce; the average fall of the London fix was $57, with an 18-year low of $283 in December. The perceived safe haven for investors in 1997 was US government debt and the dollar, rather than gold. Increased confidence in the dollar, combined with low inflation in the major industrial countries, induced investors to reconsider gold as an inflationary hedge. Official sales escalated, investors sold gold short, hedging persisted, and mine production added to the volume. Declining demand in Asia because of the region's economic crisis, and the speculation surrounding what proportion of its reserves the European Central Bank (ECB) would hold in gold, adversely affected the gold market.

The marked expansion in central bank sales throughout 1997 unsettled the already nervous market. In total, the official sector sold a substantial amount of gold in 1997 – more than double the average for the previous decade. In 1997, the Netherlands Central Bank disclosed that 300 tonnes of gold had been sold in 1996. Then Australia announced the sale of two-thirds of its reserves. A further blow was the announcement that the Russian Finance Ministry had sold 31 tonnes of gold.

Fear of official sector sales produces the same negative effect on sentiment, and the gold price, as actual sales do. Some market experts believe that central bank holdings are more mobile, and less price sensitive, than those held by private investors. Prices did fall in 1997 as a result of central bank sales, but the actual amounts sold were in fact less than the total sold in 1992 or 1993.

A Swiss government advisory panel recommended in October 1997 that the country sell over half of its gold reserves, and abandon the constitutional link between gold and the Swiss franc. Following this announcement, the gold price dropped from $323 to $306 an ounce. Proceeds of the sale would go towards compensating refugees from Nazi Germany in an attempt to distance Switzerland from accusations of converting looted Nazi gold during the war.

Then in December, Argentina disclosed a previously secret sale of virtually all its gold reserves. Nevertheless, the price began to recover in the first weeks of 1998, until the Belgium Central Bank revealed it too had secretly sold over half of its gold reserves. The price sank below $290 an ounce.

In the 1990s, the metal has acted out of character, like a commodity. The price has tended to reflect demand from fabricators of jewellery and electronics. Some commentators hope that, in the late 1990s, the Eastern Bloc nations might provide a stimulus to the market, as they seek to back their currencies with bullion. These optimists also highlight gold's traditional popularity in Eastern Europe as a store of value, and they anticipate a rise in private hoardings there. When the Baltic states successfully persuaded the Bank of England to return their pre-war reserves, enthusiasts for the metal claimed renewed interest in gold's monetary role.

Support for this claim is seen in Russia, where gold is often used as a form of money. The Russians have been minting gold roubles to steady their own currency and to stabilise the economy. Gold output has been rising in the Krasnoyarsk and Khabarovsk territories, the Irkutsk and Amur regions, and the Evanki republic. The Chairman of the Russian Federation's State Committee for Precious Stones and Metals hopes that Russia can sustain gold production at an annual rate of 160 tonnes.

Central banks in other parts of the world can use methods other than outright sales to 'mobilise' gold reserves. Indirect means of mobilising gold reserves include call options on reserves, and low-interest gold loans to producers. Reserves can also be physically disposed of through the minting of bullion coins. A group of gold mining companies, led by Barrick Gold, is set to employ this method by minting a Millennium gold coin. It hopes to drive up the price by absorbing the gold supply in this way.

17.1.3 Recent developments in the silver market

Most of the world's silver comes from Mexico, Peru, Canada and the US. Experts estimate that total world silver production since the year 4000 BC is in the region of 40 billion ounces. Silver tends to be the most volatile in price of all the precious metals, and since the early 1990s the silver market has been in deficit. In 1980, the price reached a record high of $52.50 an ounce, but dropped to a record low of $3.51 11 years later in 1991.

In 1997, there were significant developments in the silver market. Prices became volatile, demand continued to outstrip supply, and the shortfall began to have a substantial effect on market sentiment. Consequently, wealthy traders took speculative positions and acquired stocks of silver.

Silver began 1997 at $4.74 an ounce and ended the year with the price at $6.39. In the course of the year, the market showed considerable fluctuations, sparked by a series of events. These included the Asian financial crisis, and reported shifts in demand. For example, early in that year, consumers in India sustained their purchases of silver at an increasing rate, and silver imports initially rose. As pressures increased on supply and the price went up, Indian buyers dropped out of the market, choosing instead to buy gold artefacts at more attractive prices. When the silver price reached a 9-year high in December 1997, the gold price was at an 18-year low.

17.1.4 Other precious metals

Platinum, palladium and rhodium have industrial uses in manufacturing and jewellery fabrication, which make them prone to the effects of world recession. About a third of platinum output goes into catalytic converters for the automobile industry, but this demand is highly susceptible to the development of better technologies. In early 1992, the market faltered when a US company announced a breakthrough which eliminated the need for platinum. Prices recovered when later reports showed that the new device was merely an add-on to existing converters.

The miniaturisation of electronics is detracting from physical demand for these metals. Conversely, higher sales volumes of devices such as digital pagers and cellular telephones has partially offset the decline. Meanwhile, palladium's prime role is as a catalyst in the electronics and the automobile industry. Demand is susceptible to the effects of substitution, but its use in industry is rising substantially. Increasingly, the main use for platinum is in jewellery manufacture, accounting for 44 per cent of the total in 1998. Demand for platinum jewellery is mainly in Japan, but Chinese demand has grown significantly over the past five years.

In the 1990s, the 'wild card' in the market for platinum and palladium has been the uncertainty of supplies from its main producers. Labour unrest in South Africa has affected this sensitive market, and political and economic problems continue to beset the other major producer, Russia. Nine years ago, South Africa produced 75 per cent of the total world output of platinum, and the former Soviet Union 20 per cent. Demand reached record levels in 1991, but so did supplies. Russia increased exports by a third, causing a fall in prices to a six-year low. Russia is the main producer of palladium, supplying 70 per cent of it in 1998. South Africa is the second major source and most of the remainder comes from North America.

Changes to the organisational structure of Russian government agencies led to export delays of platinum group metals at the end of 1996. This stoppage lasted for the first six months of 1997, and the supply crisis resulted in significant price increases of these metals.

In parallel, demand for platinum from fabricators increased during 1997. Platinum jewellery has been popular for more than two decades in Japan, and is now becoming more so elsewhere. In China, sales doubled in 1997, and US demand increased by 75 per cent. Total demand for platinum jewellery rose by 5 per cent in 1997, offsetting the decline in Japanese demand and the effects of the Asian financial crisis generally.

Turbulence in the platinum group metals' market continued throughout 1997. Despite the Russian export delays and the 1.2 per cent fall in the total platinum supply, several years of oversupply, and bank sales, prevented an immediate impact on the price. However, by May 1997 it became clear that supply problems would continue, and the price began to rise. The year began with platinum at $370 an ounce; it reached $475 in June, but closed the year on $364.

In early 1997, palladium hovered around $125 an ounce, rose to $239 in August, and ended the year at $200. These price fluctuations eventually led to the market for these metals breaking. By June 1997, only one investment bank was quoting forward platinum prices, and palladium could be obtained solely on a spot basis. The options market had closed, and the spot price rose higher than the forward prices. Palladium's price fell towards the end of 1997 when Russian supply resumed unexpectedly.

Rhodium similarly plays a crucial role in the automobile industry, which accounts for 90 per cent of the metal's sales. Admittedly, the use of rhodium in catalytic converters is in decline, and demand fell in 1997. However, Johnson Matthey's *Platinum 1998 Report* argued that the supply of this exotic member of the platinum family was abnormally high in 1997, and that emerging uses could cause demand to pick up in the coming years.

17.1.5 Gold coins

Thus, investors who wish to secure an interest in precious metals such as gold, silver, platinum or palladium have a choice of media. Most are ill-suited to ordinary investors. For example, gold jewellery makes a memorable gift, but does the buyer really want to ask his or her spouse to sell the Patek Phillipe to pay a child's tuition bill? The alternatives include:

- Buying bullion, which comes in bars made by fabricators and is usually kept in a bank vault. This incurs expensive storage and insurance charges.
- Avoiding the cost and risk of keeping gold bars under the bed, by using the services of commercial banks that hold the metal for their customers in 'gold statement accounts'. When a customer wants to draw on his or her account, the bank advances the cash equivalent of the gold's value at the prevailing price, less commission.
- Speculating in gold futures contracts through a commodities broker. This approach is for gamblers who, undaunted by the wild swings in gold prices in the past, think they can predict future values, or gain a turn by hedging.
- Investing in mining stocks through equities of companies that mine gold and other precious metals, or diversified funds that specialise in mining companies. Mining stocks have not been stellar performers of late; in 1996, few funds recorded significant growth. Over the past three years, gold mining stocks have lost almost two-thirds of their value. Mining companies drove costs down by 15 per cent in an attempt to improve share prices and achieve an operating profit because of the low gold price. In 1997 alone, gold shares fell by around 45 per cent. Performance of funds can vary widely, as can annual charges and management fees.
- Buying government-minted coins, such as sovereigns from the Royal Mint or American Eagle coins produced by the US Treasury. (Rare coins are another matter; they are usually considered as collectables. See Chapter 19.)

Of these possibilities, gold coins are popular as bullion investments. The majority of individual investors who physically own gold hold only coins, according to the World Gold Council. Enthusiasts believe that 'when the price of gold moves, collectable coins move faster and further'. Coins generally track the gold price within a few percentage points lower than the bullion spot price. In practice when gold prices fall, bullion coins can be worth even less. For example, in 1997 the average return on bullion was −14.6 per cent, and the return on coins even worse.

Nonetheless, many countries mint bullion coins. Examples are the Russian Chervonetz, the Mexican Peso, the Austrian Corona and Philharmonic (it has a fiddle on the obverse), the Luxembourg Lion, the Australian Nugget, the South African Krugerrand and others enjoying culturally redolent names. So, Mauritius has its Dodo; France, its Napoleon; China, its Panda; Canada, its Maple Leaf; Japan, its Hirohito and its Akihito.

The Royal Mint's Britannia depends upon an aesthetic appeal (as a Coin of the Year) to justify a premium over its bullion value. The coin is struck in 22 carat gold, and on one side depicts Britannia standing amid the waves brandishing her trident; on the other, she holds a shield and olive branch. Although the Britannia competes with the American Eagle, it has a significant difference: the US Mint produces many tens of thousands of Eagles, while the Royal Mint usually limits production of the 1, ½ and ¼ ounce sizes. Over the past couple of years, the limit was raised and the issue limit of the ounce coin was 1,750; but the four coin collection of bullion proof Britannia coins was just 750. The set sells for £1,045 and individual ¼ ounce coins for £135. However, the retail price seems high, given that bullion today (June 1999) sells at approximately $260 an ounce. A recent issue from the Royal Mint is the Diana, Princess of Wales gold proof memorial coin with a mintage of 7,500; it has been selling at £595.

More than 3m gold American Eagles, of all denominations, were sold in 1998. A *New York Times* article reported on 3 May 1999 that the low gold price is attracting many American investors to gold coins. The increase in sales of the American Eagle bullion coin is partly a result of bargain hunting because of the low price, but also because of fears of computer problems associated with the year 2000 Millennium bug, together with an eventual US stock market reversal. Last year, gold coin sales in the US rose by 120 per cent, and in the first quarter of this year sales are even higher than that of the same quarter in 1998.

Gold to produce the American Eagle must come from US mines. The US Mint does not sell these metals directly: they are sold in bulk to wholesalers, who sell to the general public at the spot price plus a small premium. These coins are all legal tender (ie genuine coins produced in limited quantities) so they could eventually attract the interest of collectors. Demand might then exceed supply.

Another example is the Australian 'kangaroo', launched in March 1991 as 2 ounce and 10 ounce bullion coins and 1 kilogram 'nuggets', which are 99.99 per cent pure gold. The largest coin has a face value of A$10,000 (more than £4,000), but dealers link sales prices of the coins to the market value of bullion. The 1 kilogram nugget is the heaviest legal tender since South Sea islanders used large stones to pay for goods.

In earlier decades, the Krugerrand was largely responsible for gold coins' success. In 1978, South Africa sold the highest amount ever recorded by any country in a single year. Since trade sanctions disappeared, the South Africans have re-launched the Krugerrand internationally.

Until recently, a general deterrent for the UK private investor wishing to invest in gold coins, or for that matter wafers and bars, was a liability to pay VAT. Although investors could avoid the tax, by buying and holding gold offshore, UK demand for this form of investment collapsed after the Chancellor imposed the tax in 1982. However, in March 1999, the Government announced a VAT exemption for investment in gold, to be introduced on 1 January 2000. From that date, investors throughout the EU will be able to buy gold bars, wafers and coins exempt from VAT in line with a new EU Directive.

As with all purchases of precious metals, experts advise buyers to deal only with reputable sources. Four years ago, an advertiser in Florida promised to turn a $60 investment in gold coins into $9,200 within a short time. Trading watchdogs in the state described the plan as 'nothing more than a classic pyramid scheme'. Prudence also dictates that, when selling gold coins, the investor should check prices with several bullion merchants or coin dealers. Prices can vary 5 per cent or more from one dealer to another. Even with gold currently trading at around $260 an ounce, 5 per cent can be substantial.

17.1.6 Silver, platinum and palladium coins

In this decade, silver coins have become popular with mints. Dealers and traders sold more than 5.3m silver dollar American Eagles between December 1990 and March 1991, a record volume for a silver bullion coin. One factor in the success of the Eagle was the anticipated rise in silver prices. Another was patriotism during the Gulf War. Also, investors favour silver coins and bars to hedge positions in silver futures and shares of companies that mine silver. In 1998, sales of the silver Eagle were up 17.1 per cent on the previous year.

The latest entrant is the Canadian silver dollar, which together with a gold Can$100 coin went on sale from 1 March 1996, with a limited mintage. For example, the gold coin commemorating the Klondike gold rush is in a limited 'edition' of 35,000, although the 1996 proof silver dollar is more widely available; it records the 1811 arrival of the McIntosh apple-growing family in Canada.

In April 1995 the British Royal Mint launched a £2 silver coin to commemorate the 50th anniversary of the United Nations. However, discerning collectors and traders are beginning openly to challenge the Mint and its promotion of commemorative coins to collectors and investors. Many experts claim that they would not usually form part of a serious collection, and that they represent a poor return on investment. Dealers generally estimate that the realisable value would be no more than 40–60 per cent of the original price. Glendinning, the specialist coins and medals' auctioneer, also contends that the supply of commemorative coins considerably outstrips demand. Whereas their production was once a rare event, the mints have launched many new issues in the past two decades.

Investors can buy a silver version of the Royal Mint's UN coin for £26.50. Base metal and gold versions of this coin have been available since late 1995. Another Mint product is a silver 36-coin collection, priced at £1,200, with each coin representing a UN Member State. The coins are in limited production, and purchasable on a monthly subscription basis. The Royal Mint commemorated the Queen and Duke of Edinburgh's Golden Wedding with a silver proof Anniversary Crown. It sells at £32.50, and the Mint issued 75,000. A mintage of 350,000 silver proof of the Diana, Princess of Wales memorial coin has been issued, also priced at £32.50.

Both the silver Kookaburra (released April 1990) and the platinum Koala feature in Australia's bullion coin programme. The Koala is one of only a few platinum bullion coins currently on the market. One of the earliest was the platinum Noble from the Isle of Man, minted originally in 1983. Following that example, the Australian Gold Corporation selected platinum because of the metal's rarity. Only about 5m ounces of platinum are produced worldwide annually, compared with 40m ounces of gold. Japanese buyers account for about 50 per cent of world demand for platinum, and the designers chose the Koala image on the coins partly to develop sales in Japan. According to the Gold Corporation, the day after the coins appeared there, dealers sold 4,093 ounces of the platinum Koalas at prices averaging $515 per ounce. The coin is available in 1 ounce, ½ ounce, ¼ ounce and ⅒ ounce sizes, with nominal values in Australian dollars of $100, $50, $25 and $15. Australia has also issued the Emu, a legal tender coin minted in palladium.

The US Mint introduced the platinum Eagle bullion coin in 1997. Sales directly benefited from the high investor interest in platinum generated by the events of 1997. A further boost in demand arose from a US rule change in January 1998. For the first time, US investors could include platinum in their Individual Retirement Accounts (IRAs). In total, the US silver and platinum Eagles hold almost 80 per cent of their markets, and in 1998 the platinum Eagle won the Most Popular Coin in the Year Award.

Russia issued a giant 1 kilo (32 ounce) silver coin in 1995. It was minted to commemorate the 50th anniversary of the end of World War II. The coin bears the first ever depiction of Stalin on a Soviet or Russian coin, and the denomination is 100 Roubles. Members of the Russian parliament reserved the first 1,000 of the 1,500 coins issued. According to the Russian Mint's website, less than eight of the original mintage remain in the vaults.

Russia also markets a set of four historical commemorative coins, two made of silver, one of platinum and another of palladium. The full set has been selling for about £500. As the Russians urgently need hard currency, and have been aggressively selling palladium coins to collectors and metal speculators. The content is 99 per cent palladium, and the price 20 per cent above the metal's daily spot market price. Carrying the image of a ballerina, the coins bear a face value of 25 roubles. The coin contributes to what the Russians hope will be a long-lasting series of 'palladium ballerina' coins. Of 30,000 minted, 3,000 were of proof quality.

Knowledgeable dealers believe that the palladium coin serves as an important long-term precedent, and that palladium could be the investment metal of the next century. Only three countries (Russia, South Africa and the US) have enough palladium reserves to mine the mineral commercially, but other countries (Bermuda, France, the Isle of Man and Tonga) have produced special-issue commemorative coins manufactured from imported metal. The Russian coins are just one case of the increasing competitiveness with which foreign mints are seeking customers. Mexico, for example, has been offering the Mexican Rainbow Proof Coin collection consisting of a set of gold, silver and platinum coins. When the Mexicans launched them, they priced the first year's coins bearing the date 1989 at £440.

17.1.7 Selected forms of investment in valuables

Various bodies offer alternatives to investment in physical gold and other precious metals. Some institutions have 'certificate programmes', through which a private investor can specify how much to invest (usually a minimum of £500 or $1,000). The institution then puts all the orders together and buys ingots at the going market rate. The institution then divides the purchase between the investors, issuing certificates to each. Suppliers can subsequently arrange delivery and storage. Prudence dictates that investors should make certain that the organisation that they are dealing with is trustworthy; that they make the purchase in their individual names; and that they receive proof of ownership.

Other forms of investment have recently affected the gold market, helping to change its structure. The growth of speculation in the futures and options market has been an area of some controversy. The price of gold has declined gradually in real terms over the past five years, and some commentators see a vicious circle in the effects of hedging by producers. To cover future price rises when they open new mines, owners sell gold forward; they raise gold loans that they will repay later at a fixed rate. The more traders cap prices, the greater the incentive for producers to hedge to protect their profitability. Other analysts disagree, pointing to a reduction in hedging by mining companies when the market plunged to a seven-year low. Whether or not hedging by producers has a counter-productive effect, the options and futures market provides flexible instruments for speculators to exploit any short-term volatility in the gold price.

The World Gold Council attributes the declining gold price to the growth in hedging. Graham Birch, head of gold and mining at Mercury Asset Management, agreed. He argued in a *Financial Times* article in May 1998 that hedging has been a major factor in the weakening of the gold market, affecting the stock value of many gold companies.

In North America, 50 publicly traded and closely watched firms mine gold as their exclusive or primary line of business. These firms have the same exposure to oscillations in the price of bullion; their output is a globally traded, volatile commodity. They can manage this exposure using a diverse set of instruments, including forward and futures contracts, gold swaps, gold or bullion loans, rolling forward commitments called spot deferred contracts, and options. Perhaps most important, firms in the gold mining industry now reveal details of their risk management methods. Quarterly reporting gives investors extensive information on firms' use of forward sales, swaps, gold loans, options, and other explicit or embedded risk management activities. The data enable analysts to measure the risk, and dampen volatility.

A spot deferred contract is a long-term forward sale of gold in which mines can choose annually whether to deliver against the contract or wait to deliver the gold. Ultimately, they must deliver the gold committed under this contract, but the mine has the option of deciding whether to defer delivery, perhaps because spot prices exceed the contract price. The mine would agree a new delivery price that covers the market forward price plus the loss that the mine would have borne had it met its forward commitment. Thus, spot deferred contracts are similar to rolling one-year forward contracts, except that the former ensures that a credit-worthy mine has long-term access to forward contracting (at market rates). A mine reduces the risk of being unable to roll over an existing forward position. If a mine were to roll over a forward contract in which it had a loss, it would have to record the accounting loss on the contract at the rollover. With a spot deferred contract, mine owners roll forward these losses until the ultimate delivery of the gold, and defer accounting losses.

Firms that apply insurance strategies use either exchange-traded, or over-the-counter, gold put options. Alternatively, they dynamically replicate 'puts' by trading forwards and futures. Thus, firms can choose from a rich menu of risk management instruments that allows them to customise their gold price exposure.

Mining equities and funds offer the investor an alternative route. Shares in technologically proficient mining companies with large reserves and low production costs may on occasion be more attractive than investing directly in their physical output.

17.2 HIGHLIGHTS OF THE PREVIOUS YEAR

17.2.1 Central bank sales and related factors

The price of gold sank to a new depth of $273 in 1998, the lowest for 19 years. According to the World Gold Council, the average annual price of $294 was $37 less than the 1997 average. Depressed by central bank sell-ing, the Asian and Russian financial crises, speculation over the ECB's future gold holdings and the strength of the US dollar, the gold price remained low throughout 1998.

At the beginning of 1998, the gold price stood at $280 an ounce, and from January to May held at roughly $300. By September, a combination of Russia's domestic economic problems, the scandal surrounding President Clinton in the US and various other factors pushed the price back towards the $280 level. Then, in September, following the news that the US hedge fund Long Term Capital Management (LTCM) had almost collapsed, the price pushed upwards again to $290. In early October, as the US dollar fell against the yen and the German mark, trading in gold increased and the price climbed to $305. By the middle of the month, the dollar had stabilised, but the gold market interpreted a further cut in US interest rates as evidence of concern over the global financial crisis, and gold reached the $300 mark for the final time in 1998.

For the next two months the price fluctuated between $280 and $290, and concern over the confrontation between the US and Iraq pushed it up to almost $300. Then, with news of the continuing weakness of the yen, it drifted down to $290. Reports that Switzerland had passed the legislation to break the link between the Swiss franc and gold, together with a pessimistic global outlook for commodities generally, saw gold end the year much as it had begun on $287 an ounce.

Central banks' gold sales continued unabated throughout 1998. Although very little information was made public, sentiment remained depressed by the threat of further sales. The Czech National Bank was the first to announce gold sales in February, closely followed in March by the announcement of Belgium's fifth sale since 1989. Canada sold almost 18.5 tonnes of gold reserves between July and November. The crucial question overhanging the gold market in early 1998 was what proportion of reserves the ECB would hold in gold. In June 1998, the gold market faltered when the ECB president announced that gold would comprise between 15 and 20 per cent of total reserves. Speculation had previously put the figure at nearer 30 per cent, just over the Euroland members' average gold reserves, and compared to the US proportion of 52 per cent of reserves in gold. Finally, in July, when the ECB disclosed the actual amount of gold would be 15 per cent, sentiment improved as a more optimistic view of gold's role following the introduction of EMU developed.

Another pressing problem for the gold market is the Swiss government's decision to sever the link between the Swiss franc and gold, possibly leading to the sale of half of Switzerland's reserves – more than 1,300 tonnes of gold. To implement this decision, a referendum is first required, as the Swiss constitution would have to be changed. As the last major country to have a currency linked to gold, and the world's third largest gold owner, a Swiss sale would be a major blow for the gold market. The sale would provide the means for the Swiss to fund their state pension system, predicted to go into deficit by 2004. It could also help create a solidarity fund to help victims of the Nazi holocaust. According to a recent report, the Nazis shipped most of their gold through Switzerland to other neutral states, purchasing supplies and materials to manufacture arms from these countries. Switzerland received around £300m in stolen gold from the Nazis.

A further potential threat to the gold market over the past year has been the proposed International Monetary Fund (IMF) sale of approximately $30bn of gold, to help pay off Third World countries' debts. Worryingly for the market, a recent study by the US Federal Reserve posed an additional risk in concluding that central banks should sell their gold, as it is cheaper than mining for new gold. This has led to speculation that the US, the world's second largest gold owner, could change its gold policy and start to sell.

Over the past two years, the Russian economy has suffered successive severe crises. In early 1998, when share prices fell by more than 40 per cent, the Russian Central Bank tried to restore stability and avoid devaluation by raising interest rates to 150 per cent. The crisis in Asia, together with declining oil, gas and gold prices, had a severe effect on the Russian economy. Russia's Central Bank has generally run contrary to the trend of other central banks by increasing its gold reserves in the past two years. The central bank has pushed for this legislation to enable it to build its reserves and assist the mining industry. Russian commercial banks can now export gold directly following the introduction of new export regulations, in a bid to liberalise this heavily centralised sector. When banks began shipping gold and silver to London for sale, the gold price reacted predictably by falling sharply. Russian political and economic events clearly have the potential to affect the market sentiment on gold. Thus, earlier in 1998, when President Yeltsin decided to sack his entire cabinet, the gold price wobbled. When, in August 1998, Russia's sudden financial meltdown sparked anxiety for the global economy, the gold market, fearing that Russia would be forced to sell gold, induced the 19-year low.

Gold demand during 1998 was stronger than the market had anticipated. Demand in the World Gold Council's key markets reached 2,712 tonnes over the year, only 11 per cent less than that of the record level set in 1997. Indian demand rose by 11 per cent, and in the US by 18 per cent to a market high. Demand for gold fell by 10 per cent in China, and grew by 5 per cent and 3 per cent in Saudi Arabia and Japan respectively.

China and India are the gold jewellery industry's two primary targets. Chinese investment and jewellery demand for gold has increased substantially in the past few years. Recent moves by the People's Bank of China have changed the pricing structure for gold, bringing it into line with international markets. However, the effects of the Asian financial crisis, coupled with the fact that 1998 was the Chinese Year of the Tiger, caused declining demand. In China, Hong Kong and Taiwan aggregate demand fell by 23 per cent. Chinese communities consider holding traditional gold-giving ceremonies, such as weddings and engagements, unlucky in the Year of the Tiger.

In India, the country which currently consumes more gold than any other, lower prices and increased availability led to a new record in gold demand in 1998 for the fourth successive year. Total gold consumption for the year was 815 tonnes. Demand increased by 11 per cent on 1997's figures, which in turn had seen an increase of 45 per cent on the previous year. Rural India's banking system remains undeveloped and villagers buy gold in good harvest years as it can easily be sold for cash. Demand slackened in the second half of the year when 60 per cent increases in import tariffs, together with the depreciation of the rupee, raised the price. The reintroduction of import tariffs in India is believed to have led to the resumption in gold smuggling.

Since 1980, gold has lost 67 per cent of its value. However, gold mines continue to produce 2,400 tonnes of gold each year, and central banks still hold thousands of tonnes in reserves. Most central banks continue to hold at least some of their reserves in gold. Central banks often lease gold, generating around 2 per cent interest. This is far less than can be gained from US Treasury Bills, but more than that currently earned on Japanese government bonds. According to the World Gold Council, the US economy may be flourishing now, but this was not the case in the 1970s. Moreover, the financial crisis in Asia showed how confidence can be lost in formerly economically successful countries. The World Gold Council argues that although central bank sales are significant for the gold market, more crucial factors are US monetary policy, the strength of the dollar, and the increase in supply from mines.

17.2.2 Other precious metals

Demand for silver fell by 2 per cent in 1998 because of the high price, the strength of the US dollar, and the Asian financial crisis. Total supply to the market fell by 2 per cent despite the fact that official sector sales of the metal increased seven-fold to over 50m ounces. However, according to the *World Silver Survey 1999* by Gold Field Mineral Services, the silver market had a structural deficit for the tenth consecutive year. Fabrication demand outstripped supply from mine production, thereby depleting the above-ground stocks of silver by 105m ounces. The average silver price in 1998 was $5.53, an increase of 12.7 per cent on the previous year's average of £4.91. However, the increase was not as high as many analysts had assumed, and was concentrated in the first four months of the year.

News broke in February 1998 that US stock investor Warren Buffet had acquired one-fifth of the world silver supply. The low prices earlier in 1997 and the emerging shortfall had attracted him. This coincided with the publication of CPM Group's survey of the silver market. It revealed that silver stocks were now only 20 per cent of the 1990 level. As a result, the price jumped to $7 an ounce, and Mr Buffet recorded a paper profit of $260m – a 40 per cent return on his investment.

After peaking at $7.81 in February, silver had fallen to $5.30 an ounce by May 1998, and the market's buoyancy seemed over. Although hopes that Warren Buffet would move in to buy more of the metal did not materialise, the imbalance between supply and demand promoted further price variability and volatility. Variability measures the amount and volatility the frequency of price changes. The market became increasingly jittery amid great concern that stocks of silver could swamp the market at any time.

By August 1998, the price of silver was less than the average at which Warren Buffet had bought 20 per cent of the world's supply, and analysts were predicting a net loss for him. As the world's second richest man, Buffet was capable of sustaining such a loss in his investment. However, many smaller investors who had followed his lead into the silver market when the price was high have made substantial losses. Towards the end of the year, price fluctuations and the volume of silver in the market led experts to conclude that Buffet had sold a large proportion of his silver holdings. The price fell to a low of $4.69 in December.

Scarcity of platinum and palladium combined with political and economic instability in Russia (the world's second largest producer of platinum and foremost of palladium) resulted in a volatile year for these metals. In 1998, 70 per cent of palladium came from Russia, and its role in supplying platinum can make the difference between a surplus and deficit in the world market. Russian supply has become increasingly inconsistent since 1997, when the metals' agency was stripped of its power to authorise exports. Delays and increased bureaucracy have ensued. Crucially, there was a simultaneous escalation in industrial demand for palladium. Russia retains an unknown quantity of palladium stocks, and prices of palladium and platinum have become more volatile. Historically, palladium sold at around one-quarter of the price of platinum, but prices have now converged.

Demand for platinum in the developing world is accelerating, particularly in China. According to Johnson Matthey's *Platinum Report 1999*, demand for platinum rose by 4 per cent in 1998 to only 50,000 ounces short of the supply. A 70 per cent increase in Chinese platinum jewellery manufacture accounted for much of the demand. Jewellery manufacturing is now the major consumer of platinum. The Japanese account for the majority of platinum jewellery demand, but it has been decreasing of late. Chinese demand for both industrial uses and for jewellery has grown from zero five years ago to 620,000 ounces.

Investment in platinum mining shares is also increasing. Shares in some of the South African mines have risen by around 140 per cent, and Mercury Asset Management has invested 13 per cent, or $119m, of its Gold and General unit trust in South African platinum shares. Platinum mining companies' operating margin was 26 per cent last year, compared to 19 per cent for gold.

In early 1998, reports spread that palladium had begun to trickle through from Russia. The inflated price of palladium immediately fell sharply on the news. Reduced supply again in April saw the asking price to lease palladium for one month become 200 per cent of the spot price. By May,

Russia's export problems remained unresolved. Platinum rose to $403 an ounce, and the palladium price was, for the first time, higher, standing at a record $417. This followed the publication of the *Platinum Report 1998*, which recorded a 21 per cent increase in demand for palladium in 1997.

Resumption of Russian platinum sales pushed the price of the metal back to $360 by the close of 1998. Palladium too ended the year on the lower level of $325, as supply increased in the latter part of the year. Dealers in London claimed they had no official knowledge of where the palladium coming onto the market originated from, but guessed it was from Russia.

7.3 COUNTERFEITS AND FRAUDS

17.3.1 Counterfeit coins

One problem of purchasing coins made from gold bullion or other precious metals is the risk of forgeries. In the 1970s, when inflation was soaring upwards, interest in UK sovereigns was so high that the Mint found itself unable to produce enough. As a result, dealers increased the premium (the difference between the face value and the metal value). The coins began to sell at almost one and a half times their face value. The opportunity attracted Middle Eastern forgers, although, in practice, the vendors and buyers could easily detect the counterfeit coins.

Controversy over the long-running 'Hirohito' coin scandal still has residual effects on market sentiment in Japan. Originally issued in 1986 to commemorate the 60th anniversary of the late Emperor's accession to the throne, the Japanese police alleged in 1990 that 100,000 were Middle Eastern fakes. Coin dealers affected by confiscations denied any conspiracy or crime. The affair took a new turn when a UK dealer began civil action against the Japanese government for the return of seized coins. The dealer alleged that the Tokyo police, contrary to their statements, had effectively abandoned their investigations in 1990. As a result, confidence in the Hirohito coin collapsed and investors cashed in 3m coins worth 300bn yen at their face value.

The Hirohito coin scandal caused a delay in the issue of the Akihito coins (called Heisei after the new emperor's era). In the event, the authorities decided to release only 2m coins; the original plan was to issue 3.8m Heiseis. To discourage forgers, the coins contain 30 (not 20) grams of gold. This amount represented about 50,000 yen worth of gold in a coin that the Japanese sold for 100,000 yen. However, despite the Hirohito scandal and the delayed issue, the Japanese bought most of the 2m coins.

17.3.2 **Gold mine frauds**

Fraud has also beset precious metal investing. Typically, promoters sell interests in gold mines that are nearly worthless or non-existent. Telephone salespeople may call offering gold not yet mined. They say they will sell it for $100 under the going price.

Such frauds are an international problem. One commentator believes that there are 'probably thirty to forty gold mining scams going on now'. He cautions investors to be distrustful of salespeople who offer interests in gold mines. Typically, they promise gold for perhaps half the market price; the explanation is usually that the mine owner has a special process or patented techniques for extracting the metal.

New fingerprinting techniques developed by scientists, led by Watling and Herben at the Western Australian Department of Minerals and Energy Centre, should make salting of gold mines, a technique used since the mining industry began, a problem of the past. 'Salting' is the addition of precious metals from one mine to another, to give the illusion of great discoveries of gold, as happened in Kalgoorlie, the centre of a new Western Australian gold rush. A new mine suddenly was found to contain ores with a gold content ten times higher than normal. Watling presented evidence at a conference in 1994 to prove that the gold came from two sources, and that one was added artificially.

This now perfected process will give every mine a unique fingerprint. The fingerprinting technique will affect not only salters of mines and gold thieves, but also fraudsters who claim that gold ingots originate from a specific mine. Watling hopes that experts will fingerprint much of the world's gold so they can identify its origins with certainty, and gold will no longer be an untraceable international currency. Watling is applying the same technique to diamonds from De Beers.

However, even such advances do not always prevent fraud, as investors in the Busang mine on the island of Borneo, Indonesia, found to their cost. In February 1997, a small but reputable Canadian mining firm, Bre-X, hailed it as the biggest gold discovery of this century, with 71m ounces worth £15.5bn. In May 1997, it turned out to be the biggest illusion since the days of Houdini. The company collapsed, and $6bn in share value was wiped out. In May 1999, the defrauded investors were outraged when the Canadian police announced they would not be pursuing the case due to lack of evidence. However, the Ontario Securities Commission has filed civil charges against Bre-X's chief geologist. The company's chief executive and the geologist at the Indonesian site are both now dead.

Samples from the site had been tampered with to boost their gold content. Mining consultants, Strathcona Mineral Services Ltd, showed that the find was not economically worthwhile. Strathcona's president, Graham Farquharson, wrote in a letter to Bre-X's chairman: 'The magnitude of the tampering with core samples that we believe has occurred ... is without precedent in the history of mining anywhere.' The effect has been to reduce investment interest in unit trusts that hold shares in gold mining and exploration companies. Mining companies have cut their expenditure on exploration because of lower interest by investors together with the drop in commodity prices. It was Mark Twain who, during the 1849 gold rush, remarked: 'A mine is a hole in the ground with a liar standing next to it!'

17.4 OPPORTUNITIES AND COSTS

17.4.1 Investment potential

Who should buy gold, in what form should investors purchase it and how much should they invest in the metal? 'It depends on the investor' says one dealer. 'Many large portfolios might have at least a small percentage in gold. A person who has little money to invest and is conservative should concentrate on gilts. If you are more aggressive, you could have a larger holding in gold.' These recommendations seem optimistic, given gold's resistance in recent years to the anxiety factor. For many investors who still wish to hold gold, coins make sense, because they are easier to sell than bullion. Alternatively, investors can buy precious metals in bars or wafers which may, for an extra price, have decorative stampings. A 100-ounce gold bar is about the size of a brick. Dealers sell wafers in various weights, down to a few ounces, although premiums are higher on smaller unit weights. Hoarders could store gold coins, bars or wafers in a safe-deposit box or home safe. Anxiety over the approaching millennium has fuelled a surge in consumer demand for gold and silver bullion as a hedge in the event of Y2K computer problems with banks and the economy. Coin dealers report a huge increase in the volume of their sales during 1999.

The safest way to buy gold, either in coins or bars, is at a high street bank, which will reduce the risk of theft, increase security and avoid VAT, if the owners hold the gold in offshore branches. However, investment gold transactions after 1 January 2000 will be exempt from VAT. Some banks offer gold purchase programmes, and (given adequate security) may be willing to finance these purchases. If an investor buys on credit, the bank will want to keep the gold in its vault and charge for storage. For example, some clearing banks in Jersey will deal in Kruggerands and Maple Leaf coins for mainland customers. Reportedly, they charge £1.50 per coin for the service, with a minimum charge of £10. Insurance during transit is 50p per coin. Storage is 25p per coin per quarter (minimum charge £5 per quarter). Insurance for storage is 0.175 per cent per annum of the gold's value, with the minimum premium set at £35.

17.4.2 Costs of ownership

Among other factors, the transaction costs put off some investors. Other deterrents have been the imposition of VAT, storage expenses, and the lack of dividends or interest from precious metals investments. Investors should remember that, unlike bank deposits and securities, gold's value depends on changes in the general market for bullion. Storage, dealing and insurance costs can erode profits from investments in gold bars or coins.

17.4.3 Advisers

Even to investors who have good reasons for buying precious metals, financial advisers offer words of caution. Anyone who buys gold or another precious metal, or gemstones, should use a bank, a specialist trading house or a reputable dealer. In any event, making sure he or she can obtain possession of the asset when he or she needs it is important for the investor. In times of great financial crisis, banks may be closed.

In Britain, investors can buy gold coins through dealers, precious metal brokers, investment consultants, some banks and jewellers. They sell and buy gold sovereigns and half sovereigns in quantity, and the products of other countries' mints. Advantages can flow from choosing coins in popular demand. The premiums charged (ie the difference between the price of the coin and the value of the bullion it contains) are higher for coins that sell in low quantities.

Until the recent fluctuations in the gold market, many financial advisers suggested that individual investors interested in gold would be wise to choose shares of gold mining companies or gold unit trusts. In contrast to coins, ingots, futures or options, gold stocks represent a productive asset (ie a company) and may even pay dividends. Typically, the shares of gold-mining companies rise two or three times the percentage increase in gold prices. Over the past three years however, the gold price has dropped by 40 per cent, and gold mining stocks by almost 33 per cent.

17.5 TAXATION

17.5.1 Tax planning

The income, capital gains, capital transfer and inheritance tax considerations reviewed in Chapter 18 on arts and antiques generally apply to valuables. The same advice applies to careful tax planning.

17.5.2 VAT

From 1 January 2000, when a new EU Directive comes into force, transactions in investment gold throughout the EU will be exempt from VAT. Investment gold refers to gold bars weighing more than one gram and with a fineness of at least 995, to non-numismatic coins of a purity greater than 900, to gold-related securities and to forward and future transactions.

Before 1982, purchases of bullion coins did not attract VAT if the coins were still legal tender in their country of issue. Following the Exchange Control (Gold Coins) Exemption Order 1979 and the Value Added Tax (Finance) Order 1982, there are now two main ways for UK private investors to buy gold bullion coins. One is to pay the VAT, which would make it more difficult to realise a gain from the transaction. The other is to buy the coins overseas and store them there at a cost.

Dealers may promote other approaches in advertisements or through direct mail circulars, but investors should treat them with caution. In the UK, when VAT-registered traders (who buy and sell gold coins by way of business) sell bullion coins back, the dealer who buys them should pay the VAT on the transaction directly to HM Customs & Excise.

On 1 April 1993, the Chancellor of the Exchequer introduced a special scheme for accounting and paying for VAT on gold transactions. The scheme applies to certain supplies of gold that are liable to VAT at the standard rate. Under this current scheme the buyer and the seller treat a standard-rated supply of gold as a taxable supply for registration. Under the terms of this scheme, the buyer must account for the output tax that the seller charges when supplying the gold. The buyer retains the right to claim input tax credit in the same VAT accounting period in which the supply takes place. VAT leaflet 701/21193, 'Gold and gold coins', available from HM Customs & Excise, offers guidance. This leaflet will be altered in the coming months to reflect the abolition of VAT on purchases of investment gold in the EU from 1 January 2000.

The forfeiture provisions of the Customs & Excise Management Act apply, even if the smuggled gold is found in the hands of an innocent purchaser. It is, therefore, in the best interest of buyers to satisfy themselves that importers have complied with the regulations before agreeing to complete a purchase. The questions to ask are: Where has the gold come from? Who has imported it? Have they paid VAT on it? Why are they selling it? How is it delivered? Is a quick settlement demanded? Is the seller new to the gold market? Does he or she regularly supply large quantities? What references can he or she offer? Such basic checks on the history and reputation of the supplier, and the documents, are clearly advisable in view of the growing number of frauds.

VAT regulations will continue to apply to silver and platinum. As in the gold and silver markets, zero-rating for VAT applies only to transactions between wholesale traders. In the past, zero-rating was not necessary as transfers of metal among traders in London were insignificant. The rapid rise in demand for platinum has increased the need for speedy inter-trader movements of metal.

17.6 PREVIEW OF THE YEAR AHEAD

17.6.1 Demand and supply

The status of gold has declined since the end of the Bretton Woods Agreement in 1971. Recent announcements of the sale of reserves by the UK Government and the IMF signal a change in the way governments use central bank reserves, and a change in gold's status. Even in the US, academic opinion is changing and a sale of some of the Federal Reserve's $11bn in gold (53 per cent of total reserves) now seems more likely.

The key argument for an individual or a central bank for investing in gold is whether it has a role to play as an 'asset of last resort'. Expert opinion on the matter varies. Continued uncertainty and turbulence in global financial markets, and concern at the risk of a breakdown in the financial system on 1 January 2000 because of computer problems, could cause an expansion in the demand for physical gold. This would increase the price of mining companies' shares, and drive up the price. According to Richard Scott-Ram of the World Gold Council, there is a negative correlation between the performance of stocks and that of gold. He argues that there is a 30 per cent probability that if, for example, US stocks fall, the gold price will climb.

Analysts point out that the falling price since the late 1980s, coupled with the fact that recent international financial and political crises have not led a significant number of investors to return to the traditional 'safe haven' of gold, have damaged the metal. Neither the economic crises in Asia, Russia and Latin America, nor the collapse of LTCM, have impacted on gold demand and lifted the price, supporting the view that gold is now just another commodity.

However, as Steven Bell, Chief Economist at Deutsche Bank, commented in a recent *Financial Times* article, gold as an asset is most relevant in times of high inflation and interest rates. In the low inflationary 1990s, it is not surprising that governments and central banks should prefer to invest more fruitfully than hold onto gold.

In a presentation earlier this year, Andy Smith of Mitsui argued that gold has never kept its value over long periods. He claimed that the average real price per ounce has been about $281 since 1560, albeit with various wild swings causing a standard deviation from the average of $84. Historically, buying by central banks has caused the price increases.

Some analysts believe that there could be a shift in favour of gold. The deficit between supply and demand is set to continue growing, mine production is declining, and an eventual shortfall is possible. Supporters of gold argue that central bank sales have to end sometime, and investors' sentiment will then change. The trend towards over-selling and over-borrowing of gold has started to reverse, and hedging has declined.

A mining analyst from T Hoare agrees that the gap between supply and demand in the longer term could rise significantly. Bobby Godsell, chief executive of Anglogold, believes the gold market has an optimistic future. He points out that hundreds of millions of individual investors buy gold. Moreover, he argues, in a global economy, with a single reserve currency, it is ill-advised for central banks not to hold some of their reserves in gold. Increasing jewellery demand and limited production could further sustain the gold market in the long term.

17.6.2 Central banks' sales

The main factor to set against optimism is the activity of the official sector. Central banks, particularly in EU countries, have little incentive to maintain their reserves at current levels. Bankers now prefer to seek higher returns on reserves than that of gold. This is one of the few roles left for central banks within EMU. A widely reported prediction suggests that the prospect of European Monetary Union may eventually lead central banks to become net sellers by the turn of the century. Central banks may well continue selling gold reserves for the next ten years, despite reassurances from the World Gold Council to the contrary. There is a deficit between new supply and demand for gold, but official sales could more than compensate for the shortfall, in the next decade at least. In the absence of a major change or world calamity, there is no impending significant boost in the gold price.

Over the past decade central banks have sold 6,700 tonnes of gold. Some conspiracy theorists believe there is an international campaign by central banks to keep the gold price low, as it is the only real alternative to currencies. A group of US investors called the Gold Anti-Trust Action Committee advances this view on its website. John Wilson, head of the Canadian mining company Placer Dome, agrees to a certain extent. He said in a recent *Financial Times* article that there is a concerted effort by central banks to hold down the gold price, thereby keeping inflation down, although he did not believe that there is a correlation between the two. However, other economists, including Paul Fields of Gold Fields Mineral Services, completely reject this conspiracy theory.

The UK Treasury astonished the gold market in May of this year by announcing the intended sale of half of the UK gold reserves. Surprise at the unexpected sale and its timing shook the market more than the sale itself. Gold lost 10 per cent of its value following the announcement, falling to a 20-year low in June 1999. Gold mining shares were badly affected, dropping by more than one-quarter on average. The currencies of the major gold producers have also been hit, particularly the South African rand. The FTSE Gold Mines Index fell by more than one-quarter and the North American gold mines index by 29 per cent.

Some analysts are not surprised at the UK decision to sell half of the country's gold. A higher than average proportion of the country's reserves are held in gold, 43 per cent. However, in a letter to the *Financial Times*, Haruko Fakuda, the recently appointed Chief at the World Gold Council, disputes this. She argues that in gross terms, the UK has reduced its gold holding from 17 per cent to 7 per cent – on a par with Albania. This compares with Germany's 33.2 per cent, France's 43.5 per cent and 51.3 per cent in the US. Some traders now fear that the big gold holders could follow the UK and become sellers this year.

Rhona O'Connell, an analyst at Hoare & Co, believes that the advanced warning of the sale will offset the effect on the market in July when the first auction takes place, because the auctions will be conducted publicly every two months, and not released onto the market quietly as other banks have done in the past. Some industry insiders are now calling for official gold sales to be centrally conducted throughout the year, and marketed through a central international selling organisation.

Switzerland struck a major blow to gold's role in the international monetary system in 1998, as the link between the franc and gold was severed and the intention to sell over half of the country's gold was announced. This threat overhung the gold market until June 1999 when the Swiss parliament rejected the constitutional amendment necessary to sell the gold. However, the Swiss ban's view is that the sales will go ahead eventually, probably in early 2000.

Following a five-year campaign, the IMF has finally agreed to sell up to 10 per cent of its gold reserves to fund an initiative to help pay off Third World countries' debts.

17.6.3 Silver, platinum and palladium

Australia is set to replace the US as the world's third largest producer of silver by the year 2000, because of the development of the Cannington mine. Coinage demand in particular has increased substantially already this year.

However, in 1999, the silver deficit is expected to narrow further to a mere 144m ounces. Investment demand is expected to rise in 1999, which could push up the silver price and mine production.

Ted Kempf of the CPM Group believes that there is sustainable future demand for silver. It is a diverse metal used in jewellery, cutlery, X-rays, film and electronics – almost anything with a switch has a small amount of silver in it. In India and East Asia demand did fall in 1998; however, people there often invest in silver and other precious metals as a hedge against devalued currencies. The Asian financial crisis had less impact on silver than on gold and platinum, because in Japan there is little demand for silver jewellery.

Bill Davis of Sunshine Mining believes that the continual supply deficit improves the outlook for silver over the next 12 months, compared with other metals. However, this was the reason why Warren Buffet invested in the silver market, and reportedly later made a massive loss on his investment. The Silver Institute's Survey for 1999 warns against too optimistic a view of silver's prospects; the market is complex and prediction is difficult.

Platinum and palladium have recently led the precious metals' sector. Palladium and rhodium tripled in price in the past two years. Use of these metals in autocatalysts is set to increase as environmental standards are raised, particularly in the US. As ever, for palladium and platinum, much will depend on what happens to Russia's economy in the next 12 months. Norilsk, Russia's palladium producer, claims to have agreed a long-term export licence, and the Russian government did grant a 5 per cent export licence in April 1999. However, a supply deficit is expected well into the year 2000. No-one knows the exact size of Russia's palladium holdings, and this produces continuing market uncertainty. Political crises in Russia also cause instability in the market. When President Yeltsin sacked the fourth government in 14 months, the prices of these metals rose on the news.

Leading palladium producers in South Africa and North America are expanding production in the coming year to try to meet rising demand. The 14 major palladium mines are expected to increase supply between now and 2001, and six new mines are set to start up by the same year.

Analysts warn, however, that as the price of palladium converges with that of platinum, the metal's future is in danger as palladium has been favoured for its cheaper cost. Although palladium is technically superior for manufacture of autocatalysts, manufacturers are aware of Russia's inability to meet demand, and nickel is a good substitute in some industrial uses. One of the major autocatalyst manufacturers, Degussa-Huels, has reportedly developed a platinum-based catalyst which can be used as an alternative to those manufactured using mainly palladium. This new autocatalyst meets the EU's 2005 requirements for low emissions, and the US's even lower targets. Platinum is also a popular metal for use in many medical implants. Such developments can only lead to higher platinum prices in future.

As supply problems continue, a serious global shortage in platinum group metals is likely. Johnson Mathey's *Platinum Report 1999* predicts that platinum will fluctuate between $350 and $390 an ounce between now and the close of the year. Palladium could trade in the range of $340 to $420 an ounce, if not higher, in the same period.

Demand for the metals will remain strong well into the next century. Currently, palladium demand stands at 8m ounces, while supply is only 5m. Russian exports continue for the moment, but the *Platinum Report* believes the metal could run out in the next few years.

17.7 CONCLUSION

Gold Field Mineral Services argues that it is not the quantity of gold mined annually which determines its supply, but rather what happens to the gold already in existence. It acknowledges the possibility that the market could become accustomed to central bank sales. If the chance of further sales was no longer perceived as a threat, a more positive view of gold could develop. Improved sentiment would also prevent producers from hedge-selling at every rally.

However, few analysts now forecast large price rises for gold. Of course, pessimists might take into account the late Sir James Goldsmith's prediction of a 'meltdown' in the global financial system, and purchase bullion bars or gold coins. Or, if the new euro stumbles in 1999 or later, some investors could seek shelter in precious metals against erratic movements in the European currency and financial markets. There is some evidence that US investors have been buying gold and silver coins because of fears over the Millennium bug. But for now, analysts generally believe that investments in, for example, unit trusts holding mining equities will outperform the physical commodity. Lower production costs mean some gold mining companies remain profitable, despite the recent fall in the share prices.

Paul Walker, a director of Gold Fields Mineral Services, told the *Financial Times* that in the light of the gold sales by the UK, the IMF and other countries, there is little to be optimistic about in the immediate future. The gold price could fall to below $240 an ounce in the coming months. At the recent World Gold Conference in London, Kevin Crisp of JP Morgan told delegates that gold is likely to trade in much wider ranges in future. He expects swings of between $100 and $150 over a matter of months. Also at the conference, Peter Ward of Lehman Brothers warned the industry of the consequences for the market as private investors may begin to question why they are holding onto gold as the world's major holders of the metal begin to dispose of it.

Gold has been steadily losing its value since 1971, and it is now worth two-thirds less now than it was then. Over the past 20 years, prices of other investments have increased significantly. Stocks have risen by 1,537 per cent since 1980, and bonds by 698 per cent. Arguably in the next century gold could follow the downward trend of silver over the past six centuries, to its current position as a non-monetary metal. Silver has recently seen its lowest level in six centuries, while gold, though stable by comparison, now stands at only half of its average level for the past two centuries.

Platinum, palladium and rhodium are likely to remain fascinating, if risky, investments. These metals will probably sustain their market in the jewellery, automobile and electronics industry, with rhodium remaining resilient to the development of substitutes. Even with alternatives reducing the platinum content of catalytic converters, continuing environmental concern for greenhouse gas emissions is likely to increase the number fitted to new cars. On the supply side, whether Russian supply of these metals is sustained or not, a sustained long period of stable supply is necessary before the market loses its fear of another stoppage.

17.8 OTHER VALUABLES

7.8.1 Diamonds and De Beers

Apart from precious metals, investors can also consider gemstones like emeralds, sapphires, semi-precious stones and diamonds. In investment terms only diamonds are significant, and the Central Selling Organisation (CSO) still dominates the market. This is the London-based marketing organisation of De Beers.

Only about one in six of diamonds mined finds a use in rings or other jewellery, but these account for most of the diamond output's value. Buyers put the remainder to industrial use. The market's performance therefore largely depends on the success of its promoters in stimulating demand. To this end, De Beers spends large sums on advertising and sales promotion, a concerted effort to persuade more women and men to buy and wear diamonds as jewellery. One result has been to stimulate demand through retail jewellers, but the markups make it difficult for the investor to achieve gains. The addition of VAT accentuates the problem.

Yet, over the decades, De Beers has succeeded in mass-marketing what was once an aristocratic luxury without greatly diminishing its value. Diamonds remain 'the gem of gems', though millions own them. De Beers' aim is long-term stability and prosperity for the industry. In its view, price fluctuations would undermine confidence in the value of diamonds. So far, the strategy has succeeded. However, it is vulnerable to persistent recession and threats to the world-wide cartel, as more governments wonder about alternative approaches to marketing diamonds other than through the CSO.

De Beers has kept firm control over the supply and price of the world's diamonds for nearly a century. However, diamond prices have not always kept pace with inflation and, for a time, Russia stood accused until recently of breaking faith by flooding the market with bootleg gems and synthetic diamonds. Furthermore, the cartel is struggling to gain control over the output of mines in Zaire and elsewhere, which could deflate values. Rough diamond exports from Russia, which recently destabilised the market, have now subsided and the pressures have ceased; in October 1997, Russia signed a 13-month contract with De Beers and joined the cartel, and extended the agreement in 1998 until 2001. A three-month dispute between South Africa and De Beers in the first part of 1999 will have some impact on supply this year, but it was resolved in June.

17.8.2 The market

Antwerp, the medieval Belgian city, is the world's diamond-trading capital, home to about one-third of De Beers' hand-picked buyers and accounting for 60 per cent of all transactions. Traders experienced a slump in 1992, when falling demand and the Angolan civil war disrupted government control over freelance miners in the Lunda Norte region. The net result was a massive flow of Angolan diamonds, produced outside the cartel in recent years by the UNITA faction.

In 1998, when it emerged that over 6 per cent of the world diamond supply was in the hands of UNITA, the EU imposed sanctions on the faction in an attempt to stem increased diamond smuggling. Smuggled diamonds were apparently being sold in the streets of Antwerp and, to a lesser extent, in London. Angola is the world's third largest producer of diamonds, which are of a high quality. The EU acted to prevent a possible world slump in the diamond price – a disaster for jewellers' diamond producers, but also for millions of small investors in diamond jewellery whose assets would quickly lose value. Since then, diamond production in Angola has lessened.

Antwerp's industry association, the Diamond High Council, is confident that the US market will continue to grow and that the Japanese market will also recover. However, a question still hangs over Europe's resurgence. One major threat to Antwerp's monopoly is emerging competition from other diamond centres, mainly in the Far East.

From 1992 until 1996, Japan surpassed the US as the world's largest market for diamond jewellery. In 1967, only 6 per cent of Japanese brides received diamond engagement rings; in 1995, the level was 77 per cent. According to Toshiyuki Momozawa, president of the Jewellery Trade Centre in Tokyo, 'De Beers gets the credit for this. They took the same concepts they had used on the Americans and convinced the Japanese that the diamond lasts forever; it is a good investment and is the only kind of engagement ring.' However, there is now a trend towards platinum jewellery causing anxiety in the diamond trade.

Diamonds are not necessarily a good investment. Although some larger diamonds hold their value and may even appreciate, smaller stones of a carat or less can be money losers, especially if bought at marked-up retail prices. In 1989 wholesalers sold a top-quality one-carat stone for $18,000; in February 1996 similar stones were selling for about $15,700, a 14 per cent decline. By far the best diamond investment during those years would have been in paper form, that is, De Beers stock, which had improved in value over the years.

In 1997, the economic crisis in Asia reduced demand for diamonds, and had a serious impact on De Beers' share price. Sale of diamonds was the lowest for six years. The company responded by cutting diamond sales by half, in an attempt to stabilise the market. The CSO halted the supply of rough diamonds, to compensate for the virtually non-existent demand in Japan and South East Asia, and to prop up the price.

There has been an element of success in this tactic, but an influx of polished diamonds from Asia has contributed to oversupply. Nonetheless, in the first half of 1998, the restrictions on sales led to a revival in De Beers' share price. However, demand remained low and diamonds continued to pour into the CSO. At the year end it emerged that diamond sales had dropped to an 11-year low. Japanese demand fell a further 20 per cent on the previous year, and in Hong Kong imports were down

40 per cent on 1997 levels. De Beers continued with the policy of holding back sales of rough diamonds to promote market stability. Diamond sales were down 28 per cent to $3.3bn in 1998, and the stockpile grew to $4.7bn, despite De Beers holding back the sale and imposing production quotas on diamonds. In early 1999 the diamond market began to improve and in June De Beers announced a sharp recovery in sales of uncut diamonds. Sales had increased by 44 per cent on the previous year when sales were deliberately restricted to offset the effects of the Asian financial crisis. The recovery reflects improving confidence among the diamond-cutting centres in the CSO, which has allowed the group to increase sales throughout the first half of 1999. Analysts believe the effects of problems in Asia are levelling out and forecast that global demand will increase by around one-third, and De Beers' 'Millennium' marketing is expected to prove successful. Japanese demand is expected to turn in the coming year.

In the longer term, the outlook is promising; in particular, the plan to brand diamonds could lead to an increase in price levels. De Beers is test marketing laser-branding the own-name diamonds in the North of England. There is also an emerging trend towards two diamond markets; one for the larger, high-quality stones, and the other for small diamonds.

Dealers are focusing on the US where demand remains strong, with a growth rate of 8 per cent. The US market accounts for 35 per cent of diamond sales, and demand increased there by 7 per cent in the first half of 1998 on the previous year, and again in 1999 first-quarter sales were up by 8 per cent. Some analysts are warning of over-reliance on the US market. Diamond dealers also covet the potential of China, with its young, growing and newly prosperous urban population of 280m. Mark Cockle says: 'Its safe to say that every company is looking for a new Japan', and 'China could be another Japan and America rolled into one.'

17.8.3 Diamond production

Russian mines produce top quality diamonds, and the country has some newly discovered diamond fields. However, an acute shortage of cash constrains opportunities to add to the supply. In turn, that exacerbates the political uncertainties and the weakness of the rouble. Russia's progress is likely to have a radical impact on both the domestic and world markets by the turn of the century. Now, the Yakutia-Sakha Republic accounts for 99 per cent of the former Soviet Union's total diamond production. Analysts expect mining to deplete these fields by 2010. However, the newly discovered fields in Asiatic Russia, around St Petersburg and in the Karelian Republic, could bring riches. De Beers conservatively estimates that just one field will yield 250m carats.

The output of gem diamonds from the new fields is much higher than the Yakut fields' output, which is in turn better than the output of gem stones in South Africa. The diamond content of the Yakut ore ranges from 0.6 to 4 carats per tonne of ore, with 2–3 carats per tonne on average. Industry sources predict that an annual production of between 3 and 6m carats is likely over the next 30–40 years. Prospecting and developing the fields are likely to be both expensive and time-consuming. Nevertheless, American, British and Australian investors have already placed and won tenders to develop five diamond-bearing areas. However, in the diamond trade as elsewhere in Russia, bureaucracy prevented the export of rough diamonds in the first few months of 1998.

Russia and South Africa also face competition from other countries. For example, Australia is now a large producer of diamonds. Most of the stones are industrial grade only, but a proportion are of gem quality. Australia's Argyle diamond mine also produces rare stones, a few of which have sold for more than US$1m a carat. In other parts of Africa diamond production is increasing and in 1998, a diamond co-operation agreement was signed between Russia and Namibia. The Russian diamond monopoly Almazy Rossii-Sakha (ALROSA) disclosed its intention to expand operations in Africa, particularly in Namibia and Angola. A diamond co-operation agreement was signed between Russia and Namibia in early 1998.

17.8.4 De Beers and Russia

A new contract signed in October 1997 healed a threatened breach between the De Beers' cartel and Russia, sustaining trade worth £1bn a year. It leaves De Beers as 'the sole and exclusive buyer of all rough diamond exports from Russia', according to the authoritative *Diamantaire* newsletter. Alongside the agreement is a deal under which western banks, headed by NatWest Markets, advanced funds to ALROSA. Russia has stressed that recent agreements with other African countries will not break the contract with De Beers.

Russia's successive economic crises led to the multi-billion dollar diamond industry to extend the marketing agreement with De Beers until 2001, under which ALROSA will sell roughly 50 per cent of its output through the cartel. Some analysts had predicted that Russian rough or uncut gem diamond stocks might run out as early as 1998, but that was before the Archangel diamond company discovery worth $2.4bn in the North of the Federation. This could be the world's richest diamond mine.

To increase production, De Beers has already embarked on a four-year project to double the Orapa mine's annual output in north-east Botswana to 12m carats. De Beers also agreed a deal in March this year with the international mining company BHP to sell 35 per cent of the output of Canada's first diamond mine near Yellowknife, which the group hopes will stabilise the market in the long term.

17.8.5 Investment

The traditional image of diamonds as a good investment is not as appealing as many perhaps imagine. While other commodities fluctuate in price, influenced by the weather and economics, the price of rough diamonds has stabilised or risen. Given that price performance, and the financial strength of De Beers, investment in diamonds should be secure. However, De Beers deals only in rough diamonds, and sells only to about 150 diamond dealers, a select client list. Membership is by invitation. Outside this narrow market, prices for cut and polished diamonds rise and fall, sometimes dramatically.

With valuables like gemstones, which vary in quality, investors face problems. To follow the recommended practice in alternative investment markets, investors should purchase the best. The difficulty is that the best is becoming scarce and very expensive in many classes of alternative investments. Diamonds are no exception. One of the consequences is interest in other gemstones, such as sapphires, which are almost as durable as diamonds. A Sri Lankan government agency and the Gemological Institute of America have jointly developed a grading system for sapphires. An established grading certificate is an important supporting document when buying or selling diamonds or sapphires. Other gemstones, for example emeralds, are less appealing, because miners are still extracting them in large quantities.

Diamonds are a compact way of holding wealth, with their long-term trend appreciation slightly above that of inflation. Experts can more easily examine large loose stones, free of jewellery settings, for flaws, colour, 'fire' and brilliance, and comparing stones is easier. An internationally recognised organisation, such as the Gemological Institute of America or the Diamond High Council of Antwerp, should certify and seal the gems.

SOURCES OF FURTHER INFORMATION

See end of Chapter 19.

18

ART AND ANTIQUES

JOHN MYERS AND HELEN BAIRD
Solon Consultants

18.1 INTRODUCTION

18.1.1 A form of alternative investment

Bring and buy works of art and antiques! Why? Ultimately, as any auctioneer, dealer and lover of art and antiques will say, it is not their investment or exchange worth but their civilising and aesthetic values that are important. Also, the promoters of these 'alternative investments' confidently advocate these tangible assets as sound purchases for 'financially secure and intelligent buyers'. The assets they have in mind are, ideally, works of artistic, cultural or historical significance, that is, items that are 'museum-worthy by any standards', which will appeal to collectors. Advocates of these purchases generally recommend clients with money to spare to allocate to 'traded artefacts' up to 10 per cent of their capital (excluding the equity value of their main home). These advisers declare that possessions such as works of art and antiques can protect their clients against inflation and currency fluctuations.

On occasion, larger institutional investors and corporate bodies also buy paintings, sculptures and antiques to diversify their holdings of securities and real estate. The apologists argue that these investors can afford to ride out slumps lasting up to a quarter of a century, if beneficiaries can wait and the eventual return is adequate. Pension funds and similar bodies are generally free from tax on their gains in art and antique markets. On the other hand, these assets cost money to insure, conserve and store. Capital appreciation has to be substantial to make up for these costs and the interest foregone.

Nonetheless, buyers often see art and antique objects as investments, the values of which can rise and fall as critics and curators appraise anew the aesthetic, historic or functional worth of a school, genre or work. Other factors that prompt the eager are TV and press features, active marketing by auction houses and dealers, and ingenious ways to improve the liquidity of alternative investments. Specialist sales, fairs and exhibitions, magazines for collectors, the track record of works sold in each field, and the findings of art historians, sway decisions to buy. However, to allow values to 'mature', prudent advisers counsel buyers to keep items for years, even for decades. Speculative trading in works of art and antiques is, they say, too risky, with too volatile rewards to justify gambling on perfectly timing a purchase and a sale. Even experts make mistakes in picking the undervalued piece that is sure to re-enter fashion next month or next year.

18.1.2 The dividends

Advocates of alternative investment argue for including fine art and antiques in private or funds' portfolios as long-term investments on grounds which are, essentially, those of the economist: while the number of buyers in the markets goes up, the supply stays static or declines. On the one hand, the flow of 'discoveries' or 'retrievals of lost works' is restricted. On the other, valued items disappear through fires, thefts and other calamities; and, perhaps more significantly, museums and galleries steadily drain from the market the works they obtain and keep. Of course 'coffin chasers' (ie house clearers and others who deal with collections left after death) generate a regular supply and 'receiver chasers' have other sources, respectably illustrated by Phillips' sale of Asil Nadir's office furnishings for £4½m. In theory, the problems of Lloyd's Names should also have ensured a steady flow of art on to the market. Christie's offered a way through Coutts & Co for Names to use works of art as collateral, so that they could obtain bank guarantees for 'funds at Lloyd's' purposes.

The proponents of this market believe it appeals to individuals and institutions looking for assets that are in growing demand and diminishing supply, thus promising a long-term upward movement in prices. This argument seems to have gained wide acceptance among the cosmopolitan buyers who attend major sales and create an international demand for authentic items of quality. Evidently these buyers are confident that works of art and rare antiques are safe homes for spare capital, or revenue otherwise subject to tax, though the works bring their owners no income and involve some costs and risks. Many deny an investment motivation. Such motives degrade the purity of endeavour among aesthetes, who seek a cultural dividend, the delights of living with satisfying works that give pleasure. Equally, boards of directors and partnerships buy works of art to improve their standing in society, or to enhance their own and their employees' working environments. The prime movers in these firms will claim that investment is no more than a secondary motive.

Experts concur with the analysis. Nevertheless, they point out that works of art and antiques, unlike shares, have no clearly defined market, no bourse to provide verifiable price indices. One ordinary share in a company will be identical to another of the same category in the same company, but individual works of art and antiques will vary in many respects. These variations in detail, provenance, condition and quality, and the divergent circumstances and terms of sale, mean that like objects will differ in price. As John Andrew remarked two years ago in *The Independent*, 'Add the effects of restoration, repairs, alterations, copies and fakes to the pricing formula and a minefield appears.' He went on to suggest that: 'The biggest trap to snare the unwary in the field of antiques is a lack of knowledge. The prudent individual who carefully researches before buying a consumer durable, or seeks professional advice when investing money, generally throws caution to the wind when buying antiques.'

Andrew gave informative examples of costs and rewards. Four Charles I silver lockets, genuine antiques, bought for £905 in about 1982, sold at auction for a net sum of £1,764 in 1995, an equivalent annual return of 5¼ per cent compound interest, well below the 10 per cent per annum compound increase in the *Financial Times* Share Index over the same span. He also mentioned a silver salver made in Sheffield in 1895, bought in January 1983 for £185, and sold in early 1997 for £350. This equated to a 4½ per cent compound annual return. However, between 1983 and 1997, the stock market rose at a compound annual rate of 12 per cent. Of course, these figures do not allow for the pleasure dividend that an owner of fine antiques gains from possessing them.

18.2 PREVAILING TRENDS

18.2.1 The market's performance

In the 1980s and early 1990s, collectors paid spectacular prices for works of art; millions for a fine Impressionist or an Old Master. Many people outside the art world, and some inside, consider it absurd to pay £20m or more for a painting. Some experts dismiss this view, arguing that the doubters fail to take account of the 'edifice of values that provide a logical basis and grounds for such prices'. Others recall Euripides: 'Man's most valuable trait is a judicious sense of what not to believe.' The evidence is ambivalent.

The Art Sales Index shows that, over 20 years, the average price for works by Cézanne, Degas, Manet, Monet and Renoir sold at auction rose from £37,000 to £271,000, equal to a compound annual investment return of 10 per cent.

Comparable figures come from the Antique Collectors' Club, whose records date back to 1968. The increase in antique furniture recorded between 1997 and 1998 was 4 per cent, but this fell to 2 per cent in the 1998–99 auction season. Yet high quality furniture by a first-class maker with a stately home provenance can still fetch record prices, as shown by the Hackwood Park sale in April 1999. Buyers have become more selective, and prices are weakening for attractive items that just fail to qualify as top rate antique furniture. In other words, bargains are available for discerning buyers.

Generally, the art market seems to have performed less well than the club figures for antiques would indicate. The Art Market Research Index, calculated on a base of 1975 = 1,000, recorded a substantial recovery from the decline of recent years, as the chart in Figure 18.1 reveals. In December 1989, the Art 100 Index stood at 8,609; by June 1996, it had fallen to 3,885. The chart plots the equivalent annual compound rate of interest for £1,000 invested in 1975 and realised in the year shown. The rate fell from 16½ per cent for a work held from 1975 to 1989 to 6¼ per cent for a work held from 1975 to 1996. Some improvement progress was evident in 1997 and a considerable improvement was demonstrated in 1997 and again in December 1998, when the Index rose to 8,403 – a rise of more than 16 per cent.

Figure 18.1 Art Market Research Index: equivalent compound interest per cent per annum

18.2.2 The fundamentals and the opportunities

Markets for art and antiques have developed considerably in recent years, especially over the last two decades. Negative and positive factors have affected growth. At times, investors chose to buy tangible assets because of failures of stock markets and interest-bearing securities to protect their capital against inflation. Immediately after the October 1987 Stock Market crash, auction houses' sales attracted record volumes of works, for which bidders paid record prices. Sotheby's, for example, sold van Gogh's *Irises* for £30m. The same artist's *Portrait of Dr Gachet* brought the highest price at auction for a work of art; the auctioneer took a bid of £50m in May 1990, at the peak of the art boom.

With a spread of higher disposable incomes and an increase in leisure expenditure, a demand has emerged for assets which have a worth and an interest beyond their monetary cost. Social changes have also made an impact: for example, dealers and auctioneers report that young, wealthy buyers have been entering the market for works of fine art, such as paintings, prints, ceramics, engravings and sculptures.

As noted above, popular TV programmes, features in newspapers, magazines and books have stimulated wide interest in the hunt for works with hidden value. Admittedly, fewer antique shops can afford today's retail rents and overheads, but antique centres and antique fairs have burgeoned, placing many sellers in one location.

At times, antique markets attract large crowds, as anyone visiting London's Portobello Road on Saturday morning can testify. Dealers come from all parts of the country, and start trading between themselves almost at the crack of dawn. Other London street markets are Camden Passage (on Wednesdays) and Bermondsey (on Fridays). Paris has its flea markets and, in America, antique fairs in Atlanta and other centres of wealth are popular. The enthusiasts in Georgia start at about 5 am and stand in line for the early risers' pick of antiques and collectables.

Choice pieces can pass through several hands on their route up-market via dealers outside the main centres and street markets to a major auction or a listed antique shop. The more reliable dealers belong to the London and Provincial Antiques Dealers' Association or the British Antiques Dealers' Association. Their members usually offer a receipt with a full description; if it proves incorrect, the buyer has a basis on which to claim a refund.

Analysts of alternative investments have studied the ways the markets work. One place to chase bargains is the car boot sale, where the discerning might find 1960s designer objects. Another start for the sifting process might be a house clearance. The trash can go to the local tip, and ordinary bric-à-brac to a second-hand fair. The inlaid metal match-box case that is left seems unusual, and might really be a jewelled gold piece from the Fabergé workshop, worth thousands to a connoisseur at the top of the pyramid, who can trace its history from the St Petersburg archive. Or, of course, it might be a mass-produced design, or sometimes a forged or stolen piece.

Also gaining in popularity are international antique fairs. Some are well known and fashionable; for example, the eight-day March art and antiques fair at Maastricht is now in its 12th year. In 1997, when the 10th anniversary fair attracted 50,000 visitors, so many planes arrived that they caused an aerial traffic jam; by 1999, the number of arrivals had gone up to 70,000. Buying and selling was reportedly active. However, few sales are concluded at the fair, to avoid the complexities of Dutch VAT regulations. Moreover, fewer Asian buyers attended; they went instead to the four-year-old Asian Fair in New York, also run in March. Other events include exhibitions and fairs at the Royal Academy in London, Chelsea Town Hall and Olympia, and the British Antique Dealers' Association fair at the Duke of York's headquarters in King's Road, Chelsea.

18.2.3 Market weaknesses and strengths

More people are entering the art and antiques market. To what extent can they rely on the assets they buy proving a worthwhile investment, given the repugnance of monetary motives to the aesthetes? In truth, auctioneers and dealers who profess horror at the idea of buying a painting as an investment were, on occasion, the same auctioneers and dealers who persuaded buyers to invest large sums of money in the late 1980s, sometimes in second- and third-rate works, only to see them plunge in price. Values for first-class objects stayed reasonably solid, and bidders are paying high prices for exceptional works. Handsome short-term profits are now in evidence, and recent sales have demonstrated that high quality works of art with a sound provenance can still perform well as long-term investments.

Observers in recent years have noted a flight to calibre and bijou quality, and away from large-scale but second-rate works by famous names. As a result, investing in art is no longer limited to the monied rich with conservative tastes. Impressionist and Modern paintings by leading artists can still command a premium, but auctioneers and dealers are also reporting strong sales to buyers with eclectic tastes; they have been fuelling reviving prices in the contemporary art market. Auctions of post-war and contemporary art have a growing appeal to collectors, and many lots have fetched far more than their pre-sale estimates. Indian and South East Asian buyers have been evident. Observers have noted a shift away from Chinese artefacts. One factor has been the decline of Hong Kong as a source; far less Chinese material is coming onto the official or unofficial export markets. Another is the prevalence of fakes from China, some of which are difficult to uncover even with scientific tests.

Reliable provenance, quality and freshness to the market remain crucial factors in the sale of art and antiques. It is worth noting that the areas which have withstood the slump over recent times have been those which appeal to the connoisseur rather than the speculative trader. An increase in private buyers was noticeable at auctions in London and New York, when falling prices attracted knowledgeable collectors. Of late, they have included few Japanese bidders.

One reason for their absence is that hundreds of high-priced paintings are reportedly languishing in Tokyo, Osaka and Kyoto bank vaults as their owners wait for markets to reach new peaks. These banks have been under official pressure to dispose of the works of art they bought in good times, or later acquired as collateral for borrowers whose businesses subsequently failed. Estimates of the value of the art vary between £5bn and £20bn, which include paintings by Chagall, Picasso, Renoir, Andrew Wyeth and Japanese artists. However, some commentators believe that the collections include fakes and stolen works. Reportedly, the Art Loss Register recently approached a Japanese bank enquiring about works by Picasso and Sisley, which had been stolen or looted.

Trade sources suggest that some works have been secretly sold to dealers at a loss. Another factor is that the Japanese art market has been preoccupied in recent years with a series of scandals. Reports of debts, bribes, tax evasion, fraud and jail sentences do little to build confidence.

18.2.4 Protecting alternative investors

Questions can arise about the true value of a work of art when buyers seem to be paying telephone number sums at auction. The prices paid reflect partly the increasing number of exceptionally wealthy individuals who can afford to spend a considerable amount to purchase a work of art. *Forbes* estimates that the collective wealth of the top 200 'working rich' is almost $1 trillion, more than double the figure in 1989. The published analysis suggests that perhaps a few hundred people might today pay more than £10m for a work of art. For them, the main attractions can include the market's performance and the opportunities to 'collateralise' art, a development that, until a few years ago, seemed to have a bright future.

Experience of the last slump in prices is still instructive. After several years of rapid escalation, demand for works sold at auction declined amid controversy over Sotheby's leveraged sale of *Irises* to the Australian entrepreneur, Alan Bond. The arrangement led to accusations that auction houses were artificially inflating prices. The J Paul Getty Museum later bought the painting for an undisclosed sum, after Bond failed to pay off his £16m loan from Sotheby's. The rate of interest on such loans was as much as 4 per cent above prime.

The once-popular loan system inflated prices, whether the borrower secured the painting or not: like a roulette player with chips on house credit, he found it tempting to raise the stakes. Pre-financing by the auction house created a synthetic floor, while a dealer who stated a price set a ceiling. If the borrower then defaulted, the lender recovered the painting, wrote off the unpaid part of the loan against tax, and chose a better time to offer the work for resale at its new inflated price.

Apart from lending money to foster buying, some auction houses gave guarantees to sellers. The practice added to critics' concerns about the ethics of the trade. If a collector has a work of art that an auctioneer wants to sell, the latter can issue a 'guarantee' that the collector will obtain, say, £3m from the sale. If the work does not make £3m, the collector still receives the payment, but the work remains with the auction house for later sale. Guarantees are a strong inducement to sellers, but clearly risky for the auction house.

Leading dealers dislike the system of guarantees and loans. They argue that it creates a conflict of interest. One dealer is on record with the comment: 'If the auction house has a financial stake with both seller and buyer, its status as an agent is compromised. Lending to the buyer is like margin trading on the stock market. It creates inflation. It causes instability.' The advocates defend the policy as 'right, proper and indeed inevitable'. They claim that guarantees are given 'very sparingly'.

Persistent criticism can lead to government controls and levies, which test the industry's stability. These factors and growth in alternative investments have encouraged auction houses to examine their own practices and develop the range of services they offer, sometimes leading to controversy. Conflicts of interest and claims of sharp practice have focused the attention of regulators, as has the incidence of outright fraud and theft. Unethical behaviour has come under the scrutiny of the media and authorities in several centres of the art trade. For example, reports have focused on 'puffing the bid' – fictitious bidders inflating the price by displaying false interest.

Scandals have also emerged from the trade in art and antiques, which has traditionally thrived in the 'informal economy'. In Spain and Italy, for instance, operators in a lively black economy have poured money into art. For these buyers, art and antiques represent a store of value, a haven for assets and a form of currency. Their interest supports the market internationally, especially in fields which appeal to Latin tastes. However, many in the market, as well as in government, have become increasingly concerned about the growing internationalisation of art theft and fraud, and not only in the EU. The Japanese police have strengthened supervision of art dealers. They suspected that artworks were being used in tax evasion and as 'stage properties' in large-scale economic crimes.

Similarly, in the early 1990s, a Swiss government report expressed concern at the country's role as a transit centre for objects of questionable origin – perhaps not a novel feature of the Swiss financial scene – and for 'money laundering operations'.

A few years ago, in the US, there was a contest between the auctioneers and consumer affairs bodies, which is still worth keeping in mind. Teams of officials pored over leading auctioneers' records, identifying exotic-sounding practices like 'bidding off the chandelier' (the puffing by fictitious bidders to drive up the price) and the more normal 'buying in' (leaving a work unsold because it does not reach the seller's undisclosed reserve price). Stiffer controls have been applied in the US, including some governing loans. The New York State legislature also took a close interest in the art market. It shared with the city's Consumer Affairs Department concerns about chandelier bidding, the undisclosed reserve and auction houses' lending practices. The consumer affairs code now requires that 'if an auctioneer makes loans or advances money to consignors or prospective purchasers, this fact must be conspicuously disclosed in the auctioneer's catalogue'.

According to a US official, in the past these were 'gross irregularities' in some art auction houses. At the time, chandelier bidding amounted to 'an industry practice, both above and below the reserve'. Critics have also been concerned about the practices of not announcing buy-ins and of keeping reserves secret. The auction houses contended that, if bidders knew the reserve, it would chill the market. Art dealers, lobbying the authorities, maintained that the reserve should be disclosed and that bidding should start at it.

The English poet, Shelley, in his *Adonais*, wrote 'Month follow month with woe, and year wake year to sorrow'. When he penned these lines in 1821, Shelley might almost have had in mind London auction houses a century and three quarters later. In 1997, they suffered a surge of hostile media reports accusing them of dealing in looted works of art, of chandelier bidding, and smuggling. Auctioneers have also been under fire for accepting items that are 'not quite genuine'.

Two years ago, the BBC's *Watchdog* programme criticised Bonhams for an alleged failure to enquire properly into the background of two lots in its 'Rock and Pop' sale. Channel 4's *Dispatches* programme challenged Sotheby's alleged involvement in a smuggling case. Clearly, auctioneers have been wise to introduce rules, which require them to handle only objects that have secure export papers and provable provenances (ie reliable records that show the history and previous ownership of a piece).

The media *causes célébres* have reinforced press criticisms that auction houses sell art on less than fair conditions. Godfrey Barker put the point forcefully two years ago in an article in the *Daily Telegraph*: auction houses, he claims, typically 'say to all 50,000 buyers who pass each year through their gilded doors, "All goods are sold with all faults and imperfections and errors of description. Buyers should satisfy themselves prior to the sale as to the condition of each lot and should exercise and rely on their own judgement as to whether the lot accords with its description".' He argued that the conditions of sale are unfair, and compare poorly with measures to protect buyers of consumer goods. Barker suggests that auction houses try to keep their conditions of sale under wraps, and that, when a disaffected bidder has a complaint, he or she may settle out of court. His article claims that '100 to 150 cases a year in London are muffled in this way'. In contrast, art dealers comply with a code which generally leads to refund without question.

British antique dealers have demanded reform in the way auctioneers sell works of art and antiques. They believe that a code of conduct should include clauses on:

- legal responsibility for the authenticity of goods sold;
- a ban on chandelier bids;
- auctioneers declaring an interest when they have given guarantees;
- preventing auctioneers charging commissions to both buyers and sellers;
- withholding from auction staff details of bids received in advance ('commission bids').

For their part, the auction houses have sought to demystify the auction process to reassure the new breed of collectors and investors. They have employed capable people to explain the significance of the terminology and the practices, and the business of reserves. Representative bodies try to set standards and to control their members' practices with professional codes. Yet dealing in art from a gallery or an auction house is perhaps not a profession; instead, it is like a trade or a financial service. Its critics argue for regulation, for setting up an independent regulator, an art industry equivalent to the Financial Services Authority. The auction houses and dealers have doubts about these ideas; some outsiders think they have merit.

18.2.5 Continued internationalisation

Despite these uncertainties, buyers around the world have been persuaded by plausible arguments that alternative investments might protect them against calamity. As a result, many of the markets for art and antiques have become more international; since the 1970s, North American, Continental European, Middle and Far Eastern investors have begun to frequent sales rooms in great numbers.

A few years ago, rich art buyers revived Russia's market. Prime among them, in Moscow and St Petersburg, were banks, which had made immense profits in 1992 and 1993 from trading currencies. The most notable were Inkombank, Stolichay, Alpha-Bank, Voznozdenie, Menatep and Moscovia. Seven years ago none of them owned significant paintings; today they hold Old Masters and contemporary art. Self-promotion is one reason why the banks bought. Another was their anxiety to store value in what appears, for now, to be a stable international currency – art. What mattered most were special tax provisions that favoured investors in 'outstanding art collections' (a heritage measure to keep great art in Russia).

International developments have had a further effect. In recent years, London's traditional dominance as the centre for art and antiques sales has been challenged, in particular by New York, Geneva, Frankfurt and Paris, which nowadays are attracting important specialised sales. London still accounts for a significant proportion of art sales in the EU, but regulatory changes are putting at risk London's strength in the art world.

In some alternative investment markets, furniture being one example, the vigour of American demand has meant that market prices have been set mainly in New York. Generally, the mobility of alternative investments, combined with the wider geographical spread of dealers and auctions, should mean that prices are less vulnerable to the effects of inflation and volatile exchange rates.

18.3 NATIONAL HERITAGE ISSUES

18.3.1 Export controls

The establishment of the EU has caused concern over the possible repatriation of artworks to their countries of origin. However, this concern is not a recent phenomenon, and governments have tried in various ways to prevent objects of long-standing cultural value and national heritage works, whatever their origin, from leaving the country permanently.

How does the export licence system work in practice? Owners of heritage works of art and antiques have to allow for the imbroglio of export review when planning a sale in world markets. Consider typical cases. With the same objective in mind, the Export Review Committee delayed the sale of a late Rembrandt painting, *Portrait of an elderly man*, to a Dutch buyer. To keep the work in the UK will mean British galleries and institutions raising £9.3m in just three months. A month earlier, in February 1999, the new Tate Gallery of Modern Art on Bankside, London, and the Scottish Gallery of Modern Art in Edinburgh, with the help of the National Art Collections Fund, had raised £1.2m to buy Joan Miró's *Head of a Catalan peasant*. In May 1999, Arts Minister Alan Howarth placed a temporary bar on the export of a terracotta sculpture of *The executioner of St John the Baptist* (1478) by Andrea del Verrocchio, in line with a recommendation by the Reviewing Committee on the Export of Works of Art. They drew attention to the sculpture's significance for the study of Verrocchio's working practices, and as an example of outstanding aesthetic importance. The deferral is to enable British museums and galleries to raise more than £1.6m.

This export licensing system is designed to strike a balance between the various interests concerned in any application for an export licence – for instance, the protection of the national heritage; the rights of the owner selling the goods; the exporter or overseas purchaser; and the position and reputation of the UK as an international art market. However, the licensing system's main purpose is to keep in the UK cultural goods considered to be of outstanding national importance.

Under the extant system, the Waverley rules, the reviewing committee advising the Culture Secretary can recommend a moratorium on the granting of an export licence for up to six months. As in the case of the Verrocchio sculpture, the delay allows British institutions the opportunity to purchase. The success of this system depends, however, on these bodies having, or raising, adequate funds to meet the high prices of works deemed of national interest. In 1991 the Secretary of State resorted to placing long-term export bans on several items, limiting their potential market value.

The criteria defined in the 'Waverley Report on the Export of Works of Art' (1952) depend on the answers to three questions. Is the object so closely connected with British history and national life that its loss would be a misfortune? Is it of exceptional aesthetic importance? Is it of exceptional significance for the study of some particular branch of art, learning or history? The Waverley Committee recommended a minimum age limit of 100 years in 1952. Committee members did not want to discourage 'the vigorous two-way traffic that we should like to see, bringing important works into the country to fill the many notable gaps in our collections'.

Subsequently, the Government adopted a lower age limit, of 50 years. Under the present export licensing controls, works produced more than 50 years ago and valued at or above defined monetary limits fall within the control. Exceptions are an artist or a producer's own works that he or she plans to export. The artist or producer's spouse, widow or widower has similar rights. Advocates of the 50-year rule believe that it properly allows the authorities to decide whether a work meets the Waverley criteria, whether or not its artist or producer still lives.

The export control can apply to all works of cultural significance, including archives, manuscripts, sculpture, machinery and so on. In practice, the effect of the export control can differ according to the nature of the object. Many national treasures are valued out of the reach of all but the wealthiest investor, but government heritage policy is likely to affect the art and antiques market as a whole, and EU policies, reviewed below, even more so.

18.3.2 Export controls – revisions

Under the arrangements announced in the Spring 1998 Budget, no acceptances in lieu require expenditure by the Department. Instead, the Revenue accepts items in lieu of taxes without seeking reimbursement from the Secretary of State. In practice, the Revenue's Capital Taxes Office (CTO) refers offers of apparently 'pre-eminent' or 'historically associated' objects to the Museums & Galleries Commission, which takes opinions from independent experts. The Commission then advises the Secretary of State whether an item is suitable for acceptance in lieu of taxes. The advice covers the pre-eminence, condition and value of the item, and any conditions that apply to the offer. In addition, the Commission makes recommendations on the lodging of the item, both temporary and permanent.

A few years ago, the then Department of National Heritage consulted the museums and art trade worlds on several important issues:

* Estimates of a fair market price for export-deferred works of art. In particular, the Department has sought opinions on a proposal to exclude a dealer's commission from the fair market price, where the commission is on a sale to a connected third party.
* Whether any extra conditions attach to a private offer from a UK buyer to purchase an object under export deferral.
* Whether the National Heritage Secretary should encourage an owner to prefer a public offer to a simultaneous offer from a private source.
* The application of the Waverley rules to works by living artists.

Controversy over the fair market price arose when the Reviewing Committee considered Jean-François de Troy's painting *La lecture de Molière*. The members expressed reservations about the inclusion in the fair market price of the dealer's commission charged by the applicant to its related US company. The Committee also urged the Secretary of State for National Heritage only to take account of private offers, if the UK buyer has given satisfactory undertakings. These should include assurances on public access, proper maintenance, a minimum retention period and, for a collection or set of objects, the integrity of the collection. Consultation led to changes in the private offers policy, which imposes strict conditions on a private offer to purchase an object under export deferral.

In another case, the Reviewing Committee considered an application to export *The Painter's Room* by Lucian Freud (1943). This was the first occasion on which a work by a living artist had come before the Committee. Sotheby's had applied for a licence to export the painting to a purchaser in the US. The value shown on the export licence application was £515,812.50.

The Department of Culture, Media and Sport's Expert Adviser came from the Tate Gallery. He stated why he felt that the work should stay in Britain, asserting that *The Painter's Room* was a vital *oeuvre* from Freud's first phase, and the largest picture that he had painted to that date. The painting 'declared arrestingly the preoccupation with concentrated realisation of motifs from observation that would be a central feature of his art over the succeeding half century. Memorable in its clarity and strangeness, it was Freud's first key work.'

Against that, Sotheby's argued that the painting stood as an early work within the scope of Freud's output, and was stylistically atypical. 'The depiction of such an estranged world and the absence of human beings, were not characteristic. Later works do not bear any resemblance, and Freud's style quickly evolved into a more realistic and dramatic one.' The painting did not identify with the style upon which Freud built his reputation. It stood more as curiosity than as an established and characteristic work.

For tactical reasons, the Reviewing Committee submitted no recommendation. In due course, the Secretary of State for National Heritage decided to defer a decision for two months, hoping to see an offer at the recommended price of £515,812.50, or higher. The Tate Gallery announced a serious intention to raise funds for the purchase, extending the deferred period to four months. Later, the owner refused separate offers to purchase from the Tate and the Chatsworth House Trust, at the stated price. The National Heritage Secretary therefore refused the export licence.

This case prompted the Reviewing Committee to express reservations about deferring a decision on a licence for any living artist's work, whatever its merit. The members felt that Freud's painting raised an important point of principle: whether the export of works by living artists should stay under control. However, they noted that removing such works from UK export control would not prevent action under EU regulations that govern trade in cultural goods.

The Reviewing Committee felt that the system could act to a living artist's detriment. Suppose a painter or a sculptor is important enough for heritage conservationists to oppose its export. Probably the artist already enjoys an international reputation, and the value of the artist's work might rise if buyers learn that his or her work is 'of national importance'. A licence deferral could allow national galleries to fill gaps where public collections do not already cover the early part of an artist's *oeuvre*.

In practice, the market for the artist's work is unlikely to fall merely because the Secretary of State might not issue an export licence. It also seems unlikely that many works will come before the Reviewing Committee. The Freud painting was the first by a living artist to come before it in 42 years. If more do come forward, it is doubtful if matching offers would be forthcoming for all living artists' works subject to licence deferral.

On the other hand, the Waverley Committee's original arguments in favour of the higher limit support the exclusion of works by living artists from the regime. Any restriction on the export of work by living artists could limit the spread of their international reputation. Nor would the export controls apply to artists who export their own work. Many of these artists are under contract to sell their output through dealers, who would be subject to export licence controls. Anomalies could then arise. A dealer, or an overseas buyer, could evade the controls by selling the work back to the artist. He or she could export it legally under his or her own name and then resell it to the new owner, bringing the control into disrepute.

Export controls apply not only to the work of artists but to the archives of authors, musicians and other public figures. They might prefer to sell their papers through an agent. The latter would be subject to controls and might reduce the price offered because the Department might withhold a licence for the early part of the archive. Agents might also see advantages in breaking up a collection of papers. The Government now seems likely to update the Waverley Committee rules, in the light of such problems.

Despite these constraints, there is still a constant flow abroad of works of art. According to the latest Reviewing Committee report, only about 50 per cent of items stay in this country after the committee has recommended that an export licence be deferred. A key factor is a paucity of public resources to help fund purchases.

The Heritage Lottery Fund's grants for items of over £100,000 in value are awarded at up to 75 per cent, leaving a museum to raise at least 25 per cent of the cost. That can be quite substantial. For example, on a £5m painting, a price which is not unusual, the museum would have to raise £1.25m from its own resources, which may be difficult. In the case of the National Art Collections Funds (NACF), its financial resources, which come from its members and by legacies, are limited. Nevertheless, the NACF contributed nearly £263,000 – half the price – to the purchase of Hugh Douglas Hamilton's 18th century pastel of Canova in his studio. It met all the Waverley criteria and is now in the Victoria and Albert Museum, having originally been destined for the Getty Museum in

California. The National Heritage Memorial Fund, which is a fund of last resort, has been cut from £12m in 1993–94 to only £2m in 1997–98. The Government now intends to increase that by £1m per year for the next three years. Even so, it will still be only half what it was five years ago.

These arrangements can underpin the market for high quality works. However, non-charging museums, when making an offer for a deferred item, must include 17.5 per cent to cover VAT. That puts them at a disadvantage against overseas buyers. Those rules are governed by EU directives.

The inheritance tax concession for conditionally exempt items, allowing the owner of a small house to give public access by prior appointment, has been changed. Now, the Government intends to organise exhibitions across Britain, so that 20,000 works of art kept in private houses, and whose owners benefit from tax relief, can be seen by the public. The new scheme effectively closes the loophole by which some private owners failed to honour promises to put their collections on show in return for exemption from tax. Owners can defer inheritance tax if they promise to let the public view their works. About 56,000 works of art are now granted exemption from inheritance tax under these conditions. Of these, some 20,900 are in private homes, where many owners are reluctant to invite the public. Under the new arrangements, the Government will meet the insurance costs of protecting the art against theft or fire.

18.3.3 Art and the EU

The EU has affected the movement of works of art both out of the EU and between the member states. Since January 1993, imports and exports have been subject to spot checks only at member states' frontiers, making illegal trade much harder to detect. Some countries, notably Spain, Greece and Italy, fear the loss of many important works. The UK Government's prime concern is that trade restrictions will harm the country's art trade, while auction houses anticipate endless bureaucratic wrangles.

An EU export licence is now necessary to export a cultural object out of the Union, if its value exceeds a stated threshold. These thresholds are defined by age and value, much as they have been under UK export rules. In some cases, the thresholds are comparable with those set for a UK licence; in others the threshold is set at a higher level, as the chart below shows. For comprehensive details contact the Department of Culture, Media and Sport, tel: (020) 7211 6164.

Table 18.1

Category by type and age	Threshold (£)
Elements forming an integral part of artistic, historical or religious monuments which have been dismembered and which are:	
more than 50 years old, but less than 100 years old	no licence required
more than 100 years old	zero
Manuscripts more than 50 years old, including maps and musical scores	zero
Architectural, scientific and engineering drawings produced by hand, more than 50 years old	11,900
Arms and armour, more than 50 years old	39,600
Drawings by hand on any medium and in any material, more than 50 years old	11,900
Portraits or likenesses which are more than 50 years old, of British historic persons	119,000
Paintings in oil, tempera or other media, which are more than 50 years old (excluding portraits), of	
British historic persons	119,000
Books which are:	
more than 50 years old, but less than 100 years old	no EU licence required
more than 100 years old	39,600
Collections and specimens from zoological. botanical, mineralogical or anatomical collections	39,600

Auction houses also face what has been described as 'an unprecedented threat' from three new areas of legislation:

- *Droit de suite* – a levy on the resale of contemporary art. The EU wants to apply it to Britain, but dealers say it would devastate the international market in 20th-century painting in London, worth about £300m a year.
- *Unidroit* – a treaty which returns 'stolen' goods. The *unidroit* agreement, which has been signed by a number of governments, covers stolen or illegally exported cultural objects. The British Government has been pressed to sign the treaty, which would allow original owners to reclaim artefacts, on proof of origin.
- The imposition of value added tax on art imports into the EU after 1999 – a pressing issue. Until 1994, there was no import VAT in the UK and dealers in London could persuade sellers from across the world to send their works of art there.

Droits de suite

Payment of artists' royalties, known as *droits de suite*, varies across Europe. Eleven EU Member States already pay *droit de suite* royalties (at rates of between 3 and 5 per cent of the selling price) to artists or their families up to 70 years after the artist's death. The European Commission wants to introduce a scale of royalties, with beneficiaries securing 4 per cent of the first €50,000 (£32,000), falling to 1 per cent for works selling for €200,000 (£130,000) or more. Only the UK, Ireland, Luxembourg and Holland have yet to bring in the *droit de suite* system.

These *droits de suite* sums are payable by the seller, direct to the artist or his or her estate, provided the sale is over a threshold figure and the work is still in copyright (ie produced by a living artist, or one who has died within 70 years). The European Commission is seeking to extend this system. Supporters argue that the levy assists artists; opponents, including the UK Government, argue that it is a disincentive to trade. London dealers fear that its introduction would shift trade to the US and Switzerland, 'devastating a thriving international market in twentieth century painting, worth about £300 million a year'. A survey by the Department of Trade and Industry has estimated that *droit de suite* alone could rob the UK of an annual £68m in art sales and 5,000 jobs in the art trade.

In March 1996, the European Commission proposed harmonising national systems that cover 'resale rights' for artists. The purpose is to allow artists to share profits when dealers trade at high prices in a work by an artist who had originally sold it at a far lower price. The proposal applies to pictures, collages, paintings, drawings, engravings, prints, lithographs, sculptures, ceramics and photographic works. In 1997, the European Parliament and Council drafted a new directive on the resale rights that will benefit originators of works of art.

Anthony Browne, chairman of the British Art Market Federation, described the imposition of *droit de suite* as the biggest threat to the UK art market today. It would have applied to about 16 per cent of UK sales last year had the rule been in place. The Federation concluded in a recent report that sellers would opt for New York and other non-EU centres if the UK implements *droit de suite*. However, Mr Browne states that in practice many artists do not bother trying to collect a percentage each time a work is sold because it is an expensive process. Moreover, there is only significant trade in an artist's work once he or she becomes established. In France, Picasso and Matisse gain the most because their estates are administered by lawyers, capable of dealing with the bureaucracy involved.

In February 1999, European ministers put off a vote on an art directive which would give artists royalties every time their work goes under the hammer at auction. The UK contends that the move could adversely affect the London market, and give an unfair edge to competitors outside the EU. The annual turnover of this 20th century art in the London market is close to £400m. The British Art Market Federation estimates that 75 per cent of this business comes from clients who bring works for auction from outside Europe. These clients might easily move to Switzerland or the US.

Unidroit

A recently introduced EC Directive on the return of 'cultural objects' has been a focus of controversy in some member states. This Directive entails the forming of central authorities or 'art tribunals' in each country. They would have the power to demand the return of an item illegally exported, with compensation if the buyer had exercised due care in the purchase.

This right of return expires after 75 years for public collections and 30 years for private collections. Because the legislation is not retroactive, the British Museum will not be compelled to relinquish the Elgin Marbles.

However, other relevant changes are in train. Museums, galleries and private collectors are likely to face scrutiny now that Swiss banks have agreed to pay Holocaust survivors. In December 1998, delegates from 45 nations and the world's leading art directors agreed a set of principles for seeking out looted art and returning it to the heirs of the original owners. The search for Holocaust-era art could affect every great museum collection in the world. A spokesperson for New York's Museum of Modern Art estimates that: 'approximately 110,000 pieces of art worth $10bn to $30bn are still missing. It is my belief, because of these large numbers, that every institution, art museum and private collection has some of these missing works.'

In this context, J&H March & McLennan, London insurance brokers, have developed a policy to protect museums from losses arising from disputes over who rightfully owns a work of art. The broker is providing cover in conjunction with the Hiscox syndicate from Lloyd's of London. The policy covers costs of defending legal actions over 'defective title', and losses that arise to a maximum of $50m (£20m) if a judgment goes against the museum, so that it has to return the artwork. The policy is limited to permanent collections, including items on loan and away on international exhibition. It does not extend to work of dubious provenance.

VAT

In December 1993, the member states reached agreement on the harmonisation of VAT payable on sale of works of art imported into the EU. The Seventh VAT Directive on works of art took effect on 1 January 1995. Its effect is to tax works of art imported into and sold within the UK, which has the largest art and antiques market within the EU.

Britain's negotiators had sought to maintain the country's status as an international centre. The basis for taxing works of art, which had applied in the UK (ie VAT on the auctioneers' commission and premium, but not on the whole price) now applies throughout the EU.

For items imported from non-EU countries into the UK, the rate of VAT was 2½ per cent from 1 January 1995. This special rate applied until 30 June 1999. Britain has now come into line with the rest of the EU and charges a rate of not less than 5 per cent, in spite of criticisms in a 1998 review for the EU on the increase. London market auctioneers and dealers feel that the effects will be harmful. Confirmation of their fears came in a sale of institutional assets. The British Rail Pension Fund decided not to sell in London a pair of Canalettos and 22 other paintings. Sotheby's auctioned them in New York in January 1997. The fund had begun investing in art in the 1970s, and spent £40m on about 2,400 pieces. It has now disposed of more than 2,200 for £150m, showing a positive annual return of 5½ per cent above the retail price index. Selling the Old Masters in New York represented a departure; earlier sales by the fund had mainly been at Sotheby's, London. As a result of the decision, BR's pensioners are more than £6m richer, while London auction houses and dealers are worrying more about VAT.

The British Art Market Federation contends that artwork imports from outside the EU have fallen by 40 per cent since the imposition by the EU of 2½ per cent VAT. If the Government has to implement all the measures in full, auctioneers contend that Britain will lose a lucrative source of revenue and employment. The industry's annual turnover is £2.2bn, and it employs 40,000 people. A limited exodus from Bond Street in Central London has already begun. Pace Wildenstein, a large firm of art dealers, has sold its Bond Street premises. Phillips opened premises in both New York and Geneva in 1996 'so that we are covered whatever the outcome'. However, business now seems to be improving, and dealers are returning to the thoroughfare. See also **18.7.5** and **18.10.1**.

Art Sales Index figures on auction sales, quoted in a report by MTI to the European Commission indicate the scale of art sales by auction houses in Europe and North America. MTI recent estimates for the Commission put the total level of sales of art and antiques between €21.2bn and €24.8bn (£14bn–£16bn). The large range of the estimated total sales arises because not much reliable data are available on dealer sales. Auction houses generate about a quarter of the total turnover. However, MTI calculates that a quarter of all art market sales are 'inter-trade', ie between auctioneers and dealers and between dealers and other dealers. This would mean that the net global expenditure on art and antiques would lie between €16bn and €18.5bn. Almost half the sales are in the US, and a further 28.5 per cent in the UK.

Table 18.2

Auction room	Lots sold	Turnover €m	Average value € per lot
Christie's, New York	4,391	435	99,157
Sotheby's, New York	4,471	350	78,193
Sotheby's, London	7,615	238	31,202
Christie's, London	4,842	207	42,710
Christie's East, New York	1,952	104	53,023
Christie's Amsterdam	2,738	24	8,563
Francis Briest, Paris	971	18	18,641
Christie's, South Kensington	5,779	17	2,994
Phillips, London	2,229	16	7,358
Tajan, Paris	1,667	15	9,058
Piasa, Paris	838	13	15,155
Finarte, Milan	1,241	11	9,106
Viaa Grisebach, Berlin	627	11	18,182
Lempertz, Cologne	1,227	11	8,639
Dorotheum, Vienna	2,364	10	4,315

Source: *Report on the introduction of the 7th directive on competitiveness of the Community art market compared with third countries' art markets*, MTI study for DG-XX of the European Commission 1999.

London dealers estimate that 40 per cent or more of artworks sold (by value) come from Switzerland, America, Japan and outside the EU. Thus, it will make sense for many to buy and sell through New York. New York accounts for 40 per cent of world art sales, and is growing, while London accounts for 30 per cent and is falling.

The art trade elsewhere in the EU, apart from Paris, is mainly domestic, so that London dealers see an envy of London's status as a world centre since the 18th century. Published estimates show that the London market turns over around £2.1bn a year, compared to £3.5–£4bn for the EU as a whole, Britain included. Britain's art market accounts for between 60 and 70 per cent of the entire European art market. The British themselves may not be large-scale buyers of art, but the London market is like the City is to international money markets: an entrepôt.

Take a Japanese collector who intends to sell a modern painting. If he chooses to make the sale in New York, and attracts a bid of $4m, the buyer will pay the auctioneer 15 per cent on the first $50,000 and 10 per cent on the rest ($402,500) on top of the hammer price. The seller pays 2 per cent, plus expenses – probably a figure in excess of $100,000. The same transaction in London would attract the same costs, but the buyer would have to pay an additional 5 per cent import tax on $4,502,000

($225,100). The seller meanwhile would have to pay an additional 2 per cent *droit de suite*.

Thus, to carry out the transaction in London would cost over 60 per cent more than it would in New York. This position was to apply in 1999, when the existing preferential treatment of London was meant to cease; however, a decision from the European Commission is still awaited. Already, the 2½ per cent import tax has caused measurable damage to the London trade. The UK's imports of art and antiques are already on the decline; the trade fell by 28 per cent in 1996 to £665m.

See also **18.7.5** and **18.10.1**.

18.4 HIGHLIGHTS OF THE PREVIOUS YEAR

In 1998, the art market continued to thrive. In December 1998, Sotheby's auctioned items from the Hiscox Insurance Group's collection. Twenty-eight Modern and contemporary British works of art sold for more than £2m. The company recorded useful gains in the sale. For example, in 1987 it paid £71,500 for David Bomberg's *San Miguel, Toledo*; in the Sotheby's sale it went for £161,000 (equivalent to an 8 per cent a year compound rate of growth). In 1984, Hiscox bought a still life by Roderic O'Conor for £55,000; 14 years later, it went for £276,500 – a compound annual growth rate in value of 12 per cent.

A private dealer, vor Braka, advised Hiscox on its collection. He was an active bidder at the Sotheby's sale, paying £914,500 for Lucian Freud's small *Portrait of Frank Auerbach*, which represented a 26 per cent annual compound rate of growth over 13 years.

In a sale in Autumn 1998, the US collector and chairman of Condé Nast (Si Newhouse Jr) sold a Mondrian abstract painting, covered in strips of coloured sticky tape, for $40m (£25m). The buyer, the Dutch National Art Foundation, funded by the Dutch National Bank, has donated the work to the Gemeentemuseum in The Hague. The transaction was highly controversial. Dr Bob van der Boogert of the Rembrandt House Museum in Amsterdam reportedly commented: 'This was a set-up organised in the back rooms by high officials. It is outrageous. It does not reflect the wishes of the Dutch people. The majority actually hate Mondrian. It is also an unfinished painting. On the free market, it would never have made such a price. We could have acquired at least two good Rembrandts for that money.' Letters of protest have flooded Dutch newspapers.

The amounts at stake at the top of the art market are again rising. The year 1998 saw a run of exceptionally high prices for works of art. In the autumn, Christie's sold van Gogh's *Portrait de d'Artiste Sans Barbe* (1889) for $71.5m (£45m), the third highest price for a work sold at auction. A Paul Cézanne painting, *Still life with curtain, pitcher and bowl of fruit*, attracted a final bid of $60.5m (£37.8m) at a Sotheby's New York sale in May 1999. Amadeo Modigliani's portrait of his mistress, Jeanne Hebuterne, painted in 1919, sold for $15.1m (£9m) at a Sotheby's New York auction in November 1998.

Demand has also been increasing for works by LS Lowry, partly because of the scheduled opening in 2000 of the Lowry Centre in Salford, and the interest of wealthy collectors. Exceptional works by Lowry have gone up in value from £50,000 to £500,000 in just a few years. The beneficiaries of the upward trend in values include the Princess Helena College, near Hitchin in Hertfordshire. The school put its Lowry work, *May Day*, up for auction in 1998, and secured a six-figure sum for a painting the school had thought worth only a tenth of the sales price.

18.4.1 Museum financing

The balance is shifting in top range art and antique markets towards museums and galleries. They are mounting massive exhibitions and launching 'museum stores' that profit from art and antique merchandise. Art museums have become big business around the world, and especially in America, where reduced revenue from the public purse and corporate parsimony have prompted cultural institutions to seek other sources of funds.

Many museums and galleries in America have large endowments and collections of almost immeasurable value. Yet they suffer from seesaw support; up and down attendances, membership and other sources of income. So these institutions are shifting to new forms of financing, for example to large bond issues; to underpin these issues, they are seeking credit ratings. The first to try the approach was New York's Metropolitan Museum, which, in the 1980s, suffered substantial cuts in New York City funding. In 1987, with support from a State educational authority, the Museum floated a $40m issue. By 1993, the Museum was able to refinance its debt, and secure another $22m at preferential rates. The issues were successful; by early 1996, the Museum had won a higher rating from credit agencies, as did the Art Institute of Chicago.

Reports are becoming more common of innovative financing by museums and galleries, and raised credit standing. As an example, Moody's Investors Service now rates New York's Museum of Modern Art as A1 for an issue of $34.7m (£21m) of debt. Cultural institutions across the Atlantic and in other parts of the world have learnt how to operate in debt markets, without the cushion of government backing or costly bond insurance programmes. New York's Natural History Museum and Boston's Museum of Fine Arts are among other cultural institutions that have used publicly traded debt to finance capital projects. One benefit is a lower interest rate than banks charge for loans. The bonds are tax-exempt, offering investors and savers advantages; they do not have to pay Federal taxes on the income. American investment bankers have been struck with 'museums and galleries' strong balance sheets, low debt, and efficient financial management of large-scale events'.

These institutions apply their borrowing mainly to capital projects. However, they do not offer their collections as collateral. Nor do the agencies treat these assets as formally available for debt servicing; but the credit raters nevertheless feel that, in straitened circumstances, the institutions could sell some works of art from their inventories. The American experience might well be a precedent for the UK, although it would probably require changes in the charities' law. Arts Minister Mark Fisher, in a recent speech, renewed the Government's commitment to the state funding of museums, albeit with likely increases in admission prices to come after the Government's review on the issue.

Some other public museums are experiencing organic growth. Perhaps the most spectacular growth has been in Seattle. To house new donations of art, three major art museums there have added 200,000 square feet of floor space over the past five years. The largest, the Seattle Art Museum, a showcase for contemporary art, has tripled in size, added 2,556 pieces of art and put an additional 8,000 new members on its rolls since 1991. The greater purchasing power of art museums could have a substantial impact on world markets.

18.5 PURCHASING ART AND ANTIQUES

18.5.1 Quality and provenance

The consensus of expert opinion is that the buyer should be concerned with the features which establish a work as one of quality. The condition of a painting, for example, is an important factor, as is its provenance, ie its origins and history. An investor who acquires a work (which he or she plans to hold for some years before disposing of it, possibly in an over-seas market) will want to make sure in advance that its ownership, authenticity and quality are established beyond reasonable dispute, and that it is marketable.

When negotiating to buy an asset, the investor therefore needs to go fur-ther in his or her investigations than would be necessary merely to check that the vendor has a good title to the piece. The research carried out into the history and previous ownership of the work should also indicate clearly the probability that it is a genuine item. A bill of sale which includes a full and authentic dossier of the purchase will be helpful both for the purposes of an inventory of assets and an eventual disposal. Preferably, the dossier will be endorsed by valuers of repute, who will be in a position at some time in the future to verify the statements made.

These precautions are advisable for several reasons. Basically, they provide the buyer with evidence that the vendor has a good title to the piece. Equally, the research is important because there are frauds and forgeries in the alternative investment market, as well as reproductions and 'restorations' which can be difficult to distinguish from the genuine article. Occasionally, the forgery may turn out to have a high value in its own right, but on the whole the investor needs to take due care that the work's authenticity has been verified. It is also important to bear in mind that certificates may be counterfeited.

18.5.2 Fakes and forgeries

Dealers and auction houses take steps to reduce the risk of forgery and mistaken identity. Some offer the buyer a five-year guarantee against forgery. Because the largest houses trade in volume and compete intensively for material, they can sometimes be an unwitting conduit for fakes, particularly in ill-documented but now increasingly expensive areas of art. In sectors of the market where fakes are relatively common, some will inevitably turn up at auction; and where the rewards can be measured in millions of dollars, fakes will breed.

Successful fakers may discredit sections of the market and even distort history, but it is sometimes the 'experts' more than the artists who are to blame. When anyone dares to pry into their secret world, they close ranks. Many did so when Tom Keating, Britain's most celebrated forger, faced criminal charges over a handful of his 2,000 or more fakes. The same pattern of events occurred when another trickster, Eric Hebborn, was accused of faking many drawings by Old Masters. Nothing is guaranteed; even the *Mona Lisa* may not be the original. Leonardo's masterpiece went missing from the Louvre for 11 months in 1911 after an audacious theft, and some people still claim that a copy was substituted for the real work. In 1985, the J Paul Getty Museum in California reputedly paid $7m (£4m) for a 6th century BC Greek statue, known as a *Kouros*, only to find that experts could not substantiate its provenance, and it was very likely a fake, possibly made by one of Rodin's assistants in Paris in about 1900. The handiwork of some well-known forgers has itself become sought after. A case in point is that of Keating, whose works have fetched up to £27,500 at auction. One buyer, however, paid

£1,500 for an 'original' Keating only to find that it, and its certificate, were themselves fakes.

Nobody can say for sure how much of the art on the market has dubious origins or how many 'wrong' artworks find their way into Britain's salesrooms. Some experts believe that half the items sold on the market may not be 'right'. Dealers, auctioneers and gallery curators privately admit that faking is on the increase. In the case of most paintings by Cézanne and Seurat, provenance is impeccable and there is no reason to believe they are fakes. Then again, hundreds of fake post-Impressionist works have been turned out over the years and an unknown percentage of them are on the walls of leading galleries all over the world.

As Keating demonstrated, fakes are frequently first rate; several of his 'Samuel Palmers' are still regarded by some people as 'among Palmer's finest works'. In the Netherlands, the Rembrandt Research Project, set up 15 years ago to distinguish true Rembrandts from works produced by pupils and followers, had by 1994 reduced the Dutchman's *oeuvre* to less than half the previous total. Elmyr de Hory, an exuberant Hungarian, fooled the market for years with a profusion of faked Picassos, Matisses and Modiglianis and, at the time of his death, had no idea what had happened to a batch of skilfully forged Old Masters.

In recent years, money launderers have discovered that buying and selling fakes can double their profits. Colombian drug barons were the first, but now the Russian mafia has cornered the market in fake icons. This led to the murder of 30 icon dealers in 1996. Dealers have to cope with innumerable forgeries. Of course, the art world dislikes discussion of widespread fakery. A book on the subject (*Fakes, Forgers and the Art World*, published by Richard Cohen Books in 1995) met with the studied hostility of members of the art establishment. Publication was halted at the last moment by the publisher on the advice of lawyers, and a second firm agreed to publish only after some specific allegations about people still in the business were modified or omitted from the text.

Who are the fakers? They are usually talented artists who are consumed by the belief that their genius has gone unrecognised and are bent on revenge. Hebborn was born in Romford, Essex, in 1934. While a student in the 1950s he undertook work as a part-time restorer and discovered a gift for filling in missing bits of pictures in the style of the original artists. Later, after he studied works by the Dutch painter Willem van de Velde, he attempted a van de Velde of his own and signed it with the artist's name. He redrew his preparatory drawing on to an old canvas and prevented paint seeping into the age cracks by filling these with a jelly like substance that resisted his paintbrush and would later dissolve in water. He took care not to use colours such as zinc white and Prussian blue that were not available in van de Velde's day and the paints he did use were ground in a clearer oil than linseed and had a mixture of artificial resin added. He copied a signature from a photograph.

Hebborn was not exposed until 1978 when a curator visiting the Pierpont Morgan Library in New York noticed something odd about a drawing of a boy supposedly by Francesco del Cossa, the 15th century Italian artist. The ink lines had been scratched over with what appeared to have been a 20th century razor blade. A long investigation ensued and Hebborn's career as a forger was at an end, or so the establishment claimed. He had the satisfaction, however, of knowing that three sets of 'experts' had pronounced his Cossa an original.

The way a scam unfolds is revealed in the example of de Hory, who worked closely with an unscrupulous couple, Fernand Legros and Réal Lessard, in the 1960s, passing off bogus Dufys, Dérains, Modiglianis, Vlamincks and Matisses. Their tactics, de Hory once revealed, were to secure expert opinions, if possible, from the artists' surviving relatives, such as Jeanne Modigliani and Alice Dérain, or to forge them. The fraudsters also paid impoverished collectors to certify that they had previously owned the pictures. Alternatively, they would put a painting in an auction and, if nobody bought it, they had only to pay the handling fee to reclaim it – a small price for the picture's appearance in a reputable catalogue as genuine.

One of the century's greatest forgers was Hans van Meegeren, a Dutchman who throughout the 1930s and early 1940s specialised in superbly crafted fakes of the 17th century master Johannes Vermeer. He was generally successful (though less so than the dealers who profited from his activities) and stumbled only after it was suggested in 1945 that he had handed over a Vermeer, *The Woman Taken in Adultery*, to Hermann Goering, an act of criminal collaboration. Van Meegeren retorted that he had knocked off the Vermeer himself and then sold it to Goering, thus hoodwinking the Nazi, and to prove this he produced *Jesus Preaching in the Temple*, without models and in the presence of six witnesses, to a standard that astounded the experts.

Fakers provide the artefacts, but dealers and valuers provide the market. Keating, who died in 1984 after a spectacular career, insisted that he had always been quite open about his forgeries. 'It was other people that weren't,' he said. After he was exposed in 1976 and under investigation by Scotland Yard's art fraud division, dealers and auctioneers became singularly reluctant to talk. The art market is built upon confidence: when trade is going well, business prospers, but a scandal can easily start a downward spiral. Keating's 'crude daubs', as he called them, made it more difficult for dealers to convince buyers of the value of a unique, original production of a famous mind. A few scribbles by a master are worth far more than a fine painting by an unknown artist or a forger.

Faked art continues to be sold, alongside and often indistinguishable from the real thing. A Fabergé egg sold in good faith by Christie's in 1977 for $250,000 as an imperial egg (one of only 57 in the world) was denounced eight years later by the same company in New York. Reportedly, about $5m was paid to the buyer's estate in compensation and costs.

Recently, controversy has surrounded the authenticity of one of van Gogh's eleven *Sunflowers*. In 1987, Christie's sold it to the Yasuda Fire Insurance Company for £24.75m, making it the world's most expensive painting. In 1998, in a Channel 4 documentary, journalist Geraldine Norman alleged that it had been painted by van Gogh's friend, Claude-Emile Schuffenecker. Experts from the van Gogh museum disagree. In early 1999 a conference at the National Gallery in London discussed the painting's provenance, but opinion remained divided on the issue. Another art historian claimed in April 1999 that at least 30 van Gogh's are fake.

Most cases against fakers or their associates hinge on the intention to deceive, which has to be proved. Auctioneers will normally offer recompense for fakes only if the buyer can provide proof, usually within five years, and even then only if it can be demonstrated that the saleroom was not reflecting general opinion at the time, or that they could only have uncovered the truth by unreasonably expensive scientific means.

18.5.3 Crime and punishing losses

The editor of the magazine *Trace* estimates that, every year, thefts of antiques and works of art amount to at least £500m. Apparently, thieves familiarise themselves with the antiques and arts market while serving sentences; police sources report that the *Antiques Roadshow* is the most popular TV show among prisoners. The value of recovered items put on show by the police goes up to more than £1m for a necklace, and large sums for pieces taken from stately homes.

Some of the Metropolitan Police art and antique unit's cases are unusual and instructive. At the trial of John Drewe, more details emerged of his ingenious scheme to sell forged paintings as genuine works. A forger, John Myatt, faked paintings by Roger Bissière, Marc Chagall, Nicolas De Stael, Jean Dubuffet, Alberto Giacometti, Henri Matisse, Ben Nicholson and Graham Sutherland. Drewe then falsified the archives in galleries and museums, on which dealers rely to verify the provenance of a work they intend buying. Drewe found private galleries that had gone out of business, doctored their records, and meticulously forged old catalogues, using ink and paper of the period. He inserted the spurious records, with detailed references to faked paintings, into the gallery and museum archives, and substituted photographs of the forgeries for pictures of obscure, little-known pieces by famous artists. He used an old typewriter to create slips, identifying photographs of the forgeries as originals, which he pasted into the archives. He also forged a gallery stamp, and used it on the back of documents.

The case prompted detailed scrutiny of documents that buttress claims. For instance, appraisers focus on labels affixed to frames, which purport to chronicle a painting's itinerary from museum to gallery, to owner, to dealer, to saleroom. Letters, extracts from critics' reviews and curators' reports, invoices, receipts, insurances, bills of lading, customs declarations, all lend support to assertions that the work is genuine, and is worth a large sum. Doubts can arise when the sources are critics and curators who are no longer alive, or auction houses and galleries which have gone out of business. Prudent dealers now carry out the type of investigation that merchant bankers, accountants and research specialists conduct when a client buys a company; today, many art experts launch a 'due diligence' enquiry.

Clearly, it is unwise to accept without checking that any provenance is bona fide. Of course, an error in the provenance does not prove that a painting is a forgery, but it is advisable to take care. The due diligence process usually means verifying original documents, contacting the experts and critics cited in the support materials, and studying catalogues of an artist's work. To reduce the risk, collectors can also take advice from an art foundation that specialises in a named artist. For a fee of £250 or more, depending on the costs incurred in checking the work, an expert will supply a 'photo certificate', which includes a signed opinion and a photograph.

Fears about paintings with false provenance have affected sales. In some sectors, evidence of large-scale fraud and forgery has brought a market to a virtual stop, as happened, for example, with some Russian avantgarde art. Art historians have disputed the origins of paintings sold at auction and, in December 1996, Sotheby's withdrew six Russian avantgarde paintings at short notice. A gulf between the opinions of Russian and western experts is making it difficult to authenticate pictures that are in demand. The buyers affected are mainly rich western collectors of works by such artists as Malevich, Rodchenko, Popova and Exter. Their works belong to experimental schools that sprang up during the turbulent years between 1905 and Lenin's death in the early 1920s. Fakes make for a factious and fractious market. Given a lack of consensus on the authenticity of works, few major auction houses will now sell these controversial paintings.

The forgers and fraudsters of these Russian works rely on the muddled paper trails left by the artists, who lived through the dark days of the century's history. Stalin denounced experimentation in art as in music and literature, and artists died, or went to labour camps. Their works festered in musty storerooms, or vanished altogether.

Generally, the cognoscenti worry that fakes are widespread. In some categories, some claim forgeries are almost as numerous as the genuine article. Many doubtful paintings, these experts believe, remain undetected in private collections and great museums. A recent book tells of a Yugoslav forger, who allegedly 'sold a museumful of fakes to the Tito government'. Out of almost 4,000 items, the author believes, all but a few dozen are of disputable origins. Yet the collection is still open to the public in Zagreb. Even more spectacularly, according to this book, a Mexican fabricator has faked an entire phase of ancient Inca art, many of the artefacts being on show in American galleries.

18.5.4 Choosing an adviser

When making a purchase, it is usually helpful to have details in a dossier about the artist to whom the piece is ascribed. In the art market, for instance, it is common to use the names of artists to denote works 'in the style' of a particular painter, or paintings by unidentified members of a school associated with a famous artist. Therefore, not all paintings listed in an auction catalogue under the name 'Manet' will be by that painter; it is important for buyers to appreciate the esoteric distinctions employed by the specialists in auction houses to indicate the provenance of a work.

Ideally, those chosen to advise should have a wide knowledge of the field. Thus, a specialist offering guidance on the purchase of works of art should also be able to direct its installation, placement and maintenance. Ideally, he or she should have a background in art history, curatorial experience, an intimate knowledge of the art market, and up-to-date familiarity with trends in prices and values. In addition, care should be taken to check that the adviser has a good understanding of handling, shipping, conservation, restoration, insurance and security. Curators of art galleries and museums will sometimes indicate formally which dealers specialise in particular areas.

18.5.5 Exporting art

An intending buyer of art or antiques should keep other precautions in mind. Suppose, for instance, that the plan is to send an item out of the UK; authorisation may be needed. Some categories of antiques, collectors' items and other artefacts do not need a specific licence. They are covered by the Open General Export Licence (Antiques), which does not need to be applied for. Exporters need only inform customs officials by naming the licence in export documentation. A Specific Export Licence must be applied for (from the Department of Trade and Industry) by those wishing to send historic manuscripts, documents and archives of any value out of the country. Any object covered by the regulations which exceeds the thresholds of age and value will need a UK export licence.

Licence applications have to be accompanied by a black-and-white photographic copy of the item; and the decision whether to permit export will be influenced by independent advice. Where the item is regarded as part of the national heritage, the issue of a licence may be delayed or refused on the advice of experts in the field. The procedures may include reference to the Department of Culture, Media and Sports' Arts and Libraries' Reviewing Committee on the Export of Works of Art, described at **18.3.1** and **18.3.2**.

In the past, many licence applications have been made; few have been rejected. For example, in one recent year, 6,550 applications were made for export licences with a total value of £963m: only 24 failed to receive approval, subject to an offer to purchase at a specified price being made by a public collection in the UK within a reasonable time.

It is prudent to bear the requirement in mind when deciding to acquire a work of art or an antique of exceptional interest. When these items come onto the open market some foreign buyers may be deterred by the inconvenience and delays of up to seven months in the review procedure, and by the inherent risk that their offer will merely represent the buying-in price for a domestic museum. The absence of such foreign buyers could mean lower bids and less attractive gains when the time comes to dispose of the item.

18.5.6 National heritage bodies

The National Gallery
The National Museums of Scotland
The Ulster Museum
The National Trust for Places of Historic Interest or Natural Beauty
The Historic Buildings and Monuments Commission for England
The Trustees of the National Heritage Memorial Fund
The Historic Churches Preservation Trust
Any local authority (including National Park authorities)
Any university or university college in the UK
Any museum or art gallery in the UK which exists wholly or mainly for the purpose of preserving for the public benefit a collection of scientific, historic or artistic interest and which is maintained by a local authority or university in the UK

The British Museum
The National Museum of Wales
The National Art Collections Fund
The National Trust for Scotland for Places of Historic Interest or Natural
    Beauty
The Friends of the National Libraries
The Nature Conservancy Council
Any government department (including the National Debt
    Commissioners)
Any library the main function of which is to serve the needs of teaching
    and research at a university in the UK
Any other similar national institution which exists wholly or mainly
    for that purpose and which is approved for the purpose by the
    Commissioners of the Inland Revenue.

18.6 CHARACTERISTICS

18.6.1 Prospects of capital appreciation

Can alternative investments be justified by private investors or by
trustees and fund managers with powers to buy fine art or antiques?
Essentially the question is whether the capital appreciation over a period
of, say, 10 years, 25 years or even longer will warrant the diversion of
funds and the expenditure incurred in holding the asset.

Frequent reports in the press of record-breaking prices paid for pieces at
auction may seem to support the case for alternative investment. In 1989,
as the market approached a peak, some 10- and 20-year investments
paid handsome dividends. The increasing number of investments which
have provided significant capital appreciation short-term also represents
an interesting trend that helps to endorse the advocates' case for buying
arts and antiques.

Their counsel to both private and institutional investors is to buy the best
examples that can be afforded and to take expert advice from a reputable dealer or appraiser. They suggest that an artist's early work will,
in general, be less valuable than later, more mature, examples.
Reasonably enough, they also point out that prices can fall, as happened
with Georgian silver after a boom in the 1960s, with 19th century fine art
in the mid-1970s, and with many categories of art and antiques in the
early 1980s and the recent 1990s. However, even expert advice is falli-
ble, particularly where attribution is concerned. A case in point is the
work of Rembrandt, which has suffered the attentions of a Dutch government committee (see **18.5.2**). The majority of works once attributed to

him have now been reattributed to his pupils. Works have lost up to 90 per cent of their value, and the controversy has spawned a 'Save Rembrandt Society'.

18.6.2 Art as investment

One sector of the alternative investment market comprises investors who are nervous about the future. Some works are low in weight, small in size and high in value: they are portable, easily concealed and readily negotiable in markets around the world. Those who fear political, economic, social or tax repression in their own countries tend to regard alternative investments as a means of safeguarding their wealth.

Some market sectors, on occasion, seem to meet demanding investment criteria. Conversely, anecdotal evidence could make enthusiastic bidders at auctions pause. According to one press report, a battle tableau by Ernest Meissonier, a much-favoured painter of a century ago, sold in London in 1892 for £20,700; again in 1913 for £6,300; and again in 1964 for £4,340. Lazare reports that John Singer Sargent's oil sketch *San Virgilio* sold for £7,350 in 1925 and just £105 in 1952. A scholarly study of London auction transactions between 1952 and 1961 found that the average work appreciated just ½ per cent a year, a poor return in anyone's passbook. More recently, a painting by Henry Fuesli, an 18th century Swiss/British artist, bought by Rudolf Nureyev in 1988 for $1.16m, was sold in January 1995 for $761,500 (£488,141).

To set against these warning illustrations, there are some promising examples of the gains to be made. Paintings by the Scottish Colourists, SJ Peploe, JD Fergusson, Frances Cadell and Leslie Hunter, have shown an average annual appreciation rate of 19 per cent from 1975. Similarly, Renoir's *Tête du Femme* was sold for £1.35m in 1987 and exchanged hands again in 1988 for £1.98m (an appreciation of 35 per cent in one year).

18.6.3 Costs of ownership

Typically, rates of return are only attractive if owners are prepared to put a value on the pleasure of holding such works of art in their home or place of work. The investment may also be justified if the money used for the acquisitions would have been taxed at a high rate. Nevertheless, some items could have been a poor investment for the buyer, after taking into account outlays to meet insurance premiums, dealers' or auctioneers' commissions, any liability to capital taxation or VAT, the interest foregone, and security and maintenance costs. The lack of income flows means that buyers of alternative investments are dependent on capital appreciation; yet they have to deduct the following costs from any gains they may achieve:

(1) costs of acquisition and disposal, including premiums and dealers' commissions;
(2) holding costs (insurance, storage, etc);
(3) valuation and provenance research fees incurred;
(4) revenue and possible tax benefits foregone by tying up capital in the asset;
(5) the value of time spent dreaming about the market and, increasingly, the advice of market experts or consultants;
(6) capital gains tax payable on realisation of the asset, or inheritance tax payable on its transfer.

Substantial gains are necessary to justify such an investment in financial terms; or, alternatively, the investor has to be convinced that the assets he or she acquires can be relied upon to sustain their worth in times when traditional investments fail. Figure 18.2 shows how much an investment of £1,000 must grow to produce the equivalent of 8 per cent compound between 1997 and 2007. The interest rate represents an inflation rate of 3 per cent, and a target annual return of 5 per cent. In other words, the painting bought at auction for £1,000 net in 1997 should fetch a net sum of £2,159 in 2007 to match these targets.

18.6.4 The Chester Beatty collection: a precedent

In 1991, 13 paintings from the collection of the late Sir Alfred Chester Beatty were offered at auction. They included works by Toulouse-Lautrec, Dégas, Renoir and Chagall. The trustees had previously considered donating van Gogh's *Sunflowers* to the nation: instead they sold at auction for £24¾m. Had they donated it, the family would have received £5½m under the Government's acceptance in lieu scheme. That returns a quarter of the tax deducted as an incentive to donate works of art to the nation.

The sale at auction was subject to combined inheritance and capital gains taxation. The capital gains tax of £3.07m was calculated as 30 per cent of the difference between the valuation and the sale price at auction. The inheritance tax was levied at a variable rate (between 65 and 80 per cent) because the painting had been exempted at the time of an earlier death in the family. Otherwise the rate would have been 60 per cent. At the 80 per cent rate, the balance left for the family would be £3–3½m, probably not enough to settle the full tax on the estate.

Figure 18.2 Increase in values required equivalent to 8 per cent compound per annum

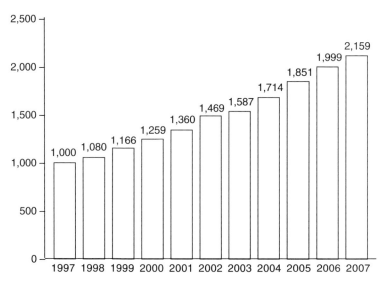

Note: 8 per cent includes 3 per cent inflation and 5 per cent compound interest per annum

Table 18.3 Increase in values to match compound rates of 5 per cent (inflation); 10 per cent (rise in art markets); and 12½ per cent (share markets)

Year	Inflation 5% €	Art 10% €	Shares 12½% €
2000	10,000	10,000	10,000
2005	12,763	16,105	18,020
2010	16,289	25,937	32,473
2015	20,789	41,772	58,518
2020	26,533	67,275	105,451
2025	33,864	108,347	190,026

18.6.5 Buying at auction

Sales to meet tax bills provide auction houses with a flow of works to offer. Many people who like the idea of buying at a sale worry that they will find it hard to conform to usual practice, that a sudden twitch will leave them with an unexpected heirloom and an unwelcome bill. The pace can be fast, the enthusiasm contagious, and bidding strategy complex. The amount paid is also likely to include extras, such as a 10 per cent buyer's premium and VAT on the auction house's services.

In reality the buying process often begins a month or more before the sale date. Catalogues appear and can be bought on subscription, by order or at the auctioneer's offices. The descriptions of items have various nuances; for instance, only information printed in bold type may be guaranteed. There will be an estimated price range, but no disclosure of the secret minimum bid acceptable to the vendor, the 'reserve'. Critics ask, 'Is this secrecy necessary?' Should buyers be told whether they are bidding against an actual rival or the consignor's reserve? Auctioneers argue that the confidential reserve is a defence against the collusion of 'auction rings'. It is only worth organising a ring when the participants know that the reserve is low enough to ensure a good profit.

Before the sale, lots are commonly exhibited. They are sold 'as seen', so it is important to study the condition of an item in advance. Before bidding at many major auctions, it is necessary to register, ie to give name, address and bank reference. A 'client card' for previous registrants can speed the process. At the auction, the registrant may take a pre-reserved seat and a bidding number. It is, in practice, virtually impossible to bid by accident. Just when to start bidding is a matter of strategy. Some buyers come in early and raise quickly to deter competitors; others wait to avoid inciting other bidders with their keenness. Care is advisable when the bidding pace seems unusually fast, or the auctioneer does not indicate the source of the bid. Often he or she will say 'on the left' or 'the bid is with me' or some similar words that convey the origin and authenticity of the bid. Payment may be cash, approved cheque or, in some instances, by credit card.

18.6.6 Independent sources of information

Research pays off before buying at auction or through a dealer. An independent source of information on the prices of paintings sold at auction is the Art Sales Index. This lists the results of auctions for about 60,000 items each year which were sold for £500 or more. Using this source, an analysis has been made of transactions for a representative selection of 20th century Modern masters. The analysis showed a compound rate of appreciation in excess of 14 per cent per annum between 1971 and 1991. Such rates of growth have made it easier to argue the case for the allocation of funds to alternative investments.

The growth of interest which has already taken place has prompted the development of improved sources of information on available media, prices and the advantages and limitations of particular types of investment. There are already computerised databases providing information to help determine sound investments. 'Artquest', provided by the Art Sales Index, holds details on paintings, drawings and sculptures which have been sold at public auction around the world. Another recently developed database is the 'Thesaurus of Fine Art Information'. This allows dealers, collectors and museums who subscribe to it to search through details of forthcoming auction sales, for any category of antique or collectable of interest. The gradual evolution of a more or less formal infrastructure of information sources in the alternative sector of the investment market will add to the understanding of the opportunities and prospects.

These sources and others show when the average annual appreciation over the past 40 years has outstripped the rate of inflation, although there has been considerable volatility from artist to artist and from sale to sale.

18.7 TAXATION

18.7.1 Tax planning

To attain positive returns, investors should plan to avoid unnecessary tax liabilities. For instance, if the investor eventually wishes to contend that isolated purchases are for the purpose of building up assets as long-term investments, then it is mandatory to record the acquisition of chargeable assets in his or her tax returns. This step would help to support a claim that capital gains, not income tax, should be the basis for calculating any future liabilities when, despite the parity of the rates of tax, there are advantages in doing so for the individual taxpayer.

The private investor may also face claims by the Inland Revenue that purchases and sales of alternative investments are 'adventures in the nature of a trade'. This would lead to an income tax liability if the investor has been carrying on the trade on his or her own account, or to a corporation tax liability if he or she has set up a company for the purpose.

18.7.2 Capital gains

Alternative investments are subject to the general law on capital gains tax, although there are special exemptions. In broad terms the amount of the chargeable gain is the difference between the cost of the asset and the sale proceeds, less an adjustment for the inflationary element of the gain accruing since March 1982. For any asset held on 31 March 1982, it is possible to base the cost of acquisition at its market value on that date.

There is however no charge on unrealised gains from assets held by an individual at his or her death.

Special considerations apply in the case of works of art and other alternative investments. Thus, a gain accruing on the disposal of an asset which does not exceed £6,000 (from 6 April 1995) is generally exempt from capital gains tax with marginal relief (see Capital Gains Tax Act 1979, s 128). In this connection the exemption on articles which provide a gain of not more than £6,000 (eg individual pieces of antique silver) would become relevant.

Exemptions also arise for individual objects of artistic, historic or scientific interest (and collections of such objects), which are accepted by the tax authorities as forming 'an integral and major part of the cultural life of this country'. These are often referred to as 'national heritage property'. Under the *douceur* arrangements (see **18.7.4**), gifts of such alternative investments to national heritage bodies (and gifts of these alternative investments to charities) are not charged to capital gains tax. In the case of sales, the notional capital gains tax liability is one of the factors relevant in calculating the sale price that can be negotiated. There is a similar exemption applying to gifts of qualifying heritage property made for the public benefit.

Where national heritage property (accepted as such by the Commissioners of Inland Revenue) is transferred by way of gift from one individual to another, or where such property is transferred into or out of settlement, the transfer is treated for capital gains tax purposes as giving rise neither to a gain nor to a loss, provided that appropriate undertakings are given with regard to location, preservation and access. This means that any gain is carried forward, and will be chargeable when the donee disposes of the property in a manner which does not qualify for conditional exemption.

18.7.3 Inheritance tax and estate duty

Inheritance tax replaced capital transfer tax with effect from 18 March 1986. It was introduced in the 1986 Finance Act and applies to gratuitous transfers by individuals. The major difference between capital transfer tax and inheritance tax is the treatment of lifetime transfers. Outright transfers between individuals are exempt if the transferor lives on for seven years. Gifts made within seven years of death are charged at death rates, but the charge is tapered where the gift occurs more than three years before death.

The charge on death is retained within inheritance tax, as are most of the exemptions and relief available under capital transfer tax, including transfers between spouses domiciled in the UK. Trust-related transfers remain subject to the full range of charges at the time the transfers are made. The cumulation period for all chargeable transfers has been reduced to seven years and the threshold below which tax is not chargeable is £223,000 (from 6 April 1998). A flat rate of 40 per cent replaced the former four-rate system.

Estate duty applies to property inherited before 13 March 1975. This may still be relevant to the sale of objects which have been previously exempted from estate duty. Estate duty will not be charged if exempted objects are sold by private treaty to a national heritage body or have again been transferred on a death and have been conditionally exempt on that occasion. Special rules apply when property which has previously been exempted is sold after 6 April 1976. The way in which this property is taxed depends on what had happened since the original exemption was granted – either capital transfer tax or inheritance tax or estate duty only may be payable. This is a complex issue and is dealt with fully in Appendix III (p 46) of *Capital Taxation and the National Heritage* (see bibliography at the end of Chapter 19).

18.7.4 Tax liabilities in practice

The Treasury has become more flexible about the art it will accept in the form of heritage sales to museums as a means of saving tax. When inheritance tax is due on an estate, the acceptance in lieu procedure may allow owners who are liable to pay the tax to instead offer objects to the Commissioners to satisfy the tax owed, in whole or in part.

On receiving a suitable offer, the Revenue's CTO refers it to the Museums and Galleries Commission. After the Commission has taken opinions from independent experts, it advises the Secretary of State whether the property offered is suitable for acceptance in lieu. Qualifying property under these procedures includes pictures, books, prints, archives, manuscripts, works of art, furniture, craft objects, historic objects, scientific objects, and other items. A case in point arose in March 1999, when the Treasury accepted a masterpiece by Van Dyck, the *Portrait of Cesare Allesandro Scaglia*, in lieu of inheritance tax, thus ensuring that it will stay in this country.

Once an item is deemed suitable for the scheme, the Revenue works out the tax by a reduction of 25 per cent of this charge (known as the *douceur* or sweetener) of the normal inheritance tax liability. This arrangement allows the vendor to offer an item to the nation, and to satisfy all tax liabilities on the estate. For example, if the market value of a work of art is estimated at £1m, the normal liability for inheritance tax would be £400,000. The net market value would therefore be £600,000. The *douceur*, at 25 per cent of the normal tax liability, would be £100,000, and the tax settlement value would be £700,000. Accordingly, the vendor can make savings on his or her tax bill than if he or she sold it on the open market.

In this way, museums can often buy chattels for perhaps 70 per cent of their full value. The problem is that museum purchasing grants have been frozen for the past seven years, and the National Heritage Fund and the National Art Collections Fund have limited resources.

The Commissioners of Inland Revenue exercise their powers under the National Heritage Act 1980, the Inheritance Tax Act 1984 and supplementary Finance Acts. As indicated above, they may accept certain property, in whole or part, in lieu of inheritance taxes (and its predecessors, estate duty and capital transfer tax), and of liability to pay interest on these taxes. Objects can only be set against inheritance tax, not against capital gains tax. The Secretary of State for Culture, Media and Sport has first to agree that the property is 'pre-eminently of national, artistic, historic or scientific interest', or has important historical associations, taking account of its valuation and condition and the benefits of adding it 'to a national, local authority, or university collection'. However, the standard which has to be applied has changed. Since the implementation of the Finance Act 1998, the same criteria now apply to chattels: they must be of museum quality and must be 'pre-eminent for their national, scientific, historic or artistic interest'

The Culture Secretary also has the power to direct the placing of this property, and can permit accepted items to remain *in situ* if they are so closely connected with a building or context. The Royal Commission on Historical Manuscripts advises on the location of records, archives and manuscripts. Chattels accepted in lieu therefore belong to local museums, galleries or public libraries, and are effectively lent back to the original owner. *In situ* offers must provide for public access, and the public has a right to see these items. In March 1998, the Secretary of State announced new measures to strengthen and extend public access to these assets. All objects should be made available to the public, without the prior appointment previously required. Owners are also obliged to 'publicise their undertakings, and disclose any other information relevant to the public access'.

Under the old arrangements, the Secretary of State would reimburse the Commissioners for the tax forgone. In its accounting, the Revenue would treat this payment as tax due. From July 1985, the Department of Culture, Media and Sport and the Revenue could draw sums from the reserves to cover the cost of large, important items. However, in the Spring 1998 Budget, the Chancellor announced new arrangements whereby the Revenue now accepts property in lieu of taxes without seeking reimbursement from the Secretary of State. The Secretary of State does have to report to the Chief Secretary to the Treasury when offers are expected to be in excess of £10m in any single year, or if one offer is likely to exceed £1m.

18.7.5 VAT

HM Treasury has produced the Value Added Tax (Works of Art etc) Order 1983 (Sl No 809), which exempts from VAT disposals of works of art and other objects (including manuscripts, prints and scientific objects) which are of national, scientific, historic or artistic interest, or which have an historical association with a particular building. To qualify for exemption, these heritage objects have to be disposed of by private individuals in the course of business either as private treaty sales or as gifts to one of the approved lists of public galleries and similar institutions, or in settlement of tax debts under the *douceur* arrangements. This change is also now incorporated in the Value Added Tax Act 1983, Sched 6.

On 1 January 1986 a new harmonised system of customs duty and temporary importation reliefs came into effect under the Value Added Tax (Temporarily Imported Goods) Relief Order 1986 (Sl No 1989). The relevant HM Customs & Excise Notices are 36l and 712. The latter is an information 'package' about the VAT second-hand scheme for works of art, antiques and collectors' pieces (mainly for dealers in fine art and antiques who are VAT-registered). VAT leaflet 701/12/89 gives guidance on 'Sales of antiques, works of art etc from stately homes'. The new regulations apply to works of art brought in primarily for exhibition but later sold. VAT leaflet 701/36/86 also contains guidance on the insurance of second-hand goods such as works of art.

Problems can arise with temporary importation. For example, according to an MTI case study for the European Commission, a London-based Old Master dealer bought a painting at auction in New York for €146,700. He brought the item back to the UK, under a temporary importation bond, which was 'debited' with €3,750 (2½ per cent of the purchase price). He then took the painting to the Maastricht Fair in the Netherlands, but required an export licence before it could leave the UK. The dealer applied for this licence, stating that the picture was worth €219,000, and took it to the Netherlands. On arrival, he had to 'debit' a further €9,500 from his temporary importation bond, to take account of the Dutch regulation, which applies import VAT at 6 per cent. No buyer emerged in Maastricht, so the dealer took the painting back to the UK, where he had to apply for a 'credit' to his bond of €7,665. Eventually, he sold the picture to a Swiss client for €219,000, resulting in a further application for a 'credit' of €5,475 to the bond.

While the dealer was waiting for the 'credits' to be applied to his temporary bond (about six months), he had to turn down the opportunity of purchasing two pictures, as to take them would have meant having to apply for an extension of his bond, with the associated costs that brings. In addition, as a result of the picture being sold eventually to a Swiss client, the net benefits to the UK authorities as a result of import VAT was zero.

This case is typical. Although a dealer can move freely within the Community items which already have import VAT paid on them, items placed under temporary import have not technically been imported. Thus, each time they move between member states they are treated as potential imports. Each time a seller crosses a border, he or she needs to process changes to the temporary import bond. In many cases, the time involved in waiting for the processing of each change can be considerable. Many dealers point out the cost implications of processing changes to the temporary import bond each time a border is crossed, as well as the cost of operating a bond, which is often a bank overdraft facility.

From the beginning of 1995 changes occurred arising from the first stage of implementing the EC Seventh VAT Directive. Further changes followed the Royal Assent to the Finance Act. The measures affect dealers in works of art and antiques. From 1 January 1995, VAT on all these goods has been accounted for on the margin between their buying and selling prices. Details of the new arrangements are explained in HM Customs & Excise VAT Information Sheet 1/95 which supersedes Information Sheet 3/93, dated 1 June 1993. The new arrangements require traders registered for VAT who make supplies of second-hand goods to traders registered for VAT in other member states to submit EC sales lists showing the full net value of any supplies made. Full details appear in HM Customs & Excise Notice 725: *VAT: the Single Market*.

The Finance Act 1995 introduced a 2½ per cent effective reduced rate of VAT on imports of those works of art and antiques which are currently fully relieved from VAT at importation. Details can be found in HM Customs & Excise Notice 712. The relief previously afforded by reg 47 of the VAT (General) Regulations ceased to be available and such importations become subject to VAT at the standard rate. Supplies of goods through auctioneers and agents who act in their own names will be treated for VAT purposes as supplies both to and by them. A special accounting scheme will allow auctioneers who sell works of art and antiques to calculate their VAT on a margin basis. A new VAT Notice 718 gives more detailed guidance on these changes.

New VAT anti-avoidance regulations were introduced in July 1997, which apply to the margin scheme. The new measures will prevent businesses from using the margin scheme for goods obtained under the rules for transfers of a going concern. These goods would have been eligible for the margin scheme prior to the transfer, and are therefore ineligible after the transfer. This is to block an annual loophole of £1.5bn. HM Customs & Excise updated VAT Notice 718 in June 1998. It covers margin schemes for second-hand goods, works of art, antiques and collectors' items. Briefly, the update clarifies the purchase value where goods obtained as a transfer of a going concern are sold under the margin scheme.

The works of art eligible for the margin scheme include:

- Pictures, collages and similar decorative plaques, paintings and drawings, executed entirely by the artist's hand, with some exceptions.
- Original engravings, prints and lithographs produced in limited numbers from plates executed entirely by the artist's hand.
- Original sculptures and statuary in any material, executed entirely by the artist (subject to certain provisos).
- Tapestries and wall textiles made by hand from original designs in limited numbers (not more than eight copies).
- Industrial pieces of ceramics executed entirely by the artist and signed by him or her.
- Enamels on copper, executed entirely by hand, limited to eight numbered copies, bearing the signature of the artist or studio, with certain exceptions.
- Photographs taken by the artist, printed by him or her, or under his or her supervision, signed and numbered, and limited to 30 copies.

Antiques are defined as objects, other than works of art or collectors' items, which are more than 100 years old. See also **19.6.2**.

In October 1995, HM Customs & Excise issued a revised edition of VAT Notice 702 (imports and warehoused goods). It replaced the January 1994 version, and reflected changes from the EC Seventh VAT Directive. These include new ways to value imported and re-imported works of art, antiques and collectors' pieces.

Subsequently, HM Customs & Excise sought views on the procedures that affect people who import their personal assets into the UK. These assets can include valuables, works of art, antiques and collectables. Details of the forms and procedures appear in Customs Notice 3, *Bringing your belongings and private motor vehicles to the UK from outside the EC*. The Department has canvassed views on the unnecessary problems that the procedures can cause, and ways to improve them. Documentation can be onerous when such moves occur. It is worth checking on any changes that emerge from the consultation.

See also **18.3.2** above.

18.7.6 Stamp duty

Stamp duty is normally payable only when the transfer is of an interest in an alternative investment, and not when it is the work itself which is being transferred, since chapels are transferable by delivery and no document is required to effect a transfer of the interest.

18.7.7 PAYE and national insurance

Regulations are in force to prevent employers avoiding PAYE and national insurance payments by remunerating their staff in kind. These regulations cover gifts of precious metals, fine wines, diamonds and other assets for which 'trading arrangements' exist that enable employees to swap assets, often for cash.

18.8 MECHANICS

18.8.1 Suitability

Research on individuals' investment preferences indicates that works of fine art and antiques, perhaps not surprisingly, only begin to figure to a significant extent in the portfolios of the wealthy. Initially, investors concentrate on property, building society investments, insurances, unit trusts or investment bonds, and possibly equity investments or gilts or National Savings certificates.

Thus, the more esoteric investments tend to be bought when extra capital is available. Neither individuals nor pension funds have so far engaged in the purchase of alternative investments as a routine policy, although the British Rail Pension Fund was, at one time, an exception; the Fund invested approximately £40m in 2,400 works of art, but its trustees and managers subsequently decided not to make any more purchases in this market.

In November 1988 the BR Pension Fund disposed of 31 museum-worthy pieces of silver for £2m, having paid £400,000 for them ten years previously. In 1989, the Fund sold paintings and sculptures, including works by Manet, Renoir, Monet, Picasso, van Gogh and Cézanne. Altogether the items put on sale realised £38½m, leaving the pensioners with more than £30m after paying all expenses and commissions. In 1990, the Fund sold its collection of 19th century continental 'European art' and Victorian paintings for £6m compared with its mid-1970s purchase price of £1.2m. One of a batch of 16 Old Masters owned by the Fund, which were sold at Sotheby's in December 1994, went for £3.4m, compared with a purchase price of around £150,000. The Fund has seen a 14⅓ per cent annual cash rate return and a 6⅔ per cent real rate of return, but later sales have generated lower returns. (See also **18.3.2**.)

In general, pension fund investment managers see a problem in the marketability of such assets. It is not easy to convert alternative investments into cash at short notice without sustaining losses. In addition, pension fund trustees and investment advisers are cautious about committing themselves to a line of action which might be criticised in the future. Trustees and investment advisers say that it is difficult to obtain accurate valuations on a regular basis and, even when valuers can supply a dependable service, there are few reliable and independent indices on which they can compare their portfolio's performance, as they can with equities. There is also a lurking suspicion that funds should not be invested in areas which are regarded as unsuitable for investors who may need income or capital at short notice, and which cannot be readily converted into cash.

On the other hand, the infrastructure for making alternative investments is gradually being established, and in the course of the next few years there may be improvements in the information sources and the indices available to investors and trustees. A well-publicised example is the service provided by London-based art investment managers Poensgen Sokolow. They produce the quarterly Art Market Analysis, and offer portfolios of important works with starting prices of around £10m. The improvement of the information facilities and the build up of reputable sources of impartial market intelligence might eventually help to make such alternative investments attractive, both for individuals and for investment managers with responsibilities for closed funds such as small self-administered pension schemes.

18.8.2 Sources of information

For the moment, the sources of information and intelligence are diverse and scattered. There are, in each of the areas of alternative investment, several specialist journals. In addition, there are various societies or clubs, which give the collector access to specialist knowledge. Auctioneers produce useful catalogues which highlight pieces coming onto the market; and those interested can find out about the prices paid at these sales.

The specialist journals and some of the directories produced by associations of dealers and auctioneers identify the areas in which particular firms are knowledgeable. The dealers will usually charge high commissions to cover their costs of holding expensive assets for periods, which can sometimes be prolonged, before a buyer emerges. Auction sales are, on the whole, a source of more competitively priced items, although many of the leading London firms now charge a commission to both vendors and buyers.

It is, however, becoming more difficult for the private collector to keep pace with developments in his or her chosen fields of alternative investment. Although London remains an important centre of trading activity in art and antiques, many important sales are nowadays being held outside the UK, which has become a net exporter of such pieces. In earlier times, collectors could rely on a steady flow of fine works.

One development which will undoubtedly help in the dissemination of information is the Internet, which gives access to art, artists and major museums world-wide. Art and the Internet might seem strange companions. While art is traditionally considered material culture – paintings, sculpture, etc – the Internet is the realm of the immaterial, the virtual, the unreal. But recently there have been exciting artistic developments on the Internet. New websites featuring gallery tours, excellent computer art reproductions and links to artists are appearing daily. However, this new approach is unlikely to signal the end of art as everyone knows it. Museums will not permanently shut down, and real art will not go out of style. When photography was invented around 160 years ago, some visionaries insisted it was the end of painting. Events proved them wrong. Similarly, the World Wide Web is unlikely to bring 'real' art to its knees. Most of the websites emphasise that they do not replace art, but rather enhance the enjoyment and understanding of it. Frequent 'surfers' of the Internet will be aware of art-related websites. For the uninitiated, the Internet can be a threatening place, and it may seem easier to pick up a book than to fight a path through the Web. But many of the really interesting websites have material not available in books.

For anyone linked to the Net simply wanting to find out what art resources are available, the easiest approach is a keyword search tailored to a specific medium, artist or museum. However, keyword searches often produce lists of possibilities too copious to follow at one sitting. Does one want to visit the Louvre or the Metropolitan Museum of Art or the Smithsonian? It is all possible in a virtual sense. At http://www.metmuseum.org/ the surfer can take a tour of the Metropolitan's collection, with spectacular computer reproductions of its famous artworks. The Web browser can also update him- or herself on the museum's plans, sign up for membership and shop in the museum store. Most museums with rich endowments have sites like this on the Internet.

Websites are advantageous to museums for a number of reasons. First, they are useful advertisements. Viewers can see almost any of the works in the museum's collection, even if the works are in storage. Also, more sensitive objects like drawings and textiles are often hidden away for years for preservation purposes. Through the Internet, visitors can see them without risking damage to the works. Not all websites correspond to actual museums. There are a number of Internet services that maintain only virtual collections of art. Time Warner's 'ArtsLink', for example, contains an 'Artist in Residence Program', a site that provides selected artists with exhibition space on the Internet. There, the viewer can see artworks and read the artists' biographies and statements. A printmaker, Francis Crisafio, has a home at this site, contactable through Time Warner's home page at http://pathfinder.com/twep.

There is virtually no end to the on-line resources available on the arts. Only a fraction has been mentioned here. To avoid the intimidation of the sheer abundance available one should start slowly, perhaps by taking a leisurely tour of a favourite museum or completing a keyword search of a popular artist. Then an enquirer can roam around art on the Internet. Another approach is to use CD-ROMs of art directories, featuring artworks and artist information. These services are updated regularly and are available on subscription.

18.8.3 Advisers

In recent years the established London firms have experienced competition in specialised fields from provincial dealers and auctioneers. To keep abreast of news and intelligence on alternative investments today requires a complex web of contacts and information sources. In this context, it is important to locate one or two specialists among the dealers and in the auction houses, who can be relied upon to assist the dedicated and wealthy enthusiast.

To a degree, investors seeking advice on specific pieces can depend upon appropriate museums or art galleries, where curators are normally willing to give an opinion on the quality and authenticity of a work. Curators are also likely to be familiar with the market and with dealers who specialise in a sector, although they are usually reluctant to recommend a particular firm. Curators do not normally give opinions on market values.

Leading auctioneers are more willing to express a view on the price a piece might command if offered for sale, and specialist dealers also have opinions on the value of an item in their field of expertise. Such valuations are important if the investor plans to make a sale; they will help him or her to arrive at a sensible reserve figure.

Dealers and auctioneers are generally keen to offer help, in particular to itemise and appraise assets. At the outset, their valuers advise on insurance cover and the security of precious items, pending sale. They then prepare a full inventory of the chattels, identify those which are of value, and make arrangements for the disposal of the residue. Any gifts or bequests will also be valued for inheritance tax purposes, and recommendations will be made on the handling of any works which have national or historic interest. The experienced auctioneer or dealer also advises on how best to sell items for disposal.

Given that the market for art and antiques has become international, it is important to choose with care a time and a place when specialist collectors are likely to be at a sale. The valuer will charge a fee, and the auctioneer or dealer will be thinking of a commission on sales.

Before confirming instructions for an inventory and appraisal, it is advisable to discuss the eventual consignment contract for an estate, which may include important pieces. Some firms in the art and antiques market refund part of their valuation fee if any of the items they appraise are sold through their auction or dealing rooms within a year or so of the appraisal. There may also be opportunities to negotiate lower commission rates on sales. Within the trade, auctioneers and dealers are often prepared to cut their selling commission from 10 to 6 per cent, with scope for reductions in standard rates when the estate is large and valuable.

A further point to bear in mind when negotiating commission rates is the possibility that an item at auction may not reach the reserve price suggested by the valuer. In some instances, the auctioneer may be willing to make no charge to the vendor, or levy a reduced commission, if a lot fails to sell at the reserve which the firm has recommended. Auctioneering and dealing in art and antiques are highly competitive businesses and many firms are willing to consider special terms when an estate contains worthwhile items.

For buyers who use the services of dealers there are often the attractions of 'buy-back' offers. These usually have many caveats attached to them. Dealers may undertake to buy back at a price geared to their valuation at the time of the repurchase; or they may only be willing to commit to buy back at the original price paid by the investor. Almost no dealer is willing to purchase at the original price plus inflation since the date of the transaction; if any do make such an offer, the buyer might well consider it prudent to make such checks as he or she can that the firm is likely to be still in business at a future date when a resale might be contemplated.

The professionals who advise on alternative investment can also help when it comes to reviewing a portfolio. To offer sound advice, they should be in close touch with the market trends, so that they can recommend optimum times for the disposal of pieces which have reached a current peak in value. Equally, they should be well placed to identify pieces coming onto the market which would make a collection more representative and therefore more valuable in terms of the chosen theme.

18.8.4 Commercial galleries

New collectors may not necessarily understand the more recondite points of aesthetics when collecting art, but they are often keenly aware of the financial implications. They are also conscious of the social benefits of being a part of the collecting 'realm', and the prestige of owning museum-calibre works. In this context, one American dealer offers a useful checklist for those entering the art market for the first time:

- Use the expertise of dealer-owned galleries which represent the artists they exhibit. Ask for biographical materials on the artists. Seek advice from individuals in the art industry.
- Let the dealer know which artists are of interest, so that he or she can send details of exhibits and new works. Probably, the collector will then have early and first-hand information, and a place on a special list for private previews.
- Galleries do not always display all their inventory. It is worth asking to see the 'back rooms', and putting questions to knowledgeable staff.
- Dealers seldom give a 'collector's discount' to occasional buyers. However, in major centres, it is not uncommon for dealers to offer perhaps 10 per cent discounts. Most works are marked up substantially to allow for price negotiations.
- Whenever possible, view a one-person exhibition to see several pieces of an artist's work. This should reveal the depth of an artist's vision and quality of his or her work.
- Take time and advice when making a purchase. Most dealers will hold an item for 24 hours or longer, or offer first refusal.

Commercial galleries normally put on three kinds of exhibition: one-person shows, theme shows, and exhibitions from stock. Galleries tend to show from stock at the quieter times of year. From the standpoint of the exhibitor, the one-person or theme show is the best way to achieve the preferred effect: they allow the gallery to suggest the cultural significance of an artist's work. A few galleries can put on first-class exhibitions from stock because their backroom holdings are strong. They are able to mount exhibitions of acknowledged masters, or works that can reasonably be described as 'museum quality'.

Some of the galleries and dealers are promoting art and antiques as alternative investments because they believe there are worthwhile opportunities to create and manage portfolios. They contend that the investor can specialise in one or two categories of investment but still spread the risks by diversifying the selection within these categories. In addition, they suggest that it is possible to use market intelligence and research to time purchases and sales to maximum advantage and to build up interest among potential bidders.

18.9 MAINTENANCE

18.9.1 Safeguarding the investment

A prime consideration in the mind of the investor who buys works of art or antiques ought to be security. Robbery, accidental damage, fires, floods and other catastrophes remove many works from the market each year, usually forever. Computer systems are now being introduced to log details of missing works such as the Art Loss Register and the New York-based International Foundation for Art Research. Their aim is to deter robbers by making details of stolen works quickly available to auction houses, dealers and collectors.

The immediate conclusion is that a purchase should be held safely. For economic reasons, a bank vault may be considered when items are not continuously on display. Even when the items are bulky, the cost of hiring vault space will be far lower than the valuation and subsequent insurance premiums for pieces held in less secure places. In other cases, the collector's pieces should be insured against all risks, and the items in a collection should be revalued at five-yearly intervals, or more frequently, to ensure that the insurance cover is adequate.

18.9.2 Insurance

Brokers and insurers who carry out these valuations with the aid of expert dealers or auctioneers will at the same time advise on cost-effective outlays on security measures, ie expenditures which will bring more than just compensating savings in premiums. The valuers will, in particular cases, photograph pieces in a collection to provide a record in case of damage or loss.

A point to note is that the London head offices of insurers charge travelling and subsistence expenses, so it is usually sensible to contact the nearest regional office. However, if the item is a specialised work of art, a prudent course is to consult fine art brokers. They may advise that it is unnecessary to insure well-known items against theft, giving substantial savings in premiums, on the grounds that any subsequent disposal by the thief in the art market would lead to his or her capture. For example, in 1994, the gang that removed, in 50 seconds, one of Norway's greatest icons, Edvard Munch's painting *The Scream*, from Oslo's National Gallery were captured when they tried to sell it to members of the Metropolitan Police's art and antiques unit, who masqueraded as unscrupulous dealers.

By and large, burglars usually avoid stealing such items unless they already have a buyer or can realise the value of precious metal or

The last few years have illustrated that if art is a market it is a highly knowledge-intensive one. To make informed judgements, the prospective investor needs expertise or access to it. A connoisseur's intuition, and familiarity with the *patois* of the auction house and dealer, are as vital as knowing what is on sale, where, and when. As the French art expert Jacques Attali pointed out, 'nobody is in a position to establish laws for a market as unstable and as irrational as this. Each work of art is singular; each motivation is unique; each transaction has its own requirements.' In the coming years, he says, buyers will become increasingly discriminating. The supply of recognised works of art will diminish, but new types will appear on the market. The art market will become 'a kind of avant-garde of museums, a selection process of what may subsequently become part of our collective memory'. It is in keeping with his remarks to add the footnote 'investments can damage one's financial health'.

18.10.3 Internet trading

On-line auctions over the Internet are attracting growing interest. The Interactive Collector (http://www.icollector.com) runs Internet auctions that allow collectors to bid on-line for works of art, antiques and collectables from auction houses and antique dealers. Its auction service enables a collector to search catalogues for lots for sale at auction houses across the globe and submit a pre-bid by e-mail. A reference channel covers archived catalogues enabling enquirers to search lots from auctions that have taken place at auction houses across the globe since 1994. An art price guide enables free searching of auction records of art sales from 800 auction houses in 40 countries from 1987 to 1998. A supporting publications service reviews art and antiques industry magazines and newspapers, and a directory enables the on-line enthusiast to view the stocks of 60 dealers or more and the holdings of 60 galleries or more from around the world. A 'live chat' facility enables participants to discuss matters of interest or to put questions to industry experts.

The main auction houses are also entering this on-line marketplace. Christie's, Sotheby's and Bonhams have set up websites, and are augmenting telephone bidding with television and Internet links. They expect electronic bidding to develop a substantial share of the market, described by Antony Thorncroft in the *Financial Times* as 'a stolid, press-button, secretive, couch-potato market'.

The French department store tycoon, François Pinault, has acquired Christie's, opening up prospects in the Paris market, which the European Commission is working to free from protectionism. The transfer of ownership also increases resources to invest in new forms of trading.

Meanwhile, Sotheby's has signed up a network of 2,800 dealers to use its Internet services, and entered into an agreement with Amazon, the Internet firm. Amazon is investing about £28m in Sotheby's; they will jointly run a website offering rare coins, books, sports memorabilia, stamps, jewellery, toys, dolls and post-1945 collectables. Amazon has software to run live Internet auctions, which will allow its customers to bid for works of art sold by Sotheby's using the Web. Buyers will often be able to watch as auction sales unfold, and send in bids by e-mail.

Internet services are rapidly gaining momentum. Nonetheless, some experts are sceptical about the prospects. Neil Stuart, secretary of the Society of London Art Dealers, reportedly holds the view that guarantees of provenance, condition, title and payment will assume even greater importance with the introduction of real-time, on-line bidding: 'We are dealing with high-quality, high-priced items. The guarantees will have to be very clear and will involve the auction houses taking even greater responsibility than they have now.'

SOURCES OF FURTHER INFORMATION

See end of Chapter 19.

19

COLLECTABLES

JOHN MYERS AND HELEN BAIRD

Solon Consultants

19.1 INTRODUCTION

19.1.1 Collectables as alternative investments

Investors in alternatives look for safe havens for their hard-earned funds, but with an eye to pecuniary and gratifying rewards. Collectables, many now believe, can satisfy these objectives. The number of desirable items is small, and values increase whenever the demand for them exceeds the supply. Prices can be low enough for individuals of modest means to choose a field in which they can build collections and become experts. Generally, the marketplace is driven by these individuals, not by investors. Collectables also offer scope for applying ingenuity and imagination; an existing set can be thematic, but then divided and combined with new examples to form a fresh topic.

As David Hirsch pointed out in *Stamps* (4 June 1994) the key to success in investment in collectables is insight. He believes that, if a collector develops the confidence to spot a good buy and act on his or her judgment, he or she should fare well. Hirsch advises against following the flock and merely buying what is popular today. A good investment should hold its value regardless of how it is viewed at one moment. Buyers should heed advice from experts, but act only if the case is convincing. The major worry for investors *qua* investors is the trap of viewing holdings as a hobby. A collector 'needs' items to complete a collection. In contrast, an investor 'needs' nothing, and acquires items solely on their merits as investments. If the purchases perform double duty as enjoyable collection items, that is a plus, and a reward in kind if the financial element fails.

In the high reaches of the market for collectables are items that qualify as 'conditionally exempt' pieces. The Inland Revenue publishes a register of these items on the Internet at http://www.cto.eds.co.uk. A free leaflet, IR 156, *Our heritage – your right to see tax exempt works of art* is also available from the Revenue and on the Internet at http://www.inlandrevenue.gov.uk/forms_pubs/index.htm. The Revenue hopes that the World

Wide Web site and the leaflet will improve public awareness of the register and rights to see the objects it lists. On the register are 22,000 entries that cover many items of national, scientific, historic or artistic interest. Among them are works by Leonardo da Vinci, Dürer, Titian, Rubens, Van Dyck, Manet, Monet and Picasso. British artists represented include Hogarth, Reynolds, Gainsborough, Stubbs, Constable, Turner, Moore and Hepworth. Other entries refer to Chippendale and Adam furniture, silver by de Lamerie, and clocks by Tompion.

Figure 19.1   Items of tax exempt works of art on public view

Source: Inland Revenue: items accepted giving tax exemption.

Objects like books, manuscripts and scientific collections, of national, scientific, historic or artistic interest, can qualify for conditional exemption from inheritance tax. To gain tax exemption, the owner has to agree to keep the object in the UK, preserve it and allow reasonable public access to it. The Revenue will charge inheritance tax when the owner persistently fails to keep the agreement.

To comply with the new public access provisions introduced in 1998, an owner must now allow viewing of the object without appointment and make it available on request to public collections on short-term loans. To qualify for exemption, the item must now be of pre-eminent heritage quality. Objects feature on the Revenue's computerised register, updated monthly. The register describes each item, and gives the name and address of a contact point. It also gives the broad location, usually the county, in which each object is normally available for viewing.

Payments for exempt collectables are the high part of a framework for

Figure 19.2 Cost of living extremely well

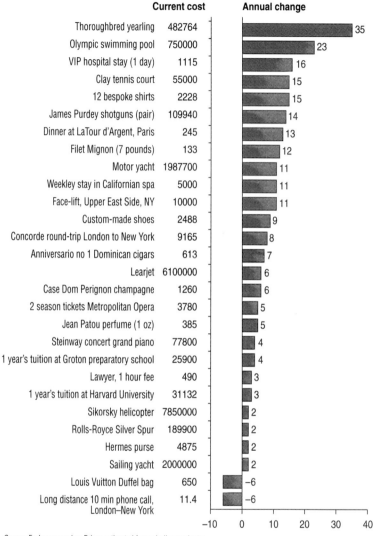

	Current cost	Annual change
Thoroughbred yearling	482764	35
Olympic swimming pool	750000	23
VIP hospital stay (1 day)	1115	16
Clay tennis court	55000	15
12 bespoke shirts	2228	15
James Purdey shotguns (pair)	109940	14
Dinner at LaTour d'Argent, Paris	245	13
Filet Mignon (7 pounds)	133	12
Motor yacht	1987700	11
Weekley stay in Californian spa	5000	11
Face-lift, Upper East Side, NY	10000	11
Custom-made shoes	2488	9
Concorde round-trip London to New York	9165	8
Anniversario no 1 Dominican cigars	613	7
Learjet	6100000	6
Case Dom Perignon champagne	1260	6
2 season tickets Metropolitan Opera	3780	5
Jean Patou perfume (1 oz)	385	5
Steinway concert grand piano	77800	4
1 year's tuition at Groton preparatory school	25900	4
Lawyer, 1 hour fee	490	3
1 year's tuition at Harvard University	31132	3
Sikorsky helicopter	7850000	2
Rolls-Royce Silver Spur	189900	2
Hermes purse	4875	2
Sailing yacht	2000000	2
Louis Vuitton Duffel bag	650	−6
Long distance 10 min phone call, London–New York	11.4	−6

Source: Forbes magazine. Prices estimated from similar products

prices in alternative investment markets. Another strut in this framework is the movement in the costs of living extremely well. *Forbes* magazine each year measures shifts in these costs, illustrated in Figure 19.2. Wealthy individuals with spare cash found that the cost of living extremely well rose by 6 per cent in 1998, three times the rate of inflation. The Forbes index has recorded the cost of living extremely well since 1976. Between then and now, the prices of luxury goods have increased on average by approximately 480 per cent.

Investors in such pieces can be collectors, but a collector should not think of him- or herself as an investor. It may happen that way, but the outcome is accidental. Nevertheless, some advisers feel that a significant portion of almost any client's savings for the future should be put into collectables. The argument is that these investments can complement other forms of investment, but not replace them.

The fashionable urge to collect seems to extend to an ever-widening range of items with memorable, nostalgic, or merely eccentric qualities: classic postage stamps, old cars, numismatic coins, Oriental carpets, banknotes, scrips, medals, vintage wines and spirits, musical instruments, playing cards, *objets de vertu*, bric-à-brac, scientific instruments, and printed items, to name but a few. The enthusiasm for collecting such items has stimulated the formation of many bodies, including the Ephemera Society, which was set up in 1975; its growing membership, running into thousands worldwide, come from as far afield as Alaska and Latvia. The Society benefits from a lively range of activities and publications, and holds a number of fairs each year.

Despite this evidence of enthusiasm, many investors remain wary of collectables. Caution is, of course, sensible when considering esoteric investment media, but several factors have recently made them more appealing. Players on the stock markets are constantly aware that equities can be volatile. Every threat of a crash can send shareholders scurrying to spread their risks. In times of uncertainty, collectables can offer a hedge against escalating prices; for many people with catholic tastes, they warrant a small proportion of an investment portfolio.

Collectables in common with art, antiques and valuables can attract wealthy buyers from all quarters of the world. They use their cash or borrowing power to diversify their assets, in the manner of new Renaissance merchant princes. Quality of life is one aim. Another is to spread risks. The buyer of an alternative investment compares an opportunity to buy a collectable with the uncertainties involved with stocks and shares. When equity markets teeter on the edge of a fall, an art deco ornament or a rare musical instrument might hold its value, or perhaps record spectacular gains.

A case in point was one example of a Venini glass vase which, in the 1960s, sold through a department store at £20. Six years ago, at a Geneva sale, a bidder paid 176,000 Swiss francs (£70,000) for it. The glass had original qualities. Valuers thought the transaction anomalous; successive appraisals of other Veninis offered for sale were too low. The appraisers recalled that a bidder who had paid £500 for a Venini glass vase in 1978 could not find a buyer to take it off his hands at a higher price. He chose not to sell at the time, and was wise to wait: at an auction in 1984, the same vase fetched £25,000, twelve times the auctioneer's estimate, equal to an annual compound rate of return of 92 per cent. In 1987, another Venini vase attracted a successful bid of £52,000. The pre-sale estimate was less than half that amount. A more recent case is a Lucie Rie pot originally priced 20 years ago at about £500 and now valued at £5,000, a more typical annual compound interest rate of 12 per cent.

Another example came to light at a Geneva sale of 20th century collectibles. French and Japanese dealers bid strongly for a delicately carved glass table lamp. A Japanese dealer paid 1.58m Swiss francs (£675,000) for a lamp, originally produced commercially by Daum and Louis Majorelle less than a hundred years ago. The seller had bought it about 20 years ago for less than £5,000, a compound annual rate of appreciation of 30 per cent.

Art deco pottery and ceramics are becoming increasingly fashionable, valuable and affordable for many collectors. Early 20th century design was inspired by the new technology of the period and was radically different from the typically ornate Victorian style. Demand for Clarice Cliff's work has intensified. She was perhaps the signature ceramics artist of the time, and much of her work is rare and unusual. Her work is broadly classified into landscapes, geometrics and florals, with variations of design within each category. Some collectors are interested in one set of designs, others in particular items.

In 1983, a Clarice Cliff crocus sugar shifter would cost £40; by 1995 it had risen to £150, representing compound interest of 11.6 per cent; today it trades at £300, a compound interest of 26 per cent. At the lower end of the scale, an Autumn Crocus side plate costs only £30, because it is the designer's most common pattern. However, a teaset for two in the same pattern sells for £1,500, when two or three years ago it could have been acquired for £750, producing compound interest of 32 per cent. Many smaller Cliff pieces have increased in value by 300 per cent over the past three years. In February 1999, Christie's sold the Daniel Brodie Hogg collection for £201,699, more than double the pre-sale estimate. The most sought after Cliff pieces are her Age of Jazz figures. In March 1997, Sotheby's set a record by selling one of the figures for £12,650. The following November, Christie's sold a table centrepiece modelled as a drummer and oboe player for £13,800, double the estimate.

Even reproductions of Cliff's work are collectors' items. The Wedgwood Company own Cliff's designs, and six years ago reproduced two of the Age of Jazz figures, which then sold for £175 each. Now the pair can fetch up to £5,000. This year is the 100th anniversary of Cliff's birth, and Wedgwood celebrated with an exhibition of her work at the Visitor Centre in Stoke-on-Trent. Many of the pieces on display are from private collections and have never before been publicly viewed. This exhibition, along with Leonard Griffin's recent biography of Cliff and a major sale of her work in mid-July, have helped to sustain continued interest in her work.

These collectables are undoubtedly exceptional examples and illustrations from markets in a wide range of media may give a more balanced picture.

19.2 DEVELOPMENTS IN COLLECTABLES' MARKETS

19.2.1 Vintage stock certificates

Collectables with obvious appeal for the alternative investor are vintage stock and bond certificates. Enthusiasts and scripophilists will pay five- or six-figure prices for a rare item, as happened in 1991 when a collector laid out £70,000 for a Bank of England promise-to-pay bill, issued to back loans to the Russian Imperial government. The certificates' value lies in their historic and aesthetic appeal, and in the signatures which appear on them, not their face value. Thus, an 1856 share certificate of the American Express Company, signed by Mr Wells and Mr Fargo and with a nominal value of $500, recently sold for £500.

Certificates from the early industrial revolution are in high demand, particularly those of shipping and railways enterprises. Some collectors hold on to pre-Communist bonds from former Eastern bloc countries in the faint hope that the certificates will eventually be redeemable. They recall 1991 when the then Soviet government paid 54 per cent of the face value of devalued bonds. However, the compensation settlement had a time limit. Dealers then received a mass of certificates from owners who missed out, causing a slump in the market for Russian bonds. The trade in vintage bonds from other pre-revolutionary regimes should be an area for speculation. Occasionally, collectors seek modern shares, if they are of a particularly interesting or unusual design. Printed shares are increasingly rare because of electronic trading.

19.2.2 Rare books

Collectors have amassed books since the times of monasteries and chain libraries. From the Renaissance to the French Revolution, books were popular among readers for what was in them, not for their packaging. By the time Jane Austen's novels were entertaining England, the *nouveau riche* had begun to see books as artefacts that conferred a desired status on their owners. Some buyers began to value the printing and binding more than the content.

The market for collectable books is segmented. One sector is the 'first edition market' – a specialised field. With some works, a book's value may depend as much on the presence and quality of its dust jacket, as on its other qualities. Scott Fitzgerald's *The Great Gatsby*, for example, had a typographical error on the jacket of its first edition, but only on a few copies. With this error, a copy might fetch £3,000; without, a mere £30–£250. In July 1998 Christie's auctioned a first edition of Chaucer's *Canterbury Tales*. Published by William Caxton in 1477 at Westminster Abbey, it is one of only a dozen left in existence. Experts expected that the book would fetch £700,000, but it sold for £4.6m ($7.5m), a record for a printed book sold at auction. Another rare book sold at the same auction fetched £771,000 – double the estimate. The *Recuyell of the Historyes of Troye* was the first book printed in English by William Caxton at Bruges in 1474. A first edition of Kenneth Grahame's *The Wind in the Willows* sold at Sotheby's in November 1998 for £44,000, three times the auctioneer's estimate. Only three copies of the book have been auctioned in the past 25 years. Other currently sought-after first editions are those by Samuel Becket, Sir Arthur Conan Doyle, George Orwell and Graham Greene.

A 16th century prayer book sold in July 1999 for £8.5m, the most expensive illuminated manuscript ever sold at auction. The work is considered a masterpiece in Renaissance manuscript illumination and is thought to have been published in Belgium in 1505. The Conaro Missale, part of the same collection, sold for £2.86m, setting a record for an Italian manuscript. The recent controversial sale of some of Jewry's most valuable and important books and manuscripts, which included one of the two copies of the Ashkenazi prayer book, fetched a total of $3.8m in New York this year.

Inscriptions in books by the author or a famous owner, or a relative, or an influential friend of the author, can also enhance values. In 1991, Sotheby's sold a copy of the late Graham Greene's rare first novel, inscribed with a message to his wife, for £13,200. The price was double the previous record for this volume, set a year earlier. In other cases, inscriptions have increased values by even more. For example, one of four presentation copies of the first edition of *Tess of the D'Urbervilles*, inscribed by Hardy to Alfred Austin, is valued at £45,000.

In collectable books, as in other areas of the market, it has been works of the finest quality that have withstood downturns. As noted in Chapter 18, the art market declined in the 1990s. Standard reference works or *catalogues raisonnés*, on the other hand, have experienced little change in demand. These volumes have more than aesthetic appeal, they are in constant demand from art dealers, and can fetch four figure sums at auction. The attractions of rare works have also weathered the recession. A successful book sale at Phillips raised more than £500,000, with the main attraction being manuscripts by David Garrick, the 18th century theatre luminary. Another generally successful area has been antiquarian textbooks. Christie's sale of the Loughlin collection, of mainly 16th to 18th century works on mathematics and other sciences, did well for the vendors. The highest price, £280,000, was for a finely bound copy of du Bellay's 1549 *Instructions sur le Fait de la Guerre.*

The advice to collectors of rare books could easily be restated in many other fields of alternative investment: 'Buy the best of what you like. Rely on your own instinct, but work closely with knowledgeable dealers. Develop a collector's eye by looking at a large number of books. Browse in specialist shops. Search out auctions, fairs and even car boot sales.'

One of the latest trends in collectables is the 'hypermoderns', ie books which have been published within the last two decades, or even the last two months. For example, an original copy of John Grisham's *A Time to Kill*, his first mystery, will fetch more than £500 today: of the 5,000 printed, the publisher destroyed 3,000. Meanwhile, in American hypermodern-speak, the author 'garped', a term used to describe a breakthrough book derived from *The World According to Garp*, the book that made John Irving's mark with critics, readers and collectors.

19.2.3 Numismatic coins

Rare coins have recently been treated almost on a par with the holding of shares and bonds, and some brokers, particularly in the US, have optimistically recommended them to their clients as a substitute for stock market investments. This is particularly so in the lead up to the year 2000 as some brokers in the US capitalise on investors' concern about the financial implications of the Millennium bug. Numismatic coins are recommended for their portability, privacy and performance. The market for coins has been greatly enhanced by a wider acceptance of a grading system. Agreed methods of categorising coins according to their quality help to structure the market for collectors and investors. With this help, enthusiasm for coin collecting is reviving somewhat. 'The interest in coin collecting has never been as great since the late 1960s and early 1970s,' according to Mark Rasmussen of Spink, the coin dealers.

The heyday for coin collecting began pre-decimalisation. In the early 1970s, collectors examined coins they received in change to fill date-runs of denominations, which were soon to vanish. The practice became almost a national obsession and, in a decade of high inflation, it became fashionable to put money into collectables, as savings in financial instruments did not pay a real return. The sharpest rise in prices for British historical coins occurred in 1973–1974 when the stock market was collapsing. Although the coin market paused for breath in the first few months of 1974, it then started on a steady upward climb. Five years later prices for English coins had increased on average by 150 per cent. 'Casual' date collectors became numismatists, and began to build sets of historical coins, only to drop out of the market in the late 1970s and early 1980s. Rare coins of quality had become too costly to collect.

Before the end of the 1970s, two interrelated factors had caused prices to rise further. Investment buying in the US gained impetus when buyers could invest in collectables, via retirement plans, and receive tax relief on their purchases. The Reagan administration cut out this concession in 1980. Booming bullion prices also helped. In January 1980, silver peaked at $52.50 and gold at $835 an ounce. Many coin dealers trade in bullion as an adjunct to their main businesses. The profits they were generating from this activity were substantial. As coin markets were buoyant, they channelled money into their coin dealing operations. The price for US historical coins rose sharply until, inevitably, the bubble burst; in the first half of 1983 prices fell. Those who had purchased coins as an investment were disillusioned, while many genuine numismatists had long since stopped adding to their collections. The specimens they sought were financially out of reach.

The most important determinant of value is a coin's condition, within a range from mint state to poor. An uncirculated 1887 silver crown bearing the Jubilee portrait of Queen Victoria would sell for around £60. However, a coin with signs of wear on its raised surfaces would be worth only £10 and, in a poor state, £2–3, putting in question the value of coins as an investment. When hopes of monetary gain outweigh the interest in coins for their own sake, problems are likely. But for the connoisseur, coins can tell enchanting stories and reveal a nation's history.

One enthusiast reminds audiences that coin collecting is the oldest collecting hobby, traceable to the invention of coinage in the 7th century BC. He comments: 'Most people are drawn into the hobby for a variety of reasons. Pride of ownership and desire to expand or complete a collection once it is started are sufficient for many collectors. For others, the profit motive is a prime incentive for collecting coins. The rest may enjoy their coin collections because they have an interest in art, history, geography or science.'

Financial traders would like coins to become respectable as the basis for investment funds they are setting up. A typical institutional scheme requires an initial tranche of capital, say £50m, to fund dealing in collectable coins. The essence of the plan is to acquire enough coins which will appreciate over a short enough period to generate worthwhile returns for the investor. A key question is how to calculate 'worthwhile'. Some coins will gain in value, others will lose. Whatever happens, the fund has to meet its overheads, which include storage, insurance and regular valuation of the portfolio. One analyst estimates that sets of coins need to appreciate, on average, by more than 40 per cent to give investors a 20 per cent return. In the case of one such fund, the promoter's filings with the US Securities and Exchange Commission contend that similar types of investment vehicle have previously achieved returns of this figure or more, a claim that the prudent will treat with caution.

The promise of success is echoed in fresh price records at coin auctions. An early record price paid for a coin was for an American doubloon, dating from 1793, sold in 1979 for £250,000. Rare coins have a long-established market among collectables, but with rarity goes a high premium. A 1982 gold coin issued when British Forces relieved the Falkland Islands sold for £2,200. It was in mint condition and one of only 25 struck. At a Christie's sale, an 1890 halfpenny sold for £1,380. This ordinary halfpenny is stamped with the word 'Oakley' on its obverse and is deformed by a bullet shot. Apparently, Annie Oakley, the great American sharpshooter, used to shoot coins thrown up in the air. These were then stamped with 'Oakley' and given to the audience. In June 1999, a new record for the highest price paid at auction was set for a gold coin when a very rare $20 Double Eagle gold piece, commissioned by Theodore Roosevelt in 1906, fetched over $1m. A record price for a silver coin was set in 1987 when an 1804 Eliasberg Specimen silver dollar was sold for $1,815,000. When another 1804 silver dollar is auctioned later in 1999, it is expected to realise in excess of this record and could be the first US coin to sell for more than $2m. The coin, from the Childs collection, was once presented to the Sultan of Muscat by an agent of President Andrew Jackson, and is believed to be in excellent condition.

Over the last two years the rare coin market has also attracted a share of the controversy caused by aggressive selling practices. Some dealers in the US have sought to encourage investment in coins by establishing certifiable grades of quality. Associated with this is the practice of 'slabbing'. Coins graded by one of two grading houses, the Numismatic Guarantee Corporation or the Professional Coin Grading Service, are sealed in plastic 'slabs'. However, the market in slabbed coins is not strong and, in at least one case, the Federal Trade Commission repeatedly indicted the PCGS for making false claims about the objectivity and consistency of the grading.

Certification of quality, if performed consistently, could show pointers to how the market in collectables might develop. Through the American Numismatic Exchange some coin dealers have sought to create their own version of the modern stock market. The Exchange enables dealers to trade over a computer network. Investors can buy and sell as they wish through the network, without having to wait for auctions and sales. Critics argue that coins are not equities, they are 'limited edition objects', so values tend to be set on a subjective basis. Nor, they argue, are coins liquid assets. Investors should allow for delays in finding a buyer who will pay the 'right price' for a rare coin. On occasion such delays can be prolonged.

Advocates of the coin bourse claim that it will help to stabilise a volatile market. In theory, if such a bourse develops, it might trade in coin futures and coin options. Equally, it could conceivably extend its remit into other alternative investments. Syndicates and funds could be set up to trade in certificates backed by physical assets, hedged on the Exchange. An information infrastructure could follow, as the traders and investors seek better intelligence on the fundamentals and technical performance of particular assets. These ideas may seem far-fetched but informal coffee-house trading years ago in the City led to the spectacular and speculative commodity, insurance and shipping markets of today. At the time, they seemed unlikely propositions.

19.2.4 Phonecards, trading cards and cards carrying artwork

Printing cards at times seems like printing money. They are 'instant collectables', fancy goods mass-produced for a few pence and retailed to collectors at premium prices. Nowadays, the main market comprises plastic telephone cards; glossy trading cards; and even cards that reproduce works by international artists. They satisfy the basic requirements of mass-market collectables: they are small, easily stored, easily displayed, issued in sets, and durable. Instead of limiting editions by setting a closing date for orders (really just a feeble justification for using the term 'limited edition'), card-makers strictly control editions by stated numbers, deliberately creating scarcity and boosting resale value among collectors.

Private publishers of telephone cards have developed an instinct for alluring commemoratives, and are becoming as responsive as the brasher trading cards to the latest comic book, film and television crazes. BT itself has promoted issues, featuring Pink Floyd for example. Worldwide, telephone cards are one of today's fastest-growing collectables, with more than four million collectors worldwide. Japan's 1.3 million telephone-card collectors now outnumber its stamp collectors. The Germans, with one million collectors, are Europe's keenest. France has 800,000 and Britain 75,000, of whom two-thirds are reckoned to be children.

In Britain, prices for limited-edition telephone cards are rising steadily. A set of two privately printed BT cards of Garfield, the strip cartoon cat, is worth perhaps £150 if unused. When the 20-unit cards were issued only three years ago, mainly to collectors, each of the 482 sets (a few of the 500 made were scrunched in manufacture) carried the premium price of £11. They would buy £2 worth of telephone time. Most of the balance is profit for the publisher. So it is hardly surprising that the original anorak-imaged collector-publishers have been joined by promoters of commercial products, charities, sports teams, schools and regiments, all keen to coin their own currency.

Promoters account for more than a score of new cards a month through BT and its suppliers. BT charges £2.16 each for a minimum permitted order of 1,000 five-unit promotional cards. One of Britain's most valuable privately published telephone cards was a money-spinner for members of the Messerschmitt Owners' Club. The club published 500 five-unit BT cards (50p worth of telephone time) at £11 each. Club members bought 300, collectors the rest. Three years later, they are worth more than £150 each unused. One of Britain's biggest telephone card dealers, Kevin Baker of Spalding, Lincolnshire, published 1,000 sets of three five-unit cards for a Romanian relief charity. They cost him £7 a set to produce and sold for £15, of which a proportion went to the charity. These cards are now worth £35–40 a set. Kevin Baker comments: 'Because of the rapid development of the hobby, there isn't a single card in existence that is not going to go up in value. As more card phones are installed, production runs are bound to increase, but there will always be a finite number of early editions as small as 500.'

Major companies have less interest in limited editions than in mass advertising. Kellogg's issued three million 20-unit advertising cards two years ago. So far, they are not worth much more than their £2 face value. However, 5,000 Coca-Cola advertising cards in a 1993 Icelandic edition, micro-chipped for exclusive use on trawlers, are worth about £30 a card to collectors. A card with a captive clientele is BT's own 20-unit 'For use in HM prisons only'. Outside the prisons, they sell for a mere 25p in used condition. Unused ones could be worth £8–10. BT's 20-unit *Beano SOS* cards, to enable children to call home, cost £2 each new. America now has sets of erotic telephone cards, with antique Oriental paintings of copulation or other sensational images. Non-erotic BT took an airbrush to its 1993 artwork for Sloggi bras: the £10 card is worth £15 today.

World-record prices for cards, both ancient and modern, have little to do with the smartness of publishers and everything to do with the age-old combination of rarity pursued by wealth. One of BT's trio of first-ever commemoratives, a 900-strong edition of 100-units for the 1987 Muirfield golf championship, is worth £2,500 unused. A Japanese collector paid £28,000 for a said-to-be-unique used and battered Taiwanese definitive (standard-issue) telephone card of 1983. The most expensive card, bought for $451,000 (£250,000) at Sotheby's New York five years ago, is an American card for Piedmont cigarettes of 1910, showing the baseball ace Honus Wagner. A non-smoker, Wagner forced Piedmont to withdraw the card, but this one survives.

19.2.5 Collectable cars

Classic cars have a more limited appeal, but demand remains cosmopolitan. A Porsche 959, a Ferrari F40 super car, or the Bugatti Royale may attract bidders from almost any part of the developed world. Their chances of gain have been considerable, as are the prospects of losing money. Within a single year, 1988–89, the price of some Aston Martin DB6s rose tenfold, from £10,000 to £100,000. Prices then fell, however, and eventually moderated to a lower 'realistic' level, at least 50 per cent below the peak figure.

The frenetic activity in the market sprang, to some extent, from wealthy, middle-aged British enthusiasts, nostalgic for their youth. Foreign buyers also stoked the price furnace. These buyers have not disappeared, although ageing Rolls-Royces and Bentleys still glut the market. In 1997, Sotheby's sold a pre-war Silver Ghost for £249,575. Fondness for the highly charged sports car is undiminished, and old Ferraris, Jaguars, Maseratis and MGs continue to command high, but not hyped, prices. The record for any car sold at auction is £6.4m for a Ferrari GTO sold by Sotheby's in Monaco. Old family cars with character – the Volkswagen Beetle, the Morris Minor, the Mini-Cooper – are attracting a new generation of enthusiasts willing to pay around £5,000 for a model in good condition. Winston Churchill's Austin 10 sold for £66,400.

Buyers of classic cars are encouraged to drive them. Unless it is a museum-quality machine, an ageing vehicle could benefit by being fired up to full running temperature on a regular basis. If it costs too much to insure the car for the road, the buyer is advised to change the oil periodically, to jack up the car to protect the suspension, and take other steps, such as dehumidifying the garage, to prevent deterioration. According to claimed, if not acclaimed, experts, the trick is to pick the few vehicles, or to find a whole new class of collectables, that will increase in value. Some specialists believe that old vehicles can offer investment possibilities. Collector cars can be worth five- and six-figure sums. However, experts say that few vehicles are legitimate investments that can offer a hedge against inflation. A noted collector of Rolls-Royce *Silver Ghosts* cautions against even this faith in rarity. He insists that it is no more than an enthusiast's market.

The cost and relative scarcity of even the finest US models may put them out of reach for many car collectors. Generally, values have stayed high but almost flat for several years. North American magazines such as *Cars and Parts* and *Old Cars Price Guide* can help collectors follow the changes in US collectable vehicle prices. *Cars and Parts* publishes graphs every month that show the change in collector car prices, while *Old Cars Price Guide* gives prices for thousands of vehicles, based on condition. Advisers recommend that prospective buyers check the *Guide* before making a purchase, and call in an appraiser. Such moves might help a buyer to avoid over-paying.

19.2.6 Collectable wines and spirits

Some French wines, for example fine vintages of Latour, have recorded an average annual appreciation of around 20 per cent in the past 15 years. At the recent sale of the late Robert Maxwell's collection, a dozen bottles of Latour 1982 sold for £800. Bidders paid around 20 per cent above the estimate, perhaps attracted by the notoriety of the cellar's previous owner.

Some specialists believe that wines can be restored. In one cited instance, a buyer paid £425 for a double magnum of 1865 Château Lafite in 1967. Fourteen years later the buyer took the bottles back to the chateau to have them topped up and new corks inserted. Sold at auction after a few months, lots reached £12,000 per double magnum – that is, a growth in value of 25 per cent a year compound. The same connoisseur believed its value in the late 1990s would be about £48,500. In February 1998, a magnum of Château Lafite 1870 fetched £9,875 at auction in Los Angeles. It originated from Glamis Castle, the Queen Mother's family home, but had been sold to a US buyer in 1971.

A sale of whisky brought bids totalling £98,000. The lots included 14 bottles from the *SS Politician*, the ship which inspired the film classic 'Whisky Galore'. The bottles sold for £11,000.

19.2.7 Photographs

Photographic images do not come into existence primarily for exhibition and sale. Some, however, are so imaginative that they transcend the original purpose and make a photographer 'collectable'. There are two main kinds of collectable image: the 'vintage print' made for a magazine or other user at the time it was taken, sometimes marked up for publication; and modern prints made for sale or exhibition from the old negative, created with special care on fine paper and under the supervision of the photographer, who then signs the print. The Photographers Gallery in London specialises in the latter. In the gallery's early days, when it sold prints from its current exhibition displayed on a trestle table, a buyer could pick up a Bill Brandt for £50. Brandt made his name as a magazine photographer in Britain in the 1930s, famously recorded the devastation of London during the Blitz, and continued to capture historic images up to his death in 1983. Today the Gallery Print Room sells Brandt prints for between £900 and £3,000.

The cost of fine photographs no doubt discourages buyers; after all, a vandal can snip the same image from books or magazines for a fraction of the cost. Nevertheless, top quality prints signed by photographers of the *Picture Post* era, for which prices start around £200, are among the Photographers Gallery's best sellers. Nostalgia is definitely 'in' with collectors. The amazing images of New York taken in 1926, just before the Wall Street crash, by Fred Zimmermann, the Hollywood film director (of 'High Noon', 'Oklahoma!'), sell for £325–600. To attract new collectors the gallery has now introduced a plan for collectors called 'Prime Prints'. With every contemporary show it asks the photographer to prepare an edition of 50 prints of one successful image, which are marketed at £150 each. There is also a 'Patron Print Scheme' by which anyone signing up as a patron (which costs £200 and includes discounts, free publications and invitations to social events) receives one print free from a set of six specially made for the gallery by leading photographers.

Early in the next century beautifully printed photographs are likely to become a more prominent form of art exhibit, and the number of collectors in Britain will probably grow steadily. At present the UK has fallen behind North America. For example, New York has 35 galleries that are members of the Association of International Photography Art Dealers. Los Angeles and San Francisco have 23 between them, while other states combined have 32. British members of the Photography Art Dealers' Association number only five: the Photographers' Gallery, Zelda Cheatle, Hamilton's, Robert Herschkowitz, and Ken and Jenny Jacobson. All sell more abroad than they do in the home market but maybe that will change, as the collecting of photographs gains in popularity.

19.2.8 Sporting memorabilia

The aficionados of sports like cricket and golf often combine enthusiasm with a nostalgia that brings them to auctions of memorabilia. One of Bradman's personally autographed bats, or an Open Championship winner's accumulation of medals, can draw bids from connoisseurs who see the purchase as a momento of past experience, a conversation piece, and an investment. Other items such as a volume of Wisden or Joseph B Hacker's library of golf books may attract collectors, who are eager to complete or improve a set. As a consequence, the major auction houses – eg Christie's, Sotheby's, Phillips and Bonhams – often hold specialist auctions of historical sports lots. Their initiative is matched by a range of dealers, especially in the US, who will authenticate autographs of personalities and they will grade and value sports collectibles.

From the buyer's viewpoint, a drawback of cricket, for the present at least, is that its geographical coverage is not universal; the Americans are wont to say that they do not understand it. However, the Cricket World Cup and similar televised events are broadening cricket's appeal. That being the case, memorabilia bought now might well go up in value as the cosmopolitan origins of enthusiasts widen. Meanwhile, golf collectibles tend to be worth more on average, and buyers across the world may pay worthwhile amounts for sporting memorabilia of international interest.

Hunting, fishing and shooting also have a broad attraction to buyers across the world. For example, shotguns in good condition by a well-known maker can be bought at auction for a few hundred pounds, and a first-class Purdey may fetch many thousands. Decoys for hunters and fishing rods can sell for tens of hundreds, while many enthusiasts will pay far larger sums for sporting trophies, works of art and other memorabilia. For example, a bidder paid £19,000 at a Sotheby's auction of a signed and numbered John Skeaping bronze of the 1971 Derby winner Mill Reef, the item had been put on sale by the jockey Lester Piggot, who received 50 per cent more than the auctioneer's estimate for the collectibles he put on sale in November 1998.

Sporting art, and particularly angling art, has risen substantially in price in a few decades. Angling paintings show locations with an intrinsic rural charm – paintings of wild places, rivers, mountains and lakes are attractive, and often lively. Angling, however, suffers in comparison with hunting and shooting, where artists can more readily capture dramatic moments. Fine angling artists whose works today command good prices include John Raphael Smith, Francis Barlow, Henry Alken, James Pollard, Ansdell, Hardie, Barrington-Browne, Rolfe, Rowlandson, and Walker. Some famous artists also executed many paintings with an angling theme, most notably Turner, but also Zoffany, Dadd and Cruikshank.

19.2.9 Stamps

For as long as stamps have served as a government license to post a letter, philately has been popular, with many devotees touring events around the country and abroad in a hunt for a rare find. Granted, Rowland Hill might not have imagined that, almost 160 years after he had the Penny Black printed, so many stamps would be issued worldwide each year. Earlier collectors had no difficulty in forming a basic international collection that reflected their interests. They have in common a curiosity about a time, place or a person that motivated them to collect stamps with a historical ambience. In these early days, philatelists collected stamps of particular periods or countries, of postal types such as airmails, postage dues and express mail stamps. With many early stamps now expensive, and a burgeoning of new issues from virtually every country, few can expect to create a comprehensive set. Collectors are therefore turning to thematic collecting – collecting stamps that illustrate a given topic, independent of time and place.

Thematic philately attracts many new collectors, who find it absorbing if not cost-free. A true thematic collection, whatever the topic, combines frustration, elation and impatience that, like a puzzle, come together to illustrate a novel theme, and form a whole. Thematic collectors must think imaginatively, and show how apparently disparate items interrelate.

Thematics has not long enjoyed respectability among serious philatelists. Of course, collectors have a choice of many themes: the beasts of the fields, the birds of the air, the fish of the sea, the people who possess fame and fortune, endorsed by provenance. One US collector has a franked Martin Luther King stamp, issued in 1979, and has added to its value by persuading all the members of the King family to autograph the envelope. He also owns a stamp that shows the legendary jazz musician and composer Duke Ellington, first issued by the US Postal Service in 1986. Alongside the stamp are the autographs of all the members of his band.

Many countries no longer conform to the tradition that only people who are dead should appear on stamps. Post offices around the world have been eager to put stamps on sale featuring stars while they are still in fashion. Britain and the United States, however, retain the convention. British stamps depict no living person other than a member of the Royal Family. In parallel, the literature of topical or thematic stamp collecting is growing. The American Topical Association produces *Topical Time*. In Britain, Stanley Gibbons has several popular thematic catalogues. The British Thematic Association has the *Themescene* magazine and supports the yearly Thematica exhibition in London. Attendees include dedicated philatelists willing to research every item and write up the design of each stamp for an exhibition or a competition.

Collectors often have many reference books, catalogues and magazines. They collect not only stamps, but envelopes, covers, post and meter marks, and stamped postcards. In the Internet era, stamp collecting is changing its image. Philatelists are moving into the computer age, and, to promote interest among young technocrats, the Royal Mail, alongside the British Philatelic Trust and the Philatelic Traders Society, has launched the Rowland Hill Awards.

The millennium will provide a spur to the producers and the connoisseurs of fine stamps. Plans are in hand for a large international exhibition in Britain in 2000. Also, new technology can help. CompuServe provides free demonstration disks and literature at the Stampex exhibitions. New technology such as e-mail may not threaten stamp collecting unduly, as letters and e-mail seem to run in tandem, at least for now. Also, many collectors buy new issues anyway. The Internet and CD-Roms will actually help, according to Lindsay Towle of the Philatelic Traders Society.

Philatelic Software is a London-based firm which has launched StampMaster GB, costing £74.95 plus postage and packaging. It is a CD-Rom database of all stamps issued by the British Post Office from 1840 to the end of 1996, with pictures and the official National Postal Museum history and a description of each stamp. 'The system will help users to build catalogues of their own collections and work out which stamps they need to complete them,' says Angela Enoch for the firm. 'It can also be used with thematic collecting, as can our systems for dinosaur and ball sport stamp collections.'

Admittedly, stamps are not a standard item in portfolios. Like many alternative investments, they are risky and illiquid, and prudent advisers counsel stamp collectors never to rely on realising hard cash from their hobby. Yet returns can be worthwhile. In November 1996, for example, a rare stamp, an 1855 Yellow Treskilling from Sweden, sold for £1½m, a record price. That was £0.6m more than when it was on sale in 1990. An 1854 Bermuda cover – a stamp still on an envelope – sold in April 1998 for £230,000. In 1980, it went for £144,000. The world's most valuable set of stamps, 48 2p stamps from 1840, are currently on sale from Spink & Son in London for £2.75m. Thought to have belonged to the 5th Duke of Beccleuch, the stamps were apparently put in a drawer, where they lay undiscovered until 1945. Printed on 6 May 1840, the same day as the Penny Black, these blue stamps are rarer as they were only printed for one year. A single 2p blue stamp is worth around £5,000, but this set is worth more as the gum is still on them, and they are in a set.

'Globally, the stamp market is faring well, especially in Hong Kong and China,' said Robert Scott of Sotheby's stamp department. One reason for the steady rise is the influx of an aging generation into the pastime; another is the relative strength of the US and UK economies. 'A great many 40- to 50-year-olds who had stamp albums as kids are revisiting the hobby,' said Michael Laurence, the editor and publisher of *Linn's Stamp News*. According to the US Postal Service, about 20 million Americans keep stamps in sets. About 550,000 are serious collectors, who carefully research stamps and slowly build collections.

Price upswings now depend on collectors, in marked contrast with an artificial boom between 1979 and 1981, when investors fleeing high inflation pressed into the market. Prices soared. Then, in 1981, a new US federal law barred the inclusion of stamps and other tangible collectables in tax-deferred retirement accounts; they were thought too risky and difficult to value. With that change and a lessening of inflation, the market collapsed. By the end of 1991, the prices of American stamps had gone down by 56 per cent from their 1981 highs. Nonetheless, like gold, coins and other collectables, stamps can move out of phase with stocks and other financial instruments, and might help to hedge against losses in those assets.

Some people also like stamps for other reasons, including their porta-bility. A person can put them in a pocket 'and cross a border with no questions asked,' one dealer emphasised. Profits from stamps can also be difficult for the authorities to detect. Scott of Sotheby's stated that stamp collectors can enjoy 'a great deal of anonymity', a claim once made by tax haven banks. However, the required knowledge is a hurdle in the way of profit. The philatelist has to learn about individual stamps and postal history. Details such as the cancellation or the stamp gum can affect values. High markups are a factor too. 'People in the stock market pay a commission of 2 or 3 per cent on a buy-sell transaction,' one dealer revealed. 'In stamps, it can be 100 per cent or more. That's expensive, and it means you've got to hold for many years to cover the dealer charges.' Add the dangers of fraud and the illiquidity of this small mar-ket, and even a risk-prone investor might hesitate.

Defects can sharply increase a stamp's price. That Swedish Treskilling, for instance, was worth £1½m because it was wrongly printed in yellow, not the issue's standard green. In 1996, 32 cent Richard Nixon stamps had the former president's name printed upside down and his picture off-centre. One sold at Christie's for £10,000. The odds against such a find are long, but the collector will find the endeavour instructive.

19.2.10 Dolls and other pieces

For some collectors on the acquisitive trail, doll collecting is now pre-ferred to coin and stamp collecting and, for a few, it has become an addiction. Some dealers have customers who come every week to see what new dolls are on the market. At times, visits take on an air of secrecy. 'They may not all have spouses who condone their purchases,' one dealer admitted. Another mentioned a customer who hides doll pur-chases under her bed until she can ease them into her collection. A few buy only with cash, so the sale will not show up on a credit card state-ment. Occasionally, a collector moves to a larger house simply to accommodate his or her collection.

Dolls bought as an investment are most valuable when in pristine condi-tion (except for antique dolls), especially the ones that are known as NRFB dolls. Translated, that means 'Never Removed From Box'. These dolls are meant to be kept in storage or posed prettily on a shelf, accord-ing to collectors. Their value has multiplied. Rare, mint-condition Barbies, for example, which sold for perhaps $2 when they were intro-duced in 1959, are valued at more than $1,000 today, according to American dealers.

Barbie, who made her debut in 1958, is rapidly approaching middle age, but she still queens collectables. The rarest Barbie dolls can attract bids in excess of £1,000, and advisors believe that, provided an item is 'rare and of its time', it could be in demand among new century collectors; this belief is widespread. In 1996, a bidder paid £34,500 at auction for a puppet from the *Thunderbirds* science fiction series, the original Lady Penelope. In 1997, Levi Strauss paid $25,000 for an 1886 pair of jeans originally priced at $1.25, equivalent to annual compound interest of 10 per cent. Dealers and auction houses that promote this trade suggest that ephemeral products and packages could become collectors' 'desirables' in the 21st century, if they survive in pristine condition. They might be worth more with the makers' signatures added.

Men sometimes enter this world of dolls because their wives are doll collectors. Don Jensen, associate editor of *Doll News*, the quarterly magazine of the United Federation of Doll Clubs, is a doll collector and active member of the Lake County Doll Club of Illinois. He and his wife, Arlene, spread their collection through every room in their home, and display many dolls in a floor-to-ceiling glassed cabinet that stretches over one full wall in one room of their house. Jensen was drawn into the hobby partly because of his wife's interest in dolls, and partly because of their shared pleasure in antiques.

In the US, any black doll is collectable, and nun dolls, which have appeal for certain collectors, come in at least 50 different habits. According to the experts, genuine antique dolls are better left in the condition in which they were discovered.

Collecting teddy bears has been increasing since the 1970s, so much so that the term 'arctophily' has been coined to describe the activity. The market-leading German Steiff bears, particularly those pre-1914 in good condition and with loveable expressions on their faces, routinely fetch £1,000. A rare red Steiff bear called an Alfonzo from 1908 sold for £12,100 in 1989. Its provenance added to its value: it had once belonged to Xenia Goergievna, a second cousin of Tsar Nicholas II. Even rarer Steiffs, the blue and black bears, have sold for as much as £49,500 and £22,000 respectively. Another expensive bear is Aloysius, the teddy bear from the TV series *Brideshead Revisited*, for which a collector paid £50,000. Collectors are also interested in specially designed modern bears and limited editions, which are cheaper than the pre-war variety.

Apart from dolls and bears, the real gamblers bought the first national lottery scratch cards, but keep them in mint condition and unscratched. In 50 years, they could be worth more to the buyer, or his or her heirs, than the prize plus interest or so the collectors hope. Meanwhile museum and gallery shops trade in distinctive designs that could become tomorrow's collectables; and hoarders seize on children's books and toys, which they keep away from their offspring. The chances are that products handled by the young will not retain the untouched look and value of a fresh heirloom.

Some connoisseurs are confident that the largest demand in the next millennium will be for early technology and craft products. They are buying primitive calculators, contemporary packaging, and fine musical instruments. One antique dealer in Cumbria is assembling a collection of high quality Steinway grand pianos, built from 1930 onwards and, in at least one instance, rebuilt by an expert. The dealer is confident that the pianos will appreciate hugely in value over the years. American dealers agree, and 1920s Steinway grand pianos, selling for around $35,000, are in demand as an investment in the US. The most recent Phillips auction of grand and vertical pianos drew buyers from across the Atlantic; as a result, prices were significantly higher than in similar auctions earlier in 1999. At the top of the market, pianos can range up to $180,000 for the most expensive – a Fazioli from Italy or a Bösendorfer from Austria.

Another expert predicts that 'an early Sinclair adding machine costing £10 in 1996 could be worth £250 by 2006'. If he proves right, the rise in price would equal a 38 per cent annual compound interest. Yet one more forecast is that a well-designed 1970s hi-fi stack, which a collector might pay £15 for at a car boot sale today, could sell for £1,500 by 2018, that is a 26 per cent a year compound rise in value.

19.2.11 Silver

Antique silver has risen in value. For example, in America a pair of delicate 18th century wine coasters, estimated to be worth about $125,000 (£80,000) recently went to a private collector who paid $299,500 (£190,000). Fine old Tiffany silver is also popular. In the years after the American Civil War, Tiffany used mixed metals consisting of silver, copper and brass in crafting Japanesque pitchers, vases and trays, bizarrely engraved and encrusted with an assortment of reptiles, crustaceans and insect life. Europeans bought them at the 1876 Paris Exposition, and they have become valuable. A fine piece, bought for $1,000 (£625) or less in the 1970s, might easily be worth $25,000 (£15,500) today, up 17 per cent compound a year.

A set of 17th century Apostle spoons can now fetch up to £150,000, having gained 50 per cent in the past two or three years. In July 1997, a single silver-gilt Apostle spoon sold at Christie's for only £368. However, a St Bartholomew spoon, with a mark by Robert Tyte of Salisbury, went for £1,955, four times its estimate. Three years ago the value of a Henry VIII St Matthias spoon was estimated at between £5,000–8,000. Subsequently, a renowned spoon expert identified the 'S' marking on the spoon as having once belonged to William Simpson, the famous 16th century spoon manufacturer; the item fetched a remarkable £18,700. The silver spoon market comprises discerning collectors; advocates claim that these objects represent an astute, longer-term investment.

At the top end of the silver market, there is a select group of multi-millionaires who bid hundreds of thousands for the famous silver collections and pieces from the 18th century, made, for example, by de Lamerie and Thomas Germain.

Items selling for under £1,000 are at the opposite end of the market. These can be found at Christie's fortnightly and at Phillips' and Bonhams' monthly auctions. At these auctions, investors may find other silver collectibles including tea caddies and spoons, nutmeg graters and Vesta boxes. Prices of these silver collectibles have risen faster than the average. Three years ago an 1830 eagle's wing tea caddy might have been worth between £1,200 and £1,500; last year one was sold at auction for £3,800, and a set of ten George III meat platters fetched £10,500, almost twice their estimate. A George II tea caddy spoon may have cost £300 ten years ago, and £500 five years ago; now it could fetch around £700. Interest in modern silver is also increasing, particularly by early 20th century silversmiths such as Oscar Ramsden or Alwyn Carr.

Generally, British silver is prized by collectors because of its hallmark, which provides a guarantee of quality. Lorraine Turner, a silver expert from Phillips, describes the 600-year-old hallmark as the oldest kind of consumer protection for collectors. One hallmark to look out for is Paul Storr from the late 18th and early 19th centuries. Paul de Lamerie is another fine silversmith, whose pieces have fetched up to $1m. The current record price for silver sold at auction is $10.3m for a rococo tureen made by Thomas Germain. Two major silver collectors recently auctioned their collections. Last year, the Ortiz-Patino family's silver collection by Paul de Lamerie was sold in New York. Another ornate silver soup tureen, made by Juste Aurèle Meissonnier for Louis XV, was auctioned in London. The Meissonier tureen, sold by Sotheby's on behalf of Baron Heinrich Thyssen-Bornemiza, fetched $5,722,500. This set a record as the second highest price ever paid for a piece of silver at auction.

When buying silver, the auctioneers Bonhams advise examining the object for signs of repair, splits, damage or wear. This should be done under a bright light with a good magnifying glass.

Buying silver also creates a need to keep it in good order. Cleaning sterling silver may be as simple as washing it with a little soap and water, then drying and buffing it with a suitable soft cloth of 100 per cent linen or cotton. Professionals recommend buffing and polishing silver in the same direction as the manufacturer did. A magnifying glass will reveal the factory's polishing marks. Alternatively, a good way is to apply a jeweller's paste, liquid or foam. 'The art,' say antiques dealers, 'is using a polish that's relatively mild and a cloth that's very soft.' Cloths impregnated with polish can also be effective; but it is wise to avoid using the same cloth on more than one piece, because the residue from one will rub off on the next.

Stored silver is best kept behind glass, in flannel bags or in bags made from soft cloth, or wrapped in acid-free paper in acid-free, paper-lined drawers. It is imprudent to let rubber bands or plastic bags touch the collection: silver can be irrevocably harmed by contact with petroleum-based products, and plastic bags can do double damage by trapping moisture. Do not allow silver to come into contact with salt, vinegar or the juices of citrus fruits, which can be equally harmful. Expert dealers advocate bringing silver pieces out of storage from time to time – 'The more you use it, the less frequently you have to polish it'. Finally, silver is also popular with burglars, so keep insurance valuations up to date, photograph the pieces, and record any distinguishing marks, or inscriptions.

19.2.12 Memorabilia

Memorabilia, items once belonging to famous individuals, particularly those with a royal connection, continue to gain popularity among collectors. The auction of 40,000 items from the former home of the Duke and Duchess of Windsor saw 60 to 90 lots snapped up per hour. As prices soared to 40 or 50 times their estimate, excitement mounted, and even a sign reading 'Drive Carefully and Beware of Small Dogs' fetched $4,500. After just 70 seconds of frenzied bidding, the desk at which Edward VIII signed the Instruments of Abdication fetched $415,500. An anonymous buyer paid $2.3m for a portrait of the king when he was the Prince of Wales, painted by Sir Alfred Munning – almost three times the $800,000 estimate. A portrait of the Duchess of Windsor was acquired by the National Portrait Gallery for $107,000.

The Christie's auction of 79 dresses belonging to Diana, the Princess of Wales, raised £2m in June 1997. One dress alone fetched £136,000, a record for an item of clothing. Following her death, a collector who had paid $25,300 for a dress hoped to resell it for $250,000, anticipating a 1,000 per cent profit. Even the catalogue from the original dress sale became a collector's item; Lord Archer auctioned it for charity at £50,000 in October 1997. Another famous dress, the Union Jack one worn by former Spice Girl Gerri Haliwell, was bought for £41,320 last September.

Last year, the US sale of items once belonging to President John F Kennedy raised $9m. Among the items were Kennedy's notes and dictation from the Cuban missile crisis, and notes made during the fatal trip to Dallas in 1963. A scrap of paper with a line from his inauguration speech written on it sold for $40,250 – almost ten times the estimate. Kennedy's signing pens went for $48,875, his comb for $1,265, and his sunglasses for $46,000. Gold buttons from his blazer sold for $18,400, along with a photograph of him in the blazer. Despite these high prices, the sale failed to realise the record $34.5m sale from the estate of Jacqueline Onassis three years ago.

Sotheby's recently sold a five-page letter written by Marilyn Monroe when she was 16 years old for $43,120 (£25,540). The notebook in which Paul McCartney wrote the lyrics for the song *Hey Jude* sold for £111,500. At the same charity, John Lennon's corduroy jacket fetched £9,200. At another sale in New York, Lennon's spectacles sold for $25,875. At the same sale, a jacket once belonging to Elvis Presley fetched almost $60,000, four times the estimate. The charity sale of a selection of Eric Clapton's guitars in June 1999 this year fetched a total of £3,230,000.

19.2.13 Recent record prices for collectables

Collectables have generally continued to escape the worst effects of recession in the arts and antiques market. However, prices did fall. Now, optimists and dealers see signs of recovery in trade buying, and highlight successful sales at which collectors paid spectacular prices. On the other hand, rare books and coins, toys, glassware, ceramics, jewellery, basketball cards and Hollywood posters have continued to sustain interest, and rarity almost always attracts bidders. Opulence, intricacy, ethnicity, authenticity, and the bizarre excite buyers.

Perfume bottles, biscuit tins, slot machines, costumes, dolls and typewriters are items cherished as never before. In the US, memorabilia related to slavery and American historical manuscripts are fast becoming favourites. Eighteenth century costumes are particularly sought after by both private buyers and museums. A hoard of Old Masterprints found inside a trunk that was home to a family of mice sold at Sotheby's for £587,952, more than twice their estimate.

Unusual early film posters have become highly collectable. In April 1999, a rare 1933 vintage *King Kong* poster sold for $244,500, the second highest price ever paid for a movie poster. The record was set in 1997 when a poster for *The Mummy* sold for $453,500. Other movie memorabilia including Oscars are increasingly sought after. In June 1999 Michael Jackson paid $1,542,500 for David O Selznick's Oscar for Best Picture of 1939 for *Gone With the Wind* – five times the pre-sale estimate.

Collectibles from the James Bond films also remain popular. The steel-rimmed bowler hat worn by the villain Oddjob in *Goldfinger* sold for

£61,750 in London last year at a sale devoted to Bond memorabilia. The sale realised two and a half times the estimate. Among other items selling well over their estimate was a Rolex Oyster Perpetual watch worn by Roger Moore in *Live and Let Die*; it went for £21,850. The popularity of the film *Titanic* prompted enthusiasm for memorabilia from the fated liner. In November 1998, two menus from the ship were sold for £19,550. The sale realised £62,200, four times the estimate. Other items included a fragment from a lifebelt which fetched £6,900, and a letter written by a passenger on board before the ship sailed for £9,775. The following month a sale realised $68,500 for a set of eight telegrams written by Bruce Ismay, managing director of the *Titanic*, detailing the disaster.

Packaging has become another popular collectable item, and recent sales have featured biscuit tins produced between the 1870s and the 1930s, the great period of the British tin. Shaped tins tend to be the most prized, with the best examples fetching prices in the hundreds of pounds at auction. One, in the shape of an ocean liner, recently went for £880.

19.3 FUTURE DEVELOPMENTS

19.3.1 Potential areas for investment

The recovery of market values in London has revived interest at the top end of the classic car market. Quality vintage Edwardian and veteran cars may now increase in value from a reduced level. Apart from cars, collectors are currently displaying an interest in areas as diverse as 20th century ceramics and photographic equipment. An early Leica, with its mystique of Henri Cartier-Bresson, André Kertesz and 1920s Paris, may be worth thousands in mint condition. Even the humble box camera, the 'ordinary' Kodak which sold for £3 in the 1890s, can fetch £1,200 today.

Other collectables that *Antiques Roadshow* valuers favour include dolls, toys and the memorabilia of the early cinema. Dolls could fetch from £10 to £150,000; a 1939 German triplate Mickey Mouse £12,000; and film posters may reach between £35 and £70,000. Collectors today tend to go for modern 'antiques', from teddy bears to comics and rock memorabilia. There is a diversity of choice to suit the taste and pocket of eclectic collectors. It might still be possible for a single enthusiast to create a sustainable market for a new collectable by writing the first textbook along the lines of Michael Bennett-Levy's work on pre-war television and Graham Turner's *Fishing Tackle: A Collector's Guide*, published seven years ago.

19.3.2 **Far East markets**

Economic changes in the 1980s and 1990s have created a cadre of afflu-ent Chinese businessmen, who are becoming active at the art and antique auctions within the country and beyond its boundaries. China's growing class of rich entrepreneurs are spending their wealth on Mandarin and Cantonese antiques that they can appreciate, and believe will appreciate. Until these buyers came into the market, Chinese porcelain and jade, fine paintings and calligraphy had ebbed to the west and Japan in the backs of lorries, and the holds, boots and cases of smugglers, traders and collec-tors. The tide is beginning to turn. Local antique shops in Beijing and Shanghai are finding customers among the well-off, and Chinese auction houses are focusing on the local market. Sotheby's and Christie's now have representatives in Shanghai, and Christie's also has a representative in Beijing. However, neither conducts auctions in China, and there are no plans to do so in the near future. Both auction houses hold frequent auc-tions in Hong Kong.

At a Beijing auction in 1996, a Chinese businessman paid 18m yuan (£1¼m) for a seven centuries old painting from the Northern Song dynasty. However, regulations and uncertainties currently constrain both traders in antiques and currency transfers, leaving the upper reaches of demand in the hands of Taiwanese and Hong Kong dealers and collec-tors. Also, it is difficult to assess how much of China's artistic heritage of calligraphy, paintings, porcelain, and jade stays hidden in private hands. Exporting these pieces would mean bypassing laws, with severe penalties, that are strict in the letter if not in their application. Pieces more than 200 years old are marked in auction catalogues to show that the regulations forbid their export. In reality, many that the local auc-tioneers do sell soon feature in auctions or dealers' showrooms outside China. This smuggling problem might lessen as local buyers increase their wealth, confidence and cosmopolitan ventures, and the authorities make the regulations workable.

Partly in anticipation of such events, a stronger demand has emerged since 1996 for Chinese artefacts at American and European auctions. Another factor is the size of the Chinese population outside China. The UK has about 170,000 Chinese, with 50,000 in London. The majority are from Hong Kong, with significant numbers from Malaysia, Vietnam and Korea. Research published in April 1997 by the Policy Studies Institute shows that the Chinese are more likely than any other group in Britain, including whites, to earn £500 or more a week.

For some collectors, furniture from China allows them 'to savour life of a cultivated genre'. Records reveal early Chinese furniture from the Shang Dynasty (16th to 11th centuries BC), which archaeologists found in tombs. Designs evolved from dynasty to dynasty, until styles matured in the era of Elizabeth I, when the furniture makers started to use central Asian hardwoods and shippers began to trade with China. These designs featured unique paints and woods. Experts esteem furniture made of 'light huanghuali or yellow rosewood, and the dark zitan or purple sandalwood'. In the 1930s, Sinophiles began to collect elegant pieces of Bauhaus simplicity, which remained in short supply until the 1980s, when the bootleggers increased their trade in Chinese art and antiques. Auction houses and dealers now expect to see a growing demand for these items in China and across the world.

For Asian collectors of Chinese antiques, Yuan, Ming and Qing ceramics and high-quality Imperial works of art attract the most interest. Jadeite jewellery (antique or new) is another important category. Early excavated porcelain produced by early dynasties has recently emerged from China, helping to change western perceptions of the scope and allure of Chinese pottery. Sotheby's devoted a week in June to Asian art sales, including many Chinese pieces, reflecting collectors' growing interest. Meanwhile, the Chinese are generally convinced that, by the end of the decade, coin and stamp prices will have rocketed worldwide. Until the reent crisis, industrialisation has been tilting the world's economic axis towards South East Asia. British auctioneers predict that in China alone the demand for coins (and telephone cards) will rise 20-fold in two to three decades. In the past five years, the number of Chinese stamp collectors has soared to 30 million. In the next century, investors seeking new collectables may ask: how much will they pay in Asia? The region could influence future taste and force up prices.

The Chinese also want impressive coins from any source and banknotes that were printed for China-based Dutch, German or French banks, or by the American Banknote Company or Britain's Bradbury Wilkinson, supplier of Hong Kong's paper money. Dealers predict that Chinese spending preferences will soon extend to stamps and coins of all nations. Sotheby's expects China's most expensive stamp, an 1897 overprint, to double in value before the end of the century. It was worth only £1,200 20 years ago. In May 1995, Sotheby's sold one for £143,965 at its first Hong Kong stamp sale. Even in the west, where the stamp market has been at a low ebb since 1979, a stamp can fetch more than £1m (see **19.2.9**). Sotheby's expects that South East Asian stamp prices will continue to rise.

Western dealers hoping to become rich in Asia are having to come to terms with the region's varying taste and uncertain wealth. The Chinese are reluctant to buy excavated antiquities, second-hand jewellery or sapphires (blue is the colour of death). Unlike the Chinese, the Taiwanese buy western-style art, much of it, paradoxically, originating in Taiwan.

Japanese taste is the most westernised. Some western speculators have
been dabbling in collectables abandoned by the Japanese, when recession
struck their economy, in the hope that they will return to the same markets. These include posters by Toulouse-Lautrec, Paris school paintings,
and Galle and Daum glass. Turkish money troubles have also aided speculators. Nonetheless, prices of the brilliant red, green and blue Iznik tiles
of the 16th and 17th centuries, coveted by Turks, are only slowly moving up from bargain levels.

19.4 PURCHASING COLLECTABLES

19.4.1 Strategies

Collectors need to plan their strategies. Do they intend to become expert
collectors, who gain thrill and pleasure out of the artefacts in which they
invest? Or will they instead rely upon dealers to feed their hobbies or their
alternative investment portfolios? If the latter, the player should realise
that he or she will miss out on the social ambience of the market, which
helps to keep real enthusiasts 'in the know'. According to a 1996 survey
by the US Collectables and Platemakers Guild, 'New collectors are the
key trend that industry executives see shaping the future', a trend that
applies equally in Europe. 'Eighty percent of the industry executives sur-
veyed expect company sales to increase in the short term, and new
collectors coming into the marketplace are identified as the primary reason for growth.'

However, the survey also refers to the 'greying' of many 'antiques
categories and some collectables categories, as one of the major 1990s
developments in the antiques marketplace'. Greying implies that most
collectors in a category are over 55 years old. To sustain demand, the
market will need enough entrants to replace collectors who lose interest
or die. Equally, if collectors follow trends, and shift their loyalty to the
next hot collecting craze, a category may decline in appeal, and pieces
fall in value. At one time, collectors and dealers saw these shifts as part
of the natural interplay of demand and supply in the antiques market.
They did not worry, because they believed that everything would eventually recycle. Generally, it did – until the 1990s. The present decade has
demonstrated that the recycling of a collecting category is no longer certain, at any rate in the medium term.

Nevertheless, the Guild's researchers conclude that 'Collecting is a
hobby of the "empty-nesting" years, after children have left home. With
the large "baby-boomer" generation reaching 50 years old, the total

number of collectors could grow rapidly by 2000.' According to the specialists, the targeting of baby boomers by the 'desirables' industry depends largely on the appeal of nostalgia for the 1960s and later pieces, but means a decline in enthusiasm for 1940s and 1950s material, especially in the toy sector. Affordability is one reason. Many objects from this era are expensive. Another reason is the collecting base itself. New collectors in their fifties are seeking material from the late 1960s and 1970s.

In America, the 'collectables industry' expects to see extra sales through expanded and new channels of distribution. 'Electronic retailing, including TV shopping and computer shopping on the Internet's World Wide Web, and expansion of direct response marketing, including categories, direct mail, newsletters and other direct communications with collectors, are opening opportunities to build collections.'

19.4.2 Collectable cars

Intending purchasers of unique cars should probably buy through a private transaction after placing a classified advertisement in a car magazine, or from an enthusiast who belongs to a specialist automobile club. Some experts believe that, when buying cars, auctions can be particularly hazardous. They argue that there may be scant opportunity to inspect the car, and they suggest collectors need an iron will to avoid being swept away by the bidding excitement.

Another simple recommendation is not to buy a car unseen. It is advice that applies equally to many other alternative investments. Skilled salesmen may give 'cast-iron assurances that there will never be another chance to buy a car like this again, and urge the investor to send money without delay'. As a cynical commentator put it: 'Two weeks later, you will find a pile of rust on your doorstep. The chance of a lifetime comes along about once a week.'

Experts suggest that collectors should use a price guide and employ an appraiser to assess an intended purchase. 'Let someone else take a bath on the restoration,' says one cynic in the field. Buyers are also advised to check motoring publications on the availability of parts for an out-of-production vehicle. Costs in addition to the purchase price include, of course, storage, insurance and maintenance.

19.4.3 Predicting future collectables

Predicting what will become the collectables of the future is a tricky exercise. Paradoxically, in the design world, the objects that fetch the highest prices at auction are not necessarily the best. The real 'timeless classics' of the 20th century are never going to fetch high prices because they have remained in production. Design failures, on the other hand, especially fiascos such as the Sinclair C5, already have rarity and curiosity value. Should environmental awareness finally put paid to the combustion engine in the coming decades, collectors may even accord 'alternative' designs pioneer status. Perhaps society's very existence 50 years hence will depend on a revolution in energy consumption, in which case disposable goods such as throwaway cameras would become 'obsolete relics of a crazy age'.

More advances in software, information, literature, music, and so on, will be coming into everyone's lives via a computer screen. So how, for example, will digital recording on CD-ROM affect collecting vinyl LPs and EPs? In an article in *Record Collector*, Ted Owen is adamant that vinyl is worth collecting, particularly rare or superior quality pressings: 'If you see a rare record, buy it, whatever the price, it's still an investment and is bound to go up in value.' Condition is always critical, so storage can be a problem, even with smaller items such as records. 'The general tendency is for people to want to get rid of something just when it's at its lowest value,' says the owner of Vinyl Exchange, a second-hand record shop in Manchester. 'We see it time and time again; troops of doleful, slightly balding men in their mid-30s whose wives have made them clear out their punk collection due to lack of space. If they could only hang on until there's no longer a glut, they might have something that other people want.'

19.5 TAXATION

19.5.1 Tax planning

If purchases can be justified as requirements of a business, for instance acquisitions of furniture or wall decorations for an office, investors paying high rates of tax may obtain benefits. They may be able to offset the costs of acquisitions as legitimate business expenses, but with a corresponding liability on disposal. If, on the other hand, the chattels which form the alternative investment portfolio are not regarded as income-producing, the owners will not normally be able to secure income tax relief in relation to insurance premiums or maintenance expenses.

19.5.2 VAT

A uniform system of VAT calculation for trade in second-hand goods took effect in the EU on 1 January 1995, when the Seventh VAT Directive came into force. Commercial transactions now carry VAT levied on the profit margin, while transactions between individuals are not liable to VAT. Second-hand cars are now defined as those more than six months old or with more than 6000 km mileage (twice the previous lower limits). The UK is allowed a transitional period up to 30 June 1999 at the latest, during which VAT will be charged at the reduced rate of 2.5 per cent. The changes to VAT explained in **18.7.5** also apply to collectors' items and second-hand goods. Collectors' items are defined as:

- Postage or revenue stamps, postmarks, first day covers, pre-stamped stationery and the like, franked, or if unfranked not being of legal tender and not being intended for use as legal tender.
- Collections and collectors' pieces of zoological, botanical, minerological, anatomical, historical, archaeological, palaeological, ethnographic or numismatic interest.

19.5.3 Sets of collectables

The investor may want to avoid acquiring 'a set of similar or complementary things' rather than a number of separate items which do not constitute a single set. The definition may affect future tax liabilities if the value of the set would exceed capital tax thresholds, whereas the individual items would be exempt. Thus the Inland Revenue is of the opinion that a collection of postage stamps per se constitutes a single set, although, in their view, the stamps of one definitive or commemorative issue would not necessarily do so.

An issue is whether the acquisition of a set or sets of collectables is a mere hobby or a bona fide investment. Implicit in the question is whether expenses will be deductible. On balance, if the collector buys strictly for investment and capital gains, and keeps accurate records including purchase dates, prices, provenance and current values, then it may be possible to make a case for deducting certain expenses (eg insurance, relevant publications, even travel to sales and auctions). In the majority of cases, however, the collector will be trying to create legal and tax history, in itself an expensive hobby.

When a collection is sold at auction, or after exhibition at a dealer's shop, the authorities may also be interested in the gains secured. In a case where someone has purchased collectables 'under the table', without a clean provenance, the Revenue may argue that the cost basis is zero. The gain would, therefore, be 100 per cent. The advantages of documented evidence are clear. Where the authorities take the view that efforts were being made to evade payment of tax, the legal penalties can be serious, even if the action was in truth innocent.

19.6 SUITABILITY AND MECHANICS

19.6.1 Risks

Snares await buyers. Markets may be thin. Collectables can be difficult to sell quickly, and meanwhile they pay no interest. Instead they can soak up steady outlays in insurance, storage, and maintenance. Repairs and restoration can also be expensive. To refurbish a good piano that a musician will want to play could cost £15,000. It might cost £60,000 to renovate a Ferrari, and only the reckless would drive it along the road. The car has a hand-formed aluminium body. If a passer-by leans against the fender it can easily dent. Despite such costs and risks, enthusiasts still pay massive sums for rare vehicles. Two years ago, a 1936 Mercedes-Benz 500K Roadster, a stunning automobile, went at auction for £1.6m. It was not in first-class condition. According to one report, rats had eaten through the upholstery. A butcher had left it sitting in his shed, unused, for more than 30 years. Originality means a great deal with great cars.

19.6.2 Precautions

Independent advisers who specialise in collectables recommend that an investor should carefully check a dealer's reputation before deciding to employ his services. They suggest that enquiries should be pursued to find out how long the dealer has been in business, and to what professional organisations he belongs. In practice, it is also prudent to make sure that the collector fully understands what is being offered and promised.

To take coins, by way of illustration, questions might be asked about the grade of the coin, and the backing for any assurances. Does the dealer guarantee to buy back an investment? If so, at what price, and on what terms? Are there, for instance, any deductions affecting buy-back warranties? Is a service charge levied? With collectables of any value, it may be worth seeking a second opinion on quality and provenance, before confirming a decision to buy. Familiarity with sales and the publications in the field will also reveal whether an asking price is in line with the market, or well above it.

Equally, in this market as in others, it is wise to avoid letting the marketplace dictate what to collect. Anyone can enjoy the thrill of buying low and selling high, but playing the collectibles market is a reliable way to lose money. Sound advice is to join a collecting society before buying anything. There are now societies and clubs for almost every conceivable collectable. Most such bodies publish newsletters and rosters of members with interests in common. These members usually know the reputable dealers, and can help to vet a purchase. Another judicious step is to attend specialist auctions. These events are often a good way to meet people who are knowledgeable, and to sharpen a collecting instinct. Museum curators can be very helpful people to speak to, and many larger museums hold opinion afternoons. Cataloguing a collection is also sensible, even from the very beginning, after a few purchases. The records help keep track of purchases and sources. Insurance is another necessity to protect the investment, and most insurance companies demand a catalogue before they will issue a policy.

19.6.3 Other risks

Trading collectors' pieces over the Internet is gaining in popularity. The World Wide Web offers more information on alternative investment opportunities than ever before. However, the Internet is an unregulated market, and the new opportunities add to the risks. Investors should be as wary of offers on the Internet as they would be about any unsolicited mailshot.

The Financial Services Authority has compared the Internet with 'a galactic car-boot sale: anyone from anywhere in the world can offer anything for sale'. As with any unregulated marketplace, those with established reputations will be pitching for business, with newcomers offering enticing deals. Investors will find false bargains, scams and frauds. Also, the Internet makes it easy, and will soon make it easier, to buy and pay for goods and services from foreign organisations, almost without being aware that they have their base abroad. So, before making a purchase, a buyer needs to know about the firm. Where is its base? Which authorities regulate it? Which country's laws will apply if a dispute occurs? Rights differ from place to place. For example, in some jurisdictions, when a firm fails, the liquidator holds clients' assets separately, and the firm's creditors do not have access to them. In other countries, the liquidator pools all the assets, and then shares out the proceeds between the owners and the creditors.

Crime adds to these risks. Sophisticated criminals are now targeting 1960s and 1970s collectables, according to the arts and antiques unit in New Scotland Yard. The unit's analyses suggest that burglars are taking pieces that, a decade ago, most people would have said were junk. The *Antiques Roadshow*'s experts have told the world, including breakers and enterers, that items that fell out of fashion years ago are now back in demand, and valuable. Auction houses have detected a similar market opportunity, and have opened outlets to deal with contemporary pieces.

The Metropolitan Police's unit enquires into art crime and manages a database of art and antiques reported stolen. Its *Bumblebee* imaging system came into operation in 1991, and now details thousands of stolen artefacts, worth from £100 to £½m that came to the unit's notice. Other European states have national art and antiques databases, and plans are in train to set up an EU system. Britain has still to integrate records of stolen art and antiques from police forces across the country. Yet law enforcement experts estimate that the purloining of paintings and other collectables represents a £5bn global industry, second only to narcotics in breadth and scale. In Britain alone, robbers make off with £½bn in such valuables each year.

Readers of this chapter may seek not only to protect their wealth but to increase it by buying rare stamps, fine wine, memorabilia, or other exotic objects. Many make worthwhile gains through these alternative investments; others lose a small fortune. Vast disparities can arise in risks. Firms that offer money-making opportunities of this kind may claim unrealistically high rates of return; businesses and advisers regulated by the Financial Services Act would find it difficult to make similar claims.

In alternative investment markets, highly speculative activities are often loosely regulated. and run by individuals, or firms, operating as unlicensed traders or brokers. This is the usual case in the UK, and means that:

- it is unlikely that anyone has vetted the people running a scheme to see if they are honest, competent and solvent;
- the firm does not have to follow the special rules and codes that apply to authorised firms, and help to ensure that they treat investors fairly;
- if a transaction goes wrong, no guarantees exist that anyone will look into complaints;
- if the firm fails, investors have no rights to claim compensation from authorised funds, and probably no access to any other compensation arrangements.

The first step for an alternative investor is therefore to make sure that a firm is legal. UK law generally requires authorisation of firms that formally run investment businesses. However, if such a firm has a current authorisation in another EU country, it may use its European passport to run an investment business lawfully in the UK. To operate an investment business without proper authorisation can be a criminal offence.

To check the status of a UK business, contact Financial Services Act regulators, and the Financial Services Authority's Central Register (tel (020) 7929 3652). The FSA will advise enquirers to take full details of the salesperson, and to record his or her name, the firm's name, the full address, and the telephone and fax numbers. Equally, keeping all documents received is wise, including the envelope. If the firm is not authorised and should be, the FSA investigations' department would like to know about the matter.

When a firm can trade without authorisation, the investor must rely for protection on his or her own efforts, for example, by going through a checklist of commonsense questions. Usually, the greater the reward, the greater the risk. If the return is so much higher than is on offer elsewhere, why is the firm letting outsiders in on it?

Is the firm seeking money for a legitimate purpose? The scams are often ingenious, and sold by experts. Illegal operators know how to take advantage of weaknesses (including greed). They also know how to exploit vulnerability. If an investor sends money to illegal operators, he or she is unlikely to make a profit or ever recover the money. If the money goes out of the UK, restitution is even less likely. Many firms that operate illegally either collapse or the authorities put them out of business. In these cases, investors often find out too late that all their money has gone. Sometimes, the firm took the money in high management fees; often, the firm has lost or removed all the investors' money. In any event, the sums laid out have vanished at a cost, on occasion, of people's life savings, with scant hope of compensation.

If the value of a product, and the possibility of selling it at a high price, are based on rarity, will this scarcity continue? Can those behind the firm show evidence of the expertise they claim? What is the true level of risk, and is it acceptable? If the money is lost, what will be the effect on the investor's life style? What will happen to a guaranteed return, if the responsibility for delivering it lies with the firm and the firm fails? How long has it been, and will it be, in existence? The firm can only fulfil promises to buy something back if it and the money are still around.

19.7 CONCLUSION

In this field of alternative investments, the vital step is to decide whether to be an investor or a collector, or both. Those who take the trouble to understand a particular market well, and be a player, can gain the knowledge to be a specialist collector. In practice, only a limited number of people have the enthusiasm, dedication and resources to pursue the opportunities on a systematic basis. As indicated, these markets for collectables are also social networks. The participants derive much pleasure from being involved in this network. Keeping in touch with fellow devotees is rewarding in the interchanges and in the exchanges.

The investor will quickly learn that he or she has to spend time studying the subtle connotations of hallmarks on metalware, manufacturers' symbols on ceramics, makers' names on antique clocks, the marks of well-known furniture craftsmen and many thousands of other characteristics which influence the attribution of collectors' pieces. Those for whom time is scarce will quickly recognise that they need to specialise and to enlist the services of a specialist. The real collectors develop a burning fervour and could scarcely stop, even if they wanted to, or were forced to by circumstances. In essence, to be a mere investor is to miss out on the social rewards, and to enjoy only vicarious or second-hand advantages. But then collectables are after all second-hand.

SOURCES OF FURTHER INFORMATION

Bibliography (for Chapters 17–19)

Sponsoring the Art: New Business Strategies for the 1990s, The Economist Intelligence Unit ((020) 7830 1000)

Art Sales Index 1995–6 (28th edition), Art Sales Index Limited (01932 856426)

Art Market Bulletin, Art Sales Index Limited (01932 856426)

The Guide to the Antique Shops of Britain 1996–7, compiled by Carole Adams, Antique Collectors Club (01394 385501)

Guide Emer 1999 (bi-annual European guide), available from Mr G Gillingham, 62 Menelik Road, London NW2 3RH ((020) 7435 5644)

Capital Taxation and the National Heritage, The Board of the Inland Revenue, London 1986 (amended 1988)

The Ephemerist (quarterly), Ephemera Society ((020) 7935 7305)

The Death Tax, Towry Law (01753 868244)

Works of Art: A Basic Guide to Capital Taxation and the National Heritage, Office of Arts and Libraries, 1982 (out of print)

Works of Art in Situ: Guidelines on In Situ Offers in Lieu of Capital Taxation, Department of National Heritage, 1984 ((020) 7270 3000) (out of print)

Gold to 2000, The Economist Intelligence Unit ((020) 7830 1000)

Diamonds: A Cartel and its future to 1996, The Economist Intelligence Unit ((020) 7830 1000)

Works of Art: Manuscripts and Archives. Basic information for Exemption from Capital Tax, Office of Arts & Libraries, 1991 (out of print)

Works of Art Private Treaty Sales: Guidelines from the Office of Arts and Libraries, Department of National Heritage, 1986 ((020) 7270 3000) (out of print)

Gold 1997, Goldfields Mineral Services, Greencoat House, Francis Street, London SW1P 1DH

Picture Guide to the UK Art Market 1997, Duncan Hislop, Art Sales Index Limited (01932 856426)

Official Review Antiques Price Guide 1996, Tony Curtis (ed), Lyle Publications

Millers Antique Price Guide 1996, Alison Starling (ed), Reed Consumer Books Ltd, Michelin House, 81 Fulham Road, London SW3 6RB

Art Newspaper, TG Scott Subscriber Services, 6 Bourne Enterprise Centre, Wrotham Road, Borough Green, Kent TN15 8DG (01732 884023)

Gold Demand Trends (quarterly), World Gold Council ((020) 7930 5171)

Platinum 1996, Johnson Matthey plc, New Garden House, 78 Hatton Garden, London EC1N 8JP ((020) 7269 8400)

USEFUL ADDRESSES

Arts Council of England
14 Great Peter Street
London
SW1P 3NQ

Tel: ((020) 7333 0100.

Oriental Ceramic Society
30b Torrington Square
London
WC1E 7JL

Tel: ((020) 7636 7985.

British Antique Dealers
    Association
20 Rutland Gate
London
SW7 1BD

Tel: ((020) 7589 4128.

Royal Academy of Arts
Burlington House
Piccadilly
London
W1V 0DS

Tel: ((020) 7439 7438.

Ephemera Society
8 Galveston Road
Putney
London SW15 2SA

Tel: ((020) 8874 3363.

Royal Fine Art Commission
7 St James Square
London
SW1Y 4JU

Tel: ((020) 7839 6537.

Incorporated Society of Valuers
    and Auctioneers
3 Cadogan Gate
London
SW1X 0AS

Tel: ((020) 7235 2282.

Society of Antiquaries of London
Burlington House
Piccadilly
London
W1V 0HS

Tel: ((020) 7734 0193.

Wine and Spirit Association of
Great Britain (Inc)
Five Kings House International
1 Queens St Place
London
EC4R 1XX

Tel: ((020) 7248 5377

Association of Professional
Numismatists
11 Adelphi Terrace
London
WC2

London and Provincial Antique
Dealers Association
535 Kings Road
London
SW10 0SZ

Tel: ((020) 7823 3511.

The Standard Catalogue of UK
Telephone Cards, from:
Kevin Baker
PO Box 364
Croydon
Surrey

Tel: (01316) 20846.

BT Collectors' Club
Post Point 05A 2S
Delta Point
35 Wellesley Road
Croydon
Surrey
CR9 2YZ

British Antique Furniture
Restorers' Association
The Old Rectory
Warmwell
Dorchester
Dorset
DT2 8HQ

Tel: (01305) 854822

Antiquarian Booksellers'
Association
Sackville House
40 Piccadilly
London
W1V 9PA

Tel: ((020) 7439 3118

Society of London Art Dealers
91 Jermyn Street
London
SW1Y 6JB

Tel: ((020) 7930 6137

Association of Art and Antique
Dealers
535 Kings Road
Chelsea
London
SW10 0SZ

Tel: ((020) 7823 3511

British Thematic Association
107 Charterhouse Street
London
EC1M 6PT

Thesaurus Group Ltd
Mill Court
Furrlongs
Newport
Isle of Wight
PO30 2AA

Tel: (01983) 826000

Sotheby's
34–35 New Bond Street
London
W1A 2AA

Tel: ((020) 7493 8080

Christie's
8 King Street
St James's
London SW1Y 6QT

Tel: ((020) 7839 9060
Fax: ((020) 7839 1611

Phillips Fine Art Auctioneers
101 New Bond Street
London W1Y 0AS

Tel: ((020) 7629 6602

20

TAX BENEFICIAL INVESTMENTS AND SAVINGS

MIKE WILKES

Pannell Kerr Forster, Chartered Accountants

20.1 INTRODUCTION

The most important consideration of savings planning is to identify appropriate investments which offer good value; tax benefits and privileges represent only one aspect of this.

An investment which is appropriate for one person may not necessarily meet the needs of another in different circumstances. Some of the questions to ask are:

(1) How long can the savings be tied up?
(2) Are the savings for a particular purpose (school fees, daughter's wedding, retirement, etc)?
(3) When will the money be needed?
(4) Is income required?
(5) Will fluctuations in stock market and/or property prices be such a worry that the investments become unattractive?

You may also want to strike a balance. The criteria for investing the short-term part of the portfolio should be different from the method of investing in more volatile investments on a longer-term basis. Striking the right balance is one of the hardest aspects. If savings are fairly modest they may have to be invested on a conservative basis – and the return will reflect this. At the other extreme, high net worth individuals who have covered all their short-term requirements may deploy a proportion of capital in more risky investments which offer the prospect of a very high return.

Once these decisions have been made, the next step is to identify investments which meet the specifications and offer good value. An investment may offer good value if the managers' charges are reasonable and the tax treatment is favourable.

This chapter starts by looking at tax privileged investments from the standpoint of the most cautious investor who may want access to capital at short notice and who is, therefore, not well disposed towards investments which may fall in value from time to time. Then a look is taken at tax privileged investments which involve a degree of risk arising from fluctuations in The Stock Exchange, etc. Finally consideration is given to bank deposits and 'near cash' investments, most of which involve little or no risk but do not have a privileged treatment. Many of these investments are provided by the government through the department of national savings or local authorities.

20.2 TAX PRIVILEGED INVESTMENTS

20.2.1 TESSAs

One of the government's more successful innovations was TESSAs (tax exempt special savings accounts). These were available to any individual resident in the UK and aged 18 or over. Although, following the introduction of individual savings accounts (ISAs), new TESSAs could not be opened after 5 April 1999, those in existence on that date can continue to run for their normal term. They can therefore run in parallel to ISAs, and on maturity, the capital element can be paid into the cash component of a new ISA, and will not restrict the allowable annual subscription limit. The previous tax rules will still apply to continuing TESSAs.

The investment normally runs for five years. It offers a secure return since the money has to be deposited with an authorised bank or building society and the risk of capital loss is therefore remote. The investor can withdraw his or her capital within the five-year period but the tax benefits are forfeited if such withdrawals exceed certain limits. Subject to this, the benefit of having a TESSA is that the investor receives tax-free interest.

The maximum amount which may be withdrawn during the first five years without jeopardising the tax benefits is the interest credited to the account less the savings rate of tax of 20 per cent, which would have been deducted if the account had not enjoyed its special tax exempt status.

Example

Louise deposits £3,000 in a TESSA on 6 April 1998. In year one the bank credits interest of £195. The interest has not borne any tax. Louise can withdraw £195 less 20 per cent notional tax, ie £156.00, without affecting the exempt status of the account. The remaining £3,039.00 will continue to attract tax-free interest. However, if Louise withdraws £156.01 the bank will have to account to the Inland Revenue for the tax of £39.00 and the account will thereafter be treated as an ordinary deposit account. Once five years have elapsed, Louise can withdraw the entire amount with no tax consequences.

There were limits on the maximum amount which could be invested in TESSA. An individual could invest up to £3,000 in the first year and up to £1,800 each year thereafter, subject to the total not exceeding £9,000. Alternatively, an individual could have invested up to £150 per month.

Prior to 6 April 1999, the whole of the capital (up to the maximum of £9,000) of a maturing TESSA could be reinvested in a follow up TESSA, provided that the new account was opened within six months of the maturity of the original account. Individuals who invested less than £9,000 in the first year of their second TESSA account could continue saving over the next four years, within the usual limits for each year, subject to the overall limit of £9,000. If however the maximum was invested, no further investment was permitted.

An individual cannot have two TESSAs at any one time. However, the above limits apply separately for husband and wife. The terms under which banks and building societies accept deposits for TESSAs vary. The government regards it as a matter of choice of whether the deposit carries a rate of interest which is fixed for five years or a variable rate. TESSAs are 'portable' so investors can transfer their savings from one financial institution to another without losing tax benefits. However, the investor should check the level of any transfer penalty.

20.2.2 National Savings fixed interest certificates

These are another investment which provide a totally tax-free return. However, the yield reflects this and so ISAs offer better value for most people.

National Savings certificates are a five-year investment but they can be encashed early, although this involves surrendering a small amount of interest. The 52nd issue of National Savings certificates is now available and if held to redemption (ie five years) give an overall net yield of 3.85 per cent.

Once certificates have matured, they attract tax-free interest at the national extension rate (currently 2.1 per cent) until they are redeemed.

Practical aspects

The certificates may be a suitable form of savings for children but children's bonus bonds are likely to be a far more attractive proposition for small savings. They are not, however, suitable for non-taxpayers or for short-term savings; but for the investor paying tax at the higher rate, the certificates may be attractive.

Application forms are available from most post offices and banks.

Between £100 and £10,000 can be invested in the 50th issue, plus up to £20,000 reinvestment of earlier issues which have matured.

Holdings should be reviewed from time to time, particularly since new issues may carry more attractive rates of capital appreciation than those already held. A review of holdings should certainly be made at the end of the specified period.

Any number of certificates can be cashed at one time, on at least eight working days' notice, and repayment forms are available at most post offices and banks.

20.2.3 Children's bonus bonds

As the name suggests, these bonds are specifically designed for children and are intended as longer-term savings, as the bondholder can retain the bonds up to the age of 21. The current issue (Issue O) has a guaranteed tax-free return of 4.85 per cent if held for five years. Anyone over 16 can purchase bonds for anyone under 16, and children under 16 who wish to purchase bonds for themselves will have to ask a parent or guardian to sign the application form. The maximum total holding in all issues of children's bonus bonds is £1,000 per child (excluding interest and bonuses) regardless of the number of donors, and can be purchased in £25 units. Shortly before each five-year period ends the next guaranteed interest rate and bonus is advised. No action is necessary unless it is decided to cash in the bond. Once the bondholder is over 16, the next offer of interest rates and bonus is for whatever length of time remains until he or she reaches 21. The bonds can be encashed at any time, with one month's notice, but there is a loss of interest unless this is at a five-year bonus date, or at age 21.

As with savings certificates, this investment is particularly suitable for parents, as the interest is not aggregated with their own income for tax purposes, even if the growth in value produces interest in excess of £100 per year.

20.2.4 National Savings index-linked certificates

As with National Savings certificates, these certificates are guaranteed by the government. They cannot be sold to third parties.

There is no lower age limit for holding these certificates, although encashment is not allowed until a child reaches the age of seven, except in special circumstances.

If a certificate is encashed within the first year, the purchase price only is repaid. If the certificates are held for more than a year, the redemption value is equal to the original purchase price, increased in proportion to the rise in the RPI between the month of purchase and the month of redemption. In the event of a fall in the RPI, the certificates can be encashed for the original purchase price. After the death of a holder, indexation can continue for a maximum of 12 months.

The latest issue (15th) guarantees a return above the rate of inflation for a five-year term by offering extra tax-free interest of 1.65 per cent as well as indexation. The amount of extra interest credited to the holding rises in each year of the life of the certificate and is itself inflation-proofed.

As with national savings certificates, capital appreciation is exempt from income tax and capital gains tax.

Certificates are suitable for individuals who do not need immediate income but are seeking protection in real terms for the amount invested. Higher rate taxpayers in this category will find the certificates particularly attractive. The investment limit here is £10,000 with a minimum of £100, in addition to holdings of all other issues of savings certificates.

Application forms are obtainable from most post offices.

Comparison with cash element ISAs

There may be circumstances where index-linked certificates could provide a better return than ISAs. Interest rates are affected by a number of factors other than the rate of inflation. If you are pessimistic about the likely rate of inflation over the next five years index-linked certificates offer a low risk alternative.

20.2.5 Premium bonds

Premium bonds are guaranteed by the government. They cannot be sold to third parties.

Any person aged 16 or over can buy the bonds, and a parent or legal guardian may buy bonds on behalf of a child under 16. A bond cannot be held in the name of more than one person or in the name of a corporate body, society, club or other association of persons. Prizes won by bonds registered in the name of a child under the age of 16 are paid on behalf of the child to the parent or legal guardian.

The minimum purchase for a bondholder aged 16 or over is £100. Above this amount you can buy bonds in multiples of £10, up to a maximum of £20,000 per person.

No interest is paid, but a bond which has been held for one clear calendar month following the month in which it was purchased is eligible for inclusion in the regular draw for prizes from £50 to £1 million. Bonds can be encashed at any time, and all prizes are totally free of UK income tax and capital gains tax. Although the top prize may not compare favourably with potential National Lottery winnings, unlike the lottery the original stake will never be lost.

20.2.6 Personal equity plans

PEPs were introduced by the Chancellor of the Exchequer in the 1986 Finance Act to encourage wider share ownership by individuals in UK companies by offering investment tax incentives. Successive Finance Acts introduced changes which made PEPs even more attractive. PEPs have been replaced by ISAs with effect from 6 April 1999, and although when the announcement was first made it was feared that existing PEPs would be severely restricted, the original proposals were revised following representations. As a result existing PEPs will be able to continue, almost as before, with the same tax advantages as ISAs, although no further subscriptions can be made after 5 April 1999.

Anyone who was over 18 years old and resident in the UK for tax purposes was able take out a PEP. Crown employees working overseas were deemed to be resident for this purpose. Should a plan holder subsequently become non-resident, the plan can be maintained and its tax benefits preserved.

The tax benefits take the form of total exemption from capital gains tax and income tax on the appreciation and investment income earned from equities, unit trusts and investment trusts held within the plan. However, from 6 April 2004, it will not be possible for the plan manager to reclaim the 10 per cent credit attached to dividends from UK equities. A plan can be terminated at any time and the funds withdrawn without loss of the tax benefits.

There are two distinct types of plan: general plans which have been available since the introduction of PEPs, and single company plans which were first introduced on 1 January 1992. Single company plans allow investment only in the shares of one designated company, and are subject to an additional condition that substantially the whole of the cash subscribed to the plan, or from the realisation of plan shares, must be reinvested in plan shares within 42 days.

There is no restriction on the investment switches that can be made within the fund and no liability to income tax or capital gains tax arises. A PEP can be transferred from one manager to another.

The cash held within the PEP can be held on deposit. The interest earned is paid gross and is exempt from tax provided that it is eventually invested in plan shares or units.

Although no relief was available on the investment into the fund, the plan is virtually a gross fund in the same way as a pension fund. There is an important advantage over most pension funds in that all proceeds are tax free when drawn whereas at least part of what emerges from a pension scheme is taxable. It is therefore a useful addition for individuals to enhance retirement benefits. The fund can be used in the same way as a pension, ie tax-free cash can be taken or the fund could be used to purchase an annuity.

PEPs are not 'no risk' investments but in the past a combination/selection of unit/investment trusts and direct investment in bluechip or 'alpha' stocks have generally produced a reasonable return where the investment was kept for between three and five years (see also Chapter 3).

20.2.7 Individual savings accounts (ISAs)

The Government issued a consultative document in December 1997 which heralded the phasing out of TESSAs and PEPs, and their replacement with ISAs. Although it was originally intended to be a simple tax-saving vehicle to encourage saving by all sections of the community, the administration involved has proved to be difficult to understand, and initial take-up has not been as wide as the Government had hoped.

Any UK-resident individual aged 18 or over can take out an ISA, and all investors are exempt from income tax and capital gains tax on the income and gains arising from investments held within the scheme. ISAs can be comprised of up to three separate elements: cash investments, stocks and shares, and life insurance. All three components can be provided by a single financial institution ('maxi' ISAs) or separately by different providers ('mini' ISAs). A maxi ISA provider must offer stocks and shares, and may offer cash and/or insurance. A mini ISA provider can offer one or more of the three separate components. It is only possible to invest in one mini ISA of the same type in the same tax year (eg one cash mini ISA), and similarly it is not possible to invest in a maxi ISA and a mini ISA during the same tax year.

Where an ISA contains a UK equity component, either in the stocks and shares element or to back a life insurance element, an additional 10 per cent tax credit will be available until 5 April 2004.

The maximum annual investment, which can be made into either a maxi or a mini ISA, is £5,000, or £7,000 for the first year that ISAs are available (1999–2000). However, the maximum investment which can be made in each individual component is different for maxi and mini ISAs, as shown below:

Maxi ISAs:	Maximum amount which can be invested	
	1999/2000	*2000/01 onwards*
Stocks and shares	Up to £7,000	Up to £5,000
Cash	Up to £3,000	Up to £1,000
Insurance	Up to £1,000	Up to £1,000
Overall investment cannot		
exceed	£7,000	£5,000

Mini ISAs:	Maximum amount which can be invested	
	1999/2000	*2000/01 onwards*
Stocks and shares	Up to £3,000	Up to £3,000
Cash	Up to £3,000	Up to £1,000
Insurance	Up to £1,000	Up to £1,000
Overall investment cannot		
exceed	£7,000	£5,000

Example

> Anthony decides to invest in a maxi ISA on 14 July 1999. He wishes to invest £4,000 in the stocks and shares component, and £3,000 in the cash element. Because he has already invested the maximum of £7,000, he is unable to make any investment in the insurance component.

It is intended that the scheme will run for ten years, but will be reviewed after seven years to decide if any changes will be needed after the expiry of the ten-year period.

It will be possible to make withdrawals from the account at any time, without loss of tax relief.

Although it will not be possible to transfer shares acquired under a public offer, or on the demutualisation of a building society, as part of the annual subscription, this restriction will not apply to shares acquired from an approved profit-sharing or savings-related share option scheme. In addition this latter transfer will not attract an immediate capital gains tax charge.

20.2.8 Insurance policies

Insurance policies are another type of tax privileged investment. Investors in qualifying policies are not subject to any tax on the maturity of the policy. For further discussion see Chapter 14.

437

20.2.9 Friendly society investments

Friendly societies issue qualifying insurance policies and there is no tax charge for investors when such policies mature. In this respect the position is no different from policies issued by insurance companies. The difference lies in the way that friendly societies are treated for tax purposes. Friendly societies are treated favourably as they are not normally subject to tax on life assurance business and this has generally enabled them to produce attractive returns.

Friendly society policies are, however, essentially a long-term investment since the surrender value can be very low where plans are cancelled or surrendered before the ten-year term has expired, as penalties tend to be heavy and frequently the charges on friendly society plans are high.

The maximum premiums are very low. The maximum annual limit is £270, or £25 per month, but some societies do permit a lump sum investment to be made to cover the full ten-year plan. Policyholders must be between the ages of 18 and 70.

At least 50 per cent of the underlying fund of a friendly society must be invested in narrower range securities as defined in the Trustee Investment Act 1971. This could restrict the investment performance but on the other hand it offers a lower level of risk. All investment income and capital gains within the fund are free of all UK tax, which enhances the rate of return.

The Policyholder's Protection Act 1975 does not extend to friendly society plans and, unfortunately, there is no compensation scheme in the event of a friendly society having financial difficulties.

20.2.10 Pension policies

Personal pension policies and additional voluntary contributions to approved pension schemes are among the most favourably treated of all investments. Full tax relief is available for the individual's contributions and the fund enjoys total exemption from tax. This is discussed in Chapter 15.

20.2.11 Enterprise zone property trusts

These trusts are effectively collective schemes whereby an individual acquires an interest in a portfolio of properties located in one of the designated enterprise zones. The minimum investment is usually £5,000 but unlike the Enterprise Investment Scheme investments (see **13.5**) there is no maximum, and it is therefore possible for investors to shelter very large or exceptional income during a tax year. Investors are issued 'units' or 'shares' but in law they hold an interest in the properties as members of a syndicate.

The investment is allowable as a deduction from the investors' taxable income to the extent that the managers invest the cash raised by them to construct buildings or purchase newly constructed and unused buildings within an enterprise zone. There is usually a small part of the investment which attracts no tax relief representing the cost of purchasing the land on which the building has been constructed. Generally this is between 5 and 10 per cent of the total investment.

Example

> Stuart invests £100,000 in an enterprise property trust on 3 March 1998. He has income of £75,000 which is subject to the 40 per cent top rate.
>
> The managers of the trust invest all the money raised in qualifying property before 6 April 1998. The land element is 10 per cent. Stuart, therefore, gets a tax deduction of £100,000 × 90 per cent, ie £90,000. This deduction saves Stuart tax of £36,000 so the net cost of the investment is £64,000.

Current yields on such investments are between 6 and $7\frac{1}{2}$ per cent of the gross investment. The income is paid gross and is treated as rental income for the investor. The final investment return on such an investment is difficult to predict. Investors should expect to retain their units for a term of 25 years. A disposal within this term could give rise to a clawback of some or all of the income tax relief given in year one (although no such clawback need arise in the case of a gift).

The yield becomes more attractive when one compares it with the net cost of the investment, after tax relief. Thus if the trust yielded 6 per cent on the gross cost, the yield on Stuart's net cost becomes 9.7 per cent.

These investments are tax privileged because of the relief due to the investor when he or she makes the investment. However, they are not risk free as the investment produces income only if the properties are fully let. In practice this risk can be minimised.

The trust managers can generally secure rental guarantees of at least two years where they buy properties from developers. Sometimes the developer offers a further guarantee which in the short term provides effectively a guaranteed income. In many cases the managers buy enterprise properties which have been 'pre-let' and this means the investor is securing a guaranteed income, usually with upward only rent reviews for a 25-year period. If good rent reviews are achieved the capital value of the investment can be expected to appreciate.

Investors may also take a qualifying loan to acquire the units, the interest being set first against the rental income from the properties and any surplus is then available to be set off against any other Schedule A rental income for the same year. The balance of any unused interest relief is available to carry forward against rental income of future years.

In addition to the long-term nature of these investments, it is often difficult to dispose of the units as there is no established market through which units can be bought and sold. The managers do, however, offer to assist investors on a matched bargain basis.

Planning in later years

One planning possibility involving the use of these investments relies upon the fact that the clawback (or 'balancing charge') need not arise on a gift. Thus, Stuart might transfer the shares in the enterprise property trust to his wife if she is not subject to the 40 per cent rate. If she had no other income at all she would have only a small tax liability on the rents she received of £6,000 per annum.

20.3 CONCLUSION

Some of the tax benefit investments offer the prospect of outperforming inflation. The return on a TESSA and cash element in an ISA might very well be 6 per cent or more per annum. PEPs or ISAs invested in a range of equities should produce a comparable return over the medium to longer term. Index-linked national savings certificates are guaranteed to do so.

The return on some of the other privileged investments looks less attractive. Where savings certificates have matured the current rate of interest added (2.1 per cent) barely keeps pace with the current rate of inflation.

The various types of deposit schemes offer a poor long-term return to anyone who cannot enjoy the income gross. They are, therefore, sensible investments for married women with little or no other income, but less attractive for a person who is subject to tax at 40 per cent. That is not to say that these investments are not appropriate from time to time as a way of investing money short term or to secure a known commitment or liability.

21

INVESTOR PROTECTION

PETER HOWE, LLB

Barrister, Company Secretary, Allied Dunbar Assurance plc

21.1 INTRODUCTION

The Financial Services Act 1986 was enacted following widespread concern at the collapse of a number of investment firms in the early 1980s. The legislation is based on the recommendations of the late Professor Gower who, on behalf of the government, carried out an investigation which revealed a lack of consistency (and in some cases the absence of any controls) in the regulatory systems controlling different types of firm.

Professor Gower's approach was to recommend regulation only in so far as necessary for the protection of investors and that the regulatory structure should remain flexible so as not to impair market efficiency. The aim was to introduce a consistent regulatory structure which would produce a 'level playing field' (ie rules which do not put some firms at a competitive disadvantage compared with others). His view was that regulation should not try to do the impossible by protecting investors from their own folly but rather to prevent reasonable people from being deceived.

Finally, Professor Gower recommended self-regulation by the industry as preferable to the regulatory system in the US where the Securities Exchange Commission is a government agency. Although the UK system is backed up by statute, the day-to-day regulation of investment businesses is currently undertaken by self-regulatory organisations the boards and committees of which include practitioners drawn from the various types of investment business which operate in the market.

The Financial Services Bill was enacted in 1986 and brought into force by a number of Commencement Orders. The key provisions were implemented in 1988. A two-tier system of regulation was introduced with the creation of a Securities and Investments Board (SIB), responsible for several self-regulatory organisations (SROs) which are referred to in the paragraphs below. They each produced their own rules and determined their compliance and monitoring approach.

21.2 HIGHLIGHTS OF THE PREVIOUS YEAR

21.2.1 Financial Services Authority

The FSA (previously the Securities and Investments Board) was given responsibility for supervising banks by the Banking Act 1997. When the Financial Services and Markets Bill (FSMB) is passed, probably in the summer 2000 (a date known as N2), the FSA will regulate building societies, insurance companies (including Lloyd's of London), friendly societies and credit unions. In the meantime, the existing regulators are responsible, although staff who have transferred to the FSA which 'supplies' their services back to these regulators do most of the work.

In preparation for N2, the FSA published for consultation Principles for Businesses which it is envisaged will replace the current set (see **21.3.4**), but from which they are unlikely to differ substantially. It intends to publish a separate statement of Principles and a Code of Individual Conduct when the FSMB becomes law, binding on those individuals who require the approval of the regulator before they carry on certain roles. The Principles will form the basis of the FSA Handbook, which will consolidate and harmonise the enormous volume of current rules and guidance of the various regulators.

Following the publication of the FSMB, significant concerns were expressed at the scope of the FSA's proposed powers and accountability. Amendments have been proposed to meet these concerns, and a joint committee of Parliament set up to report prior to the Bill commencing its legislative stages. Issues have included ensuring that the exercise of powers meets the requirements of the European Convention on Human Rights and the extent to which consumers and 'practitioners' should have an input to the regulatory process. The possibility of the FSA being made accountable to a parliamentary committee has also been canvassed.

The Treasury published a key consultation document in February 1999 on the scope of regulated activities. The approach is to rationalise the existing legislation as far as possible whilst retaining the substance of current regulation. Changes have been proposed, however, to the regimes applying to Lloyd's of London and professionals such as solicitors and accountants. Areas that will be reviewed and which may in future become regulated include mortgage advice, credit unions, pre-paid funeral plans and long-term health care insurance.

The Office of Fair Trading in August 1998 started an investigation into whether the polarisation rule (see **21.4.2**) should be modified in the light of changes in the industry. At the time the rule was introduced, there was investor confusion about the relationship between product providers and the intermediaries that sold their packaged products. The issue is whether changes in agency practices since 1988 have made the strictness of the rule unnecessary and possibly detrimental to the interests of consumers.

21.2.2 Pensions review

With the substantial completion of Phase 1 of the review under which priority cases were dealt with, the FSA and the PIA have now decided on the policy for Phase 2, covering those investors who were not priority categories under Phase 1. Model guidance for carrying out this part of the review was also issued. The FSA has commissioned a high profile publicity campaign timed to coincide with firms' mailings of their clients. The FSA and the SROs are to set realistic but challenging targets with a full set of dates published in summer 1999.

21.2.3 Consumer education

For the first time in the UK, a regulator, the FSA, is to be given the statutory objective of promoting public understanding of the financial system. Recognising the complexity and lack of transparency in the financial services market, the FSA is proposing short- and long-term actions including the convening of an education forum, consumer research, a public helpline and initiatives aimed at simplifying and standardising services and products for the mass market. A possible early example of the latter approach is the 'benchmarking' of the new Individual Savings Accounts (ISAs) through the publication of cost, access and terms (CAT) standards.

21.2.4 Year 2000

The risk that computer systems may malfunction because of historical programming of date-sensitive systems which use two rather than four digits for years and fail to recognise 2000 as a leap year is the responsibility of firms' senior management. It is also an important supervisory issue because of its potential impact on markets and consumers. The FSA proposes to monitor firms' progress in addressing the problem.

21.2.5 Europe

The outgoing European Commission has proposed a five-year programme to put the financial services industry (omitted from the introduction of the single market in the early 1990s) on the same level as other industries.

21.3 BASIC FRAMEWORK

The key provision in the Financial Services Act 1986 (the Act) makes it a criminal offence to carry on investment business in the UK unless the person concerned is authorised or exempt. Investment business is defined as carrying on certain activities, eg buying and selling, advising, arranging or managing 'things' which are investments under the Act. The definition of investments includes most 'paper' securities such as stocks and shares, collective investment schemes, most life and pension policies, gilt-edged securities and futures and options. The definition excludes real property, bank and building society accounts or alternative investments such as antiques and works of art. Although most National Savings products satisfy the definition of investments they are specifically excluded.

The Act has only minor application to the regulation of occupational pension schemes which are largely governed by trust law. Financial services regulation is only concerned with the investment management aspects. In particular the Act requires trustees to be authorised (see **21.3.1**) unless they have delegated day-to-day investment decisions to professional investment managers.

Since 1 June 1997 the provision of custody services has required authorisation under the Act.

21.3.1 Authorisation

Firms carrying on investment business may obtain their authorisation from the Financial Services Authority (FSA), previously the SIB, or more likely from one of the SROs which the FSA has recognised:

(1) the Securities and Futures Authority (SFA) which resulted from a merger, in April 1991, of The Securities Association (TSA) and the Association of Futures Brokers and Dealers (AFBD). TSA regulated the activities of those who deal in, advise on or manage securities whilst AFBD regulated those who advise on or deal in futures and options, including those handled by the commodity exchanges and the London International Financial Futures Exchange;

(2) the Investment Management Regulatory Organisation (IMRO) which regulates the managers of investments including the managers and trustees of collective investment schemes, eg unit trusts and those firms providing custody services;

(3) the Life Assurance and Unit Trust Regulatory Organisation (LAUTRO) which regulates the marketing activities of life companies, friendly societies and collective investment scheme managers;

(4) the Financial Intermediaries Managers and Brokers Regulatory Association (FIMBRA) which regulates the many intermediaries who advise and arrange deals in life and pension products, collective investment schemes and other investments;

(5) the Personal Investment Authority (PIA), which became operational in July 1994, effectively merges the regulatory activities of FIMBRA and LAUTRO as well as covering some of the non-stockbroking private investor responsibilities of IMRO and the SFA. LAUTRO and FIMBRA will cease to be recognised by the FSA as SROs now that the process of transfer of membership to the PIA is complete.

Another way in which authorisation to carry on investment business can be obtained is through membership of a recognised professional body (RPB). Most solicitors and accountants obtain their authorisation from their respective professional bodies (eg The Law Society or one of the accountancy bodies) where their investment business is only a small proportion of their overall professional activities. The Insurance Brokers' Registration Council (IBRC) in the past regulated insurance brokers whose main business is general insurance but who undertake investment business so long as this does not exceed 49 per cent of their total business. Recognition of the IRBC has been withdrawn and such brokers are now in the process of applying to the PIA for authorisation.

Finally, there are firms such as insurance companies and friendly societies which obtain their authorisation under separate legislation from the Treasury or the equivalent authorities in the EU member state in which the company's head office is situated, and the Registrar of Friendly Societies respectively. These firms do not need to seek additional authorisation under the FSA although their marketing activities are subject to regulation by the PIA or, in a very few cases, the FSA.

21.3.2 Exemptions

Some firms are exempted from the requirement to obtain authorisation under the Act. These include the Bank of England, recognised exchanges and clearing houses, and members of Lloyd's.

An important category of exempt person is the appointed representative. This is an individual or firm which acts as the agent of an authorised person and for whose activities (within the limits of the authorised person's business activities) the authorised person takes legal responsibility. Although it is open to any firm which is authorised to appoint such representatives, the practice is most common in the case of insurance companies and firms that market life policies and collective investment schemes.

21.3.3 **The FSA Central Register**

The FSA is required under the Act to maintain a public register of firms authorised to carry on investment business, including a list of authorised and recognised collective investment schemes. This Central Register permits investors as well as firms to check on the authorisation status of firms including appointed representatives who trade under their own names and not that of the authorised firm which has appointed them. It is therefore possible to check whether such an appointed representative is the agent of a particular company.

The Central Register can be contacted by telephoning (020) 7929 3652 or by using New Prestel or Telecom Gold services. It is proposed to make the service available through the Internet, libraries and citizens' advice bureaux.

21.3.4 **Authorisation criteria**

In deciding whether to authorise a firm the FSA, SROs or RPBs consider such matters as whether those involved in the business are fit and proper persons having the financial resources and competence to operate the business in a way which is unlikely to result in unreasonable risk to investors. In addition, the FSA has published ten Principles (see below) which it expects all firms to observe. The breach of any principle might call into question whether the firm was fit and proper to carry on investment business.

The Principles

(1) Integrity
A firm should observe high standards of integrity and fair dealing.

(2) Skill, care and diligence
A firm should act with due skill, care and diligence.

(3) Market practice
A firm should observe high standards of market conduct. It should also, to the extent endorsed for the purpose of this principle, comply with any code or standard as in force from time to time and as it applies to the firm either according to its terms or by rulings made under it.

(4) Information about customers
A firm should seek from customers it advises, or for whom it exercises discretion, any information about their circumstances and investment objectives which might reasonably be expected to be relevant in enabling it to fulfil its responsibilities to them.

(5) Information for customers

A firm should take reasonable steps to give a customer it advises, in a comprehensible and timely way, any information needed to enable him to make a balanced and informed decision. A firm should similarly be ready to provide a customer with a full and fair account of the fulfilment of its responsibilities to him.

(6) Conflicts of interest

A firm should either avoid any conflict of interest arising or, where conflicts arise, should ensure fair treatment to all its customers by disclosure, internal rules of confidentiality, declining to act, or otherwise. A firm should not unfairly place its interests above those of its customers and, where a properly informed customer would reasonably expect that the firm would place his interests above its own, the firm should live up to that expectation.

(7) Customer assets

Where a firm has control of or is otherwise responsible for assets belonging to a customer which it is required to safeguard, it should arrange proper protection for them, by way of segregation and identification of those assets or otherwise, in accordance with the responsibility it has accepted.

(8) Financial resources

A firm should ensure that it maintains adequate financial resources to meet its investment business commitments and to withstand the risks to which its business is subject.

(9) Internal organisation

A firm should organise and control its internal affairs in a responsible manner, keeping proper records, and where the firm employs staff or is responsible for the conduct of investment business by others, should have adequate arrangements to ensure that they are suitable, adequately trained and properly supervised and that it has well-defined compliance procedures.

(10) Relations with regulators

A firm should deal with its regulator in an open and cooperative manner and keep the regulator promptly informed of anything concerning the firm which might reasonably be expected to be disclosed to it.

Source: *The Financial Services Authority*

21.4 RULES AND REGULATIONS

The Act contains only the bare framework of the total investor protection legislation. The detailed rules and regulations with which authorised firms are expected to comply are contained in rule books maintained and enforced by the FSA and the relevant SRO or RPB. The original rule books of individual SROs and RPBs were required to give investor protection which was equivalent to that given by the rules of the FSA itself. In an effort to avoid unnecessary duplication whilst preserving the ability of SROs and RPBs to make practitioner-based rules relevant to the particular business in which their members operate, some amendments have been made to the Act. These amendments have allowed the FSA to make certain core rules which are directly applicable to all investment firms (except members of RPBs) whichever SRO they belong to. The designated core rules (of which there are 40) were intended to provide a degree of uniformity and common standards which the individual SROs could supplement by additional rules geared to the activities of the firms which they regulate. Instead of having to convince the FSA that their rule books are equivalent, the new arrangements require the FSA to agree that the rule books, together with the SRO's monitoring and compliance arrangements, provide adequate protection to investors. Since these amendments were made the FSA has had second thoughts about the need to designate core rules although most of them have been incorporated into the SRO's own rule books.

21.4.1 Business conduct

The detailed rules and regulations cover a number of areas relating to the conduct of investment business by authorised persons. These include:

(1) the way in which authorised firms and their appointed representatives seek new business;
(2) the ongoing relationships between authorised firms and their customers where such relationships exist;
(3) the way in which authorised firms must deal with complaints by investors.

21.4.2 Seeking business

There are detailed advertising rules which prohibit misleading advertisements and statements and claims which cannot be substantiated. For example, LAUTRO has required its member firms to submit their marketing material for with-profit bonds and guaranteed bonds which offer potential growth in line with a stock market index but with a guaranteed return of capital if performance is poor. Where potentially misleading advertising material was found LAUTRO required its member firms to check that investors had not been disadvantaged and to compensate any that had.

The PIA has issued a reminder that advertisements for unit trusts and PEPs must give a fair indication of the nature of the investment. If an advertisement states there are 'no initial charges' or 'no entry or exit charges', it must take into account the difference between the buying and selling price, if a difference exists.

There are rules which require authorised firms to know their customer before making a recommendation or arranging an investment transaction and to make sure that any investment that is recommended or transacted is suitable, having regard to the investor's personal and financial requirements. Poor completion of 'fact finds' (the questionnaires which intermediaries normally use to get to know their customers) have been the subject of criticism by some SROs and the Insurance Ombudsman and has received significant attention in the proposals for training and competence.

In the case of packaged product investments such as life assurance, pension plans and collective investment schemes, the polarisation rule requires intermediaries to disclose in a Terms of Business letter (previously called a Buyer's Guide) and on business stationery whether they are independent from any particular product company, in which case the obligation is to recommend a suitable product from those available on the market or company representatives, who must recommend a suitable product from the product range of the particular company they represent.

Independent intermediaries and company representatives are permitted to make unsolicited calls (personal visits or oral communications other than at the investor's invitation) which cannot be made in relation to non-polarised investments. Investments which can be the subject of unsolicited calls normally give the investor cooling-off rights, enabling the investor to cancel an investment transaction within a reasonable period (normally 14 days) from entering into the contract. Detailed product disclosure rules are designed to provide sufficient information about the product to enable the investor to decide whether to continue with the contract.

From 1 January 1995 new product and commission disclosure rules for life companies have required a 'Key Features' document, setting out the essential elements of the product including charges and expenses, to be given to an investor before an application form is completed. The document must disclose the commission or other remuneration payable to the intermediary (whether independent or tied) and must give further important information, specific to the circumstances of the purchasing investor, about the product. The rules require life offices to use their own charges and not industry standard charges when preparing illustrations of future benefits and the clear disclosure to investors of the consequences of surrendering a policy before the end of its term or maturity. They also permit product providers to make charges which differ according to which distributor outlet is used to obtain the business. From 1 May 1997 these rules have applied to unit trusts and other non-life assurance packaged products.

21.4.3 Customer agreements

The rules prescribe the terms of customer agreements between authorised firms and their customers including how such agreements are made, how instructions are to be communicated and how such agreements are terminated.

There are also rules requiring authorised firms to place client money in designated trust accounts to ensure that investors' money is kept separate from other money belonging to the firm. The rules provide for the payment of interest except in specified circumstances.

21.4.4 Complaints and compensation

There are rules requiring authorised firms to operate detailed monitoring and compliance procedures to ensure that the rules are obeyed and to have suitable procedures for dealing with complaints from investors. A breach of these rules may also result in a breach of FSA Principle 9 (see **21.3.4**).

Authorised firms are required to contribute a levy to a compensation scheme established by the FSA and administered by the Investors Compensation Scheme Limited under which, in the event of an authorised firm going into liquidation, investors may recover up to a maximum of £48,000 if the firm is unable to meet its liabilities.

21.5 COMPLAINTS AND REMEDIES

21.5.1 Basic procedures

If an investor has a complaint about an authorised firm, the investor should raise the matter initially with the firm's compliance officer who is usually an employee of the firm with responsibility for ensuring that the firm complies with the rules. If the firm does not handle the complaint to the investor's satisfaction, the investor may refer the matter to the relevant complaints body. The appropriate complaints body depends upon the arrangements which that firm's SRO or RPB has made. For example, nearly all life assurance companies and many unit trust companies are members of the PIA and it is the PIA Ombudsman that would deal with the investor's complaint. Disputes between members of IMRO and their customers are dealt with by the Investment Ombudsman. It is the authorised firm's responsibility to inform the investor of the appropriate complaints body. The complaints body has a range of sanctions which can be imposed including awarding appropriate compensation for any losses suffered by the investor.

Referring a complaint to one of the relevant complaints bodies does not normally prevent the investor from pursuing any other legal remedies. In addition to bringing civil actions for breach of contract or negligence, the private investor is given a right, under the Act, to sue an authorised firm for any breach of the investor protection rules which causes the investor loss.

Individual SROs as well as the FSA have a range of intervention powers which can be used in the interests of investor protection. These include the FSA's power to prohibit the employment of persons considered to be unfit, to apply for an injunction or restitution order where a breach is threatened or where investors have suffered loss, to restrict the business of investment firms, to restrict any dealings with a firm's assets or even to vest those assets in a trustee. SROs have the power to discipline their members for misconduct and may impose fines.

21.6 OVERSEAS ASPECTS

Overseas firms are subject to the Act if they carry on investment business in the UK. Unless an overseas company is authorised to carry on investment business in the UK, it is difficult for it to market its products and services to UK investors. It is possible for the overseas firm to promote its products and services in the UK through an authorised person.

If the investment is a recognised collective investment scheme or an insurance policy issued by a recognised insurer, which it may be if the scheme or insurer is authorised in another EU member state or in a territory designated by the Treasury (eg the Isle of Man, the Channel Islands), the authorised firm may market it freely within the UK. Although such a scheme may not be subject to the UK compensation scheme it is possible that it will be subject to a compensation scheme set up in the home country or territory concerned.

If the collective investment scheme or insurance policy is not a recognised scheme, there are severe restrictions on the extent to which it can be promoted in the UK. For example, an authorised person can promote such a scheme to established customers under the terms of a subsisting customer agreement but cannot market to investors generally.

21.7 PREVIEW OF THE YEAR AHEAD

The FSA will be preparing in earnest for N2 when the FSMB is expected to be passed, probably in the summer of 2000. Many consultation papers are planned, ranging from the responsibilities of senior management to a Conduct of Business sourcebook.

A Chief Ombudsman and a panel of ombudsmen will be appointed in readiness for N2 and the details of the new compensation scheme determined.

Phase 2 of the pensions review will be high on the list of priorities and the FSA and PIA will publish the timetable for its completion. In addition, the PIA will be monitoring advice given to investors about personal pension plans in the light of the Government's stated intention to introduce a stakeholder pension in the future (see **15.8**).

One known future problem is the Year 2000 problem. The risks are predictable and can be mitigated by firms taking timely and appropriate actions. It will be a major object of the FSA to ensure as far as possible that firms take necessary steps to protect customers of financial services firms.

21.8 CONCLUSION AND FUTURE DEVELOPMENTS

The Act provides the framework for the most comprehensive investor protection system ever seen in the UK or elsewhere in Europe. In the past eleven years considerable progress has been made by the FSA and the SROs in putting the flesh on the bare bones provided by the Act.

Changing circumstances brought about by an innovative and competitive financial services industry as well as developments in Europe will require further adaptations of a system which needs to be responsive to such changes.

21.8.1 Future developments

Looking ahead, the scope for change and future development of the regulatory system is significant. The principle of self-regulation which was a cornerstone of the original Professor Gower proposals (see **21.1**) has been dealt a severe blow by the new Labour government's plans to change the system. Even before the proposed legislation takes effect it is difficult to disagree with one conclusion of the final report of the House of Commons Treasury and Civil Service Committee, which looked at financial services regulation, that: 'Whatever the Act says, and whatever the philosophy underlying the legislation, the SFA and the other SROs have now moved firmly towards acting as "Statutory regulators with practitioner involvement"'. Developments in Europe may also provide a focus for further questioning.

The implementation of the Third Life Insurance Directive will pave the way towards a workable investment protection system across member states. This process has accelerated from 1 January 1996 now that the Capital Adequacy Directive (setting minimum Community-wide levels of capital needed by investment firms) and the Investment Services Directive (enabling share dealers to operate throughout the European Economic Area with a single licence issued by their home country regulatory authority) have come into force. The European Commission proposal to create a single market in financial services over a five-year period will boost activity in this area. The adoption by member states of an investor's compensation directive and intermediaries directive will be further steps towards the creation of a regulated market in Europe. The arrival of EMU will accelerate the process.

Increasing resources will need to be expended on monitoring compliance, meeting the costs of the compensation scheme and financing the initial and ongoing costs of the training and competence proposals. These expenses, together with the cost of initiatives like the revised product disclosure regime and the setting up costs of the PIA for the retail sector, have added to the competitive pressures on investment firms. Those costs, together with the opportunities created by the introduction of EMU and a single market in Europe, are likely to produce an increasing number of mergers or take-overs and a search for more cost-effective methods of securing the distribution of financial products and services. Predictions have been made that the number of banks, life companies and independent intermediaries will reduce substantially over the next few years. New methods of distribution such as the sale of more products by telephone will occur. It is also possible that the regulators will extend their reach to mortgages and banking products not currently subject to the same level of control as investments under the Act. There are even signs that regulators may take an increasingly interventionist approach to the types of products sold by firms and the terms under which they are sold, including the price. In this environment new challenges will be created for the regulators as well as for those regulated. It is possible that the regulators will focus their attention on minimising the risk of fraud and other market failures instead of concentrating on the improvement of the detailed standards of industry practice. This is a distinct possibility for regulators whose primary concern is not with the private investor since non-private investors should, arguably, be able to look after their own interests.

The Act introduced a dynamic system capable of responding to change. There is little doubt that the system will be severely tested during the next few years.

USEFUL ADDRESSES

PIA (Personal Investment
    Authority Limited)
25 The North Colonnade
Canary Wharf
London
E14 5HS

Tel: (020) 7676 1000

IMRO (Investment Management
    Regulatory Organisation Ltd)
25 The North Colonnade
Canary Wharf
London
E14 5HS

Tel: (020) 7676 1000

FSA (Financial Services
    Authority)
25 The North Colonnade
Canary Wharf
London
E14 5HS

Tel: (020) 7676 1000

Investors Compensation
    Scheme Limited
The Cottons Centre
Cottons Lane
London
SE1 2QB

Tel: (020) 7367 6000

SFA (Securities and Futures
    Authority Limited)
25 The North Colonnade
Canary Wharf
London
E14 5HS

Tel: (020) 7676 1000

The Law Society (of England
    and Wales)
The Law Society's Hall
113 Chancery Lane
London
WC2A 1PL

Tel: (020) 7242 1222

The Institute of Chartered
    Accountants (in England
    and Wales)
PO Box 433
Chartered Accountant's Hall
Moorgate Place
London
EC2P 2BJ

Tel: (020) 7920 8100

Insurance Brokers' Registration
    Council
Higham Business Centre
Midland Road
Higham Forrers
Northamptonshire
NN10 8DW

Tel: (01933) 359083

PIA Ombudsman Bureau Limited
Hertsmere House
Hertsmere Road
London
E14 4AB

Tel: (020) 7216 0016

The Insurance Ombudsman
Bureau
City Gate One
135 Park Street
London
SE1 9EA

Tel: (020) 7902 8100

The Office of the Investment
Ombudsman
Hertsmere House
Hertsmere Road
London
E14 4AB

Tel: (020) 7216 0016

The Pensions Ombudsman
11 Belgrave Road
London
SW1V 1RB

Tel: (020) 7834 9144

INDEX

[All references are to paragraph number.]

Accommodation land, 11.4.1
Accrued interest scheme, 3.5.1
Agricultural land—
    accommodation land, 11.4.1
    amount of, 11.2.1
    annual tenancies, 11.2.4
    background, 11.2.1
    buildings, redundant, 11.2.5
        commercial use of, 11.4.5
    changes in, 11.1
    commercial investment, 12.7
    farm ownership, monetary benefits of,
        11.2.3
    finance, 11.2.6
    gross and net yields, 11.2.4
    highlights of previous year, 11.2.2
    investment in, 11.2
    investment land, 11.2.4
    land uses, 11.2.1
    let land, 11.2.4
    livestock farming, 11.2.3
    preview of year ahead, 11.2.7
    rent, levels of, 11.2.4
    soil grades, distribution of, 11.2.1
    sporting rights, 11.4.2
    stud farms, 11.4.3
    training establishments, 11.4.3
    types of, 11.2.1
    vacant land values, 11.2.3
    vacant possession, with, 11.2.3
    values, recovery in, 11.2.2
Alternative Investment Market, 3.4.3,
        3.7.1, 3.7.3
Alternative investments—
    capital gains, 18.6.2
    collectables as, 19.1.1

Alternative investments – contd
    tangible assets, 18.1.1
    valuables, see Valuables
    See also Art and antiques; Collectables
Angels, 13.10
Art and antiques—
    advisers, 18.5.4, 18.8.3
    alternative investment, as, 18.1.1, 18.2.4
    alternative investors, protecting, 18.2.4
    auction, buying at, 18.6.5
    capital appreciation, prospects of,
        18.6.1
    characteristics as investments, 18.6
    Chester Beatty collection, 18.6.4
    commercial galleries, 18.8.4
    commission rates, 18.4
    consumer protection, 18.2.4
    crime and punishing losses, 18.5.3
    dividends, 18.1.2
    droites de suite, 18.3.3
    Europe market, in, 18.3.3
    EU rules, 18.10.1
    export controls, 18.3.1, 18.3.2
    exporting, 18.5.5
    export licences, 18.10.1
    fair market price, 18.10.1
    fakes and forgeries, 18.5.2
    Far Eastern interest, 18.10.2
    financing, 18.4
    heritage issues, 18.3
    information, sources of, 18.6.6, 18.8.2
    inheritance tax, 18.3.2
    insurance, 18.9.2
    internationalisation, 18.2.5
    investment, as, 18.6.2, 18.8.1, 18.9.1
    living artists, works by, 18.10.1
    market—
        developments in, 18.2.2

Art and antiques – *contd*
  market – *contd*
    performance, 18.2.1
    weaknesses and strengths, 18.2.3
  museum financing, 18.4.1
  national heritage bodies, 18.5.6
  ownership costs, 18.6.3
  preview of year ahead, 18.10.1 – 18.10.3
  previous year, highlights of, 18.4
  private offers, 18.10.1
  prudence, 18.10.3
  purchasing, 18.5
  quality and provenance, 18.5.1
  safeguarding, 18.9.1
  sales, 18.3.3
  security, 18.9.3
  Single Market, in, 18.3.2
  taxation—
    capital gains, 18.7.2
    estate duty, 18.7.3
    inheritance tax, 18.7.3
    liabilities, 18.7.4
    national insurance, 18.7.7
    PAYE, 18.7.7
    planning, 18.7.1
    stamp duty, 18.7.6
    VAT, 18.3.3, 18.7.5
  unidroit, 18.3.3
  websites, 18.8.2
Banks—
  commercial, 2.3.12
Bond-washing, 3.5.1
Books—
  collecting, 19.2.2
  options on, 13.11
  rare, 19.2.2
British government stocks, *see* Gilt-edged securities
Building societies—
  accounts, 2.3.13
  rates of return and conditions, 2.1
Business Expansion Scheme—
  Enterprise Investment Scheme, replacement by, 13.5.1
  introduction of, 13.1
Business Start-up Scheme, 13.1
Business ventures—
  current business climate, 13.2
  generally, 13.1
  investment in another's expertise, 13.8
  preview of year ahead, 13.12
  venture capital trusts, *see* Venture capital trusts

Capital gains tax—
  alternative investments, 18.6.2
  authorised unit trusts, exemption of, 8.9
  British government stocks, exemption of, 3.3.3
  charge to, 1.11
  disposal of shares, on, 13.3.6
  indexation relief, 3.7.1
  capital loss, creation of, 1.11
  investment trusts, concessions for, 7.2, 7.7.2
  private residence exemption, 10.2.1
  racehorses, disposal of, 13.9.3
  shares, on gains from, 3.7.1
  taper relief, scale for, 1.11
  unit trusts, gains on, 8.9
  venture capital trusts, relief for, 13.5.9
Capitalisation issues, 3.4.5, 3.7.3
Cards—
  carrying artworks, 19.2.4
  phonecards, 19.2.4
  trading cards, 19.2.4
Cars—
  American, 19.2.5
  collectable, 19.2.5, 19.4.2
  European, 19.2.5
Certificates of deposit, 2.3.12
Certificates of tax deposit, 2.3.16
Children's bonus bonds, 2.3.7
Coins—
  collecting, 19.2.3
  counterfeit, 17.3.1
  gold, 17.1.5
  manufactured in other metals, 17.1.6
  numismatic, 19.2.3
  silver, 17.1.6
  valuables, *see* Gold; Valuables
Collectables—
  alternative investments, as, 19.1.1
  books, 19.2.2
  cards carrying artworks, 19.2.4
  cars, 19.2.5, 19.4.2
  Clarice Cliff, 19.1.1
  coins, 19.2.3
  comics, 19.2.8
  current developments, 19.2
  dolls, 19.2.10
  Far East markets, 19.3.2
  future developments, 19.3
  investment in, 19.3.1, 19.6
  markets—
    Far East, 19.3.2

Collectables – *contd*
markets – *contd*
new trends in, 19.3.1
mechanics, 19.6
memorabilia, 19.2.12
motives for collecting, 19.1.1
numismatic coins, 19.2.3
phonecards, 19.2.4
photographs, 19.2.7
precautions, 19.6.2
predicting future collectables, 19.4.3
prices, 19.2.13
purchasing—
cars, 19.4.2
strategies, 19.4.1
rare books, 19.2.2
record prices, 19.2.13
risks, 19.6.1, 19.6.3
sets of, 19.5.3
silver, 19.2.11
sporting memorabilia, 19.2.8
stamps, 19.2.9
taxation—
planning, 19.5.1
sets, 19.5.3
VAT, 19.5.2
trading cards, 19.2.4
vintage stock certificates, 19.2.1
wines and spirits, 19.2.6
Collective investment schemes—
administration, 4.4.2
flexibility, 4.4.2
global funds, 4.4.2
overseas investment, 4.4.2, 4.5
specialist geographical funds, 4.4.2
Comics, collecting, 19.2.8
Commercial banks, 2.3.12
Commercial property—
agricultural, 12.7
hi-tech, 12.6
industrial, 12.5
factories and warehouses, 12.5.1
general investment, 12.5.1
institutional criteria, 12.5.3
location criteria, 12.5.2
yields, 12.5.4
investment in, 12.1
investors, types of, 12.1.1
lease of, 12.2.2
leisure, for, 12.8
offices, 12.4
investment in, 12.4.2
London, in, 12.4.1

Commercial property – *contd*
purchase of, 12.2.1
rent reviews, 12.2.3
rental growth, 12.2.2, 12.2.4, 12.3
review of 1997, 12.1
shops, 12.3
generally, 12.3.1
out of town, 12.3.5
prime, 12.3.2
secondary, 12.3.3
tertiary, 12.3.4
types of, 12.2
valuation, 12.1.2
yields—
1965–97, 12.1
sector by, 1972–97, 12.3.1
See also Agricultural land
Commission—
considerations, 1.6.4
Commodities—
hedge against inflation, as, 1.5.2
types of, 16.2
Commodity markets—
ASEAN crisis, 16.5.1
base metals, 16.5.3
call and put options, 16.4.4
cash and carry, 16.4.2
cash metals, 16.4.1
characteristics of, 16.3
cocoa, 16.5.3
coffee, 16.5.3
Commodity Trading Advisors,
16.4.5
evolution of, 16.1
financial futures, 16.2.3
futures, 16.2.2
dealing in, 16.4.3
geared futures and options funds,
16.4.5
grantor, 16.4.4
interest rate market, 16.2.3
International Markets, 16.3.1
London Clearing House, 16.2.1
London Metal Exchange, 16.2.1
managed funds, 16.4.5
market liquidity, 16.2.2
market performance, 16.5
financial markets, 16.5.1
soft commodities, 16.5.3
metal market review & outlook,
16.5.2
modern, 16.1
opportunities, frequency of, 16.3.2

Commodity markets – *contd*
  options, 16.4.4
  outlook for 1999/2000, 16.6
  participation in, methods of, 16.4
  physical markets, 16.2.2, 16.4.1
  real assets, 16.3.3
  review of, 16.5
  risk, 16.4.3
  soft commodities, 16.5.3
  stock index contracts, 16.2.3
  sugar, 16.5.2
  types of, 16.2
    futures markets, 16.2.2
    metals, 16.2.1
    physical markets, 16.2.2
    softs, 16.2.1
Company fixed interest securities, *see* Listed investments
Convertible stocks, 3.6.3
Corporation tax—
  approved investment trust, 7.7.3
  unit trust, 8.9
Counterfeit coins, 17.3.1
CREST—
  introduction of, 3.4.5
Currency—
  overseas investment, 4.3.4
  swaps, 7.6.3
Custody of customer assets, 21.2.12

Debentures—
  characteristics, 3.6.3
  legal nature of, 3.6.1
  meaning, 13.3.5
  suitability of, 3.6.5
  taxation of, 3.6.4
Demergers, 3.7.3
Derivatives—
  arbitrage, 6.9
  gearing, avoiding, 6.2
  generally, 6.1, 6.10
  over-the-counter options, 6.8
  risk, 6.2
  uses of, 6.1
  See also Financial futures; Options; Swaps
Diamonds—
  De Beers and, 17.8.1, 17.8.4
  investment in, 17.8.5
  market, 17.8.2
  production, 17.8.3
  Russian, 17.8.4
  suitability of investment, 17.8.5

Diversification—
  investment policy, 1.6.1
  trustees, by, 1.6.1, 1.7.2
Dividends—
  books-closing, 3.4.5
  income and capital gains, taxation of, 3.7.1
  profits, paid from, 3.7.1
  scrip, 3.7.1
  Stock Exchange, dealing on, 3.4.5
  tax credit, 3.7.1
  taxation, 13.6.4

Emerging markets—
  changing attitudes, 5.6
  choosing a market, 5.8
  context, in, 5.3
  direct investment in, 5.7.1
  diversity, increase in, 5.6, 5.8
  education, 5.3
  example of, 5.3
  factors to consider, 5.7
  fund manager, choice of, 5.9
  funds, 5.7.2
  future influence, of, 5.11
  generally, 4.2.5, 5.1
  growth in, 5.3
  healthcare, 5.3
  individual markets, 5.5
  liberalisation, 5.3
  life expectancy, 5.3
  market catch-up, 5.3
  market statistics, 5.5
  meaning, 5.2
  new, 5.6
  nutrition, 5.3
  open versus closed-ended, 5.7.3
  opportunity, 5.3
  performance, 5.4
  premium, 5.7.3
  rules for investment, 5.11
  technology transfer, 5.3
  timing investment, 5.10
  volatility, 5.3
Enterprise Investment Scheme—
  introduction of, 13.5.1
  qualifying holdings, 13.5.9
  tax relief—
    claim for, 13.5.2
    conditions for, 13.5.3
    individuals eligible for, 13.5.3
    qualifying companies, 13.5.4

Enterprise Investment Scheme – *contd*
 tax relief – *contd*
  qualifying investments, 13.5.6
  qualifying trades, 13.5.5
  withdrawal of, 13.5.7
  venture capital trusts, 13.5.8
Enterprise zones—
 property trusts, 20.2.11
Equity market review, 21.2.11
Europe—
 investing in, 4.2.2
European Union—
 Directives, 21.2.7
Exchange control—
 overseas investors, and, 1.8.1
 suspension of, 4.1
Expertise—
 investment in, 13.8

Far East—
 investing in, 4.2.4
Farming—
 agricultural property, *see* Agricultural
  land
 livestock, 11.2.3
 monetary benefits of, 11.2
Financial futures—
 arbitrage, 6.9
 contracts, 6.3
 dealing in, 6.4
 fair value, 6.5
 FT-SE contract, 6.3
 growth in, 16.2.3
 interest rate contracts, 16.2.3
 options, relationship with, 6.6, 6.7
 outlook in 1996–97, 16.6.1
 over the counter options, 6.8
 pricing, 6.5, 6.7
 recent market performance, 16.5.1
 stock index contracts, 16.2.3
 stocks dealing compared, 6.4
 swaps, 6.9
 trading, 16.4.3
 See also Commodity markets
FIRST option bonds, 2.3.6
Fishing rights, 11.4.2
Foreign income dividends, 8.9
Friendly societies, 20.2.9
Futures, *see* Financial futures

Gearing—
 investment policy, 1.6.9
 investment trusts, by, 7.6.5

Gilt-edged securities—
 accrued interest, 3.5.1
 characteristics, 3.5.1
 commission on, 1.6.5
 dealing in—
  Post Office, through, 3.5.1
  stockbroker, via, 3.5.1
 income from, 1.5.1
 index-linked, 3.5.1
 legal nature of, 3.5.1
 long-dated, 1.5.1
 mechanics, 3.5.1
 nature of, 2.3.10
 newly issued, purchase of, 3.5.1
 pre-conditions for holding, 3.5.1
 price of, 3.5.1
 review of 1995, 3.2
 safe custody of, 3.5.1
 short-dated, 1.5.1
 suitability of, 3.5.1
 taxation, 3.5.1
Gold—
 advisers, 17.4.3
 bacterial leaching, 17.6.3
 bullion price, 17.1.2
 central bank activity, 17.2.1, 17.6.2
 certificate programmes, 17.1.7
 coins, 17.1.5
  mint bullion, 17.1.5
  silver, platinum and palladium,
   17.1.6
 counterfeit coins, 17.3.1
 IMF sales, 17.2.1
 insurance strategies, 17.1.7
 internationally, 17.6.1
 investment potential, 17.4.1
 krugerrands, 17.1.5
 limiting factors, 17.6.1
 long-term hedge, in, 17.1.1
 market, signs of revival in, 17.2.1
 mine frauds, 17.3.2
 mine production, falling, 17.6.4
 mining equities and funds, 17.1.7
 mining shares, 17.7
 ownership, costs of, 17.4.2
 precious metals, other, 17.1.4, 17.2.2
 preview of year ahead, 17.6, 17.7
  demand and supply, 17.6.1
  central banks, 17.6.2
  silver, platinum and palladium, 17.6.3
 previous year highlights, 17.2
 price rises, 17.2.1
 purchase programmes, 17.4.1

Gold – *contd*
  recent developments, 17.1.2
  silver market, 17.1.3
  spot deferred contract, 17.1.7
  tax planning, 17.5.1
  technical changes in mining, 17.6.4
  VAT on, 17.5.2
  value, loss of, 17.2.1
Government stock, *see* Gilt-edged
  securities

Income tax—
  personal allowances, 1.10
  rates from 6 April 1999, 1.10
  venture capital trusts, relief for, 13.5.9
Individual savings accounts (ISAs),
  2.3.15, 3.7.1
  life assurance, 14.2.2
  nation savings, comparision with,
    20.2.4
  tax benefit of, 20.2.7
Industrial property—
  factories, 12.5.1
  institutional criteria, 12.5.3
  location criteria, 12.5.2
  warehouses, 12.5.1
  yields, 12.5.4
Inflation—
  hedge against, 1.5.2
Information sources, 3.4.8
Insurance policies—
  tax beneficial investment, as, 20.2.8
Investment—
  another's expertise, in, 13.8
  constant review of, 1.9
  principles of, 1.1
  trustees, by, *see* Trustees
Investment adviser—
  advice of, 1.6.3
  burden of, 1.2
  limitations, recognition of, 1.2
  main responsibilities, 1.2
  personal factors, taking into account,
    1.3
  task of, 1.1
Investment business—
  authorisation to carry on—
    bodies for, 21.3.1
    criteria, 21.3.4
    exemptions from requirements, 21.3.2
  business conduct rules, 21.4.1
  complaints—
    basic procedure, 21.5.1

Investment business – *contd*
  complaints – *contd*
    compensation and, 21.2.4, 21.4.4,
      21.5
    remedies, 21.5
  consumer education, 21.2.3
  customer agreements, 21.4.3
  disclosure requirements, 21.2.2
  Europe, 21.2.5
  Financial Services Authority, role of,
    21.2.1
  intervention powers, 21.5.1
  overseas aspects, 21.6
  pensions review, 21.2.2
  recognised professional bodies, 21.3.1
  seeking, rules for, 21.4.2
  self regulatory organisations, 21.3.1
  training and competence, 21.2.3
  Year 2000, 21.2.4
Investment companies—
  unapproved, 7.8
Investment policy—
  balance, 1.6.2
  benefits generally, 1.6.7
  buying and selling prices, 1.6.6
  commission and expenses, 1.6.5
  diversification, 1.6.1, 1.7.2
  gearing, 1.6.9
  methods of investment, 1.6.8
  specialists, advice of, 1.6.3
  taxation, 1.6.4
Investment trusts—
  approval of, 7.7.1
  benefits of, 7.1, 7.13
  capital gains, 7.2, 7.6.2, 7.7.2
  characteristics of, 7.6
  constitution, 7.4.1
  constraints on, 7.1
  conversion shares, 7.3
  costs, 7.10
  currency management, 7.6.3
  flexibility, 7.2, 7.6.1
  gearing, 7.6.5
  historical background, 7.2
  income from, treatment of, 7.6.2
  introduction, 7.1
  investment overseas, 7.6.3
  investments, 7.4.2
  legal nature, 7.4
  limited company, as, 7.1
  maintenance, 7.11
  mechanics, 7.10
  overseas investment, 4.4.6, 7.6.3

Investment trusts – *contd*
personal equity plan investments, 20.2.6
preview of year ahead, 7.12
purchase of, 7.5
recent developments, 7.3
risk, 7.6.1
savings schemes, 7.10
securities, 7.4.2
shares—
  acquisition of, 7.10
  advertisement of, 7.4.1
  geared income shares, 7.4.4
  income and annuity, 7.4.4
  stepped preference, 7.4.4
  zero dividend preference, 7.4.4
specialised split capital securities, 7.4.4
split capital trusts, 7.4.3
stock market price, 7.6.4
suitability, 7.9
taxation—
  approval of investment trusts, 7.7.1
  capital gains on approved investment trusts, 7.7.2
  franked investment income, 7.7.3
  income from approved investment trusts, 7.7.3
  unfranked income, 7.7.3
unapproved investment companies, 7.8
underlying net asset value, 7.6.4
unitisation, 7.6.4
value of, assessing the, 7.6.4
Investments—
arranging and holding, methods of, 1.4
basic elements of, 1.5.1
capital and income, 1.5.1
evaluating, 1.5.2
favourable tax treatment, 1.6.4
inflation and, 1.5.2
listed, *see* Listed investments; Shares
methods of, 1.6.8
nature of, 1.5
tax beneficial—
  deciding on, 20.1
  enterprise zone property trusts, 20.2.11
  friendly society, 20.2.9
  insurance policies, 20.2.8
  National Savings, see National Savings

Investments – *contd*
tax beneficial – *contd*
  pension policies, 20.2.10
  personal equity plans, *see* Personal equity plans
  premium bonds, 20.2.5
  questions to be asked, 20.1
  return on, 20.3
  TESSAs, *see* Tax exempt special savings accounts (TESSAs)
time factor, 1.5.3
unlisted, *see* Unlisted investments
Investor protection—
authorisation, 21.3.1-21.3.4
complaints and compensation, 21.4.4, 21.5
conduct of business, 21.4.1, 21.4.2
consumer education, 21.2.3
custody, 21.2.7
customer agreements, 21.4.3
disclosure, 21.2.2
Europe, in, 21.2.5
Financial Services Authority, 21.2.1
  register of, 21.3.3
future developments, 21.8.1
investment business *see* Investment business
legislation, 21.1
management responsibility, 21.2.2
occupational pension schemes, 21.2.5
Office of Fair Trading, investigation by, 21.2.1
open-ended investment companies, 21.2.6
overseas, 21.6
pensions, review of, 21.2.2
preview of year ahead, 21.7
previous year, highlights of, 21.2
principles, 21.3.4
remedies, 21.5
rules and regulations, 21.4
Year 2000 issues, 21.2.4
Investors—
protection of, *see* Investor protection
types of, 1.3

Japan—
investing in, 4.2.3
Jewellery—
growing demand, 17.6.3

Land—
agricultural, *see* Agricultural land

Land – *contd*
  mineral bearing land, 11.4.4
  public leisure/entertainment, 11.4.5
  retail land uses, 11.4.5
  woodlands, *see* Woodlands
Leisure—
  commercial property, 12.8
  land uses, 11.4.5
Life assurance—
  beneficiaries, 14.3.7
  business, 14.2.1
  charges, 14.3.8
  contracts, types of, 14.1
  highlights of previous year, 14.2
  individual savings accounts, 14.2.3
  policies—
    benefits of, 14.6
    companies, investment by, 14.3.7
    divisions, 14.3.3
    endowment, 14.3.3
    legal nature, 14.3.1
    long-term investor, 14.3.7
    maintenance, 14.3.10
    mechanics for taking out, 14.3.9
    medium-term investor, 14.3.7
    non-qualifying, 14.3.3, 14.3.6
    pre-conditions for taking out, 14.3.2
    qualifying, 14.3.3, 14.3.6
    regular premium, 14.3.3
    single premium, 14.3.3
    suitability, 14.3.7
    taxation, 14.2.2
    term assurance, 14.3.3
    types of, 14.3.3
    unit-linked, 14.3.3
    whole of life, 14.3.3
    with profit, 14.3.3
    without profit, 14.3.3
  preview of year ahead, 14.5
  previous year highlights, 14.2
  purchased life annuities, *see* Purchased
    life annuities
  regular premium—
    characteristics of, 14.3.4
    generally, 14.3.3
    investment and protection, 14.3.4
    policy loans, 14.3.4
    withdrawal plans, 14.3.4
  single premium—
    characteristics of, 14.3.5
    encashment of, 14.3.5
    generally, 14.3.3
    withdrawal plans, 14.3.5

Life assurance – *contd*
  taxation—
    changes, 14.2.2
    life company, of, 14.3.6
    person liable for, 14.3.6
    policyholder, of, 14.3.6
  withdrawal plans, 1.5.1
Listed investments—
  advantages of, 3.9
  Alternative Investment Market, 3.4.3
  company fixed interest securities—
    characteristics, 3.6.3
    convertible stocks, 3.6.3
    debenture stocks, 3.6.1
    legal nature of, 3.6.1
    loan stocks, 3.6.1
    mechanics, 3.4.6
    pre-conditions, 3.6.2
    preference shares, 3.6.1
    qualifying corporate bonds, 3.6.4
    safe custody, 3.6.7
    suitability of, 3.6.5
    taxation, 3.6.4
  company flotations, 3.2
  comparisons, 3.3
  cost of dealing, 3.3.4
  CREST, *see* Stock Exchange
  default, security against, 3.3.1
  dividend reinvestment plans, 3.7.1
  dividends, 3.4.5
  indices—
    Bank of England trade weighted
      sterling index, 3.2
    Barings, collapse of, 3.2, 6.2
    Continental, 3.2
    FT-SE 100 index, 3.2
    London Clearing banks base rate and
      UK inflation rate, 3.2
    London FTA Government all stocks
      index, 3.2
    New York, 3.2
    sources of information, 3.4.8
    Tokyo, 3.2
  introduction, 3.1
  mergers and acquisitions activity, 3.2
  offers from companies, *see* Share offers
  options, 3.7.2
  personal equity plans, 3.7.1
  preview of 1999–2000, 3.8
  public sector—
    British government stocks, *see* Gilt-
      edged securities
    Commonwealth stocks, 3.5.2

Listed investments – *contd*
public sector – *contd*
public boards, of, 3.5.2
rate of return, 3.3.2
review of 1998–99, 3.2
shares, *see* Shares
stamp duty on, 3.4.4
Stock Exchange, *see* Stock Exchange
stockbroker services, regulation of, 3.4.6
tax advantages, 3.3.3
warrants, 3.7.2
Lloyd's—
entrance fee, 13.7.3
income and gains, 13.7.1
individual membership—
application, 13.7.2
conditions of, 13.7.3
losses, 13.7.1
members—
premium limit, 13.7.3
syndicates, 13.7.1
taxation of, 13.7.4
unlimited liability, 13.7.1
origin of, 13.7.1
preview of year ahead, 13.12
Special Reserve Fund, 13.7.4
underwriters, taxation of, 13.7.4
Loan creditors—
dormant partners distinguished, 13.6.2
Loan stocks—
characteristics, 3.6.3
legal nature of, 3.6.1
suitability of, 3.6.5
taxation, 3.6.4
Local authority—
mortgage bonds, 2.3.11

Metal markets, 16.5.2
aluminium, 16.5.2
copper, 16.5.2
nickel, 16.5.2
zinc, 16.5.2
Mineral bearing land, 11.4.4

National heritage—
bodies, 18.4.5
concern for, 18.3
sale of art and antiques to, 18.7.4
transfer of property, 18.7.2
National insurance—
contribution rates, 1.10
National Lottery—
scratch cards, 2.2

National savings—
bank accounts, 2.3.1
Bank of England, role of, 2.3.10
capital bonds, 2.3.5
certificates, 2.3.2, 20.2.2
children's bonus bonds, 2.3.7, 20.2.3
FIRST option bond, 2.3.6
fixed interest certificates, 20.2.2
funding through, 2.2
gilt-edged stock, 3.5.1
income bonds, 2.3.4
index-linked certificates, 2.3.3, 20.2.4
ISAs, comparison with, 20.2.4
pensioner's guaranteed income bonds, 2.3.8
preview of 1996, 2.5
rates of return and conditions, 2.1
review of 1997–98, 2.2

Offers from companies, 3.7.3
Offices—
generally, 12.4
investment in, 12.4.2
London, in, 12.4.1
Offshore funds—
investment in, 4.4.5
Open-ended investment company (OEIC),
4.4.4, 8.1, 8.12, 21.2.10
authorisation, 8.3, 8.8
conditions for purchase, 8.7
historical background, 8.2
parties in, 8.6
pricing of shares in, 8.5
suitability, 8.10
Options—
Black-Scholes fair value formula, 6.7
calls, 6.6
European-style options, 6.6
meaning, 6.6
over-the-counter trades, 6.8
pricing, 6.7
puts, 6.6
swaps, 6.9
trading, 16.4.4
Ordinary shares, *see* Shares
Overseas investment—
collective investment schemes, 4.4.2, 4.5
direct investment schemes, 4.4.1
emerging markets, *see* Emerging markets
equities, 4.2

Overseas investment – *contd*
Europe, in, 4.2.2
Far East, in, 4.2.4
increase in, 4.1
investment trusts, 4.4.6, 7.6.3
Japan, in, 4.2.3
market, choosing a—
currency, 4.3.4
economic activity, 4.3.1
factors in, 4.3.4
interest rates, 4.3.2
valuation, 4.3.3
offshore funds, 4.4.5
Open-ended investment companies,
4.4.4
opportunities for, 4.2
protection of investors, 21.6
unit trusts, 4.4.3
United States, in, 4.2.1
Overseas investors—
exchange control, 1.8.1
restrictions on, 1.8.3
taxation of, 1.8.2
capital gains tax, 1.8.2
income tax, 1.8.2
inheritance tax, 1.8.2
Overseas securities—
dealing in, 3.4.6

Palladium, 17.1.3, 17.2.2, 17.6.5
See also Coins; Valuables
Panel on Takeovers and Mergers—
levy, 3.4.6
Partnerships—
dormant—
loan creditors, distinguished, 13.6.2
meaning, 13.6.1
rights and liabilities, 13.6.3
taxation, 13.6.4
Pensioners' guaranteed income bonds,
2.3.8
Pensions—
benefits of, 15.11
contracted-out money purchase scheme,
15.7.7
contracts—
characteristics of, 15.6
types of, 15.5
free-standing AVC schemes, 15.7.9
highlights of previous year, 15.2
investor protection, 21.2.6
life company, tax-free gains of, 15.7.1
loans, 15.7.6

Pensions – *contd*
occupational schemes—
approval of, 15.7.5
benefits, 15.7.5
company directors, for, 15.7.5
contracting-out via, 15.7.7
contributions, 15.7.5
discretionary membership of, 15.7.5
freestanding AVCs, 15.7.9
investor protection, 21.2.6
meaning, 15.7.5
unapproved, 15.7.8
personal pension plans—
benefits, payment of, 15.7.2
contracting-out via, 15.7.3
eligibility for, 15.7.2
premium limits, 15.7.2
premiums, tax relief on, 15.7.2
protected rights contributions, 15.7.3
relief, years for which granted, 15.7.2
scheme certificates, 15.7.3
preview of year ahead, 15.10
previous year highlights, 15.2
retirement annuity contracts, 15.7.4
review of, 21.2.2
schemes, types of, 15.1
self-investment, 15.7.6
state scheme—
contracting in, 15.4
contracting out, 15.4
generally, 15.3
SERPS, 15.3
suitability, 15.9
tax beneficial investment, as, 20.2.10
transfers and opt outs, 21.2.5
welfare reform, 15.8
Personal equity plans—
cash in, 20.2.6
introduction of, 3.7.1, 20.2.6
investment trusts, investment in, 20.2.6
maximum investment, 20.2.6
rules, 3.7.1
taking out, 20.2.6
tax benefits, 20.2.6
unit trusts, investment in, 20.2.6
Phonecards, collecting, 19.2.7
Plays, backing, 13.10
Precious metals—
gold, *see* Gold
highlights of previous year, 17.2.2
long-term hedge in, 17.1.1
recent developments, 17.1.2, 17.1.3
valuables, *see* Valuables

Preference shares—
  stepped, 7.4.4
  zero-dividend, 7.4.4
Premium bonds, 2.2, 2.3.9
  tax beneficial investment, as,
    20.2.5
Private companies—
  day-to-day running, 13.3.2
  financing costs, relief for, 13.3.9
  investment, 13.4
  loans to, 13.3.5, 13.3.8
  losses, 13.3.7
  minority holdings—
    acquisition of, 13.3.1
    generally, 13.3.1
    meaning, 13.3.1
    powers of minority, 13.3.2
    protection, 13.3.2
    transfer of shares, 13.3.4
  reinvestment relief, 13.3.7
  special resolutions, 13.3.2
  taxation of investments in, 13.3.6
  uncalled capital, liability for, 13.3.3
  voting rights, 13.3.1
Private investment companies, 13.4
Property—
  agricultural, *see* Agricultural land
  commercial, *see* Commercial property
  home, purchase of, 1.6.7
  industrial, *see* Industrial property
  real, *see* Real property
  residential, *see* Residential property
Protection of investors, *see* Investor
  protection
Public sector securities—
  British government stocks, *see* Gilt-
    edged stocks
  other, 3.5.2
Purchased life annuities—
  characteristics, 14.4.3
  legal nature of, 14.4.1
  maintenance, 14.4.7
  mechanics for taking out, 14.4.6
  pre-conditions for investment,
    14.4.2
  suitability of, 14.4.5
  taxation—
    annuitant, of, 14.4.4
    life company, of, 14.4.4

Qualifying corporate bonds—
  requirements for, 3.6.4
  taxation of, 3.6.4

Racehorses—
  investment in, 13.9.1
  stallions, 13.9.2
  taxation—
    capital gains tax, 13.9.3
    income tax, 13.9.3
Real property—
  accommodation land, 11.4.1
  active leisure entertainment uses,
    11.4.5
  advisers, role of, 9.4
  costs—
    acquisitions, 9.2.3
    disposal, 9.2.3
    management, 9.2.3
  interests in, 9.1
  investment aspects, 9.1
  legislation, 9.2.1
  mineral bearing land, 11.4.4
  ownership, 9.1
  passive leisure uses, 11.4.5
  retail uses, 11.4.5
  sporting rights, 11.4.2
  stud farms, 11.4.3
  tangibility of, 9.1
  taxation, 9.2.2
  training establishments or yards,
    11.4.3
  valuation, 9.3
Residence—
  tax purposes, for, 1.8.2
Residential property—
  assured shorthold tenancies, 10.2.2
  assured tenancies, 10.2.2
  capital gains tax exemption, 10.2.1
  corporate tenants, 10.2.2
  flats—
    blocks, 10.2.3
    rented, 10.2.2
  highlights of past few years, 10.1
  holiday homes, 10.2.4
  lettings, 10.2.2
  long leasehold houses, 10.2.2
  personal homes, 10.2.1
  preview of year ahead, 10.3
  protected shorthold tenancies, 10.2.2
  Rent Acts, 10.2.2
  sale of, 10.2.2
  time sharing, 10.2.4
Rights issues—
  placing with clawback, 3.7.3
  prospectus, 3.7.3
  provisional allotment letter, 3.7.3

Rights issues – *contd*
record date, 3.4.5
terms of, 3.7.3
use of, 3.7.3

Schools fees—
TESSAs used to provide, 20.2.1
Scrip dividends, 3.7.1
Scrip issues, 3.4.5
Securities, types of, 3.6.1
Security—
comparing different types of, 2.4, 3.3
convenience, 2.4.4, 3.3.4
cost of dealing, 2.4.4, 3.3.4
default, against, 2.4.1, 3.3.1
maintenance, 2.4.6
rate of return, 2.4.2, 3.3.2
realising investment, 2.4.5
tax advantages, 2.4.3, 3.3.3
Share offers—
capitalisation issues, 3.7.3
demergers, 3.7.3
maintenance, 3.7.3
offers for sale, 3.7.3
prospectus, 3.7.3
rights issues—
prospectus, 3.7.3
provisional allotment letter, 3.7.3
record date, 3.4.5
terms of, 3.7.3
use of, 3.7.3
takeover offers, 3.7.3
time limits, 3.7.3
Shareholders—
annual report and accounts, receiving,
3.7.1
liability of, 3.7.1
members of company, as, 3.7.1
Shares—
B shares, 3.7.1
bearer—
dealing with, 3.4.5
safe custody, 3.7.1
bed and breakfasting, 3.7.1
bonus issues, 3.4.5
capitalisation issue, 3.4.5, 3.7.1
CREST, introduction of, 3.4.5
dealing in, 3.4.6, 3.7.1
demergers, 3.7.1
dividend reinvestment plans, 3.7.1
dividends, 3.7.1
income and capital gains, taxation of,
3.7.1

Shares – *contd*
listing, 3.7.1
maintenance, 3.7.1
nominee, registered in name of, 3.7.1
offers for sale, 3.7.1
ordinary—
characteristics, 3.7.1
legal nature of, 3.7.1
market price of, 3.7.1
ownership, establishment of, 3.7.1
pre-conditions, 3.7.1
suitability of, 3.7.1
taxation, 3.7.1
personal equity plans, *see* Personal
equity plans
preference—
legal nature of, 3.6.1
taxation of, 3.6.4
preview of 1998–99, 3.8
review of 1997–98, 3.2
rights issues—
placing with clawback, 3.7.3
prospectus, 3.7.3
provisional allotment letter, 3.7.3
record date, 3.4.5
terms of, 3.7.3
use of, 3.7.3
safe custody, 3.7.1
scrip issues, 3.4.5
stamp duty on, 3.4.5
take-over offers, 3.7.1
taxation of income and gains from,
3.7.1
Shooting rights, 11.4.2
Shops—
generally, 12.3.1
out-of-town, 12.3.5
prime, 12.3.2
secondary, 12.3.3
tertiary, 12.3.4
Silver, 17.1.3, 17.1.6, 19.2.11
See also Coins; Collectables; Valuables
Single Market—
art market, effect on, 18.2.8
Sources of information, 3.4.7
Split capital trusts, 7.4.3
Sporting rights—
categories of, 11.4.2
deer stalking, 11.4.2
fishing, 11.4.2
legal estate, as, 11.4.2
market trends, 11.4.2
shooting, 11.4.2

Stamp duty—
acquisition of property, on, 9.2.3
alternative investment, transfer of, 18.6.6
listed investments, on, 3.4.5
Stock Exchange—
capitalisation and rights issues, 3.4.5
commission, 3.4.5
constitution, 3.4.1
contract note, 3.4.5
CREST, 3.4.5
dealing on, 3.4.5
contract note, 3.4.5
flowchart, 3.4.5
method of, 3.4.5
settlement date, 3.4.5
TALISMAN system, 3.4.5
dividends, 3.4.5
information, sources of, 3.4.7
listing, admission to, 3.7.1
overseas securities on, 3.4.4
primary market, 3.4.2
PTM levy, 3.4.5
regulatory role, 3.4.1
secondary market, 3.4.2
SETS, 3.4.5
sources of information, 3.4.7
stamp duty, 3.4.5
TAURUS, abandonment of, 3.4.5
Unlisted Securities Market, 3.4.3
Stockbrokers—
nominee services, 3.7.1
services, 3.4.6
Stud farms, 11.4.3
Swaps—
currency, 7.6.3
meaning, 6.9
pricing, 6.9

Takeovers—
offers, 3.7.3
TALISMAN system, 3.4.5
Tax exempt special savings accounts (TESSAs)—
duration of, 2.3.14
limits on, 20.2.1
school fees, provision for, 20.2.1
uses of, 20.2.1
withdrawals from, 2.3.14
Taxation—
art and antiques, of, see Art and antiques

Taxation – contd
collectables, of, see Collectables
company fixed interest securities, of, 3.6.4
dividends, 13.3.6
dormant partnership, 13.6.4
earned income, meaning, 13.6.4
favourable investments, 1.6.4
general rule for, 1.6.4
gilt-edged securities, 3.5.1
investment trusts, see Investment trusts
life assurance, see Life assurance
loans, tax relief on, 13.3.8
overseas investors—
capital gains tax, 1.8.2
income tax, 1.8.2
inheritance tax, 1.8.2
purchased life annuities, see Purchased life annuities
racehorses, receipts from, 13.9.3
real property, of, 9.2.2
residence for purposes of, 1.8.2
traded options, of, 3.7.2
underwriters, of, 13.7.4
unit trusts, of, see Unit trusts
valuables, of, see Valuables
Traded options, 3.7.2
Trading cards, collecting, 19.2.4
Treasury bills, 2.3.17
Trustees—
appointment, 1.7
authorised investments, 1.7.4
caution, exercising, 1.7.5
diversification, 1.6.1, 1.7.2
expert advice, obtaining, 1.7.3
investments, suitability of, 1.7.1

Unit trusts—
accumulation trusts, 8.8.2
authorisation, 8.3
balanced trusts, 8.8.2
capital growth trusts, 8.8.2
characteristics—
convenience, 8.8.1
eligible markets, 8.8
marketability, 8.8.1
professional management, 8.8.1
simplicity, 8.8.1
commodity futures, 16.4.5
conditions for purchase, 8.7
constitution of, 8.6
exempt, 8.14
fixed interest trusts, 8.8.2

Unit trusts – *contd*
generally, 8.1, 8.16
historical background, 8.2
income trusts, 8.8.2
legal nature of, 8.6
maintenance, 8.11.2
mechanics, 8.11.1
minimum investment in, 8.7
open-ended investment company, 8.12
operation of, 8.1
overseas trusts, 8.8.2
overseas investment, 4.4.3
personal equity plan investments, 20.2.6
preview of year ahead, 8.15
previous year highlights, 8.4
prices quoted for, 8.6
regulation of, 8.1
specialist trusts, 8.8.2
suitability, 8.10
taxation, 8.9
tracker trusts, 8.8.2
types of, 8.8.2
unauthorised, 8.13
units—
acquisition of, 8.11.1
charge on purchase of, 8.11.1
pricing, 8.5
wider range investment, as, 8.7
United States—
investing in, 4.2.1
Unlisted investments—
building society accounts, 2.3.13
certificates of deposit, 2.3.12
certificates of tax deposit, 2.3.16
commercial banks, with, 2.3.12
comparison of, 2.4
conditions, 2.1
convenience, 2.4.4
cost of dealing, 2.4.4
default, security against, 2.4.1
government stock, 2.3.10
individual savings accounts (ISAs), 2.3.15
local authority mortgage bonds, 2.3.11
maintenance, 2.4.6
National Savings, *see* National Savings
premium bonds, 2.2, 2.3.9
preview of 1999–2000, 2.5
rate of return, 2.1, 2.4.2
realisation of investment, 2.4.5
review of 1998–99, 2.2
tax advantages, 2.4.3

Unlisted investments – *contd*
tax exempt special savings accounts (TESSAs), 2.3.14
Treasury bills, 2.3.17
types of, 2.1, 2.3

Valuables—
advisers, 17.4.3
coins, *see* Coins
commodity markets, *see* Commodity markets
counterfeit coins, 17.3.1
forms of investment, 17.1.6
generally, 17.1
gold, *see* Gold
investment in, 17.6.1, 17.6.5
jewellery—
fabrication, 17.1.3
growing demand, 17.6.2
limiting factors, 17.6.1
long-term hedge, as, 17.1.1
palladium, 17.1.6, 17.6.3
platinum—
investment in, 17.1.1, 17.7
price, 17.2.2
uses of, 17.1.3
preview of year ahead, 17.6
previous year highlights, 17.2
revival in, 17.2.1
selected forms of investment in, 17.1.6
silver, 17.1.3
coins, 17.1.6
taxation—
planning, 17.5.1
VAT, 17.5.2
Value added tax—
acquisition of property, on, 9.2.3
alternative investment, transfer of, 18.6.5
collectables, on, 19.5.2
gold and precious metals, on, 17.5.2
Venture capital trusts—
conditions, 13.5.8
generally, 13.1
introduction of, 13.5.8
nature of, 7.12
qualifying holdings, 13.5.9
tax relief, 13.5.9

Warrants—
investment in, 7.4.2
legal nature of, 3.7.2
pre-conditions, 3.7.2

Warrants – *contd*
    safe custody, 3.7.2
    suitability, 3.7.2
Welfare reform, 15.8
Wines and spirits, collecting, 19.2.6

Woodlands, 11.3.1
    market trends, 11.3.2

Zero dividend preference shares—
    investment in, 7.4.4